D0895370

WITHDRAWN
UTSA LIBRARIES

Factional Politics

Factional Politics

How Dominant Parties Implode or Stabilize

Françoise Boucek

School of Politics and International Relations, Queen Mary, University of London, UK

© Françoise Boucek 2012

All rights reserved. No reproduction, copy or transmission of this publication may be made without written permission.

No portion of this publication may be reproduced, copied or transmitted save with written permission or in accordance with the provisions of the Copyright, Designs and Patents Act 1988, or under the terms of any licence permitting limited copying issued by the Copyright Licensing Agency, Saffron House, 6–10 Kirby Street, London EC1N 8TS.

Any person who does any unauthorized act in relation to this publication may be liable to criminal prosecution and civil claims for damages.

The author has asserted her right to be identified as the author of this work in accordance with the Copyright, Designs and Patents Act 1988.

First published 2012 by
PALGRAVE MACMILLAN

Palgrave Macmillan in the UK is an imprint of Macmillan Publishers Limited, registered in England, company number 785998, of Houndmills, Basingstoke, Hampshire RG21 6XS.

Palgrave Macmillan in the US is a division of St Martin's Press LLC, 175 Fifth Avenue, New York, NY 10010.

Palgrave Macmillan is the global academic imprint of the above companies and has companies and representatives throughout the world.

Palgrave® and Macmillan® are registered trademarks in the United States, the United Kingdom, Europe and other countries.

ISBN 978–0–230–01993–5

This book is printed on paper suitable for recycling and made from fully managed and sustained forest sources. Logging, pulping and manufacturing processes are expected to conform to the environmental regulations of the country of origin.

A catalogue record for this book is available from the British Library.

Library of Congress Cataloging-in-Publication Data
Boucek, Françoise.
   Factional politics : how dominant parties implode or
   stabilize / Françoise Boucek.
      p.   cm.
   Summary: "Drawing on theories of neo-institutionalism to show how institutions shape dissident behavior, Boucek develops new ways of measuring factionalism and explains its effects on office tenure.
   In each of the four cases – from Britain, Canada, Italy and Japan – intra-party dynamics are analyzed through times series and rational choice tools"—Provided by publisher.
   ISBN 978–0–230–01993–5
   1. Political parties—Great Britain.   2. Political parties—Canada.
   3. Political parties—Italy.   4. Political parties—Japan.   I. Title.
   JN1121.B68 2012
   324.2—dc23   2012033376

10   9   8   7   6   5   4   3   2   1
21   20   19   18   17   16   15   14   13   12

Printed and bound in the United States of America

Library
University of Texas
at San Antonio

To Jan, Emilie and Louise
and the memory of my mother who would have been proud

Contents

List of Tables and Figures   viii

Preface and Acknowledgements   x

Introduction   1

1   The Theory of One-Party Dominance   6

2   Why Does One-Party Dominance End in Factionalism?   33

3   Majoritarian Democracies: Executive-Dominated Britain
    and Decentralised Canada   50

4   Case 1 – The Thatcher–Major Factional Wars over Europe   71

5   Case 2 – The Demise of Canadian Liberal Hegemony   101

6   Non-Majoritarian Democracies: Centrifugal Italy and
    Consensual Japan   123

7   Case 3 – Italy's Christian Democrats: How Factional
    Capture Bred Self-Destruction   144

8   Case 4 – The Liberal Democratic Party of Japan
    (1955–2009): End of Hegemony   183

Conclusion: How Parties Succeed or Fail to Manage
Factionalism and Stay in Power   205

Notes   214

Bibliography   228

Index   258

Tables and Figures

Tables

1.1 Party parliamentary representation and pivotal power
for a selection of government coalitions in Italy 1958–92   24
1.2 Party parliamentary representation and pivotal power
Italian coalition governments, 1983–92   25
3.1 Conservative MPs' rewards and deprivation 1979–97   60
6.1 Italy's DC – factional representation on intraparty
organs and in government in 1971   131
6.2 DC – factional representation on intraparty organs and
in government in 1986–87   132
6.3 Factions' shares of delegate votes and of normalised
Banzhaf power DC national congresses of 1949, 1969
and 1982   138
6.4 The LDP seniority system   142
7.1 Christian Democratic Party of Italy, factional strength
and pivotal power, 1946–62   148
7.2 Southern vote shares for Christian Democrats and Right
Parties, general elections 1948 and 1953 (per cent)   150
7.3 Christian Democratic Party of Italy, factional strength
and pivotal power, 1964–73   154
7.4 Christian Democratic Party of Italy, factional strength
and pivotal power, 1976 national congress   159
7.5 Christian Democratic Party of Italy, factional strength
and pivotal power, 1980 and 1982 national congresses   165
7.6 Christian Democratic Party of Italy, factional strength
and pivotal power national congresses (1984, 1986
and 1989)   171
7.7 Italian national, regional, provincial and communal
elections, April 1992–November 1993   177

Figures

2.1 Party system competition and the demand for intraparty
consent. (a) Elastic demand; (b) inelastic demand   41

2.2	The interplay between party dominance and factionalism	43
4.1	Pay-off matrix: game between conservative dries and wets; March 1981 budget	76
4.2	Maastricht game pay-off matrix	89
4.3	Game between Major and Eurosceptic rebels. Maastricht Treaty ratification 22–23 July 1993	90
4.4	European (finance) bill, November 1994 game between Major and Eurosceptic rebels pay-off matrix	95
7.1	Effective number of factions and factional power Italian Christian Democratic Party	146
7.2	The relative significance of voice and exit for DC supporters – demand inelastic for political consent with respect to quality	173
7.3	The relative significance of voice and exit for DC supporters – demand elastic with respect to quality	174
8.1	Effective number of factions and factional power Japanese Liberal Democratic Party	186

Preface and Acknowledgements

If this book was a wine it wouldn't be a *Beaujolais nouveau* given the amount of toiling away and different stages of fermentation it took to mature and bring to consumption.

My interest in the internal politics of dominant political parties dates back to the early 1990s when I returned to Britain after a decade in Canada having swapped a career in finance for political science. The ruling Conservative Party under Margaret Thatcher was then in a state of mutiny over Europe. Thatcher's internecine overthrow in November 1990 and replacement by John Major had won the Conservatives a fourth term in office in 1992 which led some academics to claim that the British political system was 'turning Japanese'. Except that within a year Japan's Liberal Democratic Party (LDP) were thrown out of office for the first time in 38 years and Italy's ruling Christian Democratic Party (DC) were imploding after more than four decades in power and in both cases internal conflict and factional defections had played a big role. Meanwhile, back in Canada the Liberals who had dominated federal politics and government for most of the 20th century had come back to power after the near-fatal implosion of the Progressive Conservatives. Was there something about longevity in office that made ruling parties prone to internal division and disintegration? I started my quest.

Writing this book has been quite a solitary journey. However, many people have helped me along the way and I want to take this opportunity to thank them. I owe special thanks to several people in the Government Department at the London School of Economics and Political Science (LSE) particularly the late Gordon Smith who fostered my interest in the study of political parties and party systems during lively discussions in his MSc seminar in the early 1990s. Gordon then encouraged me to return to the LSE for doctoral research and start an academic career later than most people as he did. He remained a friend and interested in my research until his untimely death in 2009. I am thankful to Patrick Dunleavy for his research guidance, stimulating discussions and staunch encouragement to get this work into print. Along with Keith Dowding, Patrick provided a very stimulating research environment at the LSE for those of us interested in rational choice theory and new institutionalism. They invited top rational choice international scholars to their seminar series and facilitated face-to-face discussions during 'brown bagging' lunchtime sessions in the Shapiro room at King's Chambers. Rosa Mulé and Moshe Maor helped me refine the framing of my research question and Bob Leonardi kindly shared his detailed knowledge of Italy's Christian Democratic Party (DC) and commented on a preliminary version of this volume.

For the quantitative data on DC faction representation I am grateful to Bob Leonardi and Douglas Wertman for their co-authored work which allowed me to do times series analysis and develop new measures of intra-party fragmentation and factional power. On the latter, I am grateful to Thomas Bräuninger and Thomas Köenig at the Mannheim Centre for European Social Research at the University of Mannheim, Germany. The software program they developed (in the pre-internet age) for calculating power indices enabled me to examine the structure of bargaining inside the factionalised DC and LDP in times series. I also thank Patrick Dumont, Jean-François Caulier and Nicolas Sauger for commenting on my applications of this methodology and Hugh Ward for teaching me the basics of game theory in his first methods course at the 27th Essex Summer School.

I thank the anonymous referee who commented on the original manuscript proposal acknowledging that this book addresses an important research question and features well chosen cases. I hope the book delivers on their expectations. Several country experts and party scholars have commented on individual cases and provided additional information notably Kenneth Carty, Ellis Krauss, Richard Katz, Judith Bara, Paul Webb, David Farrell and Daniela Giannetti to name only a few. Of course, any omissions and mistakes are strictly my own. Eric Acker kindly kept me up to date on developments in Canadian politics and the Liberal Party. I am grateful to my commissioning editor Andrew Baird at Palgrave for whom this volume represented one of his first projects and to Devasena Vedamurthi at Integra for seeing the book to production.

I am grateful to the friends and colleagues of the late Professor W A Robson at the LSE for awarding me the 2003 William Robson Memorial Prize to help me publish this book and other academic papers. I thank the European Consortium for Political Research (ECPR) for allowing me to organise and co-direct two workshops at the Joint Sessions (on dominant political parties in Granada in 2005 and on intraparty dissent in St. Gallen in 2011) and various panels and sections at ECPR General Conferences, notably in Budapest in 2005 and Potsdam in 2010 and I thank all the participants at these events for their constructive criticism. I also thank Peter Edmonds for capturing my vision in his illustration of the book cover. But none of this would have been possible if it wasn't for Jan Boucek who apart from his editorial and technical advice kept me focused on finishing this book in order to move on.

Introduction

Political earthquakes in established democracies often result from long-lived governing parties becoming increasingly fractious, losing their coherence and disillusioning voters.

Japan's Liberal Democratic Party (LDP) was finally tossed out by voters in 2009 after almost 50 years of continuous power. Canada's Liberal Party had ruled for 81 years since the turn of the twentieth century but was humiliatingly relegated to third place in the 2011 elections. The Christian Democrats (DC) in Italy had looked impregnable since the end of the Second World War until a slow rot ended their hegemony by the mid-1990s. And, in the United Kingdom, the Conservatives' aura as the natural party of government was shattered in 1997 by Tony Blair's New Labour landslide. India's Congress Party, Mexico's Institutional Revolutionary Party and Taiwan's Kuomintang suffered similar fates.

Particular circumstances differed in each country but internal dissent and disorder were common. In Japan and Canada, warning signs about internal discord had emerged before the final collapse and only weak opposition parties helped forestall the inevitable. Italy's experience dragged on for years while Britain's proved brutally quick.

The book's puzzle

Over time, all political parties become fractious and unpopular but this is made worse when a party monopolises government for a long time because the stakes of holding power are so much greater.

If unity is so essential for electoral success, how did two of the most long-lasting dominant parties – Italy's DC and Japan's LDP – survive for so long even though they were the most notoriously factionalised? And how did dominant parties like the United Kingdom's Conservatives

1

and Canada's Liberals lose power after much shorter periods of internal strife?

This book applies empirical analysis to investigate the factors leading some dominant parties to degenerate into fatal factionalism and others to retain power by keeping factionalism in check. The conclusion is twofold: party unity is a necessary but insufficient condition for party dominance and it is difficult to maintain in the long run.

Factional pressures are due to the following:

- First, electoral success is a magnet for aspiring politicians so dominant parties face increasing competition for election claims as long as they remain successful, putting pressure on partisan resources.
- Second, the heterogeneous nature of dominant parties increases conflicting pressures for ideological and policy claims which, in turn, raise the risk of ideological divisions and splits.
- Third, dominant parties attract careerist politicians, fanning competition in the struggle for the limited number of available positions.
- Fourth, security of office alters the balance between parties' collective goals and individuals' careers. Careerist politicians risk creating divided and entrenched loyalties which, in the long run, may trump the party's collective interests.

These propositions reveal a paradox. Factionalism can become destabilising and dangerous if factions wield a veto but factionalism can also prolong office tenure by regulating conflict to prevent exit. This book examines this paradox by studying intraparty disequilibrium in four well-known dominant parties: Britain's Conservatives, Canada's Liberals, Italy's former Christian Democrats and Japan's Liberal Democrats.

The book assumes that intraparty harmony is punctuated by crises characterised by internal divisions and factional conflicts prompting insurgencies and collective action by dissidents who mobilise against the leadership to bring about change. It argues that the institutional and strategic capacity of ruling parties to respond to dissidence is a significant determinant of their ability to stay in power. However, variables such as the state of the electoral market and the bargaining power of dissidents affect this capacity.

Theoretical/methodological approach

The theoretical propositions and empirical observations draw on structural and agential factors interpreted through the analytical perspective and methods of rational choice theory and new institutionalism including historical institutionalism.

Factional behaviour and dissident action are themselves structurally determined. Institutions (systemic and party-specific) can be manipulated particularly when the incumbent is in power for a long time. This book's four case studies show that different constitutional and organisational arrangements affect factionalism differently, either by penalising divided parties or by encouraging the formation and institutionalisation of factions, paradoxically, enabling them to become mediators in conflict resolution within political parties.

This book constitutes 'small-n' qualitative research applied to the four case studies: the British Conservative Party, the Liberal Party of Canada, the former Christian Democratic Party of Italy and the Liberal Democratic Party of Japan.

The insights and predictions are generally applicable to emerging democracies. Moreover, the general conclusions about factional management and conflict resolution inside parties are also widely applicable to all political parties including opposition parties whose ability to regain power after major defeats rests primarily on restoring party unity.

The empirical study uses the comparative method and, more specifically, the 'most different/similar system design'. It contrasts two majoritarian Westminster systems (the United Kingdom and Canada) featuring strong disincentives to factionalism and two non-majoritarian/consensus democracies (Italy and Japan) that are more receptive to intraparty pluralism and tolerant of factionalism.

However, within each type of democracy, there are significant constitutional differences which have implications for partisanship and intraparty politics such as federalism in Canada compared with Britain's unitary state and a much more concentrated party system in Japan than in Italy.

There are also key differences in party institutional arrangements for the parties examined in each democratic system which have implications for conflict regulation in these four parties. In sum, a key aspect of this book maps out the institutional mechanisms (systemic and party specific) that shape conflict resolution inside political parties.

The book's value added

This book adds substantively to the theoretical and empirical understanding of dominant party rule and factionalism. By questioning the unitary actor assumption underlying existing (albeit scarce) theories of party dominance, it offers a more complete explanation of:

- How dominant parties endure or, conversely, why opposition parties fail to compete in dominant party systems.
- Why dominant parties lose power and/or implode.

Overlooking intraparty politics may lead to premature conclusions about dominant parties' resilience and underestimate the potential for disunity.

This book offers more complete causal explanations of single-party dominance and its breakdown than conventional studies focusing on party competition. The intraparty dimension of competition is a critical factor in the emergence, persistence and decline of dominant parties. Parties that maintain harmony are more likely in the long run to stay in power than parties that don't. The capacity to maintain unity over time through the efficient management of intraparty relations represents a necessary, albeit insufficient, condition for political dominance.

Other added value:

- The conceptualisation and dimensionalisation of one-party dominance.
- The conceptualisation of factionalism and its different manifestations.
- The identification of the institutional and strategic factors leading to the development of intraparty factions and the effective management of factional conflict.
- Empirical analysis of outcomes of particular factional conflicts in specific parties.
- New measures for calculating the number and power of intraparty factions.
- The application of a variety of methods including strategic games and bargaining to analyse conflict resolution inside political parties.

The book's plan

Chapter 1 maps out a theoretical and empirical analysis of single-party dominance identifying the causal factors leading governing parties in competitive democracies to become dominant. The arguments are made from a party competition perspective but the main premise of this study is to question the unitary actor assumption of this approach.

Chapter 2 argues that party unity represents a necessary, albeit insufficient, condition for party dominance. The examination of the intraparty dimension of dominance involves conceptualising factionalism and developing the above four theoretical propositions about why long office tenure puts strains on party unity. Hence, Chapter 1's theory of one-party dominance represents this study's independent variable which is closely linked with the theory of intraparty competition and factional politics presented in Chapter 2 which represents the dependent variable.

Chapter 3 looks at structural incentives for political parties competing in majoritarian Westminster systems (Lijphart, 1999). For instance, in Britain and Canada party unity is at a premium because of the prerequisites of majoritarian institutions such as single-member plurality voting systems. The rules and procedures used by parties to select their candidates, leaders and programmes are also analysed. This is followed by studies of the factional politics of two dominant parties operating in majoritarian democracies: the British Conservative Party under Thatcher and Major (Chapter 4) and the Liberal Party of Canada mainly under Trudeau and Chrétien (Chapter 5).

Chapter 6 looks at structural incentives for political parties competing in non-majoritarian democracies using Italy and Japan to demonstrate the effect of proportional voting systems and other consensual arrangements on intraparty competition. Party rules and procedures are also examined to explain their role in institutionalising factions in the DC and LDP. The factional politics of these parties are the focus of the following two chapters: the DC in Italy (Chapter 7) and the Liberal Democrats in Japan (Chapter 8). This is followed by the Conclusion.

1
The Theory of One-Party Dominance

Why do voters in mature democracies such as Japan, Canada, Italy, Sweden, the United Kingdom and Australia keep re-electing the same party, even though there are reasonable alternatives on offer? It's understandable that black South Africans give the African National Congress (ANC) landslide win after landslide win since the alternatives are minnow parties or those connected with the old white regime. But what enables national parties in many mature democracies to dominate politics and government while retaining the consent of the losers?

This chapter identifies the conditions causing dominant parties to endure and, by implication, to lose office when these conditions cease to prevail. A theoretical and empirical analysis of single-party dominance identifies the factors leading governing parties in competitive democracies to become dominant. The arguments are from a party competition perspective, but the main premise questions the unitary actor assumption of this approach by arguing that party unity is a necessary but not sufficient condition for party dominance.

A brief review of the scholarly literature on dominant parties and dominant party systems is followed by the argument that dominance should be viewed as a temporal and spatial phenomenon. Longevity in office is a conventional device for identifying dominant parties. However, a spatial concept involves separate albeit linked arenas of competition or location. The chapter focuses on the competitive strategies of dominant parties in the electoral, legislative and executive arenas which involve a positive feedback process that creates cyclical dominance (see also Boucek, 1998).

No single theory can explain party dominance completely. This book's analysis represents a synthesis of different theoretical approaches drawing on institutional and agential factors to identify, describe and explain the different dimensions of dominance. The theoretical claims are supported by empirical evidence drawn from the book's four case studies – British Conservatives, Canadian Liberals, Italian Christian Democrats and Japanese Liberal Democrats – and other relevant cases in established democracies. This analysis is also relevant to less democratic regimes and is intertwined with the theory of intraparty competition developed in Chapter 2.

The first two sections of this chapter deal with issues of definition and conceptualisation. Section 1.1 examines old and new ways of understanding party dominance in political science while Section 1.2 looks at how dominant parties skew party competition to entrench themselves in power. The rest of the chapter studies the configuration of dominant parties' competitive strategies through demand and supply theories.

On the demand side, Section 1.3 focuses empirically on the electoral dimension of dominance by looking at societal and institutional factors to explain how dominant parties in different competitive democracies create asymmetric competition in the market for votes. On the supply side, Section 1.4 focuses on strategic or political factors drawing on median voter and coalition theories, using Italy's Christian Democrats to demonstrate the bargaining advantages of dominant parties in multiparty coalitions which are calculated with a power index.

Finally Section 1.5 looks at executive dominance to explain how dominant parties embed themselves in office by transforming the benefits of incumbency into partisan resources.

1.1 Old and new ways of understanding dominant party systems

Interest in dominant parties emerged as an offshoot of early party system typologies based on the number of parties in competition (Duverger, 1964) and sometimes on their relative size (Blondel, 1968). These typologies identified a distinctive type of party system called a predominant party system (Sartori, 1976, 1990; Ware, 1996), a multiparty system with a dominant party (Blondel, 1968) or a system of 'one hegemonial party in polarised pluralism' (Von Beyme, 1984: 263–5). The study of dominant parties and dominant party systems has moved on since then but it remains a contested field. A recent collaborative project shows a growing consistency and coherence in conceptualising, measuring and explaining party dominance at national, sub-national and intraparty levels (Bogaards and Boucek, 2010).

The main criticism of party system categories is that they set arbitrary cut-off points, providing only a simplified snapshot of the format of a party system at a specific point in time. Hence they aren't useful to examine dominant parties as discrete empirical objects since dominant parties exist in different types of party systems with different configurations, patterns of competition and dynamics as Sartori discovered when he tried to differentiate dominant parties from dominant party systems (Sartori, 1976). Italy's party system offered the quintessential example of Sartori's theory of 'polarized pluralism'[1] and was also the prototype of a dominant party system with a strong centre party.

It is unfeasible to view dominant parties and dominant party systems as separable objects of study. Typologies and categories can be valuable research tools for exploring concepts and delineating their properties but they are less helpful for studying dynamics and explaining change. They cannot explain the causes and consequences of single-party dominance and the persistence and downfall of dominant parties. For this we need methods to analyse behaviour and explain group dynamics.

Most party scholars view party dominance as a retrospective phenomenon. But for Duverger dominance was 'a question of influence rather than of strength', and a dominant party became 'identified with an epoch when its doctrines, ideas, methods, its style, so to speak, coincide with those of the epoch' (Duverger, 1964: 308). Undoubtedly Duverger's understanding was influenced by his chosen prototype – the Radicals under France's Third Republic – a very unstable and fragmented multiparty system where no single majority party government could emerge. Duverger also stressed the role of public perceptions by claiming that a dominant party is that which public opinion believes to be dominant. He suggested that a party's long-term rule is inevitably self-destructing, implying the potential destructive aspect of internal forces.

Party longevity in office and the size of a party's legislative majority (or a combination of both) is the way most scholars identify dominant parties. These variables are easily quantifiable although opinion varies about the size-of-the-majority criterion and the required length of office tenure before a party can be characterised as dominant.[2]

However, dominance can also be viewed in non-temporal terms as a multilevel concept, for instance, in reference to parties holding concurrent majorities in separate competitive arenas at a specific point in time: in the presidency and separate legislative chambers of a national polity, say, or in separate tiers of government (national and sub-national), separate spheres of influence (such as the electoral, parliamentary and executive arenas) and separate districts or constituencies within a single territory, as in the case of the French Socialist Party in 2012,[3] United Russia in 2003–08[4] and the United States in 2002–06.[5] In the United States identifying multilevel dominance would involve observing the frequency of concurrent partisan majorities in *inter alia* the US presidency, the Congress and the state legislatures. Hence a given party would be described as strongly dominant at a specific point in time if it had controlling majorities in all of these competitive arenas.

District-level dominance was first examined by V.O. Key in his analysis of Democratic partisan voting in the Southern American states (Key, 1949). This disaggregated approach linked to the concept of safe and marginal seats has been replicated in a recent study of district-level dominance in France, where the author argues that durability should not be interpreted as a mere measure of time span but prospectively as the probability of incumbent office holders staying in office (Sauger, 2010).[6]

One critic went so far as to claim that 'longitudinal' versions of dominance are 'tautological and re-descriptive', since they can only say that a party is dominant when it has continuously been in government for a specified period (Dunleavy, 2010). Rejecting the *post facto* view of dominance, Dunleavy argues that 'parties do not become dominant by holding government incumbency for prolonged or unbroken periods, but by possessing a relatively long-lasting efficacy advantage over all opponents'. Dunleavy develops an approach built around the notion of an 'effectiveness advantage' (Kang, 2004) and a 'protected core' for dominant parties drawing on my empirical research (Boucek, 2001).

One advantage of the non-temporal approach is that it addresses the *post hoc* dilemma typical of the current literature plagued by a lack of consensus about how long a party needs to be in power before it can be described as dominant (for a review, see introduction and conclusion in Bogaards and Boucek, 2010). It also avoids the inconsistency and arbitrariness of categorisation which forced Sartori to relax his threshold of three consecutive victories in order to accommodate the socialist dominance in Sweden and Norway (Sartori, 1976 [2005]: 177).

However, a purely spatial conceptualisation is problematic. First, despite its elegant modelling, it isn't clear what the 'effectiveness advantage' really means in terms of parties becoming dominant by delivering 'utility' to individual voters. Second, the model based on proximity analysis makes bold assumptions about voters' knowledge of their 'personal optima' and about their compound utility and aggregate preferences. Third, the model's capacity to identify dominant parties still needs to be demonstrated empirically. This is a big challenge because it would require developing methods for measuring 'effectiveness' in the aggregate and integrating the results into a cumulative profile that would allow prediction of the success of any party in becoming dominant and losing its dominance (see conclusion in Bogaards and Boucek (2010)). Finally, this view may not be as atemporal as implied by Dunleavy, who talks about a *'relatively long-lasting* efficacy advantage' (my italics). How long does the efficacy advantage have to last before a party can be characterised as dominant?

Single-party dominance cannot be reduced to mere categories in the classification of party systems or political regimes, but this doesn't mean that parties' longevity in office and the size of their governing majorities should be discarded as indicators of dominance. On the contrary, to ignore these variables would strip the concept of a dominant party of any substantive meaning which is why empirical studies of party dominance use length-of-tenure and majority criteria as starting points, and include one of the few formalised theories of single-party dominance (Greene, 2007).[7]

The conventional temporal approach is used because the time element is crucial to discovering to what extent and why internal disunity increases with the time in power. A party's duration in office is a meaningful variable and a good indicator of dominance. Indeed the number of successive re-elections and the closeness of particular electoral results (at the aggregate and district levels) reflect the degree and fluctuation of a party's electoral dominance and affect the cost of exit for dissidents.

A government party winning large majorities in consecutive national elections is obviously strongly dominant while a party gaining a narrow victory after several large majorities is obviously vulnerable, as in the case of the British Conservatives under John Major in 1992. In parallel, declining dominance and vulnerability may apply to a long-term incumbent whose aggregate vote at the national level may disguise loss of support in traditional regional strongholds or in sub-national elections, as in the case of the Christian Democrats in Italy in the early 1990s and the Liberals in Quebec in 1984. In sum, dominance is a relative term.

1.2   Party dominance and skewed competition

Dominant parties are found in different types of party systems, so the basic units of analysis must be parties (and sub-party groups) and not party systems. What needs explaining is the capacity for a single party to skew competition in any form of party system. This capacity is observed in the electoral, parliamentary and executive arenas of competition and involves a positive feedback process whereby repeated incumbencies allow ruling parties to capitalise on the advantages of office to entrench themselves in power (Boucek, 1998: figure 6.1). Once the conditions enabling government parties to create asymmetric competition are identified it becomes possible to explain why dominant parties emerge and persist and to predict with relative certainty their decline and breakdown.

The most useful interpretations of party dominance focus on the structure of party competition and particularly on the concentration or fragmentation of opposition forces (Dahl, 1966; Blondel, 1968; Arian and Barnes, 1974; Riker, 1976; Levite and Tarrow, 1983; Smith, 1989; Laver and Schofield, 1990; Pempel, 1990; Ware, 1996; Cox, 1997; Greene, 2007). These approaches allow the examination of coalition possibilities and the prediction of the capacity for opposition forces to coordinate action against the incumbent.

However, it is important to specify which variables make the patterns of interaction between the component parties unique and to consider intraparty dynamics given that internal dissidence and factional defection can be the decisive factors in making opposition forces more competitive.

A compelling study of Mexico's transition from an authoritarian regime under the Institutional Revolutionary Party (Spanish: *Partido Revolucionario Institucional*, PRI) dominance to a fully competitive democracy argues that dominant parties bias electoral competition in their favour. They win elections before election day without resorting to electoral fraud or repression by turning public resources into patronage goods under two conditions: a large public sector and a politically quiescent bureaucracy (Greene, 2007). The resource disadvantages of opposition parties explain why they fail to become competitors who can threaten the dominant party.

Theoretical parsimony requires abstracting out variables and simplifying complex linkages. However, the search for monocausality risks eliminating relevant explanatory variables. The resource theory of party dominance (Greene, 2007) limits its own potential for comparative enquiry by tying the durability and breakdown of dominant party rule to a country's macroeconomic fortunes on the assumption that the state plays a central role in the economy and that the bureaucracy is the captive of its political masters. Consequently, Greene's attempt to apply his theory in competitive democracies (including Italy and Japan) is less persuasive than in authoritarian regimes. It would fail to explain the dominance of the Swedish Social Democrats (SAP) in twentieth-century Sweden and that of the ANC in South Africa.

Greene rejects standard demand-side, supply-side and institutional theories which he claims don't meet the 'sufficient condition' criterion although his evidence to support this is sketchy (Greene, 2007: 18–27). He rejects cleavage theory (Lipset and Rokkan, 1967) because of its poor closeness of fit with party system fragmentation (Greene, 2007: 18). Yet cleavage theory offers a powerful and parsimonious explanation of single-party dominance in post-apartheid South Africa, where the overwhelming dominance of the ANC rests solely on the political saliency of the racial cleavage providing a strong example of 'hard dominance' (Smith, 2010).

In the end, the choice of theories and methods of enquiry to explain equilibrium dominance and its breakdown is a matter of research trade-offs which the analyst has to weigh in the pursuit of particular objectives. The accuracy of descriptive accounts is often achieved at the price of theoretical complexity and parsimony and vice versa.

The objective of this book isn't to develop a cast-iron and regime-neutral theory of single-party dominance but rather to examine the internal politics of dominant parties. Hence this chapter draws on different perspectives to identify the determinants of dominance, building on previous work where dominance was dimensionalised in reference to separate, albeit connected, arenas of party competition: electoral, parliamentary and executive (Boucek, 1998).

In each arena, the salient features of dominant parties' strategies (vote-seeking, seat-seeking and portfolio-winning) are analysed from different theoretical perspectives (sociological, strategic and institutional) and assessed with appropriate qualitative and quantitative indicators, which include the number of electoral and legislative parties, to measure the reductive effect of electoral systems on electoral and parliamentary competition (Boucek, 1998); the pivotal power of individual parties in multiparty coalitions to measure parties' bargaining power and the capacity to maximise office pay-offs; the concentration of governmental power to explain executive dominance in majoritarian and non-majoritarian systems; and so on.

1.3   Electoral dominance

The primary indicator of political dominance is, naturally, electoral strength. It is difficult to envisage a single party becoming dominant without regularly gaining more popular support than its competitors.[8]

The capacity of a single party to repeatedly skew competition for votes requires an analysis of voters' preference formation and its structural factors (societal and institutional).

Many cases of one-party dominance can be traced back to country-specific historical, political and economic conditions often associated with nation-building or regime change, including the formation of a movement for national unity or independence, a new constitutional settlement, a party system realignment following a watershed election and so on. However, for dominance to persist, ruling parties must be able to win a plurality of votes on a regular basis by mobilising large groups of voters from diverse socio-economic and geographic areas.

Sociological explanations

Mobilising voters may involve activating social divisions (cleavage theory), relying on party identification to give partisan cues to core voters (less relevant in Europe than in the United States), making 'catch-all' appeals to voters under multiparty competition or 'median' voter appeals under two-party dynamics (the latter also more relevant in the United States than in European multiparty systems with polymodal preference distributions), shaping and reshaping voters' preferences (including changing voters' societal status), making targeted appeals to swing groups of voters (risky and hard to sustain), campaigning on a party's record in government to encourage retrospective voting and so on. Given incumbents' multiple electoral strategies, it's no surprise that theorists of single-party dominance focus on the competitive failures of opposition parties (Cox, 1997; Greene, 2007).

The socio-economic structure of a given electorate and the saliency of specific societal cleavages determine whether parties appeal to voters on the basis of class, religion, language or race. These cleavages often have a regional base: the German Christian Social Union in Catholic Bavaria, the Liberal Party of Canada in French-speaking Quebec and the ANC in black South Africa, to name a few. Parties may act as brokers in mediating the interests of these different societal groups.

In post-industrial democracies, the declining correspondence between social cleavages and voting has driven parties to adopt 'catch-all' strategies. In Canada during the second half of the twentieth century, voter de-alignment and the growth of regional parties forced the dominant Liberals to abandon a style of localised 'brokerage politics' in favour of a nationwide appeal through pan-Canadian campaigns.[9] Issue cleavages can help target swing groups of voters on the basis of salient (albeit sometimes narrow) issues, as in the case of the Republicans under President George W. Bush. His 2004 re-election campaign directed family-value appeals to the Christian Right. However, such instrumental strategies can be counterproductive if they alienate moderate supporters.

If social location is a significant determinant of voting behaviour, parties may engage in social engineering by seeking to change the social structure as in the case of British Conservatives under Thatcher in the 1980s. By encouraging local authorities to sell their stock of public housing to tenants, Thatcher effectively transformed traditional Labour supporters into property owners and Conservative voters (Dunleavy, 1991: 120–1), albeit with consequences for the British economy two decades later.[10] The creation of a new working class in Thatcher's Britain was bolstered by the sale of public shares in newly privatised utilities which transformed thousands of voters into small stockholders.[11] This partisan social engineering swelled the ranks of Conservative supporters associated with private-sector employment, business and home ownership (Sanders, 1992: 188–9). In contrast, the strategy of New Labour seemed to be about turning as many voters as possible into clients of the state.

Cultivating links with specific sectional interests helps consolidate a party's core vote. For example, Japanese farmers in over-represented rural districts and businesses in the construction industry provided bedrock support for the Liberal Democratic Party of Japan (LDP) well into the 1980s. In Italy the Christian Democrats built their mass appeal by garnering the support of occupational groups and trade union organisations, including the Confederation of Small Farmers (*Coltivatori Diretti*), the Italian Confederation of Labour Movement (CISL), ACLI (Italian Christian Workers' Association), the *Movimento Laureati* (the Movement of Catholic University Graduates), the Church and the construction industry. In Sweden the SAP owed much of its pre-war electoral support to the agrarian movement within the red–green alliance and its post-war support of the labour movement, notably the *Landsorganisationen* federation and the white-collar union federation the Swedish Confederation of Professional Employees (Swedish: *Tjänstemännens Centralorganisation*, TCO) (Esping-Andersen, 1990). In Britain the Labour Party relies on the trade unions for much of its funding and its leadership selection when the party is in opposition, as demonstrated by the election of Ed Miliband in 2010 against his brother David who had much more cabinet experience.

Institutional explanations

From an institutional perspective dominance is explained primarily through the role of electoral systems. Reductive voting systems such as single-member plurality (SMP) have the capacity to skew party competition by exaggerating parties' wins and losses giving the party with the plurality of votes a commanding majority.

According to the Duvergerian logic SMP concentrates party systems, squeezes out third parties whose support isn't geographically concentrated and generates single-party majority governments (Duverger, 1964; Cox, 1997; Lijphart, 1999). It is now a canon that this hypothesis applies only at the district level, but it encompasses both the mechanical effects of voting systems (generated by the formulae used to translate votes into seats, the thresholds of representation, the magnitude and boundaries of electoral districts and so on) and the psychological effects which encourage voters to cast strategic votes when their preferred party stands no chance of winning.

Through their reductive effect on the number of parties restrictive electoral systems give dominant parties comparative advantages, as shown in a longitudinal survey of seven dominant party systems using different voting systems[12] (Boucek, 1998, 2001: Chapter 1; see also Dunleavy and Boucek, 2003). In contrast permissive electoral systems that translate votes into seats in a more proportional way are less biased towards dominant parties and less penalising towards minority parties.

SMP narrows competition by exaggerating the electoral strength of the winning party whose share of the popular vote translates into a disproportional share of the seats and by penalising third parties as long as their votes aren't geographically concentrated. In Britain this bias has benefited each of the major parties at different times (the Labour Party recently and the Conservatives before 1979)[13] at the expense of the third party: the Liberal Democrats, who have accumulated 'wasted votes' across the country since the 1970s which have marked the end of the British two-party system. From the 1930s to the 1970s the combined vote share of the two main parties stood at over 90 per cent but dropped sharply to 75 per cent in 1974 and to just 65.5 per cent in 2010.[14]

Such artificial majority victories motivated Labour and Conservatives to act as if they enjoyed dominant status and as if opposition parties were completely irrelevant. However, the disproportional character of Labour's landslide victories in 1997 and 2001 put electoral reform on the agenda. In 1997, energetic Labour leader Tony Blair won 44.4 per cent of the popular vote but 63.6 per cent of the seats giving the party a total of 418 seats and a majority of 179 seats over all other parties. Their re-election landslide in June 2001 was even more disproportional: a 62.5 per cent seat share in return for a 40.7 per cent share of the nationwide vote. This was a seat/vote ratio of 1.53 to 1, even bigger than the previous record of 1.44 to 1 in 1983 when the Conservatives' 42.4 per cent of the vote translated into 61.1 per cent of the seats.[15]

In 1964, when Britain was still a two-party democracy, Labour won nearly the same percentage of the popular vote as in 1997 (44.1 per cent versus 44.4 per cent), under another energetic leader, Harold Wilson, but ended up with 317 seats (just half the seats in the chamber), giving them a bare majority of only four seats. In 1970, Labour lost the general election with only 1 percentage point less of the popular vote than in 1964.

The growth in the number of third-party members of parliament (MPs) and the fractured state of the British electorate mean that Britain is no longer a classic two-party democracy characterised by alternating periods of single-party dominance between Labour and the Conservatives. The general election in May 2010 produced a 'hung' parliament and a Conservative–Liberal Democrat coalition. Despite the Labour-to-Conservative 5 per cent swing (the largest since Thatcher came to power in 1979) and the fact that the Conservatives won more seats than at any time since 1931, they were 19 seats short of a majority although they were still the dominant party in England.[16]

In Canada the persistence of single-party government under multiparty competition confirms that Duverger's hypothesis isn't applicable at the national level and that the presence of regional parties with geographically concentrated electorates can mitigate the reductive effect of SMP on national party systems. Despite a nearly 50 per cent failure rate of the two major Canadian parties to gain absolute majorities since World War II, single-party government remains the norm in Canada. Pressures to reform the voting system are weak because the regularity of landslide elections suggests SMP isn't dysfunctional, as it can produce government with absolute majorities. Moreover, the need for partisan coordination across geographical regions is weaker in Canada's federal system than in unitary systems such as Britain's due to the decoupling of provincial politics from national politics (Johnston, 2008).

In Canada SMP produces occasional explosions in the national party system, as in 1984, 1993 and 2011 (Chapter 5), indicating a notoriously volatile electorate but also a regionalised party system that produces some quirky election outcomes. For example in the 1993 watershed election, the Progressive Conservatives collapsed from being a majority governing party to winning just two seats in the Canadian House of Commons. This left the *Bloc Québécois* – a new separatist party advocating the country's break-up – as the official opposition. The Bloc had only the fourth-largest share of the popular vote but the second-largest share of federal seats, all in Quebec. This permitted the Liberals' sweep back into power after almost a decade in opposition with a 60 per cent seat majority but only 41.6 per cent of the popular vote.

However, another shocking election in 2011 nearly wiped out the Bloc, leaving it with only four federal seats, while the left-leaning New Democratic Party (NDP) was transformed into the official opposition as it grabbed a large majority of Quebec seats. This redrawing of the Canadian political map enabled Stephen Harper's Conservatives to be re-elected with a majority after running two minority governments and left the Liberals in third place, their lowest seat share ever.

Historically the Canadian Liberals have been direct beneficiaries of the Conservatives' boom and bust performances (Johnston, 2008), thanks to the reductive effect of SMP. An aggregate time-series analysis of the relative reduction in the effective number of parties (RRP) shows that the Liberals' periods of dominance (1935–57, 1963–84 and 1993–06) are marked by wide divergences between the effective number of electoral parties (N_v) and the effective number of legislative parties (N_s) (Boucek, 1998, 2001). The biggest gaps were found in elections when the Liberals seized power back from the Progressive Conservatives (in 1935, 1963 and 1993, when the RRP stood at 41 per cent, 19 per cent and 38 per cent, respectively). When the then Progressive Conservatives won big (in 1958 and 1984) the RRP was also very high (around 38 per cent) but, importantly, these were also majorities of the popular vote, a feat never achieved by the Liberals.

Earlier Liberal dominance had rested on concentrated support in at least one of the two most populous Canadian provinces – Quebec and Ontario, which together account for approximately 60 per cent of the seats in the federal parliament. So as long as the Liberals won big in one of those two provinces, their dominance was assured.[17] However, the 2011 election appears to have broken this pattern primarily due to the loss of saliency of the national unity question for Canadian voters.

Permissive electoral systems are less instrumental in propping up dominant parties, because they erect fewer barriers to entry. In Italy the Christian Democrats derived virtually no advantage from the mechanical effects of the list preference voting system due to the large district magnitudes[18] and no minimum threshold of entry. In Japan, however, the single non-transferable vote in multimember constituencies (SNTV) – not a true proportional system – gave the LDP a comparative advantage by skewing party competition through its 1955 multiparty merger (Boucek, 1998, 2001). Having gained 58 per cent of the vote and 61.5 per cent of the seats in the Lower House of the Diet in 1958, the new LDP cut the number of competing parties by half and established its dominance. Electoral competition became two-way contests between two unequal parties – the conservative LDP and the much smaller Socialist Party of Japan (JSP).

Moreover, as Chapter 6 explains, in both Italy and Japan before electoral reform in the mid-1990s, these voting systems generated competitive advantages for the Christian Democratic Party (DC) and LDP through the factional management of the personal vote. The factions regulated the internal competition for electoral stakes by controlling list placement (DC) and the distribution of campaign resources and by coordinating local party nomination and vote division (LDP) – a strategy that Japan's opposition parties were slow to emulate (Cox, 1997; Christensen, 2000). In Italy and Japan the new mixed-member majoritarian systems have introduced a more bipolar logic to party competition, including landslide elections in Japan in 2005 and 2009.

In general there are more opportunities for incumbents to compromise the outcomes of competitive elections in countries with weak political institutions than in fully fledged competitive democracies. But since institutions can be manipulated, it is possible for dominant parties even in competitive democracies to boost their advantage through various strategies. These include constant re-districting or 'gerrymandering' in the United States, malapportionment in Ireland (under Fianna Fáil's dominance before 1979), blocking demands for electoral reform (as in Japan and Italy in the 1980s and 1990s) and interference in the running of elections (as in Mexico under PRI dominance).

Strategic and spatial explanations

Dominant parties are notorious for being pragmatic and 'catch-all' (Kirchheimer, 1966). Orientated towards power rather than ideology, catch-all parties adapt to changing electoral market conditions in a pragmatic way to maximise support and capture the 'median' voter. There is ample evidence of long-lived government parties de-emphasising doctrine in order to broaden voter appeal. The SAP went so far as to declare in a manifesto that their party had 'never been especially interested in theoretical discussions' (Misgeld, Molin, and Åmark, 1992: 152). This was a rational strategy under Sweden's one-dimensional welfare politics which allowed the SAP to regain office in the midst of a home-grown economic crisis in 1994 related to a programme of tax rises and public spending cuts not normally associated with social democratic parties.

British Conservatives and Canadian Liberals have at different times embraced opposite sides of the same issue, for instance protectionism and free trade, state interventionism and *laissez-faire* economics as well as foreign engagement and appeasement. Conservative dominance in twentieth-century Britain has been explained through the party's pragmatism and selective use of ideology to bolster its status as the 'natural party of government' (Seldon, 1994).

After 18 years in opposition, Labour under Tony Blair learned the value of non-ideological politics. It discarded its class doctrines in the early 1990s (notably through the removal of Clause IV from the party's constitution[19]), and the Labour government adopted practical policies to raise standards in public services which Blair defended as 'what matters is what works'. In Japan weak partisanship facilitated the creation of the LDP in 1955 from a broad multiparty merger and kept the party relatively free of ideological divisions while in office for half a century. 'Rather than being narrowly and ideologically fixated on particular conservative principles, it [the LDP] has been able to tack with the prevailing strong winds and alter, even if belatedly, its previous policies when they proved to be unpopular later on' (Krauss and Pekkanen, 2011: 14).

In sum flexible politics enables parties to maintain centrist support and to embrace new issues as they emerge. The trick is to endorse issues that have wide public support and aren't redistributive and divisive: such as Thatcher's 'poll tax' in Britain (Chapter 4) and federalism in Canada (Chapter 5).

There are times when parties need to reposition policies to win new tranches of voters at the risk of polarising politics and party opinion. Downsian competition predicts that parties will compete to accommodate voters' preferences by converging on the median voter's position, which under two-party dynamics is expected to be located somewhere close to the centre of the political spectrum (Downs, 1957: 95–138).

In practice, however, parties may prefer to move away from the political centre ground to accommodate changes in electoral tastes, reshape voters' preferences or reorient the political agenda, even under two-party dynamics. For example, in the early 1980s, Thatcher's Conservatives abandoned consensus politics by moving clearly to the right with a radical programme to denationalise public services while reasserting state authority (Gamble, 1988), leaving intact the National Health Service (NHS).

By concentrating on floating voters, parties may damage their core vote if this drives some supporters towards extreme parties. The UK Independence Party (UKIP) and the British National Party (BNP) encroach on the core votes of the two mainstream British parties. UKIP's anti-Europe rhetoric appeals to some Conservative supporters on the far right and the BNP's special brand of nationalism holds a particular appeal for Labour's traditional working-class supporters who feel threatened by immigrant labour.

The Italian DC is another example of successful repositioning. After World War II de Gasperi created a successful mass Catholic party by transforming the wartime anti-fascist solidarity into Church-sponsored anti-communism. This polarised Italian politics between left and right on economic and social issues (Levite and Tarrow, 1983: 313–5) and neutered the large Communist Party (PCI), which was portrayed as a threat to democratic stability even though the two parties (DC and PCI) shared the spoils of power through *consociativismo* (Burnett and Mantovani, 1998). DC was described as 'a party for all seasons', thanks to its ability to juggle issues to accommodate shifting electoral interests (Pasquino, 1980a).

In short structural aspects of party competition can be 'endogenised' to enhance re-election prospects and prolong dominance. Parties have the capacity to manipulate salient issues to safeguard or expand their 'own' policy spaces (Robertson, 1976; Budge and Farlie, 1977; Dunleavy and Husbands, 1985: 67–70; Dunleavy, 1991, 2010: 112–44; Laver and Hunt, 1992).

Control of public information enables ruling parties to endogenise their information advantages. State broadcasting monopolies have been abolished in most modern democracies (except for Italy[20]) but governing parties can still shape public perceptions by putting their own 'spin' on political events, by initiating news leaks to selected media and by restraining public access to government information.

In the United Kingdom political spinning has a long pedigree, most recently associated with Alistair Campbell, Tony Blair's Director of Communications and Strategy.[21] Thatcher had exploited the media to win Conservative elections in 1979 and 1983, as her press secretary Bernard Ingham had cultivated close relationships with Fleet Street right-wing editors and writers of powerful tabloids. For the 1982 war against Argentina for the Falkland Islands British soldiers were portrayed as being in danger for their lives, provoking a surge of public support in favour of invasion, significantly boosting the Conservatives' popularity during their re-election campaign in 1983 (Dunleavy and Husbands, 1985: 67–70) and allowing Thatcher to reinvent herself as the warrior queen.

Incumbent governments can also restrict public access to government information by exploiting regulatory loopholes and restraining freedom of information. In Britain newspapers and publishers covering the House of Commons risk being in contempt of court if they publish parliamentary questions, answers or debates on subjects classified under 'super-injunctions'.

Finally campaign finance is another source of comparative advantage for incumbents. In many European countries parties are subsidised by the state, and campaign funding is apportioned on the basis of individual party shares of legislative seats. This gives dominant parties the lion's share of campaign finance at the expense of minority parties, who are deprived of funding if their popular support falls below a set threshold. Opposition parties' capacities to compete is hampered not only by their lack of public finance but also by limited private funding as individuals, business groups and trade unions prefer to back election winners rather than losers.

1.4   Legislative and coalition dominance

The capacity to form viable legislative and executive coalitions is a major determinant of dominance. It depends on the degree of party system fragmentation and the ideological distance between opposition parties. These factors can prevent opposition parties from forming connected winning coalitions to beat dominant centrist parties.

In most democracies the party with the largest share of the popular vote forms the government on its own or as the senior member of a coalition, which is often the case under permissive electoral systems. Restrictive electoral systems lead to single-party governments, according to the Duvergerian logic.

In multiparty systems breakdowns in single-party dominance are often due to the success of opposition forces in forming viable coalitions to unseat the ruling party. This may be due to asymmetric preference distribution, factional defections from the dominant party and so on. In Ireland in 1973 Fianna Fáil had been in power continuously since 1957, but was unseated by a coalition between Fine Gael and Labour. To regain office Fianna Fáil had to form its own coalition with the Progressive Democrats in 1989 and with Labour in 1992.

This logic also holds for non-centrist parties under asymmetric preference distribution. Laver and Schofield argue that, in theory, if parties care only about policy and if politics really is one-dimensional, then the party that controls the median legislators will be in a dominant bargaining position and will always end up in government (Laver and Schofield, 1990: 80).

In Sweden the 'bourgeois' parties formed an electoral alliance for the first time in 1976, producing the first non-SAP government in half a century.[22] Indeed the opposition parties' coordination failures and dominant parties' cohesion explain why long-term political dominance has been the rule in many West European countries during the twentieth century, particularly in Scandinavia where the distribution of preferences on the main competitive dimension – welfare state policy – was skewed to the right (McGann, 2002). This spatial configuration has allowed cohesive Social Democratic parties to become dominant by hampering the coalition strategies of opposition parties on the right, who are stretched over a broad ideological space on this issue.

1.5 Coalition dominance in practice: Italy's Christian Democrats

Executive dominance is the by-product of a party's success in building durable coalitions at both intraparty and interparty levels. The spatial positioning of a party (or faction) along the ideological spectrum and the cohesion of the dominant player are the building blocks of coalition dominance.

Sartori explains the DC's long-term rule in terms of the presence of bipolar oppositions under a model of 'polarized pluralism' (Sartori, 1976). Party systems with large centre parties facing numerous competitors to the left and right tend to perpetuate long-term rule by centrist parties. The left and right can never agree on an alternative to the centrist government party, as each is further from the other than from the government. Hence, while centrist parties do not necessarily govern alone, they govern continuously because their competitors are unable to coordinate on an alternative that excludes them.

Given these conditions, it is surprising that coalition governments in post-war Italy were frequently surplus majority coalitions and minority governments rather than the minimum winning coalitions (Laver and Schofield, 1990: 71; Lijphart, 1999) predicted by coalition theories based on rational choice (Riker, 1962).

Carrying extra passengers in a coalition may be a source of stability because it provides insurance against coalition break-ups, factional exits and uncertain legislative outcomes. In the first instance this enabled Italy's DC leaders to bind smaller coalition partners by making their exit threats less credible. A coalition withdrawal after the investiture vote would require a full-scale government resignation and thus the formation of a new one, which would be costly (Laver and Schofield, 1990: 86). Second, the extra legislative slack from a surplus majority removes leverage from factions whose policy positions on some issues may be closer to those of other parties not in the coalition. Such factions will be disinclined to defect, knowing that they aren't pivotal to government survival. Third, surplus majorities can facilitate legislative management and increase government efficiency. In Italy until 1988 the secret ballot was used frequently in the Chamber of Deputies, making party discipline difficult to enforce and legislative outcomes difficult to predict. A surplus majority increased the likelihood that party leaders could deliver enough votes on key measures.

The idea of bargaining leverage indicates how pivotal individual parties and factions are in making and breaking interparty and intraparty coalitions and consequently in maximising pay-offs. Coalition pivotality can be measured with power indices, such as the Shapley–Shubik index or the Banzhaf index, which draw attention to the notion of players who pivot, that is those who can convert losing coalitions into winning coalitions. These indices estimate at specific points in time how pivotal individual parties and factions are in forming winning coalitions or in breaking existing ones.

The normalised Banzhaf index of power used here shows the number of times a player's defection is pivotal in any winning coalition. Given the legislative strength of a given party (or faction), the index computes in how many of all the possible winning coalitions above the 50 per cent threshold that party is a necessary partner. Despite the fact that the index is policy-blind and thus assumes that all coalitions are equally probable, it nevertheless shows that parties who are decisive in many coalition alternatives have good chances of being included in government. More importantly, by identifying the dominant player in bargaining games the index goes a long way in explaining why potential minimum winning coalitions fail to materialise – precisely because of problems of policy/ideological distance between parties or factions.

The Banzhaf index is used here to calculate the pivotal power of all the parties in the Italian Chamber of Deputies over several periods and is used in Chapters 7 and 8 to analyse the interfactional bargaining structure of the DC and LDP. The results are normalised so that the total bargaining power of all the parties (or factions) add up to 1.00. The figures reported in Tables 1.1 and 1.2 show the proportion of seats and the fractional share of pivots for each of the parties competing in

Table 1.1 Party parliamentary representation and pivotal power for a selection of government coalitions in Italy 1958–92

| | Centre-Right Coalitions 1958–63 | | Centre-Left Coalitions 1963–76 | | National Solidarity 1976–79 | | *Pentapartito* Coalitions 1979–92 | |
| | 1958 Election | | 1972 Election | | 1976 Election | | 1987 Election | |
	%Seats	Power*	%Seats	Power*	%Seats	Power*	%Seats	Power*
PCI	24	.06	28	.13	36	.19	28	.21
PSI	14	.06	10	.13	9	.19	15	.21
PSDI	4	.05	5	.03	3	.04	3	.03
PRI	1	.02	2	.01	2	.02	3	.03
DC	46	.69	42	.53	42	.42	37	.36
PLI	3	.02	3	.03	2	.02	2	.03
MSI	4	.05	10	.13	6	.12	6	.07
Radicals							2	.02
Greens							2	.02

*The normalised Banzhaf index of power is calculated using the software programme designed by Thomas König and Thomas Bräuninger (Mannheim Centre for European Social Research). Total scores might not add up to 1.00 due to rounding.

PCI: Communists; PSI: Socialists; PSDI: Social Democrats; PRI: Republicans; DC: Christian Democrats; PLI: Liberals; MSI: Social Movement.

Table 1.2 Party parliamentary representation and pivotal power Italian coalition governments, 1983–92

	1983 Election		1987 Election		1992 Election	
	%Seats	Power*	%Seats	Power*	%Seats	Power*
PCI±	31	.22	28	.22	17	.14
PSI§	12	.19	15	.22	15	.14
PdUP	1	.02				
PSDI	4	.04	3	.03	3	.03
PRI	5	.06	3	.03	4	.03
DC	36	.34	37	.36	33	.43
PLI	2	.03	2	.03	3	.03
MSI¥	7	.08	6	.07	5	.04
Radicals	2	.03	2	.02	5	.04
Greens			2	.02	2	.02
Northern League					9	.09
La Rete					2	.02
Others					2	.02

*The normalised Banzhaf index of power is calculated using the software programme designed by Thomas König and Thomas Bräuninger (Mannheim Centre for European Social Research). Because of rounding, the scores might not add up to 1.00.
±Democratic Party of the Left (PDS) after 1991.
§Socialist Unity Party (PSU) after 1990.
¥Renamed *Destra Nazionale*.
PCI: Communists; PSI: Socialists; PSDI: Social Democrats; PRI: Republicans; DC: Christian Democrats; PLI: Liberals; MSI: Social Movement.

selected elections (Table 1.1: 1958, 1972, 1976 and 1987; Table 1.2: 1983, 1987 and 1992) corresponding to different types of DC-led government coalitions involving different models of interparty bargaining as a result of changes in the party system's balance of power.

The DC played a pivotal role in the formation of every multiparty government in Italy between 1945 and 1993 despite gaining an absolute parliamentary majority only once. In 1948 Prime Minister De Gasperi invited other parties to join the Christian Democrats in government to consolidate Italy's fragile democracy and to demonstrate to the American government the country's willingness to join the fight against Communism, an implicit condition for Italy's receipt of Marshall Aid. For the next quarter century Communist delegitimation became the linchpin of the DC's coalition strategies based on the so-called *conventio ad excludendum* – an unwritten agreement to exclude the anti-system parties: the Communists (PCI) and the neo-fascist (Social Movement; MSI) – from DC-led governments (Arian and Barnes, 1974: 597–9; Levite and Tarrow, 1983; Hine, 1993: 96–107). Readers will note that there is a ten-year overlap in the periods covered in Tables 1.1 and 1.2 which focuses on the declining period of DC dominance from 1983 to 1992, when the Socialists (PSI) played a prominent coalition role in keeping the Communists out. This shows how increased competition (resulting from the entry of new parties and the split of the Communists in the early 1990s) affects the coalition power of individual parties and the overall bargaining structure in the party system.

Party representation and pivotal power for a selection of government coalitions in Italy 1958–92

1. Communist neutralisation under centre–right coalitions (1958–63)
   During this period, the DC dominated the legislative party system and formed centre–right coalitions with the PSDI, the Republicans (PRI) and the Liberals (PLI). As Table 1.1 shows, the DC was strongly pivotal. For instance, in 1958, its 46 per cent seat share translated into a 70 per cent share of pivots. Of the six governments that were formed during this period, four were minority single-party governments and two were DC-led multiparty coalitions that included the small PSDI (July 1958–Feb 1959) and even smaller PRI (Feb 1962–June 1963).

2. Communist neutralisation in centre–left coalitions (1963–76)
   This period is marked by centre–left coalitions initiated in 1963, when the DC dumped the PLI in favour of PSI. This was a pre-emptive strike by Prime Minister Aldo Moro to deter the formation of a Communist–Socialist alliance which would have been strong enough to defeat the DC. However, as the PCI vote and seat shares increased and those of the DC gradually declined, the PSI became more and more pivotal to government formation. Their participation would satisfy the 'minimum winning' criterion, but the DC continued to carry surplus passengers (usually the PSDI and/or the PRI) as insurance against a PCI–PSI alliance.

3. Communist co-optation (1976–79)
   In the mid-1970s Italy went through a severe national crisis marked by terrorist violence and economic recession. This prompted the DC to engineer a *rapprochement* with the Communists, culminating in a 'historic compromise' and the formation of a single-party (*monocolore*) government of national solidarity. In the 1976 general election the Communists gained 34.4 per cent of the popular vote (4.3 per cent behind the DC) and 34 per cent of the seats in the Chamber of Deputies. While not in cabinet the PCI received

parliamentary committee memberships in exchange for their 'constructive abstention' on key bills such as the introduction of income policies.

However, the kidnap and murder of Aldo Moro by the Red Brigades in the spring of 1978 brought this DC–PCI cooperation to an abrupt end. The PCI was dumped in favour of the PSI and the PLI. As Table 1.1 demonstrates, by 1976 the bargaining structure had changed as the centre of gravity shifted to the left, translating into a significant drop in the pivotal power of the DC (from .53 to .42), whose seat share stayed the same as in 1972.

This shift in the balance of power was to the benefit of the Socialists and to the detriment of the Communists, whose share of pivots remained very disproportional to their parliamentary representation. With 227 seats in the Chamber of Deputies the Communists were no more pivotal than the Socialists with their 35 seats. As Chapter 7 demonstrates, this new interparty configuration affected the balance of power inside the DC and made factions on the left of the party more pivotal.

4. Renewed Communist exclusion and PSI inclusion (1979–92)

As the DC reverted to forming surplus multiparty coalitions that included the PSI, PLI, PSDI and PRI, the Socialists' participation became critical to government survival. The DC's bargaining leverage was eroding in favour of the PCI. Under Bettino Craxi it became a decisive partner in DC-led coalition governments. Without the support of the Communists and neo-fascist MSI (the old anti-system parties located at each extreme of the ideological spectrum) no winning coalition could be formed that didn't include the Socialists. As Table 1.2 demonstrates, in 1983 and 1987 the Socialists (PSI) and the Communists (PCI) were as pivotal in coalition terms even though in 1983 the Communists had 37 per cent more MPs than the Socialists and 53 per cent more MPs in 1987.

The PSI used this bargaining leverage to extract substantive payoffs from coalition partners and to destabilise government. They gained control of many important ministries, such as Finance, Public Sector and Defense, and the top executive: the presidency in 1981 and the prime ministership in 1983 (Craxi was prime minister until 1987[23]). To satisfy the lust for office of its junior coalition partner, the DC created new cabinet and non-cabinet posts with no particular policy responsibilities. The Socialists used their blackmail potential to destabilise governments and were responsible for four of five government crises in the early 1980s.

Party system de-alignment at the end of the Cold War put an end to these unstable DC-led coalitions by making anti-communism irrelevant. Having already lost control of the 'median' voter to the small left-of-centre Republican Party, the DC faced intense competition resulting from the split of the PCI in 1991 and the entry of new parties, notably the Northern League and the anti-Mafia *La Rete*. In 1991 the government fell when the PRI withdrew from the five-party (*pentapartito*) coalition, triggering a major realigning election in April 1992 in which the DC's share of the vote fell below 30 per cent for the first time.

This was the tipping point in the DC's collapse. Their support disintegrated in a series of local and regional elections over the next 18 months. Election defeats combined with factional disputes over constitutional reform, and wide-ranging arrests of corrupt politicians in the 'clean hands' judicial investigation brought down Italy's post-war political establishment and precipitated the implosion of the dominant Christian Democrats during their last congress in January 1994.

Party representation and pivotal power: Italian coalition governments 1983–92

Coalition dominance is also about agenda control. By controlling the structural constraints of coalition bargaining, dominant parties can use procedural devices and institutional arrangements to maximise their own pay-offs. For example an incoming Italian government must gain the approval of the legislature through an investiture vote before taking office. Such investiture decision rules favour the 'candidate government', because abstentions effectively count in the government's favour.[24]

Implicit rules for selecting the prime minister are also biased in favour of the candidate government. Conventions give the senior coalition partner a leading role in the selection and distribution of cabinet and non-cabinet appointments, the chairmanships and composition of parliamentary committees and many other important political appointments that have the capacity to embed ruling parties in government.

Until 1992 Italy's DC monopolised the chairmanships of all standing committees of both houses of parliament, managed their agendas and organised their consultations with others. Hence, in the long run, executive dominance gives incumbents agenda-setting powers and a proprietary lock-in over the spoils of office, which can be transformed into partisan resources to skew competition and maintain single-party dominance.

1.6   Entrenched dominance: transforming incumbency advantage into partisan resources

Executive dominance enables ruling parties to transform incumbency advantages into partisan resources by giving them a command over the levers of government and control of the public purse and political patronage. In authoritarian regimes dominant parties generate asymmetric resources by diverting funds from state-owned enterprises, doling out many patronage jobs to supporters and extracting kickbacks and sometimes illicit campaign contributions from domestic businesses in exchange for economic protection or state contracts. By virtually transforming public agencies into campaign headquarters, this capacity depends on a large public sector and an acquiescent bureaucracy (Greene, 2007).

In competitive democracies, especially in West Europe during the second half of the twentieth century ruling parties monopolised state resources through the expansion of the state sector. Post-war reconstruction required massive infrastructure projects under state control and led to the nationalisation of many utilities, such as water, power, transport and telephone. This extended to other industries such as steel and coal in Britain. Overall this expansion of the state meant public bureaucracies ballooned and became politicised while political elites tapped into deep reservoirs of resources to purchase consent.

In Italy, during the 1950s and early 1960s most utilities were nationalised into state-holding corporations. This gave DC politicians a deep pool of resources to spread among their clients. Fanfani in particular set up the so-called *sottogoverno*, a system of patronage distribution which consolidated the power of the DC and of his own personal faction, especially in the South where the bureaucracy was more receptive to political influence and manipulation.

Unlike in Britain and in France,[25] an Italian 'constituency for bureaucratic autonomy did not emerge prior to the democratic era' (Shefter, 1977: 443). This deprived the country of an autonomous, technocratic and expert civil service to oversee the country's modernisation. Bureaucrats were recruited and promoted not on merit but on partisan grounds. Civil servants became captives of their political masters – the Christian Democrats – and were drawn into the DC's web of clientelism, deceit and corruption.

Client–parent relationships were the major pattern of interaction between ministries and their constituents (LaPalombara, 1964), and this exacerbated factionalism (Allum, 1973: 107). A given ministry became the client of the group dominating the activity under its jurisdiction (for example *Confindustria* representing business, the Ministry of Industry and Commerce, the Ministry of State Participation and many public companies) or bureaucracies within certain departments became colonised by a parent group controlling the ministry's appointments and patronage (for example the Ministry of Education, the Catholic organisations or the Ministry of Labour and the unions).

Patronage was allocated through the *lottizazione,* based on the balance of power between political parties and factions but giving the largest party (the DC) the lion's share. Top personnel in the agencies of the *parastato,* such as the savings banks, were appointed for their partisan and factional affiliations.[26] The largest pool of patronage was the Institute for Industrial Reconstruction (IRI), Italy's biggest state-holding company set up under Mussolini in 1933 and privatised in 1992.[27] The IRI had 600 holding companies in iron and steel, shipbuilding, telecommunications and electronics, engineering, road and motorway construction, city planning, the national airline Alitalia and national broadcasting, and also held most of the shares of Italy's three large banks. The IRI gave the DC vast opportunities to provide 'jobs for the boys' and draw powerful elites into their web. But the cost was high – by 1992 IRI's debts had ballooned to 73 billion liras.

The exchange of private goods for votes became widespread during the early years of DC dominance as state resources grew on the back of the 1960s economic boom and the 1970 decentralisation programme, which transformed the regions into large depositories of economic power and lubricated the DC factional system at the grass-roots. In Italy (and Japan) the building of infrastructural projects, such as post offices, motorways and airports, offered rich rewards to partisan supporters through jobs and public works contracts. The system was administered by local barons and faction leaders inside the dominant parties. In Italy road-building contracts were divided up among DC faction leaders. They in turn took bribes in exchange for tenders in their particular regions where segments of motorways were even personally associated with individual faction leaders.[28]

In Japan, the LDP maintained a firm grip over policy and patronage through its triangular links with business and the powerful Japanese civil service described by American political scientist Chalmers Johnson as the 'capitalist developmental state' – a description that also applied to South Korea and Taiwan (Johnson, 1994). The LDP feathered its own nest by distributing 'pork' and other selective goods to its constituents:

the goods given included licenses and contracts for the construction industry controlled by the Ministry of Construction[29] and various protectionist measures such as subsidies, price supports and tax breaks (Curtis, 1988; van Wolferen, 1989; Pempel, 1990). Business lobbied the government for public contracts by pouring money into the LDP's coffers and the pockets of powerful mandarins. This badly dented the prestige and pride of Japan's public service that dated back to the samurai era of the 17–19th centuries.

Japan's patronage distribution was managed through the *köenkai*. These candidate-support networks corresponding to electoral district lines were vote-mobilising machines for individual politicians. Constituents exchanged funding, votes and canvassing efforts for political favours and services (van Wolferen, 1990: 109–43; Scheiner, 2006; Krauss and Pekkanen, 2011). This enabled the LDP to target and monitor support among voters and interest groups in individual districts and regions and was reinforced by the factions (Chapter 6). Some have argued that in the long run such clientelist arrangements weakened the LDP's capacity to expand its electoral appeal beyond its core vote (Christensen, 2000: 185). However, Krauss and Pekkanen (2011) argue that despite the decline in the memberships of the *Köenkai* years after the 1994 electoral reform they remain vibrant organisations that haven't been substituted by LDP party branches.

In Canada vast reservoirs of political patronage and public funds are provided by the Crown corporations[30] and the federal procurement system. Under the Liberals private corporations gained procurement contracts in exchange for party funding. Contributions to the Liberals were made either without public bidding or in proportion to the amount of government business received (Whitaker, 1992: 161). Private appeals to national corporations enabled the Liberals to finance their partisan activities during the 1940s and 1950s but created costly kickback scandals.

With no regular alternation in office the essential mechanism of accountability fails to function. The privatisation of incentives resulting from the abuse of patronage by self-serving politicians has led many dominant parties, including the DC, LDP and the Canadian Liberals, to become embroiled in damaging corruption scandals. In Italy the 'clean hands' investigation precipitated the collapse of the DC in the mid-1990s and in Canada the Liberals were thrown out of office in 2006 in the midst of an enquiry into a federal sponsorship scandal (Chapter 6).[31] Although the privatisation of public services in most countries puts constraints on the partisan use of state resources, British academics have argued that the emergence of quasi-governmental agencies represents a new and less transparent way of distributing patronage to supporters (Weir and Beetham, 1999: chapter 8).

Conclusion

This chapter has demonstrated that dominant parties endure because of the success of their vote-seeking, office-seeking and policy-seeking strategies which have been explained from different theoretical perspectives: sociological, institutional and strategic.

Long-lived government parties skew party competition by adapting their 'catch-all' strategies to the structure of specific electorates and institutional regimes. Under multiparty competition generated by permissive voting systems the ability to form durable government coalitions is critical to long-lasting executive dominance. This was demonstrated through snapshots of the Christian Democrats' bargaining leverage in multiparty coalition governments in post-war Italy.

Whether executive dominance is achieved under single-party rule or multiparty government, its consolidation is likely to rest on a party's capacity to transform incumbency advantages into partisan resources. This enables parties to expand their reach and build their organisational strength and consequently entrench themselves in office. However, in the long run this can be counterproductive, if the means used to achieve this feedback lead to a privatisation of incentives. The waste of public resources by self-serving politicians subtracts value from a party's brand and, in time, pushes voters and reform-minded politicians to abandon long-term incumbents in favour of opposition parties, bringing about breakdowns in single-party dominance.

2
Why Does One-Party Dominance End in Factionalism?

Squabbling parties don't win elections. Research suggests that cohesion is a good predictor of performance implying that dominant parties must be more united than rivals or at least present a facade of unity for voters. In the long run, party unity is a necessary, but not sufficient, condition for political dominance.

Theories of party dominance have ignored intraparty feuding, focusing instead on interparty competition – dominant parties' competitive strategies and/or opposition parties' failures to compete (Chapter 1). Factionalism and intraparty conflict are at best treated as residual variables in descriptive accounts of party dominance. This is surprising because splits leading to factional defections were either the immediate reasons for breakdowns in dominant party rule in Japan, Mexico, Taiwan, India and Malaysia or major contributors to dominant parties' downfall and scale of defeat in Italy, Britain and Canada. In one-party states such as China and the former Soviet Union, party factionalisation and splits are precursors of regime delegitimation and dismantling (Friedman and Wong, 2008; Ishiyama, 2008).

This chapter argues that the unitary actor assumption of party competition is too restrictive to fully explain and predict the emergence, durability, decline and implosion of dominant parties. Section 2.1 explains why the theory of single-party dominance must integrate the intraparty dimension while Section 2.2 shows that factionalism should be understood as a process of sub-group partitioning instead of a typology of sub-party groupings.

Section 2.3 develops hypotheses about why long office tenure is likely to result in disunity and identifies four reasons why a growth in defections creates conflicting pressures in long-lived government parties. Section 2.4 concentrates on the interplay between party dominance and factionalism from an institutional perspective, briefly explaining how different institutions lead to challenges to the *status quo*. These institutional arguments are examined at greater length in Chapters 3 and 6, contrasting majoritarian democracies (Britain and Canada) and non-majoritarian democracies (Italy and Japan).

Factional behaviour is also driven by the state of the electoral market which shapes incentives for party dissidents to engage or not in collective action. Section 2.5 reviews how market conditions affect the bargaining leverage of intraparty dissidents. Section 2.6 focuses on measuring this bargaining power and estimating the degree of intraparty competition.

2.1   The neglected intraparty dimension of dominance

Sooner or later, all dominant parties are likely to become losers as discontent and factional competition lead to party splits that often make opposition parties look like viable competitors. Dissidents defecting to the opposition enlarge the field of competition, giving the opposition a real chance to compete. Hence, critical defections are frequently the main drivers of regime change following long periods of one-party dominance.

In Japan, the LDP's first but brief loss of power in 1993 resulted from the defection of two dissident factions who allied to bring down the government in a motion of confidence before leaving the LDP to form breakaway parties. The members of the Mitsuzuka faction formed the new Sakigake (Harbinger Party) and the members of the Hata-Ozawa faction formed the Shinseito ('New Born' Party). In this expanded field of competition, a multiparty coalition was able to dislodge the LDP from power after four decades of one-party rule.

In Italy, the DC's rapid decline in a series of elections in the early 1990s and its final implosion in 1994 were the result of voter disaffection with a corrupt party and the defection of reform-minded DC elites frustrated by the party's failure to change. The major party realignment that took place in Italy after the fall of Communism at the end of the Cold War enlarged the field of competition and provided DC defectors with opportunities to set up or join new parties.

Factional struggles contributed significantly to ending the dominance of the Congress Party in India in 1989 (India's first 'hung' parliament), the Kuomintang (KMT) in Taiwan in 2001, the Partido Revolucionario Institucional (PRI) in Mexico in 2000[1] and the United Malays National Organization (UMNO) in Malaysia in 2008, to name only a few (Friedman and Wong, 2008). In all of these cases, declining exit costs due to shrinking partisan resources and poor performance by the incumbent provided dissidents with incentives to defect and increase the ranks of the opposition.

Any theory seeking to explain the emergence, durability and decline of dominant parties must take into account the intraparty politics of the incumbent. The office-seeking imperative puts pressure on parties to maintain a facade of unity for voters so discord in dominant party systems is often dealt with internally and behind the scenes. This transforms national elections to the incumbent's intraparty races.

The displacement of competitive politics inside ruling parties explains why in several dominant party systems voters with legitimacy concerns tolerated corrupt parties for so long and why reform movements were slow to mobilise. In Italy and Japan, intra-elite competition through DC and LDP factions gave voters a sense that opposition politics were still operating since elections produced an alternation in power between different faction leaders and political teams (Curtis, 1988: 236; Leonardi and Wertman: 1989: 92, 118, 124; van Wolferen, 1989: 138; Kohno, 1992: 385).

2.2 Factionalism defined and conceptualised

Political parties aren't monolithic structures but coalitions of individuals and sub-party groups with diverse attitudes, interests and ambitions. This creates competitive and conflicting pressures inside parties which can trigger the formation and entrenchment of internal factions, making the unitary actor assumption of party competition theories highly questionable. Although widespread, factionalism is still a relatively understudied phenomenon and its analysis tends to vary from extremely quantitative to purely intuitive and cross-national surveys are few.

The main approach to the study of factionalism as an independent variable has been to devise typologies of sub-party groups based on variables such as stability, organisation, function, role, group size and number. However, the variables characterising factions are difficult to dissociate and often turn out to be interactive (Boucek, 2009: 456–60). Classification schemes are useful tools for exploring concepts and delineating their properties but are less useful for understanding dynamics and explaining change. An alternative approach takes a non-exclusive view of factionalism by focusing on the dynamics of sub-party groups and on parties' factional politics (Boucek, 2009).

Factionalism is a process of sub-group partitioning that gives factions their specific attributes. Factions characterised differently under traditional schemes (for instance, ideological factions versus factions of interest) can act similarly – cooperate or compete – and factions characterised in the same way can act differently. For example, factions can be cooperative (as under Japan's old electoral system where LDP factions cooperated locally in the nomination of candidates and the division of district votes) or they can also be competitive in the selection of party leaders, policy and the distribution of patronage and degenerative when incentives become excessively privatised. However, there is nothing predetermined about these processes and it is possible for factions to move from competition to cooperation through institutional reforms, effective leadership, party system change and so on.

This book's case studies show that factionalism is multifaceted and transforms itself over time. It may acquire different faces in individual parties at different times under different institutional regimes. In previous work, three types of factionalism have been identified: cooperative, competitive and degenerative (Boucek, 2009: 469–78). Cooperative factionalism is often associated with party formation and regime change and is essentially centripetal and consensus building. By helping different groups coalesce while enabling them to retain their separate identities, factions may play a constructive role in building 'catch-all' parties during periods of political change and in the early stages of party formation as in the case of the DC, LDP and Canadian Liberals.

In contrast, competitive factionalism represents the splitting of existing parties into factions that are opposed rather than simply separate. By creating centrifugal forces inside parties, competitive factionalism can be destabilising. As long as it is regulated, competitive factionalism can be a force for good. It can widen voter choice where it is restricted (for instance, in sub-competitive party systems under dominant party rule). It can improve intraparty democracy by facilitating debate and communication between leaders and followers. It can contain and dissipate conflict within an organisation by giving dissenters a voice. Factionalism can provide a structure for elite circulation, power sharing and conflict resolution.

However, too much factional competition creates fragmentation and polarisation resulting in majority failures and instability. Under centrifugal competition, there is a risk that incentives will become privatised resulting in a degenerative form of factionalism. As factions become too numerous and self-seeking, they operate mainly as channels for the distribution of patronage. In time, factional capture triggers a destructive cycle of factionalism which may end in party implosion as in the case of the DC in the early 1990s.

In sum, factionalism is the partitioning of a political party into sub-groups that, depending on incentives, become more or less institutionalised and engage in collective action to achieve their members' particular objectives, usually changing the *status quo* in a given party. Factions provide a structure for intraparty competition. They are seen as support coalitions for actual or putative party leaders (Giannetti and Laver, 2009) but their degree of institutionalisation depends on systemic and party-specific incentives. Some institutions like single-member plurality (SMP) voting systems put a high premium on party unity whereas non-majoritarian voting systems promote co-partisan competition (Chapters 3 and 6). Factional objectives may contradict collective party objectives and may change over time in response to new issues, new leaders, new parties and the like. This has implications for group dynamics and organisational cohesion. In addition, the extent of institutionalised factionalism may change over time in response to constitutional changes, electoral reform, new party rules and so on, producing new patterns of intraparty behaviour and changing the direction of intraparty competition from centrifugal to centripetal and vice versa. Depending on their specific design, institutions have the potential to contain factionalism or to encourage its growth.

To understand the factional dynamics of dominant parties and explain conflict resolution requires an understanding of how political institutions shape intraparty behaviour and evolve over time. Here, institutionalism is a useful analytical framework. Chapter 3 looks at institutional incentives in two Westminster systems (executive-dominated Britain and decentralised Canada) to explain the internal politics of dominant parties (British Conservatives in Chapter 4 and Canadian Liberals in Chapter 5). Meanwhile, Chapter 6 looks at institutional incentives in two non-majoritarian democracies (fragmented Italy and more consensual Japan) to explain the factional politics of Italy's former Christian Democrats (Chapter 7) and Japan's Liberal Democrats (Chapter 8).

2.3 Why does factionalism grow the longer a party is in power?

Schattschneider and other political scientists have suggested that party disunity is the inevitable by-product of too much success (Schattschneider, 1942; Golombiewski, 1958; Duverger, 1964: 312;

Sartori, 1976: 86). For instance, Hatschek claims (as reported by Duverger) that 'every domination bears within itself the seeds of its own destruction' (Duverger, 1964: 312). Golombiewski asserts that 'party cohesion is a direct function of the degree of competition between political parties' (Golombiewski, 1958: 501) and Sartori says that 'when a party finds for itself an electorally safe situation, party unity tends to give way to sub-party disunity' (Sartori, 1976: 86).

What these authors imply is that, sooner or later, all dominant parties are doomed to fail and that long office tenure carries within itself the forces of disintegration. But what is the rationale behind these assumptions? What are the conditions that lead government parties to become fractious after a long time in office? Why should the decrease in competition in dominant party systems give rise to increased competition inside the incumbent?

It is inevitable that with the passage of time all political parties will become fractious. However, this problem is made worse for parties who monopolise government for a long time because the stakes of holding office become so great as dominant parties must deal with a growing number of competitive claims. Party unity is difficult to maintain in the long run for the following reasons:

- First, electoral success is a magnet for aspiring politicians so dominant parties face increasing competition for election claims as long as they remain successful, putting pressure on partisan resources.
- Second, the heterogeneous nature of dominant parties increases conflicting pressures for ideological and policy claims which, in turn, raise the risk of ideological divisions and splits.
- Third, dominant parties attract careerist politicians, fanning rivalries in the struggle for the limited number of available positions.
- Fourth, security of office alters the balance between parties' collective goals and individuals' careers. Careerist politicians risk creating divided and entrenched loyalties which, in the long run, may trump the party's collective interests.

2.4   Institutional incentives and factional behaviour

The above propositions assume that all things are equal on the institutional side which is evidently not true. Institutions such as electoral systems and party organisational arrangements greatly shape the behaviour of intraparty actors by providing incentives or disincentives for internal competition and factional divisions. These impact dissidents' exit costs. Institutions are understood as 'formal rules, compliance procedures, and standard operating practices that structure relationships between individuals in various units of the polity and the economy' (Hall, 1986: 19).

The parties examined in this book have been selected on the basis of similarities and differences in their institutional contexts. Majoritarian Westminster systems (Britain and Canada) are contrasted to non-majoritarian systems (Italy and Japan) through a systematic documentation analysis in Chapters 3 and 6. It is reasonable to expect that, in Westminster systems, restrictive voting systems would produce cohesive parliamentary parties, given that reductive electoral systems such as SMP sharpen partisanship and generate high expectations of party unity by voters and constituency associations who control election and selection and by party leaders who control MPs' careers. However, countervailing institutions such as federalism in Canada reduce the scope for partisan conflict and ideological divisions in national parties by devolving power to sub-national governments in policy areas such as health and education where ideological differences are common.

In non-majoritarian systems like Italy and Japan, permissive electoral systems such as the old preference list vote in Italy and the single non-transferable vote in Japan provided incentives for intraparty competition and the development of a personal vote since same-party nominees were allowed to compete for district votes and for factional endorsement to maximise their chances of winning.

By featuring differently organised parties operating in similar political systems – the centrally controlled British Conservatives versus the more decentralised Canadian Liberals, and the deeply factionalised DC versus the moderately fragmented LDP – this study is able to explore the capacity of party-specific incentives in reinforcing/countering system-specific incentives.

For instance, Japan's LDP majoritarian rules in leadership selection and regulated career advancement compounded the benefits of factional coordination under SNTV to create centripetal forces inside the party which reduced fragmentation and deterred exit. By contrast, the DC's factional system of proportionality and power-sharing generated centrifugal forces which aggravated the fragmentary pressures of the preference voting system and destabilised the party.

This small *n*-qualitative research generates causal arguments about the influence of institutional incentives and disincentives on factional behaviour to explain conflict resolution in individual parties. Consequently, it is possible to identify in a systematic way the structural conditions that lead some dominant parties to become factionalised with severe consequences for their competitiveness while other dominant parties keep factionalism and its worst consequences in check.

2.5   Factional behaviour and the electoral market

Collective action by the losers in the competition for intraparty claims is also shaped by electoral market conditions. In the long run, office security makes party cohesion less critical to government survival which means that dissidence is more likely in dominant party systems than in more competitive party systems. That is why commentators claim that excessive majorities are undesirable for efficient government. For example, Francis Pym, British Conservative MP and a 'wet' member of Thatcher's first cabinet, said in 1983 that he didn't think a landslide majority for the Conservatives would be a good thing. According to this logic, by reducing the need for party discipline, large majorities effectively lower the costs of dissent for governing parties and their dissidents. Rebel MPs know that withdrawing consent is unlikely to endanger the government's survival and their own candidate re-selection while the party leadership can appear open-minded.

However, there is a paradox in this logic. In theory, under strict rationality, we would expect that a narrow government majority would be more likely to motivate dissent since a narrow majority gives dissidents more bargaining leverage than a large majority. With their votes decisive to the government's ability to pass legislation and survive confidence votes, dissidents might reason their power is enhanced. Of course, factors such as the size and cohesiveness of a given faction and career ambitions are also likely to influence behaviour.

This means that, in theory, electoral market conditions affect dominant parties' exposure to factionalism so the state of the electoral market is a second key variable (in addition to institutions) in the interplay between factionalism and single-party dominance. These are the critical factors determining the capacity of intraparty dissidents to end dominant party rule.

If we assume for the sake of argument that the electoral market represents a market for voter consent and that intraparty actors (leaders and followers) are utility-maximising individuals, then the consumer model helps examine in theory the market sensitivity of dissident behaviour to party competition.

Figures 2.1a and 2.1b represent the market for consent under two opposite demand scenarios. In the electoral market, voters elect parties

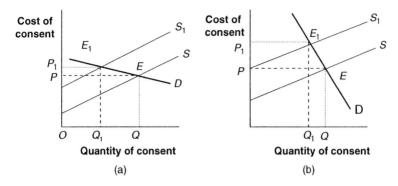

Figure 2.1 Party system competition and the demand for intraparty consent. (a) Elastic demand; (b) inelastic demand

for particular policy packages that parties promise to implement. In a sub-competitive electoral market such as a dominant party system (Figure 2.1a) where the governing party or coalition has a large working majority the losers for intraparty claims will have little to gain by threatening to defect since their support won't be pivotal to government survival. However, they may still organise as a faction to signal their discontent to the leadership. In this case, the marginal cost of factional dissent for ruling parties will be relatively low and party leaders will have considerable room for manoeuvre in dealing with internal rebellions. Under this scenario of elastic demand, dissidents and disgruntled office holders would face collective action disincentives and be unwilling to trade off voice for exit as in Italy and Japan in the 1950s and 1960s.

In Figure 2.1a, a shift in supply from S to S_1 would trigger a significant reduction in output from Q to Q_1 with only a moderate change in cost from P to P_1. Consequently, dissidents might decide instead to free-ride on the efforts of co-partisans and withhold consent from their party or abstain in specific votes knowing that their lack of support is unlikely to jeopardise the government. In this situation, a ruling party could afford to lose support from its own ranks at relatively low cost. Assuming this was a one-shot game, it would take significant levels of dissent or defection to bring about a change in price and supply and demand closer to equilibrium levels. Dissidents would have relatively limited bargaining leverage to extract demands from the leadership since their exit threats wouldn't be credible unless the group's size and cohesion were pivotal. This party competition scenario allows the leadership to overlook dissent like Tony Blair did during Labour's first three parliaments[2] or to introduce radical policies like Thatcher did in 1981 and following the 1983 and 1987 general elections.[3]

In contrast, the more competitive the electoral market is, the stronger the demand for party unity. Figure 2.1b represents a market with tight supply–demand conditions whereby demand for intraparty consent is very inelastic as shown by the steep demand curve. Under this scenario, the governing party has a narrow parliamentary majority or operates within a 'hung' parliament. A shift in supply from S to S_1 is associated with a small decrease in output but a significant increase in price. In other words, to make up a relatively small deficit in support (in party legislative voting, say, or in particular intraparty contests), the party would have to purchase extra units of consent from intraparty actors at a relatively high price to raise participation.

In such a competitive electoral market where demand for voter consent is inelastic, dissidents and discontented office holders would have good bargaining leverage. Their support would be more pivotal to government survival and their exit threats would be more credible. Under competitive market conditions, those on the losing side in the competition for intraparty claims would be in a relatively powerful position to extract pay-offs from party leaders. There is strength in numbers so this scenario would provide incentives for collective action by dissidents. In a worst case scenario they might trade off voice for exit.

A competitive electoral market raises the stakes for government parties that are divided because the costs of factional defection decrease and exit is more likely to jeopardise office tenure due to shifts in dissidents' trade-offs between voice and exit. This was the situation in Italy and Japan in the early 1990s when the political market opened up in both countries. In Italy particularly, the DC began losing support at an alarming rate between 1992 and 1994 making exit more attractive to dissidents and providing opportunities to dislodge the dominant party from power (Chapter 7).

These are contrasting scenarios at opposite ends of a spectrum and there are caveats in the logic of collective action by intraparty dissidents.

- First, party competition dynamics are different under single-party government than under coalition government since the costs of exit for dissidents are generally lower in multiparty systems than under two-party dynamics (although the gains from exit can also be low).

- Second, intraparty relations aren't one-shot games but repeated interactions where cooperation in one game often leads to cooperation in another.
- Third, the bargaining leverage and exit costs of dissidents are also determined by the relative size and degree of cohesion of the host faction and by individuals' career motivations. A small faction can wield disproportionate power as in the case of the DC where small minority factions used their blocking power in a destructive way in the 1970s and 1980s (Chapter 7). But a cohesive faction in a concentrated party may be able to use its pivotal power to influence the party agenda or prevent party leaders from making separate deals with individual faction members as in the case of John Major and Conservative Eurosceptic MPs during the passage of the Maastricht bill in 1993 (Chapter 4).

Incentives for dissident behaviour are determined by institutions and the state of the electoral market. The above scenarios may be simplified and there are differences between the political market and the workings of pure 'market economics'. In line with rational choice critics who argue that demand theory makes unreasonable assumptions about political action, some readers may question the assumptions underlying the utility-maximising calculus of party dissidents. However, by bringing together the interparty and intraparty aspects of competition, the above model is a useful heuristic tool to explain the bargaining context

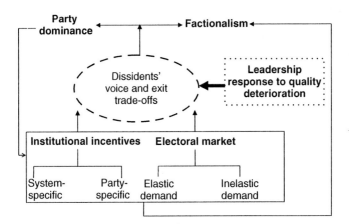

Figure 2.2 The interplay between party dominance and factionalism

shaping party dissidents' collective action and trade-offs between voice and exit.

This book's case studies show that the intervening variable in the interplay between party dominance and factionalism illustrated in Figure 2.2 are dissident's voice and exit trade-offs which are shaped by institutional incentives (systemic and party-specific) and by electoral market conditions.

2.6 Methods for measuring factionalism and analysing factional dynamics

To analyse intraparty competition, factional dynamics and parties' conflict management strategies, we need methods for identifying factions, calculating their number, estimating their power and modelling their interactions. The methodological difficulties in conceptualising factionalism through traditional categories of sub-party groups as explained in Section 2.2 mean it isn't possible to compare factionalism in a systematic way across cases on the basis of consistent variables. Empirical comparative surveys have demonstrated that many of these variables are interrelated (Janda, 1993).

In this study factionalism is viewed simply as a process of sub-group partitioning. What needs explaining is the nature of this process, the outcomes of factional competition and the management of intraparty conflict. Different methods are required to examine the internal politics of differently organised parties (deeply fragmented parties such as the DC and LDP versus more concentrated parties such as British Conservatives and decentralised parties such as the Canadian Liberals) at key junctures (major intraparty conflicts, leadership challenges, decisive elections, tipping events and so on). This study relies on selective methods that are appropriate to each of the cases examined.

The effective number of factions

Sartori calls for methods to measure 'fractionism' and to study factions as veto groups (Sartori, 1976: 74). Taagepera and Shugart acknowledge that no single index can tell how united or how fractionalised a party is internally (Taagepera and Shugart, 1989: 203). However, despite its mathematical quirks (Dunleavy and Boucek, 2003), the 'effective number of parties' index developed by Taagepera and Shugart is a good statistic that can be adapted to the intraparty arena in order to calculate the effective number of factions (N_f) in parties containing factions with identifiable memberships such as the DC and LDP. This method is less arbitrary than the one suggested by Lijphart in his study of party systems which treats each factionalised party as one-and-a-half party (Lijphart, 1999: 69–74).

The effective number of intraparty factions (N_f) takes into account each faction's relative size at different points in time. Instead of using the number of observable factions, the factions are weighted (by squaring their vote or seat shares) so that larger factions are given more weight than smaller ones. The key methodological decision is to use appropriate units of measurement. Depending on available data for any given party, the unit of measurement could be faction parliamentary memberships such as the number of MPs affiliated with each faction (as in the case of the LDP), the voting strength of individual factions on party decisional bodies like party congresses using factions' motion votes as indicators of factional strength (DC) and on party executives using individual factions' seat shares (DC), shares of appointments in cabinet based on the number and type of portfolios received by each faction (DC and LDP) or in legislatures based on factions' committee memberships and chairs and so on.

In two of the case studies presented in this volume (the DC in Chapter 7 and LDP in Chapter 8), this new measure (N_f) is used in time-series analysis to examine the structure of intraparty competition at separate intervals. It is useful to know how many factions are in competition at any one time if we want to gauge the degree, intensity and direction of intraparty competition at specific junctures during a party's time in office.

For the DC whose factions were the key actors in regulating most party activities, the distribution of support received by each faction's motions in the party national congress and national council (in the early years) is used.

For the LDP, whose factions were the main actors in electoral coordination under SNTV and whose memberships determined the subsequent allocation of government power among LDP office holders and the selection of the party leader and prime minister, the effective number of factions (N_f) is calculated by using the parliamentary memberships of each faction following each general election in both houses of the Diet although the information presented in Chapter 8 is based mainly on lower house elections. Despite the LDP factions' shadowy role during election campaigns, most party nominees openly affiliated with a particular faction when entering the race for a Diet seat and remained attached to this faction once elected.

The pivotal power of intraparty factions

The effective number of factions provides information about the structure of competition in an individual party at a particular point in time but not how powerful individual factions are at achieving outcomes in a particular coalition. To understand cooperation and competition inside parties and to explain factional defections, we need to know how powerful individual factions can be in controlling outcomes such as setting the party and government agenda, selecting the party leader, passing the government's legislation and so on.

That is why Sartori recommends viewing factions as veto groups and using game theory and coalition theory to analyse factionalism (Sartori, [1976] 2005: 70, 80). In so far as factions represent voting blocks, it is right to view factions as veto groups and to use game theory and coalition bargaining to analyse factional behaviour and explain conflict resolution. However, these are methodological tools, *not* criteria for distinguishing different *types* of factions as Sartori indicates (Sartori, [1976] 2005: 70, 79).

In very fragmented parties of institutionalised factions with stable memberships such as the DC and LDP, power indices and the tools of coalition theory are useful to examine the structure of intraparty bargaining at key junctures and to explain the outcomes of inter-factional games.

This book estimates the coalition and blackmail potential of individual factions of varying strengths through power indices which incorporate the notion of a 'pivotal player'. Power indices have frequently been applied to voting bodies such as juries, legislative committees in the American Congress, weighted decisional bodies such as the EU Council of Ministers and political parties in multiparty coalition governments. However, the power indices developed by Banzhaf (1965) and by Shapley and Shubik (1954) can also be adapted to the intraparty arena of competition in time series to measure how pivotal individual factions of varying strengths can be in influencing outcomes in particular situations.

By providing snapshots of the structure of internal bargaining over time, such methods have the capacity to explain critical defections and seemingly irrational outcomes, for instance, by demonstrating how the collective decisions of political parties may result from rational collective action in bargaining games by utility-maximising factions.

Chapters 7 and 8 use the normalised Banzhaf index of power to measure and analyse power relationships inside parties containing factions with identifiable memberships of varying sizes.

The Banzhaf measure allows the calculation of the power of individual factions (BZ_f) within fractionalised parties such as the DC and LDP and to explain factional defections in a quantitative way (the Shapley and Shubik index delivers almost identical results[4]). The index defines 'the number of winning coalitions in which the member's defection from the coalition would render it losing – which is a critical defection – divided by the total number of critical defections for all members' (Brams, 1985). The resulting scores provide an approximation of the power of individual factions in making or breaking intraparty coalitions at different points in time. This is a useful exercise. It sheds light on non-obvious aspects of intraparty life that party competition theories fail to acknowledge. By identifying critical defections, these methods can explain coalition problems and decisional dilemmas inside political parties who become excessively fragmented and polarised.

In coalition theory, the bargaining power of an individual group member or a sub-group within a larger group essentially depends on its decisiveness in making or breaking an internal coalition. The power exercised by each faction belonging to a coalition is a function of its contribution to the majority status of the coalition and the availability of acceptable alternative coalition partners. Even if the size of a faction remains stable over time, its coalition potential and pay-offs may vary because the party's factional composition may have changed. Some factions may have gained (or lost) strength inside the host party, new factions may have emerged or existing ones may have split or disappeared.

In Chapters 7 and 8, the Banzhaf power statistic calculates in how many of all the possible winning internal DC and LDP coalitions above the 50 per cent threshold a faction is a necessary partner. In other words, a partner whose withdrawal would make the coalition a losing one since it would fall below the 50 per cent threshold. This procedure is repeated for all factions represented at each DC national party congress and in each LDP parliament. Each faction receives a fractional share of total Banzhaf power in line with the relative size of its voting block and the results are standardised so that the total Banzhaf power of all the factions taken together equals 1.00. If one faction holds the totality of normalised Banzhaf power of 1.00 for itself, then all the other factions are 'dummies', unnecessary to any majority coalition.

One criticism of power indices is their 'policy blindness'. All factions are treated as possible partners in a majority bloc regardless of their ideological position. In other words, power indices don't systematically discriminate between those coalitions that are feasible because they are ideologically connected and those that aren't. In theory, constraints could be introduced to link coalition feasibility to the spatial positioning of intraparty factions that might be located in a two-dimensional space as long as there were two salient issues of intraparty division and not too many competing factions.

In practice, the blindness of power indices isn't a problem for this book's case studies since the factional competition in the DC was unidimensional[5] and factions in the LDP were non-ideological under Japan's non-partisan style of politics. It is worth noting that tools which map out the positions of different factions on different policies can also measure the depth of intraparty splits (Andrews, 2002; Giannetti and Laver, 2005; Hix, Noury and Roland, 2007) although win-set models are difficult to apply to parties containing more than three factions such as the DC and LDP (Laver and Shepsle, 1996: ch 12).

Finally, operationalising the power of individual factions in this way shows in the case of the DC the proximity of particular factions to the median voter which is relevant since the choices of DC elite and delegates at party congresses were sensitive to the party preferences expressed by voters at the previous election.

Game theory and factional politics

It is self-evident that power indices aren't appropriate to analyse group dynamics and conflict resolution in concentrated and bi-factionalised parties which don't contain formal factions organised as voting blocs. In such cases, like the British Conservatives, the tools of game theory are more appropriate to analyse and model conflict resolution representing decisions in situations of interdependent choices (Schelling, 1960: 16). Hence, intraparty conflicts can be modelled as strategic games between two or three factions with different strategies each.

Chapter 4 examines the factional politics of British Conservatives during their 18 years of dominance by analysing the strategic behaviour of recalcitrant MPs during critical votes in the House of Commons. These confrontations are modelled as 2×2 ordinal games – interactive situations involving two actors with two strategies each. Three games focus first on the cabinet battle over the deflationary budget introduced in 1981; second, the Conservatives' battle to ratify the Maastricht Treaty in

July 1993; and, third, the passage of the European Community (Finance) bill in November 1994.

Conclusion

This chapter has questioned the unitary actor assumption underlying existing but scarce theories of party dominance and has argued that the intraparty dimension of competition is a critical factor in the emergence, persistence and decline of dominant parties. The capacity to maintain unity over time through the efficient management of intraparty relations represents a necessary, albeit insufficient, condition for political dominance.

Viewing factionalism as a process of sub-group partitioning avoids the trap of static categorisation of factions and allows the analysis of internal dynamics of differently organised parties containing different types of sub-party groups. This partitioning determines the factions' specific attributes. It can change over time in response to incentives (institutional and strategic) leading to shifting patterns of factional competition and cooperation over the life of a party.

Several theoretical propositions have been put forward to explore why unity is difficult to maintain in the long run. Dominant parties are prone to factional pressures because of a growth in the internal competition for election, ideological/policy and career claims. These conflicting pressures increase the risk of dissent and defection by providing opportunities for the deprived to challenge the leadership through collective action which may involve faction formation.

Incentives to defect are shaped by systemic and party-specific institutions (Chapters 3 and 6) and by the state of the electoral market. This chapter outlined two opposite scenarios of party competition to demonstrate, in theory, how the size of a government's majority affects dissidents' bargaining leverage and costs of defection. But the case studies show that the ideological location, size and cohesion of dissident factions are also important factors in determining the credibility of their exit threats. The final section suggested different methods (used in the case studies) for identifying factions, calculating their number relative to their size, estimating their pivotal power and modelling their interactions.

3
Majoritarian Democracies: Executive-Dominated Britain and Decentralised Canada

In majoritarian democracies, power is concentrated in the centre of the political system. Centripetal forces lead the voting public to expect political parties to be strong and cohesive to deliver efficient government. This forces parties to design organisational incentives promoting unity.

A useful strategy to research how political institutions shape intraparty politics in different countries is Lijphart's conceptualisation of political systems along a single spectrum running from majoritarian to consensus (Lijphart, 1999).[1] It corresponds *inter alia* to two theoretical perspectives on representation and government. The theory of responsible party government applies in majoritarian parliamentary democracies (also called Westminster systems) such as Britain and Canada while the theory of representative government is more typical of consensus democracies (Chapter 6). That said, in Westminster systems,[2] the prerequisite of party unity derives from the norm of majority single-party government which creates incentives for careerist politicians to toe the party line in election campaigns and legislative votes. In both Britain and Canada, majoritarian institutions generate strong disincentives to factionalism in 'the party in public office'. However, incentives differ in 'the party on the ground' and 'the party in central office' (Katz and Mair, 1994) due to constitutional and organisational differences in these two countries. Intraparty behaviour is also shaped by party organisational arrangements which, depending on their design, can reinforce or mitigate systemic constraints.

This chapter looks at institutional incentives and disincentives on factionalism in political parties competing in majoritarian democracies using Britain and Canada for empirical comparison. The effects of system-specific institutions on electoral competition and legislative behaviour are considered in the first few sections covering bipolar competition, public perceptions, responsible party government, legislative voting, political careers and federalism. The final section has three parts that look at party organisational arrangements concentrating on the different rules and procedures used by British and Canadian parties to select party candidates, leaders and programmes. The objective of this chapter is to evaluate the conflict-reducing capacity of institutions before analysing the internal dynamics of British Conservatives (Chapter 4) and Canadian Liberals (Chapter 5).

3.1 The constraints of bipolar competition

In the electoral arena, party exposure to intraparty competition is primarily determined by the voting system – whether or not co-partisans are allowed to compete for district votes – which affects the number of parties, campaign behaviour and partisanship. Majoritarian democracies are notable for using 'winner takes all' single-member plurality (SMP) voting systems. According to Duverger (1964), this favours the two-party system leading to single-party majority governments assuming two-candidate/two-party contests locally and evenly distributed nationwide support – without local fortresses (Chapter 1).

Under restrictive electoral systems like SMP, parties nominate a single candidate in each district or constituency which normally ends co-partisan competition after nomination. However, in nineteenth-century Britain, the 1832 Reform Act created multi-member constituencies[3] and weak partisanship. Since MPs owed their nomination to sectional single-issue groups, legislative politics were dominated by local questions (Berrington, 1985). But the introduction by the Reform Act of 1867 of single-seat constituencies changed the logic of party competition, gave legislative politics a more partisan character as MPs' loyalty was directed away from their constituents and towards their parties (Cox, 1987) and galvanised the Liberals in 1867 and Conservatives in 1868 to establish central headquarters.

Two-party dynamics concentrate party systems (Chapter 1) and act as a powerful deterrent against party splits and defection. Bipolar competition imposes high exit costs on dissidents and careerists who disagree with their party on specific issues and high start-up costs for new parties. By dividing the left, the 1981 Labour Party's defection contributed significantly to the Conservatives' huge landslide victory in 1983 despite a lower share of the vote than in 1979 when they first came to power under Thatcher. The defection by the 'Gang of Four' who formed the Social Democratic Party (SDP) with 19 backbench MPs cost Labour the election. It was even more punishing for the Liberal/SDP Alliance which won a remarkable 25 per cent of the popular vote but ended up with just 23 seats. Labour won 209 seats with only 2 per cent more of the vote than the Alliance. Moreover, under SMP, chances are slim for party defectors winning seats as members of fringe parties or as independents. At the 1997 British general election, no seats were secured by the 1,678 candidates who stood for fringe parties or ran as independents (Norris, 1997) but such parties gain seats in European Parliament elections under more proportional voting systems.

In Canada until 1993, the third party (the New Democratic Party) was unfairly penalised by SMP leaving the two main parties (the Liberals and Progressive Conservatives) to claim the status of national organisations and the Liberals to become dominant. However, the Canadian long-standing 'two-party-plus' system of competition changed in 1993 when the *Bloc Québécois* and the Western Reform Party gained representation in the federal parliament and the Bloc became the official opposition, marking the end of Canada's third-party system (Carty, 1992).

In the US Congress, the same powerful majoritarian logic narrows the field of competition and polarises electioneering in two-party races in most districts. However, polarisation is mediated by the separation of executive and legislative powers explaining why ideological divisions in the US Congress crystallise as temporary bipartisan factions and intraparty caucuses and not as new breakaway political parties.[4]

3.2 Public perceptions and party unity

In majoritarian democracies, the normative desirability of 'strong' party government has a powerful hold on public opinion and the media putting a heavy burden of responsibility on party leaders to manage public perceptions and downplay disunity. By bipolarising voter choice and promoting single-party government, plurality voting gives partisanship a sharper edge than proportional representation and preferential voting. Strong partisanship reinforces public expectations that political parties must be strong and cohesive in the aggregate to deliver effective campaigns and responsible government.

Most social research suggests that group cohesion is a good predictor of performance and political scientists such as Walter Bagehot, Henry Jones Ford, A. Lawrence Lowell and Woodrow Wilson have argued that good governance is linked to party unity and factionalism with individualistic behaviour. To be perceived as less united than a competitor is damaging for political parties as shown by longitudinal analysis of

British attitudes towards party unity and disunity in 1965–97 (Boucek, 2001).[5]

Regressing perceptions of party unity and disunity with party popularity, I demonstrated that a strong positive correlation exists between these two variables in Britain. Although perceptions of unity and disunity used to be slightly better predictors of support for Conservatives than for Labour, in both cases the two variables are strongly correlated. Forty-six per cent of the variation in Conservative support is explained by public perceptions of unity and 53 per cent by perceptions of disunity as opposed to 36 per cent and 40 per cent, respectively, for Labour.

Historically, Labour was perceived as much more divided than the Conservatives, especially after the 1981 defection. By 1989, unity and disunity scores began to cancel out as a result of Neil Kinnock's taming of the 'loony left, John Smith's[6] organisational reforms replacing the trade union block vote at Labour Party conferences by one-member-one-vote (OMOV) and Tony Blair's party rebranding as 'New Labour'. This transformed it from a factionalised party at the mercy of trade unions into a successful electoral machine.

Concurrently, long-held views of Conservatives as a non-factionalised party (Rose, 1964) changed dramatically. They used to receive significantly smaller and mainly positive differential scores on party unity and disunity except when the leadership was challenged (in 1974 and 1989) or when the party became divided by a specific issue such as the 1981 deflationary budget and the 1986 Westland affair under Thatcher (Chapter 4). Even then, negative differentials for the Conservatives were only about a third of those of Labour.

Perceptions changed abruptly in the summer of 1989 when Thatcher polarised Conservative opinion with her anti-Europe views and the 'poll tax' which triggered street riots in 1990, leading to her eventual downfall. Europe continued to divide the Conservatives under John Major especially during the passage of the Maastricht bill (Chapter 4). By October 1992, 79 per cent of respondents felt that the Conservatives were disunited while only 14 per cent felt they were united. By July 1995, Major put his leadership on the line to stamp out dissent and 90 per cent of respondents felt the Conservatives were disunited.

My statistical analysis is corroborated by research on Conservative disunity based on the 1983 and 1987 *British Election Studies* and Labour disunity over Blair's decision to go to war in Iraq (Kam, 2009, Chapter 6).

In Canada, voters and the media are just as sensitive to party disunity and government defections but there is no continuous data to replicate the above analysis.[7] The strength of executive control in the federal government is such that party disunity is to the voting public a sure sign of a weak prime minister. The Liberals' defeat in 1988 when the ruling Progressive Conservatives were very unpopular was due to Turner's divisive leadership (Chapter 5). Individual MPs crossing the floor of the Canadian House of Commons to join rival parties are widely reported in the press although they turn out to be inconsequential and soon forgotten.[8]

Negative perceptions are heightened by a media keen to portray intraparty disputes as zero-sum games between winners and losers. In contrast, in consensus democracies, intraparty disagreements are viewed as solutions to coalition bargaining games or as moderating influences in building balanced governments.

Paradoxically, the decline in party attachments has led non-partisan voters to reward shows of political independence by MPs indicating that voters may hold two separate views of party unity. At the individual level, voters are prepared to forgive dissent and re-elect rebel MPs. A recent study of party discipline and parliamentary politics in Britain, Canada, Australia and New Zealand showed that, among other things, dissent is 'an effective vote-winning strategy primarily because it alters the opinions and voting behaviour of non-partisan and weakly partisan voters' suggesting that dissent contributes to a personal vote (Kam, 2009: 128).

However, at the aggregate level, voters value unity and expect parties to behave cohesively. This dissonance in the perceived value of party unity at the individual and aggregate levels creates a dilemma for parties in mobilising their core vote in majoritarian systems and raises questions about the legitimacy of political leaders who fail to assert their authority over party and country.

In sum, public perceptions explain why ruling parties in majoritarian democracies try to stamp out or conceal factional divisions and why some political leaders (notably Major and Brown in Britain and Chrétien in Canada) view dissent and factionalism as attacks on their authority. By contrast, Trudeau and Blair respected dissent within party ranks. 'I had no patience with tribal politics, with its exaggerated differences, rancorous disputes and irrational prejudices' (Blair, 2010: 26)

3.3   Responsible government and party unity

Party unity simplifies electorates' voting decisions and, in theory, sets the conditions for decisive, accountable and stable government. However, it puts a high premium on party unity and, by implication, constraints on factionalism. Voters see elections primarily as mechanisms for choosing a government (a cabinet, administration or executive rather than specific candidates) and only secondarily as instruments to reflect citizens' preferences or opinions (Breton and Galeotti, 1985: 1–2).

The theory of *responsible* government underlying majoritarian parliamentary democracy emphasises issues related to cabinets rather than to parliament and citizens as is the case under *representative* government more characteristic of consensus democracies. In contrast, the American model of Madisonian democracy (divided powers with checks and balances) seeks to achieve both responsible and representative government.

Responsible cabinet government assumes that parties behave as unitary actors, which provides common benefits to voters, politicians and parties. The ability to choose between distinctive party teams with differentiated (and, in theory, reliable) government mandates saves voters' information costs. Reliance on parties' collective reputations provides office seekers with campaign savings and office holders with some degree of office security. Loyalty to party rather than constituents provides government parties and opposition parties with collective benefits and efficiency gains such as the certainty of legislative outcomes.

In contrast, in the American Congress, partisanship is diluted by the division of executive and legislative powers. This creates incentives for bipartisan cooperation and co-partisan competition and directs the loyalty of national politicians primarily towards constituents and secondarily towards party. Congressional careers are neither confined to the executive nor subject to strict party discipline unlike at Westminster where career advancement is closely tied to party voting. Furthermore, in most presidential systems, incentives are shaped by presidential powers to initiate legislation, issue decrees or veto legislation from their own party without endangering the government's survival. In practice, however, presidents tend to compromise and bargain with members of their own party to maximise unity and reward legislators who support them on crucial issues.

3.4 The prime minister's disciplinary power

The British system of government was once described as an 'elective dictatorship' due to the concentration of power in cabinet.[9] This rests on two conditions: majority support in parliament and cohesiveness of the majority party (Lijphart, 1999: 12). Lijphart argues that, in theory, the British House of Commons 'controls' the cabinet because it has the power to vote it out of office but in practice the relationship is reversed since the cabinet is composed of the leaders of a *cohesive* majority party in the house [my emphasis].

Party cohesion provides the confidence to cabinet that it can stay in office and get its legislative proposals approved but only as long as the government's majority is large enough to neutralise the veto power of intraparty dissidents (Chapter 2).

The Westminster top-down model has a powerful prime minister at the apex of a national executive built upon a chain of responsibility from cabinet, to parliament and to the electorate. The prime minister controls the agenda through his monopoly over cabinet and parliament and the recruitment of personal advisers.

Some now argue that 'the premiership is best seen as a cluster of functions, rights and personnel centring on the person occupying the post of Prime Minister' and that 'the emergence of a quasi-prime ministerial department has undermined Cabinet as a whole' which does not 'correlate automatically or simply with the strengthening of No. 10' (Blick and Jones, 2010: 199–202).

Prime Ministers in Westminster systems can be vulnerable. Their power is mitigated by potential leadership threats from the second-in-command, often the minister of finance who controls the purse strings and can mobilise dissent. Under Tony Blair, this 'dual monarchy' divided Whitehall into hemispheres of interests – 'Tony's departments' and Gordon's departments' (Rawnsley, 2007). While he was Chancellor of the Exchequer, Brown starved Number 10 Downing Street of information to block Blair's public service reforms. Apparently before one budget, and in front of witnesses, Blair pleaded with Brown to 'give us a clue what might be in it' (Rawnsley, 2007). Protracted struggles at the top were common in Canada too where finance ministers attracted dissident voices (Chapter 5).

Another prime ministerial prerogative, the power to call elections, is a double-edged sword. The threat of parliament dissolution can establish order in divided parties as in Canada where Chrétien called two snap elections to pre-empt attacks on his leadership (Chapter 5). However, it can also lead to intraparty instability because without fixed-term parliaments, incumbents risk overstaying their welcome and fuelling speculation about their eventual departure as with Thatcher and Blair in Britain and Trudeau and Chrétien in Canada. In Britain, the Conservative-Lib Dem coalition government adopted a Fixed-term Parliaments Act that came into force in September 2011 (setting the date of the next general election as 7 May 2015 and on the first Thursday in May of every fifth year thereafter) thus relinquishing a key aspect of majoritarian government.

Canada's political system has been described as 'prime ministerial government' (Savoie, 1999) given the prime minister's capacity to manipulate the machinery of government. Trudeau centralised the cabinet system and manipulated federal–provincial diplomacy (Chapter 5). The Canadian prime minister can initiate policy through orders-in-council and can shut down parliament to strengthen the government's position. In 2008–10, Stephen Harper prorogued parliament twice with the approval of the Governor General to protect his minority government from no-confidence votes by opposition forces.

Collective cabinet responsibility forces frontbench MPs to defend all government policies and to speak with a single voice. This doesn't prevent frontbenchers from privately disagreeing with particular government policies but this dissent increasingly surfaces through ministerial news leaks or prime ministerial decisions to relax collective responsibility in coded messages intended to conceal dissent (James, 1995: 83–4). In 1975, Labour Prime Minister Harold Wilson allowed cabinet members to campaign both for and against the referendum on Britain staying in the European Economic Community (EEC) but two decades later, Major aggravated dissent by stubbornly refusing the promise of a referendum on Europe to Conservative rebel MPs (Chapter 4).

Prime ministerial failures to resolve cabinet conflict can be very destabilising because they can trigger a dangerous chain of events: ministerial resignations leading to leadership challenges as in Britain in 1990 (Chapter 4) and Canada in 1975 and 2002 (Chapter 5). Cabinet resignations are attention grabbing precisely because they are rare and send powerful messages of disunity, encouraging leadership factions to mobilise against the leader. That is why the incidence of sitting prime ministers being forced to depart because of intraparty conflict is relatively low.[10]

3.5 Disincentives to legislative dissent

According to Lijphart, a cohesive parliamentary party is the second key prerequisite of majoritarian democracy and cabinet government. Indeed, Westminster parliamentary systems are known for their traditionally high levels of cohesion. Career incentives put strong pressures on MPs to toe the party line, leading to few and temporary legislative factions and extremely rare party splits.

With executive authority resting on parliamentary majorities or near-majorities, norms of legislative cohesion have evolved as solutions to repeated dealings in partisan legislatures. The assumption is that MPs will toe the party line because of party affiliation, common policy preferences and career incentives. Socialisation also plays a role in shaping group behaviour in parliamentary systems. However, when these incentives fail to deliver unity, discipline is imposed by the party leadership through the 'whipping' system and, in a worst case scenario, through motions of confidence in the government (or the threat of a motion).

The need to show unity to the electorate means policy disagreements are usually thrashed out in party caucuses prior to legislative votes or in private discussions between backbenchers and their 'whips' who monitor voting. 'We have our agreements in public and our disagreements in private,' declared John Major at the Conservative Party Conference in 1993 when his party was split over ratification of the Maastricht Treaty.

Majoritarian incentives used to effectively deliver legislative cohesion in Britain. By the middle of the twentieth century, it was claimed that 'governments being defeated by their own followers became virtually impossible' (Ozbudun, 1970: 318) so that 'there was no longer any point in measuring party cohesion' (Beer, 1965: 350). An international survey covering the period 1950–62 showed complete legislative cohesion in Britain (Janda, 1979).

However, since the 1970s, parliamentary dissent has risen with an increased number of MPs voting against their parties (Ozbudun, 1970; Norton, 1978b, 1980, 1985; Cowley, 1999, 2005). Until 1970, the number of divisions seeing dissenting votes in the British House of Commons was less than 5 per cent for most parliaments.[11] But in 1970–79, British governments suffered 65 defeats compared to only five during the previous 25 years. Aggregate dissent remained high under the dominance of the Conservatives (1979–97) and Labour (1997–2010).[12]

To be sure, surveys of voting divisions can distort the significance of legislative dissent since aggregate numbers can't track the consistency of intraparty voting patterns within or across issue categories (Wood and Jacoby, 1983). In Britain under Major, 60 per cent of all Conservative dissenting votes were on the bill to approve the Maastricht Treaty (Baker, Gamble, Ludlam and Seawright, 1999: 82–4).

Under Tony Blair, there was widespread dissent over welfare and public services legislation including school academies, university tuition fees and foundation hospitals, the Iraq war and the prevention of terrorism (Cowley, 2002, 2005). In February 2003, no less than 200 MPs including 121 Labour members voted for a motion stating that the case for military action in Iraq was not yet proven. A month later, 139 Labour MPs voted for a hostile amendment opposing Blair's decision to join an American-led invasion of Iraq (Cowley, 2005). The largest government rebellion since the Liberals split over Home Rule in 1886, the Iraq war prompted two ministerial resignations including house leader and former Foreign Secretary Robin Cook. This insubordination greatly undermined Blair's authority over the Labour Party and country.[13]

Institutional constraints explain why legislative factions are rare in majoritarian democracies given the trade-offs between the advantages of faction membership and those of re-election, policy and career advancement. In the United States, however, Leon Epstein asserted that the separation of powers was the key variable in explaining the low cohesion of American parties (Epstein, 1980: 315–50). In Congress, legislative factions occasionally emerge to moderate leaders' policy orientations or vent politicians' frustrations at the incapacity of Congress' structure to achieve policy objectives (Kolodny, 1999).

3.6 Career incentives

The prime minister's control over MPs' careers and his power to call confidence votes are major deterrents against backbench dissent and factionalism.[14] However, in the long run, the capacity to reward supporters with career benefits diminishes and pushes leaders to rely more on collective incentives and threat power to keep unity within party ranks.

Leadership changes in long-lived government parties may offer a temporary buffer against dissent by providing elite turnover. To gauge this effect, I have calculated levels of deprivation in the Conservative caucus in 1979–97 covering the 1990 leadership change from Thatcher to Major. In a rejoinder to the arguments of Sections 2.3 and 2.5, this proxy measure is relative to the size of the government majority in each of the four parliaments. The rational assumption is that large majorities reduce the pool of career benefits at the disposal of leaders and may encourage grievances and dissent by the deprived. By implication, narrow majorities create conditions for cohesion by providing government stakes to a larger proportion of MPs while simultaneously increasing dissidents' bargaining leverage.

The data in the bottom row of Table 3.1 confirm expectations that deprivation levels increase with the size of a government majority since a significant number of backbench MPs miss out on promotion. Under the Conservatives' first parliament (1979–83), 42 per cent of Conservative MPs were deprived of 'paid' government posts[15] but,

Table 3.1 Conservative MPs' rewards and deprivation 1979–97

Total Number of MPs in government	First parliament 1979–83	Second parliament 1983–87	Third parliament 1987–92	Fourth parliament 1992–97
Cabinet ministers	41	34	60	48
Non-cabinet ministers*	65	65	91	72
Junior ministers**	92	71	134	114
MPs not in government	141	227	91	102
Total Conservative MPs	339	397	376	336
Rate of deprivation (per cent)	42	57	24	30

*Non-cabinet ministers include ministers of state and financial secretaries.
**Junior ministers include under-secretaries, parliamentary secretaries, whips, and assistant whips (but not parliamentary private secretaries).
Note: Each promotion to a government post counts as 1. Hence, because some members get promoted more than once, the effective levels of deprivation are likely to be slightly higher than stated above. Calculations are based on the number of seats won at the beginning of each parliament.

during their second parliament when the party had a whopping majority of 144, the level of deprivation climbed to 57 per cent.

One political scientist argued that 'the resentment of the "dispossessed" and the hunger of the "never possessed" may have contributed to Margaret Thatcher's downfall in 1990' (Berrington and Hague, 1995) This is supported by a survey in *The Times* (12 April 1990) showing that when Thatcher left office, 95 Conservative MPs elected since 1979 and earlier had not been appointed to office, while another 78 had been demoted from ministerial office.

However, after Thatcher's departure in the middle of the Conservatives' third parliament, John Major's cabinet reshuffles brought the rate of deprivation down to 24 per cent. This remained at a modest 30 per cent under the fourth Conservative administration (1992–97) mainly due to the government's reduced majority of 21 MPs in 1992. A larger proportion of Conservative backbench MPs had government posts which in theory should have lowered the risk of dissent. In practice, though, it increased the bargaining leverage of a small number of Eurosceptic MPs. A different logic exists in the Cameron–Clegg coalition government which has a majority of 37 seats giving managers in each party some leeway in neutralising potential rebels (Boucek, 2010c).

Readers should note that the size of a given legislative assembly (not simply the size of a government majority) has implications for the management of legislative dissent. This variable has a direct effect on the number of political elites appointed to government given that the size of government cabinets is relatively inelastic. There are more opportunities for career advancement in smaller legislatures such as the 150-seat Australian legislature and the 308-seat Canadian House of Commons than in larger legislatures such as the 650-seat British House of Commons.[16] In addition, lower incumbency rates in Canada make deprivation less problematic in the long run than in Britain.

A quantitative survey of parliamentary dissent in Britain, Canada, Australia and New Zealand argues that party cohesion is fragile and conditional upon the way party leaders and MPs interact (Kam, 2009). It shows that, in the long run, party leaders have been forced to rely on a mixture of strategies to offset electoral pressures: offering MPs advancement, threatening discipline or ultimately relying on a long-run socialisation to temper MPs' dissension. Harold Wilson co-opted rebels by giving them government posts in a quest to balance Labour Party factions in his administration (Piper, 1991).

In Canada, career advancement 'hinges on the internal politics of leadership selection' (Kam, 2009: 207). Liberal MPs who failed to back Jean Chrétien in the 1990 leadership contest suffered most in the 1993 reshuffle. Dissent was a principal cause of demotion and Liberal disunity at that time, fuelled by a combination of professional frustration and electoral insecurity (Chapter 5). Panel data on the career trajectories and voting records of British MPs show similar patterns between demotion and dissent (Kam, 2009, Chapter 9).[17]

Of course, prime ministers have a mighty but blunt weapon to enforce legislative cohesion: the confidence vote. This is a very dangerous way to restore order because deterrent force involves unilateral threat but bilateral punishment. While few divisions in parliament are considered matters of confidence, a vote of no confidence in parliament means the government is responsible collectively and must resign. So, to be effective, the threat of dissolution has to be credible. When the norm is not to call an election following loss of a confidence vote, then this weapon loses its deterrence value. In short, prime ministers have to be desperate to make important votes tantamount to votes of confidence and is why 'the wars fought between ministers and Government backbenchers are almost invariably limited wars, with the ultimate weapon not used' (King, 1976: 30).

However, John Major regularly used this deterrent force. The strategy preserved some essential elements of European Union (EU) policy bargains but it severely damaged his authority (Chapter 4). Politicians who sign up to confidence motions against their own parties greatly discount the future by waving goodbye to a political career, at least under the incumbent.

The case studies show that, in the long run, party leaders must rely on discipline and social norms to thwart dissent and maintain trust in a caucus whose members hold the key to their survival. A willingness to compromise with dissidents and avoid threat power can be decisive factors in resolving conflict in long-lived government parties.

3.7   Conflict-reducing federalism

Federalism entails a rejection of simple majoritarian democracy. By dampening partisanship, it can mitigate factional pressures in 'non-unitary' federal states such as Canada, Australia and India but it can also be a source of conflict.

First, by devolving policymaking to sub-national governments in redistributive politics, federalism compresses the scope for political conflict. If national governments lack jurisdiction over the provision of health, welfare and education and have limited agenda control over the economy and taxation, there will be little partisan competition and division nationwide over such ideological issues. In Canada, considerable responsibility and fiscal autonomy in these policy domains is delegated to the provinces and managed through federal–provincial diplomacy. This narrows the scope for ideological and factional divisions within national parties and disconnects provincial politics from federal politics leading to the conclusion that Canadians live in 'two political worlds' (Blake, 1985). It also disconnects national and provincial party organisations and reduces the pressures for a regional factionalisation of national parties (Carty, 2010: 150).

In 'unitary federal states' like Germany, power flows to the centre resulting in a closer alignment between partisan politics at sub-national and national levels. Parties fight sub-national elections on the basis of national issues and voters use their vote in regional contests to express opinions about the incumbent federal government. Centripetal forces on the input side produce a less pluralistic logic in Germany than in Canada because legislative powers are exercised nationally and national legislation is implemented by the sub-national governments (*Länder*) who are democratically represented in the federal parliament (*Bundesrat*). In Canada, the provinces have no formal representation in the unelected senate and provincial governments have exclusive competence over substantive policy areas. However, on the output side, Germany and Canada share fiscal equalisation to alleviate differences in the spending capacity of sub-national governments. This fundamental principle of federalism in the 1982 Canadian constitution has been a source of factional divisions in the Liberal Party (Chapter 5).

Second, federalism relaxes the constraints of bipolar competition by reducing the pressures for cross-district partisan coordination. In societies divided by ethnic, religious and linguistic conflict, federalism promotes the formation of regional parties such as the separatist *Bloc Québécois* in Canada's French-speaking province of Quebec and the Reform Party[18] in the west (Chapter 1). The Bloc even formed the official opposition in the national parliament in 1993. But multiparty competition continues to produce single-party government and distorted regional representation in the national party system which has exaggerated the Liberals' winning majorities and facilitated their dominance (Chapter 1).

Third, power sharing and consociational norms help reduce regional conflict in Canada, 'a country where geography overwhelms history' (Carty, 2002: 349). Portfolio allocation in the federal government is very sensitive to regional interests. The fisheries portfolio normally goes to a politician from a Maritime province and the agriculture portfolio to one from the Prairies. Alternation between French and English leaders has traditionally maintained harmony between Canada's two founding nations. The Liberals always appoint a special 'lieutenant' in Quebec to ease relations between the federal and provincial organisations. Pre-legislative inquiries, task forces and royal commissions remove contentious issues from partisan politics such as wage control in the 1970s, constitutional reform in the 1980s and the reduction of the national deficit in the 1990s.[19]

However, due to its ideological dimension, federalism can amplify divisions and polarise politics. In Canada, the Liberals' ideological core revolves around the issue of national unity linked to constitutional reform which has threatened to tear the party apart (Chapter 5). Since federalism is endogenous to party organisation and incentives, it also determines the way parties divide powers internally which has implications for party unity.

3.8 Party organisational incentives

Party unity is also conditioned by party organisation. The procedures for selecting candidates, leaders and programmes determine the distribution of internal power and affect intraparty relations. What matters is who holds the selection power in a given organisation for each of these activities.

Party candidate selection

The selection of candidates for political office is a key variable in the analysis of intraparty conflict. It controls the composition of the legislative caucus (Schattschneider, 1942: 64) whose unity is necessary to maintain a government in office (Epstein, 1980: 339) and it 'is a crucial indicator of power distribution within a party' (Scarrow *et al.*, 2000: 138). Duverger saw the centralisation of power as a cause of party cohesion (Duverger, 1964) but others argue that 'central control of candidate selection is not a crucial, nor even a necessary, condition of party cohesion' (Ozbudun, 1970: 339). A cross-country survey finds no significant variation between cohesiveness of voting in parliament and the selection process (Gallagher and Marsh, 1988).

All other things being equal, candidates whose nomination is centrally controlled are more likely to toe the party line in parliament (Gallagher and Marsh 1988) at least if they believe that disloyalty will deprive them of career advancement or endanger their reselection.

Is the threat of deselection a good deterrent against dissent? A study of Labour government defeats in 1974–79 showed that newly elected Labour MPs from marginal seats were more prepared to dissent than MPs from safe seats (Tsebelis, 1990). Among the Labour MPs elected in 1974, the most loyal were from safe seats than from marginal seats (114–72) while the non-loyal MPs came from marginal seats more than from safe seats (83–63) (Tsebelis, 1990: 134).

Supporting the arguments in Section 3.3, British party activists and constituency associations tolerate rebellion by individual MPs. In 1972, all the Conservative and Labour MPs (except for one) who rebelled on the second reading of the European Communities Bill were renominated and all the Labour MPs who defeated the devolution bills in the 1974–79 parliament were reselected (Norton, 1980). Recent evidence suggests that backbench MPs are more motivated by the prospect of career advancement than the fear of deselection. This is shown by the difference between the number of MPs who sign early day motions and dissent on final votes[20] and by attitude surveys of Conservative Party activists (Whiteley and Seyd, 1999).

In contrast, legislators whose nomination is not primarily determined by party but by their ability to mobilise the personal vote have more incentives to act independently and compete against co-partisans. This is mainly an effect of the voting system and divided government. In multi-seat systems, voters have a *de facto* input into candidate selection whereas, in single-seat contests, this is primarily a matter for parties and their local associations. However, there is considerable variation in patterns of delegated powers for candidate selection in individual parties which is mostly unregulated and manipulable.

In Canada, the nomination of candidates for office is a local autonomous process by constituency associations probably unmatched in other Western-style parliamentary systems (Sayers, 1999) featuring considerable geographic variations due to weak national parties. Lacking national membership programmes, the main Canadian national parties have been described as '19th c. European cadre parties' whose business model resembles flexible 'franchise contracts' (Carty, 2002). Carty suggests that these parties have traded off 'autonomy for national parliamentary discipline' by tying 'an American (mobile, plural, growing and changing) society to European-style (disciplined, centralised, closed) governing institutions' (Carty, 2002: 354).

However, nomination papers must be signed by party leaders whose power to withhold the party label from individual candidates has been enhanced by party constitution amendments in 1990. Chrétien and especially Martin used this power to establish control over the Liberal Party organisation, notably during the 2004 election campaign (Chapter 5). This threat encourages MPs to then submit to the central party's policy and decision-making authority.

In Britain, as in Canada, 'national governmental recruitment is primarily a party-oriented rather than a candidate-centred process' (Webb, 2002: 31) but, in Britain, parties are more centralised and incumbency rates higher than in Canada. This gives the party leadership more sustained leverage over sitting MPs and national party elites more of a veto over local members' candidate selection or at least a post facto veto over the choices made by local associations. The British Conservative Party works on the basis of local selection although the party's Central Office screens applicants and draws up a list of about 500 suitable candidates (Denver, 1988). The party has refrained from using an explicit quota system for recruiting minority candidates but, under Cameron, an 'A list' of some 500 approved parliamentary candidates dominated by females was compiled. It remains to be seen what the impact of coalition politics on candidate selection will be for the Conservatives and Liberal Democrats at the next general election.

Party leadership selection

Leadership selection affects leader–follower relationships and indicates what shape opposition to unsatisfactory incumbents is likely to take. However, tinkering with rules to pre-empt future conflict can be counterproductive if party members are ideologically out of step with their competitive environment (Flanagan, 1998).

Challengers' incentives to instigate leadership contests to unseat incumbents are determined by which intraparty actors have leadership-selection power: the parliamentary party or the party membership. In hybrid systems, this includes different combinations of these groups including party executives and congresses. In contemporary parties, leadership selection has now become more inclusive but was traditionally the prerogative of parliamentary elites. In the British Conservative Party, leadership selection used to be very informal – the sounding of party opinion by a 'magic circle' of senior politicians in consultation with the outgoing leader. However, in 1965, backbench MPs gained exclusive responsibility for electing the leader in run-off elections under the alternative vote system with rules modified in 1975. For victory on the first ballot the winner needed the backing of an absolute majority of MPs plus a margin of 15 per cent over the nearest rival – narrowly missed by Thatcher in 1990 (Chapter 4). While this acts as a test of confidence – a plebiscite – on the incumbent leader it can also encourage 'stalking horse' candidates to enter the race (Jesse, 1996) as happened in 1975 when Thatcher replaced Heath as leader and in 1989 when Thatcher was first challenged. Adding uncertainty, for the second-round nominations are reopened and victory requires only an absolute majority.

In 1997, William Hague introduced a parliamentary mass-membership hybrid system involving party members voting in a run-off race between the two front runners selected by MPs. This was meant to protect future leaders and sitting prime ministers from being thrown out of office in parliamentary coups. This happened in 1990 to Thatcher who had considerable grass-roots support and delivered three consecutive victories.

Empowering party members can have unintended consequences as demonstrated by the election of Ian Duncan Smith (IDS). In 2001, Hague resigned following a second Conservative defeat and IDS, a Eurosceptic MP, came second in a near-perfect three-way split of the caucus vote and ahead of Michael Portillo by a single vote. IDS had the support of 54 MPs and Kenneth Clarke 59 MPs but IDS won the membership run-off race even though Clarke was more popular with the public.

This majority failure cost the Conservatives dearly. Without a strong party mandate, IDS failed to make a mark as opposition leader and, within two years, he resigned after losing a vote of confidence called by the backbench Conservative 1922 Committee. His successor Michael Howard initiated a partial Conservative recovery at the 2005 general election (a 31-seat gain) before stepping down in favour of a younger and modernising leader. By adopting a moderate centrist approach, media-savvy Cameron made the Conservatives electable again but it took four leadership changes to achieve this.

The British Labour Party has high nomination barriers which protect its leaders against challenges but these tough eviction rules can have unintended consequences (Quinn, 2005). The lack of regular leadership reviews means the incumbent must be challenged directly. In 2007, Chancellor of the Exchequer Gordon Brown, a divisive figure in the Labour Party, even managed to become Labour leader and prime minister without any contest whatsoever since no senior Labour figure dared challenge him. In 2010, his successor Ed Miliband narrowly won the leadership against his older brother David, former Foreign Affairs Secretary, by winning a majority of the trade union vote even though his more experienced brother had majority backbench support.

Labour's institutional division of power bolstered by its 1993 reforms deter leadership challenges and explains why Labour leaders have faced fewer plots than Conservative leaders.[21] Very high eviction costs in the electoral college greatly reduce the probability of a challenge (Quinn, 2005) even when the party is deeply divided. Tony Blair was unchallenged after joining the US-led invasion of Iraq in 2003 despite a huge backbench revolt and cabinet resignations. The expense and length of a contest ensures that only credible contenders are likely to come forward. Quinn argues that had Labour used the system that deposed Thatcher, it is conceivable that Blair could have faced a middle-ranking challenger, possibly opening the way for Gordon Brown to enter a Blair-less second ballot. Since leaders generally depart when they lose the confidence of senior colleagues (as Thatcher did in 1990), it is possible that Blair too may have yielded. Thatcher lost the confidence of her cabinet only after she had been challenged by Heseltine and had failed to win convincingly on the first ballot. 'Blair was never put in that position, because the electoral college impeded stalking horses and did not permit serious candidates to wait for later ballots' (Quinn, 2005: 808).

In Canada, the internal politics of leadership selection impact directly on MPs' careers but they can also factionalise a party. Loyalties to a single leadership faction can remain dormant for a long time but may be quickly reactivated for leadership reviews (Carty, 2002), as happened with the election of Turner in 1984 and Martin in 2003 (Chapter 5).

Canadian party leaders used to be selected by conventions of party delegates chosen by activists in the constituency associations. This was a costly and corrupt process which pushed leadership rivals to develop highly personalised networks within local organisations and encouraged the development of personal factions (Carty and Blake, 1999). Recently, Canadian parties have opted for more participatory systems based on 'one-member, one-vote' with different types of membership-selection rules reflecting the different values and priorities that individual parties attach to inclusiveness and openness (Carty and Blake, 1999). Membership selection is too recent to have produced observable patterns of eviction.

For a long time, the Liberals lacked a formal mechanism for removing the incumbent leader. It's why Turner resisted stepping down in 1988 when the Liberals were deeply divided by his policy choices (Chapter 5). However, the party's 1990 constitutional amendments have made leadership reviews mandatory following each general election even if the incumbent leader led the party to victory. The current method is a procedural compromise combining a constituency proportional system of one-member, one-vote with a convention vote both of which must be won by the successful candidate.

New rules requiring votes by women and youth delegates can be manipulated by provincial party executives (and through them by Liberal leaders) since provincial executives control the distribution of membership forms to local associations and can change the rules for recruiting new party members. This is how Martin ousted Chrétien from office in 2002 (Jeffrey, 2010: 331–5). The introduction of an automatic leadership review after general elections has motivated the incumbent to call snap elections to pre-empt challenges by grass-roots revolts but it also enables challengers to capture the extra-parliamentary organisation and launch leadership bids (Chapter 5).

Party policy selection

Party programmes and election manifestos involve ideological choices and these values can divide a party and mobilise factions depending on the inclusiveness of party arrangements for deciding policy. In general, 'party leaderships are anxious to keep a tight rein on policy-making' explaining why the comparative party literature on policy selection is largely undeveloped (Scarrow, Webb and Farrell, 2000).

All else being equal, the location of intraparty ideological groups is a reflection of who has policymaking authority in a given party. In centrally controlled parties where policy discussion is the preserve of the leadership, factional pressures are more likely to surface within the top hierarchy where ministers of finance often have more say over party policy than the prime minister since they control the purse strings. This can produce rival governments like the schism in the Labour governments (1997–2010) between market-oriented 'Blairites' and statist 'Brownites' and between the 'wets' and 'dries' in Thatcher's first administration (Chapter 4).

In contrast, in de-concentrated parties, people who disagree with the party line are more likely to mobilise in the grass roots, using activists as in the case of the old militant British Labour Party in the 1970s and early 1980s and the DC in Italy in the mid-1970s (Chapter 7) but at the risk of creating decisional dilemmas.

Party conferences or congresses are the main forum of policy debate where activists try to influence policy direction. In inclusive parties, delegates may have been recruited in advance to back specific motions which can reinforce the power of factions. To circumvent veto gates in such forums, leaders may opt for membership ballots before general conferences, especially if they want to introduce radical and divisive policy changes. Blair did this to remove the totemic 'Clause IV' from the Labour Party constitution which committed the party to public ownership of the means of production, distribution and exchange. By adopting the slogans 'New Labour, New Britain' and 'for the many not the few', Blair and his top advisers put this issue in the context of party modernisation and convinced opponents like the trade unions to accept this radical change. Instead of appealing for unity in the face of party division as Major had done, Blair asserted his leadership by appealing for a mandate to modernise the party (Blair, 2010: 75–102).

In most parties, policy change is an incremental process involving consultation exercises during local and regional party conferences. The acquiescence of the party membership and caucus results from trade-offs. Members are given a say over candidate and leadership selection in return for which parliamentary leaders are left with a relatively free hand to set policy (Carty et al., 2000). Sometimes, parties set up ginger groups and thinkers' conferences, especially if redefining themselves while in opposition (British Conservatives 1975–79 and Canadian Liberals 1979–80). However, with the decline in mass parties, leaders are increasingly turning to special advisers to frame new policies and to the Internet to test public opinion about specific measures.

Conclusion

Majoritarian institutions pressure parties to behave as unitary actors because SMP voting generates centripetal competition in the party system. Voters perceive disunited parties as unfit to govern and raise exit costs for dissidents.

Centripetal competition is reinforced by a top-down responsible party model of government that directs MPs' loyalty towards the party leadership which holds the key to career advancement. This explains why parliamentary parties are more cohesive in Westminster systems than in non-majoritarian democracies although party discipline doesn't prevent legislative rebellions by dissenting MPs.

The advent of coalition government in Britain in May 2010 means that, like other mature democracies,[22] Britain now displays consensual traits that may lead to a realignment of national politics and lessen incentives for party cohesion (Boucek, 2010c).

In hybrid Westminster systems such as Canada, power sharing and federalism create more multiparty competition than in Britain but these institutions don't lessen the pressures on party unity since single-party rule persists despite the frequency of minority government. On the contrary, 'prime ministerial government' gives the Canadian prime minister even more disciplinary control over MPs' careers than in Britain which explains the absence of legislative factions in the federal parliament.

The management of intraparty conflict is shaped by party organisation. Inclusive rules for selecting parliamentary candidates, party leaders and party programmes may dissipate conflict internally and prevent faction formation but there is nothing predetermined about these patterns. This chapter has shown that measures to increase party democratisation in British and Canadian parties can have unintended consequences and may not lessen factional pressures.

Majoritarian decision-making puts a heavy burden of discipline on party leaders who bear the primary cost of intraparty dissidence as the next two chapters demonstrate.

4
Case 1 – The Thatcher–Major Factional Wars over Europe

In Britain, big election defeats had always been caused by party splits (Pinto-Duschinsky, 1972: 13)[1] and were a big part in the Conservatives' 1997 loss. This left the Conservatives flat-lining in the polls for a decade until David Cameron, their fourth leader in eight years, 'decontaminated' the brand[2] and convinced Conservatives to stop 'banging on about Europe'. They returned to power in 2010 in a coalition with the Liberal Democrats but, 18 months later, Cameron was again facing a 1990s-style rebellion by Eurosceptic MPs and wielding Britain's veto to block another European Union (EU) treaty.

Labour's 13 years in power also degenerated into factionalism but not over Europe. Gordon Brown's camp of 'New Labour' sceptics forced Tony Blair from office in 2007 despite three hugely successful electoral wins.

The Conservative Party was once described as 'pre-eminently a party of tendencies... without the firmness of factional groupings' whereas Labour had been 'a party of factions' (Rose, 1964: 110–1). These labels were swapped in the 1990s. Conservatives used to have 'its agreements in public and its disagreements in private'[3] but, under Major, factionalism over Europe became the staple of the daily news agenda, leading to their big defeat in 1997 – their worst popular vote since 1832 (30.7 per cent) and lowest seat share since 1906 (165 MPs), giving Labour a record 419 seats and its largest majority (179 MPs) since 1935.

Labour had discarded its image as an old-fashioned anti-European party beholden to trade unions and the 'loony left' under Michael Foot. In 1981, a 'Gang of Four' defected to form the Social Democratic Party (SDP) with the rest of Labour split into three factions: the Campaign Group, the Tribune Group and Solidarity. Under the young and trendy Blair, though, Labour became a modern, pro-European party – 'a campaign apparatus with a single clear goal, electoral victory' (Rose, 1997: 243)

This chapter's three sections examine the factional politics of the Conservative Party using game theory to explain the outcomes of conflicts and the impact of disunity on its dominance. Section 4.1 looks at the first Thatcher administration and its division over the abandonment of post-war Keynesianism in favour of neo-liberalism. Section 4.2 focuses on intraparty relations after Michael Heseltine's cabinet defection in 1986, the catalyst for Thatcher's downfall in 1990, and Section 4.3 analyses Major's failure to quell anti-Europe rebellions.

4.1   From conciliation to polarisation: the early Thatcher years (1975–83)

In 1975, Margaret Thatcher won the Conservative leadership through luck rather than backbench support. She entered the race as a 'stalking horse' when the expected winner William Whitelaw refused to run against the incumbent Edward Heath in the first round. She built momentum in the second round after Heath withdrew and four new contenders including Whitelaw lowered the winning threshold.[4] Heath had lost three out of four elections in nine years and his interventionist policies, economic 'U-turns', poor parliamentary relations and unfulfilled manifesto pledges created disquiet within party ranks. In 1973, the neo-liberal Selsdon Group mobilised for a leadership change.

As Opposition Leader in 1975–79, Thatcher adopted a moderate and conciliatory leadership style to prepare Conservatives for a return to power. Her shadow cabinet included Whitelaw (who became her staunchest cabinet ally) and other leadership contenders including several Heath supporters, later known as wets. Heath refused to join her cabinet, preferring to speak from the backbenches on 'the great issues of the day'.

In the early days, Thatcher played for the centre ground out of necessity even though she viewed consensus politics as 'an attempt to satisfy people holding no particular views about anything' (Campbell, 2000). Her Parliamentary Party Secretary Ian Gow guarded against any ideological *faux pas* by ensuring that Thatcher didn't alienate moderate Conservative MPs and endanger election prospects. Policy documents such as 'The Right Approach' and 'The Right Approach to the Economy' (Prior, 1986: 109) were seen as treaties between different intraparty groups (Patten, 1980). Thatcher didn't fight the rescue of British Leyland or the 1975 referendum on Britain staying in the European Economic

Community (EEC). She took a moderate attitude towards union power which Heath supporters like Ian Gilmour and Jim Prior conceded needed curbing (Blake, 1998: 324, 331). The 1979 Conservative manifesto even pledged to honour public-sector pay increases as recommended by the Clegg Commission. One academic estimated that the parliaments of the 1970s contained no more than 30 'diehard neo-liberal' Conservatives (Norton, 1987: 32).

Thatcher was biding her time while Jim Callaghan's minority Labour government disintegrated during the 1978–79 'winter of discontent's' social unrest and widespread strikes. Meanwhile, more liberal policies were being thrashed out in the Centre for Policy Studies set up outside Conservative headquarters in 1975 by shadow minister Keith Joseph to 'learn the lessons of failure of the Tory government'[5] since the Conservative Research Department wasn't trusted with this task (Boucek, 1991). This think tank, one of the earliest in Britain, re-examined Conservative policies to enhance electoral prospects and identify public expenditure savings once the 'natural party of government' returned to power. Defeat of the Labour government came in 1979 when the Scottish devolution referendum was lost and Thatcher tabled a motion of no confidence in the government with the support of the Liberals, Scottish Nationalists (SNP) and eight Ulster Unionists. She won by a single vote and, at the May general election, the Conservatives won 43.9 per cent of the popular vote, a 5.2 per cent swing from Labour, giving them a 43-seat parliamentary majority.

Testing her mettle with the wets[6]

Once in office, Thatcher was determined to reverse Britain's long-term economic decline which meant confronting the unions and sceptical cabinet colleagues in budget discussions. Before the election, Thatcher claimed she didn't want to 'waste time having any internal arguments' (*The Observer* 25 February 1979). However, her first cabinet contained left-wingers 'who had expressed scepticism in opposition about the changes in policy direction' (Holmes, 1985).

Cabinet members who favoured increased state spending to create jobs (the wets) were more experienced and numerous than Thatcher's followers (the dries) and both groups had been in the 1970–74 Heath government. The wets included Jim Prior (Employment), Willie Whitelaw (Home Office), Lord Carrington (Foreign Office), Francis Pym (Defence), Ian Gilmour (Lord Privy Seal), Peter Walker (Agriculture), Mark Carlisle (Education), Norman St. John Stevas (Leader of the House), Michael Heseltine (Environment), Lord Hailsham (Lord Chancellor) and

Lord Soames (Leader of the House of Lords). Prior himself claimed that 'the balance of the Cabinet looked better for our wing of the Party than I had dreamt possible. Looking round the table at our first Cabinet meeting, I saw that most of us had worked together in the Shadow Cabinet and had managed to restrain Margaret from pursuing her more extreme instincts' (Prior, 1986: 114).

However, Thatcher's dries were strategically placed in key economic posts: Geoffrey Howe (Treasury), Nigel Lawson (Finance Secretary), John Biffen (Chief Secretary), Keith Joseph (Industry), David Howell (Energy), Norman Tebbit (Under-Secretary), John Nott (Trade Secretary) and junior ministers such as Tom King, Nicholas Ridley, Norman Fowler, Peter Rees, Cecil Parkinson and Leon Brittan.

Barely a month after their 1979 victory, Chancellor of the Exchequer Howe delivered his first budget to establish 'sound money' and reverse high taxation, high spending and high inflation that had generated high unemployment in post-war Britain. Public spending was cut and privatisation introduced. The top rate of income tax was cut from 83 per cent to 60 per cent and thresholds were increased to 18 per cent although VAT (value-added tax, a consumption tax) was raised from 8 per cent to 15 per cent. Incomes policy was abandoned as a means of countering inflation, exchange controls were relaxed and controls of dividends and the Rate Support Grant were scrapped.

Shocked by the extreme spending cuts and the exclusive reliance on money supply targets, the wets pushed for reflationary measures and a 'softly, softly' approach to trade union reform (Prior, 1986). They wished to slow down the pace of policy change rather than make a 'U-turn' as Thatcher claimed but they had no real alternative. 'A sense of guarding a traditional wisdom, of going neither too far for the country nor too far from the post-war settlement, united men who were personally and professionally not a group at all – though the Prime Minister soon began to refer to them, disparagingly as Wets' (Middlemas, 1991: 236).

Many industrialists, bankers and Treasury officials (Middlemas, 1991: 242) backed the wets. The Director-General of the Confederation of British Industry called for a 'bare knuckle fight' (Lawson, 1992: 58) and its 1980 conference passed a motion criticising the government's policy on interest rates, exchange rates and public spending. Meanwhile, the Clegg Commission had awarded public-sector employees salary increases between 15 per cent and 25 per cent signalling a return to incomes policy.

By 1981, the wets were fretting about the deflationary budget that the Treasury was preparing for 1981–82. By leaking cabinet discussions to the media and threatening revolt, they tried to create a climate of disquiet about economic monetarism (Holmes, 1985: 80). They warned that social unrest following a13-week steel strike could trigger economic collapse during the winter of 1981. Money supply measures had driven unemployment from 1.5 million to 2 million between April and August 1980. Inflation had risen to 20 per cent on an oil price surge after Iran's 1979 revolution.

Heroes and reptiles: the 1981 deflationary budget

Halfway through the Conservatives' first parliament, Thatcher was determined to win the fight between wets and dries to ensure economic recovery before the next election. A neo-liberal programme in the middle of a recession was risky for a deeply unpopular prime minister who claimed she needed ten years to turn round the 'ship of state' and change the course of history (Blake, 1998: 340).

Thatcher hoped an aggressive strategy would signal to the wets the government's determination. In his Medium-Term Financial Strategy document in March 1980, Howe said categorically that 'the new economic direction was not negotiable' (Middlemas, 1991: 242). At the 1980 Conservative Party Conference Thatcher famously declared, 'U Turn if you want to, the lady's not for turning.' In the event, intense political bargaining during three cabinet meetings forced Howe to halve the amount of public spending cuts agreed in July and make minor concessions to mollify backbenchers (Lawson, 1992).

Things came to a head in cabinet discussions over the tax raising 1981 budget, pitting wets against dries (or 'heroes' and 'reptiles' as described by Ian Gow[7]). The pay-off matrix depicted in Figure 4.1 as a 2 × 2 ordinal game was played mainly in the cabinet although each player had backbench supporters. Player 1 (the row player) represents the dries. They are thought to have the initiative and so sit on the left of the matrix. Player 2 (the column player) represents the wets and sits on top. Each player has two alternative strategies: cooperate (compromise) or defect (not compromise).

Each player ranks the four possible outcomes according to relative preferences that are expressed in ordinal values from best to worst (the order – not the magnitude of preferences – is considered in this game). The outcome considered best is labelled 4, next best 3, next worst 2 and worst 1. Each of the four cells in the matrix symbolises a situation where a choice by the dries interacts with a choice by the wets yielding four possible outcomes displayed in the pay-off matrix. For example, the lower left-hand cell symbolises the situation in which by

Player 2
'Wets'

	Accept	Reject
Compromise	(2, 3)	(1, 4)
No compromise	(4, 2)	(3, 1)

Player 1
'Dries'

Figure 4.1 Pay-off matrix: game between conservative dries and wets; March 1981 budget

not compromising the dries obtain their first preference and the wets obtain their third preference by endorsing a budget they disliked.

Thatcher's strategic choices were: (a) No Compromise – stand firm to obtain unanimous cabinet agreement for the government budget or (b) Compromise – yield to the demands of 'wet' cabinet members.

The wets' strategy choices were: (a) Reject – refuse to take responsibility for the government budget and risk deadlock[8] or (b) Accept – take collective cabinet responsibility for the government budget.

Each actor's preferences over possible outcomes are outlined below.

Pay-offs over outcomes for Thatcher and the dries

Best outcome (4): Cabinet endorsement of the budget gives green light to the prime minister's monetarist agenda.

Next best (3): The budget is endorsed but opponents resign rather than take responsibility for tax-raising measures forcing Thatcher into a cabinet reshuffle.

Next worse (2): To avert deadlock, Thatcher reduces scope of spending cuts, delaying the economic recovery by the next election.

Worse (1): Cabinet opposition being larger than expected, the Treasury makes a 'U-turn' and reflates the economy, prompting a loss for Thatcher's 'battle of ideas'.

Pay-offs over outcomes for the wets

Best (4): The budget is significantly amended to reflate the economy.

Next best (3): The wets extract concessions[9] increasing their bargaining leverage while averting a government crisis.

Next worse (2): The wets endorse the budget to save their cabinet positions.

Worse (1): Wet cabinet members resign, the budget is passed and the act of treason ends their political careers and endangers the government's survival.

This game has a single Nash equilibrium[10] circled in the lower left quadrant of the pay-off matrix at (4, 2) which is a victory for the dries. They obtain their first preference while the wets settle for their third preference by endorsing the budget unconditionally which is what happened.

No player had an incentive to depart unilaterally from strategy because such departure would immediately lead to a worse outcome. The dries were better off choosing the no-compromise strategy whatever strategy the wets chose. In any hypothesis concerning the wets' choice, the dries are better off by choosing not to compromise. If the wets calculate that the dries will chose not to compromise, the dries gain 3 if the wets refuse to accept the budget and 4 if the wets accept the budget. If the wets calculate that the dries will compromise, the dries obtain 1 if the wets reject the budget and 2 if the wets accept the budget.

Hence, whatever the wets chose, the dries were always better off with a no-compromise strategy so theirs was dominant while the wets didn't have a dominant strategy. Their better strategy depended on the dries' strategic choice. Hence, if the dries wouldn't compromise, it was rational for the wets to compromise and endorse the budget. This variable-sum game was stable and efficient but also non-myopic.[11]

The 1981 budget was 'the turning point in the Thatcher government's political fortunes' which 'came to be seen almost as a political equivalent of the Battle of Britain: the Thatcher Government's finest hour' (Lawson, 1992: 98). The gamble paid off. At the end of 1982, inflation had been reduced to 5 per cent from a peak of 21.9 per cent in May 1980. A prolonged period of economic recovery would keep the Conservatives in power for a generation.

Ex post, the game's non-obvious institutional and strategic features explain how the dries managed to extract the wets' consent:

- First, as Howe recognised, the wets weren't a cohesive group (Howe, 1994: 170).
- Second, the wets didn't have a dominant strategy or any alternative. 'The inner wets...were not all of the same mind, or similar political purpose...and the outer wets were a still more fragmented class' (Young, 1989: 198–205).
- Third, the dries' dominant strategy was bolstered by the information asymmetry of the budget process. Its contents aren't discussed

collectively. Cabinet members are informed only on the morning of the Chancellor's Budget Statement after the Queen who is briefed the night before (Weir and Beetham, 1999: 128). This 'iron secrecy ensures the impotence of the cabinet in budgetary matters' (Mount, 1992: 121–2) giving the Chancellor a strategic opportunity to introduce radical measures with minimal opposition. The budget figures were 'completely at variance with the wets' readings of the figures agreed in the autumn' (Middlemas, 1991: 250).

- Fourth, Howe misrepresented the situation by putting the three cabinet moderates (Gilmour, Walker and Prior) in a 'prisoner's dilemma', playing one against the other by suggesting to each that the others had given their consent. By the next morning when the three cabinet members assembled, the budget had already been announced in the House of Commons and the opportunity for a rebellion was lost (Prior, 1986: 140–1; Middlemas, 1991: 250–1).
- Fifth, concessions were made to sweeten the pill for dissenters. Howe promised to give cabinet colleagues future say in policy by holding preliminary budget discussions within the Economic Policy Committee (EPC) (Prior, 1986: 140–1; Middlemas, 1991: 251). 'Margaret knew full well that the Cabinet would be a difficult one and had armed herself with a concession – in future there would be a pre-Budget discussion of Budget strategy' (Lawson, 1992: 96). Howe also brought the Confederation of British Industry (CBI) on their side by promising to reduce the National Insurance surcharge and remove hire–purchase controls.

The dries stood firm in the spring and summer of 1981 despite inflation, soaring unemployment and civil unrest, including a four-month campaign of civil service strikes. Some 364 economists signed a letter in *The Times* rejecting the government's monetarist policies. In the autumn, Thatcher was rated the most unpopular British Prime Minister with 25 per cent support in opinion polls. There were rumours of a leadership challenge and defections of ultra-loyalists including John Biffen and John Nott. When internal dissidence threatened open rebellion, Whitelaw demanded in cabinet in July that, if the wets couldn't produce an alternative leader, they had to give way as cabinet unity was paramount (Middlemas, 1991: 254). During the summer recess, tempers cooled off.

In September, Thatcher purged her cabinet of all wets and promoted junior ministers with Thatcherite attitudes. Wets were either dismissed or sent to the House of Lords (except for James Prior who became

Secretary of State for Northern Ireland) and were replaced with 'one of us' as Thatcher was fond of saying (Young, 1989). 'There was a clear sense of being bound together in a common endeavour, in which we believed, and of mutual trust' (Lawson, 1992: 123).

The 1981 confrontation advanced Thatcher's reputation for toughness. She had a long-term strategy and was willing to pay the start-up costs of an economic recovery. She became known as the 'Iron Lady', a phrase coined by a Soviet newspaper, and left no room for compromise or bargaining. Economic policy discussions were restricted to *ad hoc* groups such as the E-Committee (economic committee) or the Thursday Breakfast Group of advisers from the No. 10 Policy Unit such as Alan Walters. By the 1982 party conference, cabinet unity had been restored and by early 1983, general confidence in Britain had returned, delivering the biggest Conservative victory since 1935 with a majority of 144 seats, thanks to the voting system's quirks, a revived economy, victory in the Falklands war and a divided opposition (Chapter 1).

4.2 Deteriorating intraparty relations and Thatcher's dismissal

With dissidents stripped of bargaining leverage, the Conservatives' big majority in 1983 would simplify party management as long as no leadership challenger emerged. Most Conservative backbenchers didn't hold 'Thatcherite' values so the prime minister had to retain support of the 'pragmatic middle ground' for future confrontations. Less than 100 MPs – about a quarter of the 1983 Conservative parliamentary party – were committed free marketeers and monetarists. Some 40 to 60 MPs (10–15 per cent) were wets and up to 240 had no firm ideological commitment (Riddell, 1985: 12). The latter seemed content to 'follow my leader' as long as Thatcher delivered their re-election.

However, the lower cost of dissent under this majority encouraged Conservative MPs to express disagreement by voting against their party on issues such as the selection of House Speaker, capital punishment, higher ministerial salaries and Sunday trading. Despite occasional government defeats and dissenting votes on 17 per cent of divisions, the 1983–87 parliament was pretty united and 'the closest she has been able to create a ' "Thatcher Cabinet" ' (Norton, 1990: 45).

In January 1986, a row erupted between Thatcher and Secretary of State for Defence Michael Heseltine, revealing Thatcher's domineering style and sowing the seeds for a future leadership challenge. The issue was Westland Helicopters, a small undercapitalised British firm, which

Heseltine wanted to rescue through a European joint venture. Thatcher preferred an American solution recommended by Leon Brittan in the Department of Trade and Industry. The subsequent argument violated the norms of collective responsibility and cabinet secrecy.

Heseltine spread disinformation through press leaks prompting Thatcher to allow Brittan to leak a letter from the Attorney General stating that Heseltine was putting about untruths. The decisive moment came when Thatcher put a gagging order on Heseltine who responded by storming out of cabinet arguing that 'cabinet responsibility could scarcely apply since she had not permitted a proper collective discussion of the issue' (Lawson, 1991: 678). Under pressure from the parliamentary 1922 Committee, Brittan also resigned without admitting any blame (and subsequently being appointed European Commissioner).

Thatcher appeared to emerge unscathed from this episode as Opposition Leader Neil Kinnock failed to capitalise on it and the British public soon forgot about it. However, Heseltine's open campaign against Thatcher was correctly decoded as a leadership challenge (Dunleavy, 1995), revealing a growing cleavage in the party between Thatcherite liberal transatlantic and anti-Europe views on the one hand and pro-European interventionist attitudes embodied by Heseltine and popular in the Conservative grass roots. Moreover, Thatcher came to regard cabinet colleagues as troublesome and retreated into 'the Number 10 bunker' (Lawson, 1992: 680).

Polarising her party on Europe

An economic boom delivered Thatcher a third triumphant general election victory in June 1987, a feat not achieved by any British prime minister since Lord Liverpool (1812–27). A 102-seat majority allowed the government to continue riding out parliamentary dissent on issues such as the freezing of child benefit, the Official Secrets Act, the poll tax, eye and dental charges, football identity cards and social security benefits for the elderly in private residential homes (Weir and Beetham, 1999: 380).

Feeling secure, Thatcher neglected 'decisive issues' that generate wide party support by embodying contested principles of policy or programme direction as opposed to 'divisive issues' involving timing, amounts and contingencies (Luebbert, 1986). Instead, divisive policies[12] such as the poll tax and European Monetary Union (EMU) polarised the party, isolating Thatcher from many, including those who had been part of her coalition on other issues (Baker, Gamble, Ludlam, 1993: 425).

Trade had always been a sensitive issue for British Conservatives who split over the Repeal of the Corn Laws in1846 and Chamberlain's Tariff

Reform in 1906. Now, Europe revealed 'a tension at the heart of British Conservatism...between market rationalism and romantic nationalism' (Webb, 2000: 182). Scepticism about Britain's relationship with Europe dates back to Churchill's 'United States of Europe' speech in Zurich in1946 that delayed Britain's entry into the EEC in 1971. At the 1970 Conservative conference, Heath secured a big vote in favour of negotiating EEC membership which parliament then approved in 1971 by 356 votes against 244 and which voters confirmed by 67 per cent in a 1975 *post facto* referendum that Thatcher herself had backed.

By the mid-1980s, however, Thatcher's anti-European sentiment sharpened against increasing European integration which she viewed as a threat to Britain's sovereignty. European summits provided opportunities to flex her muscles and extract concessions, notably a substantial budget rebate for Britain in 1984. However, she remained enthusiastic about the removal of European trade barriers, seeing it as 'Thatcherism on a European scale' opposed to European Commission (EC) President Jacques Delors' internal market project which she saw as 'fortress Europe'. Still, she signed up to the 1986 Single European Act (SEA) to create a single European market by 1992 despite deep reservations about the extension of majority voting in Council (seen as a surrender of Britain's veto), greater legislative powers for the European Parliament (EP) and European competence in foreign and security policy.

However, Thatcher was wary of further economic and social integration in Europe and opposed to Britain's membership of the European Monetary System (EMS) created in 1979 as the first step towards monetary union, calling it 'a backdoor towards a federal Europe'. Cabinet agreed that Britain would join 'when the time was right' but Thatcher raised the stakes by telling colleagues that 'if you join [the EMS], you will have to do without me'. She eventually softened her line to 'until inflation was under control and maybe not even then'.

A turning point in Thatcher's anti-Europe agenda came with her September 1988 speech at the College of Europe in Bruges, Belgium. It drew attention to Conservative disunity and prompted the formation of the *Bruges Group*, a mainly Conservative Eurosceptic advocacy group. Thatcher described Delors' expansion of the EC's authority 'creeping socialism through the back door', polarising her party and narrowing its choice to Thatcherism or Europe. She alienated longtime allies such as Howe and Lawson who had the backing of the business community and the City. Howe felt like being 'married to a clergyman who had suddenly proclaimed his disbelief in God' (Howe, 1994: 538).

Howe and Lawson forced her hand at a European Council meeting in Madrid in June 1989 by threatening to resign if she didn't sign the Delors Report on a three-stage process to monetary union, calling for the entry of sterling and other European currencies into the Exchange Rate Mechanism (ERM), followed by the establishment of a European Central Bank and finally a single currency. Thatcher yielded in Madrid but promptly retaliated with a cabinet reshuffle replacing Howe with John Major[13] at the Foreign Office. Lawson remained Chancellor of the Exchequer because of his popularity with Conservative MPs and the media.

At the 1989 EP elections, the Conservatives suffered their first electoral defeat since coming to power in 1979, winning just 38 per cent of the popular vote and losing 10 seats to leave them with 35 of Britain's 81 seats.

Isolated in an increasingly disorderly party, Thatcher kept making contradictory statements regarding Britain's joining the ERM, her future as prime minister and support for her Chancellor. Lawson was angered by her reliance on advisers in the No. 10 Policy Unit, particularly Alan Walters who criticised Lawson's interest rate increases and 'shadowing the Deutschmark' in preparation for Britain's entry into the ERM which he described as 'half baked'. Thatcher backed Walters' policy of non-interference in currency markets later claiming her ignorance of Lawson's policy (Thatcher, 1995: 719), leading to Lawson's ultimatum: if Walters stayed, he would have to go.[14] Against the opinions of her own backbenchers and Chief Whip, Thatcher disowned Lawson who left in October 1989 (as indeed did Walters). Lawson was replaced as Chancellor by John Major who 'could keep the party together' (Thatcher, 1995: 719) and, in October 1990, Britain joined the ERM.

Thatcher's reputation was now damaged and her authority weakened, triggering an autumn leadership review intended to warn her about the deteriorating state of intraparty relations. Howe refused to stand so Anthony Meyer, a pro-Europe backbencher with no ministerial experience, came forward as a 'stalking horse'. Conservative MPs had three options: vote for Thatcher but let discontent linger; vote for the challenger but create uncertainty in a second round of voting or abstain and provide the 'soft optioners' with an 'honourable protest' (Clark: 1993: 346). In the event, 70 per cent of Conservative MPs voted for Thatcher, 33 for the challenger and 24 abstained. Critically, 40 MPs gave Thatcher conditional support by signing a letter indicating that she couldn't count on their future support if the *status quo* prevailed.

Thatcher ignored this warning and stayed on the offensive, declaring in parliament that Britain would never participate in the EMU even though Britain had already joined the ERM. She was prepared to use Britain's veto to oppose EMU with her infamous 'No, no, no!' At the 1990 party annual conference, her admirers chanted that she should stay in power for '10 more years' but, within a few weeks, 55 per cent of Conservative MPs declared in an opinion poll that she had become a liability.

Howe's resignation speech in the House of Commons on 13 November 1990 proved the tipping point for Thatcher's downfall. He stressed Thatcher's inability to unite the party on Europe and prompted Heseltine to bid for the leadership, claiming he wanted to 'chart a new course on Europe'. He cleverly transformed the context of the race by focusing on the deeply unpopular 'poll tax', a local property tax in the Conservative Party's 1987 general election manifesto that entailed a single flat-rate per-capita tax on every adult at a rate set by local authorities. Thatcher had to abandon it after violent riots in March 1990.

On the first ballot of the Conservative leadership contest on 21 November 1990, Thatcher won 204 votes against Heseltine's 152 votes and four short of the 15 per cent margin required for a first ballot victory (Chapter 3). At a European summit in Paris, Thatcher vowed to fight on but, on her return to London, cabinet colleagues warned of impending defeat on a second ballot. In a dramatic week, she resigned as prime minister and Conservative leader.

Thatcher encouraged supporters to back John Major who came first on the three-candidate second round but two votes short of the required majority. Major was supported by 131 MPs but Heseltine lost 21 votes from his first round showing while Foreign Secretary Douglas Hurd received 56 votes. Knowing that most of Hurd's supporters would back Major in a third round and that Thatcherite MPs wouldn't vote for him, Heseltine dropped out.[15] Major owed his victory to the decisive group of loyalists at the centre of the party (Cowley, 1996).

Thatcher's tale is one of mistrust within her party. She failed to foster common beliefs among subordinates – a necessary condition for mutual cooperation (Miller, 1992: 222) – and instead radicalised intraparty opinion, focused on divisive issues and sidelined those who disagreed with her. She failed to recognise that 'the three key constraints on a prime minister, the voters, the party in Parliament and the cabinet, could no longer be ignored or flouted with impunity' (Jones, 1995: 88). By 1990, Thatcher was considered by many as an electoral liability for Conservatives and was ousted by her own backbenchers despite grass-roots support, a 100-seat majority in the House of Commons and being the first British prime minister to have won three consecutive general elections since 1827. Her downfall continues to deeply scar the Conservative Party's collective memory.

4.3   Major versus Eurosceptic rebels

Thatcher's ousting prompted a 24 per cent jump in prime ministerial approval ratings for John Major and an 11 per cent increase in voting intentions for the Conservatives. As a former whip, Major knew the importance of negotiating, cajoling and bargaining to arrive at 'the Office view after discussion' (Major, 1999: foreword). Such skills would be needed to pacify an increasingly factionalised parliamentary party especially after the Conservatives were re-elected against the odds in April 1992 in the midst of a recession. However, the government's majority was reduced to only 21 seats and this narrow majority would raise the price of intraparty consent for the Conservative leadership and enhance the bargaining leverage of dissidents. Intraparty management was bound to get complicated.

Playing tit for tat with Maastricht rebels

Major inherited a parliamentary party with a nascent but growing element of Euroscepticism that was further fuelled by the Treaty of European Union (TEU) at Maastricht on 7 February 1992. The bill to ratify the treaty was on its second reading when the general election was called in April and it wasn't mentioned in the Conservative Party's election manifesto. During the campaign, Conservatives and Labour kept the lid on this divisive and not simple left–right issue. By the summer of 1993 when the Maastricht Treaty's 18-month acrimonious ratification was reaching its end, the Conservatives' popularity had plummeted to an all-time low of 19 per cent, a sign the party was worn out after 13 years in power.

Back in June 1992, a Danish referendum had rejected the Maastricht Treaty, prompting the British government to delay its own ratification in committee until the Danish position was clarified. This delay allowed 84 Conservative MPs to sign an 'early day motion' (EDM) demanding a 'Fresh Start' on Europe and a treaty postponement. Their strategy was to delay the bill's committee stage and fight for amendments for as long as possible. Over 40 Conservative MPs voted against the government on up to 50 of the approximately 60 divisions involved in the committee stage (*Keesings'* UK Record 6: 4).

While this was going on, Britain left the ERM on so-called 'Black Wednesday' (16 September 1992) after Chancellor of the Exchequer Norman Lamont failed to prop up sterling with three interest rate hikes in a single day and selling £30 billion of Britain's capital reserves. This cost taxpayers between £3 to £4 billion and destroyed the Conservatives' reputation as the party best qualified to run the economy, handing it to Labour for the first time.

In 1993, Eurosceptic Conservative MPs were better organised and more focused than Conservative wets in 1981. They had convergent first preferences – to block the treaty ratification – but mixed motives (career and ideological) and divergent lower-order preferences. Some were die-hard Common Market dissidents who had opposed Britain's entry into the EC in 1973 such as Richard Body, John Biffen, Roger Moate and Teddy Taylor. Others such as Bill Cash, Christopher Gill, James Craan and Richard Shepherd[16] were worried about the treaty's legal repercussions on Britain's institutions, laws and identity. Then there were the patriots like John Carlisle, Anne and Nicholas Winterton, and Tony Marlow wanting to defend British sovereignty.

One particular group of Eurosceptics comprised free marketeers opposed to fixed exchange rates and a single currency notably Nicholas Budgen and Michael Spicer who claimed this was 'a treaty too far' (Spicer, 1992). Thatcher helped this group launch a referendum movement in February 1993 with former party bigwigs Norman Tebbit, Alistair McAlpine and Norman Lamont who had been dismissed as Chancellor in May and replaced by Kenneth Clarke. This camp had cabinet sympathisers including Michael Portillo, Peter Lilley and John Redwood allegedly called 'bastards' by Major in a media interview.[17]

In the summer of 1993, Major needed to reassert his authority over cabinet, parliament and the party organisation. A survey of Conservative constituency association chairmen had revealed that a third wished Major would resign and Lamont's resignation speech in the House of Commons claimed 'the government gives the impression of being in office but not in power'. Voting intentions for Conservatives had plummeted to 27 per cent, giving Labour a 17 per cent lead and handing the Conservatives a string of by-election losses.

Some 18 months of government time and energy had been spent on brinkmanship, ducking procedural votes and accepting amendments to prevent defeat[18] over the Maastricht Treaty. After its third reading in May when 46 Conservative MPs had rebelled, the Maastricht bill was finally sent to the House of Lords who promptly sent it back to the Commons with the question of the Social Chapter postponed to a later vote. An earlier decision required that the treaty not be ratified until both Houses of Parliament had come to a resolution on the issue of the Social Policy Protocol. Finally, on 20 July 1993, the bill was enacted but ratification awaited the vote on the Social Chapter set for 22 July.

Major wanted the treaty ratified inclusive of the Social Chapter opt-out that he was proud to have extracted from his European counterparts at Maastricht[19] along with opt-outs on a minimum wage and monetary union. Emerging from the negotiating chamber at Maastricht, Major was alleged to have declared 'game, set and match for Britain'.[20]

Two votes were to be held on that July night and the Conservative government couldn't afford to lose either. The first was on Labour's amendment to prevent ratification without the Social Chapter and the second was on the government's motion to 'note' its opt-out policy. This was the pivotal moment for both the prime minister and Eurosceptic MPs. Major had staked his future on this vote saying 'it was ultimately a matter for the electorate'[21] meaning that if the government were defeated on the vote, parliament would be dissolved.

The rebels risked being deselected despite their cause's popularity with constituency associations and the public. The worst outcome was the so-called 'nightmare scenario' whereby the government would defeat Labour's amendment but would then lose its own motion forcing deliberations to continue until the government either won or abandoned the treaty (Baker, Gamble, and Ludlam, 1994: 43). Conservative rebels had made maximum use of institutional and strategic resources to defeat the government and block ratification. However, Major held a powerful deterrent (Chapter 3) with the threat of turning the vote into a question of confidence in the government, forcing recalcitrant Conservative MPs to yield.

This was a high-stake game for Major. 'For any prime minister, it was the ultimate gamble ... by whipping the Bill I was tying my fate to that of the legislation. If it fell, so would I' (Major, 1999: 342, 351). If he called a confidence vote to discipline his troops he would be ridiculed by the opposition for jeopardising his government's narrow majority so soon after winning an election. If he lost the confidence of the House he would have to dissolve parliament and probably lose an election since Labour's voting intentions had reached a 30-year record of 44 per cent. He would go down in history as the only Conservative leader (except for Neville Chamberlain) to have brought down his government from within and, like Peel, split his party.

Eurosceptic MPs weren't appeased by the opt-outs. They weren't disloyal by nature but did hold strong views about the direction of

Conservative European policy. They wanted to slow down, if not reverse, the process of European integration.

This was a two-level 'nested' game. The confrontation between Major and Eurosceptic MPs was nested in the bigger game of Westminster party politics and in EU interstate bargaining. Conscious that he was playing a two-level game, Major misrepresented the situation in the intraparty game. He told Conservative rebel MPs that defeat of the Maastricht bill would make it impossible for him to remain as prime minister which the whips effectively transformed into a vote of confidence in the government. However, in the wider interparty game, Major argued this was a vote on the principle of the Maastricht Treaty endorsed by all Social Democratic MPs except for one. In his memoirs he claims this was a question of Britain's 'reputation as an honest nation, not a matter of pride or stubbornness... I had pledged Britain's word' (Major, 1999: 363).

Given previous bluffs and counter-bluffs, it was unclear whether Major would transform the issue into a question of confidence if the government lost the vote. He had often encouraged the whips to impress on Conservative MPs the confidence nature of several crucial votes. During the November 1992 paving motion, he had apparently threatened a cabinet resignation and had even requested that anonymous government sources leak this information while he was travelling abroad (*Sunday Telegraph*, 20 November 1994).

It became apparent *ex post* that the cabinet was divided on what to do in case of defeat. However, a cabinet majority including Major's potential successors (Douglas Hurd, Kenneth Clarke and Michael Howard) favoured the prime minister's high-risk strategy of tabling a specific confidence motion that included the Social Chapter. But other frontbenchers wished to ratify the treaty whatever the result of that day's vote (possibly through a Crown prerogative). Others preferred to drop the treaty rather than ram it through parliament (Baker, Gamble, and Ludlam, 1994: 44).

The game illustrated in Figure 4.3 is a sequential game requiring a different matrix than that in the Thatcher game on Figure 4.1. In this game, the rebels had to make the first move deciding either to support or to oppose Labour's amendment to prevent ratification without the Social Chapter. In a second vote they had to decide either to support or to oppose the government's motion noting the 'opt-out'. Their strategy choice was more critical in the second vote. If the rebellion was decisive – the government motion failing to gain enough support from its own MPs – Major would have to make the next potentially dangerous move.

Having to make good on his threat Major could call a vote of confidence in the government or compromise and negotiate a deal with the rebels hoping to win their support in another vote before the next week's summer recess. Major's bargaining chips included the promise of a referendum on the single European currency,[22] a less costly ruling out of ERM re-entry or the inclusion of the rebels' objectives in his negotiating stance at the 1996 intergovernmental conference – 'son of Maastricht'.

While the rebels made the first move (in the two separate votes) their subsequent strategies would be contingent upon Major's prior choice. In other words, Major would have prior knowledge of their move before deciding whether or not to call a confidence vote. But not knowing if Major would make good on this threat if they did not support the government's motion, the rebels had to plan strategies under both contingencies in their first move. Hence, the sub-game in Figure 4.3 represents a sequence of moves in a game tree.

Each player has two alternative strategies: to compromise C or not compromise NC

The strategy choices for Eurosceptic MPs are:

C Cooperate with co-partisans and support the government
NC Pursue factional interest and withhold support from the government

The strategy choices for Major are:

C Compromise and negotiate a deal if rebellion is decisive
NC Stand firm and call a vote of confidence if rebellion is decisive

This game represents non-simultaneous play with the first player (rebels) having to plan strategies under two different contingencies. It is represented as a 2 × 4 game (Major has two strategies and rebels have four) since Major's move precedes the rebels' move in the sub-game and rebels know Major's prior choice in the final game. The matrix in Figure 4.2 gives each player's pay-offs for every pair of strategy choices.

The rebels have four strategies contingent upon Major's prior choices:

1. **C/C:** *Compromise regardless.* Compromise if Major compromises, compromise if Major doesn't
2. **NC/NC:** *Not compromise regardless.* Don't compromise if Major does, don't compromise if Major doesn't

3. **C/NC**: *Tit for tat.* Compromise if Major compromises, don't compromise if Major doesn't
4. **NC/C**: *Tat for tit.* Don't compromise if Major compromises, compromise if Major doesn't.

Figure 4.2 gives the pay-offs received by each player for every pair of strategy choices (two for Major, four for the rebels). If Major chooses to compromise (C) and the rebels choose tat for tit (NC/C), NC/C is the resultant outcome, as the choice C by Major implies the choice NC by the rebels under tat for tit. This yields a pay-off of (2,2) – the next-worse outcome for Major and for Rebels (in their eyes anyway) which is shown in the C row and NC/C column in Figure 4.2.

The implication of the preference assumptions made for Major and the rebels is that Major's strategy of no compromise is dominant giving him his first preference and the rebels their next-best preference which was indeed the outcome of the game illustrated on Figure 4.3.

The rebels made it clear that they wouldn't compromise when they helped defeat Labour's Social Chapter amendment in the first division (which was tied 317 to 317).[23] They subsequently voted against the government motion that was lost by eight votes (324 to 316 votes) in spite of Ulster Unionist support, triggering the so-called 'nightmare scenario'. Twenty-four Conservative MPs defied the whips (23 voted against and 1 abstained). 'The effect of this was to block us from ratifying a treaty that Parliament had already approved with a huge majority' (Major, 1999: 383).

The rebels' defiance in the government motion's vote prompted Major's aggressive response. After the government's defeat, he declared that the issue could 'fester' no longer and announced a confidence vote

		Rebels			
				Tit for tat	Tat for tit
		C/C	NC/NC	C/NC	NC/C
Major	C	(3, 4)	(2, 2)	(3, 4)	(2, 2)
	NC	(4, 3)	(−1, −1)	(−1, −1)	(4, 3)

Figure 4.2 Maastricht game pay-off matrix
Note: (x,y) = (Major, Rebels); 4 = best; 3 = next best; 2 = next worst; − 1 = worst. Outcome boxed-in is rational.

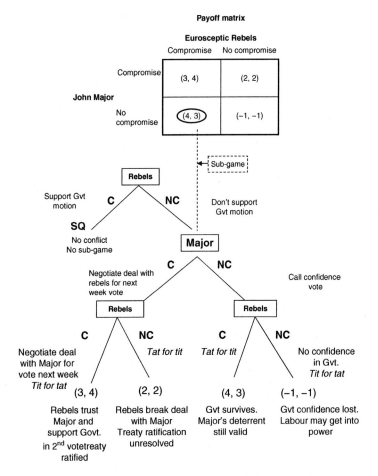

Figure 4.3   Game between Major and Eurosceptic rebels. Maastricht Treaty ratification 22–23 July 1993

Note: (x,y) = (Major, Rebels); 4 = best; 3 = next best; 2 = next worst; −1 = worst. Outcome boxed-in is rational.

for the next day. One rebel declared, 'They have been throwing sand in our face, telling us Major will not make it a vote of confidence. But now they have just done that' (*Sunday Telegraph*, 25 July 1993).

Major's no-compromise strategy paid off and the government won by 339–299 votes (with one Conservative rebel). Major obtained his most preferred outcome whereas the rebels (strongly reprimanded by their constituents) settled for second-best. With little time to coordinate their response they stayed *incommunicado* before the Social Chapter vote and left early or were absent at the 1922 Committee meeting where Major made his end-of-term speech.

Major gained a strategic advantage from the rebels' divergent lower-order preferences and exploited these divisions to break the unholy alliance between Labour, Liberal Democrats and Conservative rebels. By playing 'divide and rule' and making private deals, Major tipped the balance in favour of the government.

The whips made promises and side payments to buy the votes of some rebels including Michael Spicer, Bill Cash, John Carlisle, Michael Lord and Nicholas Winterton. The latter extracted a verbal promise that Britain would not rejoin the ERM while Douglas Hurd promised Bill Cash a role in party policymaking on Europe. Michael Spicer was told there would be 'no reprisals' (Baker, Gamble, and Ludlam, 1994) and that the rebels had fought an honourable campaign (*Sunday Telegraph*, 25 July 1993).

The rebels' blocking power lessened once the Ulster Unionists agreed to give the government their nine votes. Major had held two meetings with Unionist leader James Molyneaux the previous week when the Unionists suddenly toned down their anti-Maastricht stance. A statement by Labour spokesman for Northern Ireland Kevin Macnamara may have been the tipping point. He said a future Labour government would hold joint Anglo-Irish talks on the sovereignty of Ulster whether the Unionists decided to participate or not. 'We should give Macnamara a knighthood', one Conservative MP said, 'for services to the Conservative Party' (*Sunday Telegraph*, 25 July 1993).

As it turned out, the consequences of the Maastricht game proved unstable. Promises of 'no reprisals' were broken. For example, the party whips who had blackmailed MP Michael Carttiss to support the Maastricht bill ended up leaking details of his love life to the press (*Guardian*, 29 November 1994). In addition, rebel MPs were denied membership on Commons select committees (*Times' Diary*, 10 July 1992) and rebel MP George Gardiner was voted off the executive of the 1922 Committee.

This created a climate of mistrust within the party caucus and in cabinet which Major aggravated by maintaining an aggressive stance. He failed to acknowledge the loyalty of the rebels who had sacrificed deeply held principles for the sake of party unity and then continued to antagonise Eurosceptic cabinet members, backbenchers and the rank and file.

A survey of activists by Conservative Central Office showed a majority of three to one against the reduction of Britain's powers in the EU but, in April 1994, Major went along with a European Council decision to revise

EU voting rules and dilute Britain's veto. His attempts to appease rebels by threatening to deadlock EU affairs weren't credible. Fearing a defeat at the EP elections in June 1994, Major vetoed the nominations of two candidates as President of the EU Commission (Lubbers and Dehaene) as too 'federalist' but then approved the nomination of another 'federalist' candidate Jacques Santer. Other examples included the lifting of the European ban on exports of British beef and Britain's exemption from the European Court of Justice's decision on the 48-hour working week.

Their trust violated, Conservative rebels went on the offensive. Four months after the Maastricht rebellion, 11 rebel MPs forced the government to abandon plans to privatise the Royal Mail. MP Tony Marlow called for Major to 'stand aside and make way for somebody else who can provide the party with direction and leadership'. Major was stuck between the Euro-enthusiasts and the Eurosceptic MPs whom he could neither ignore nor appease and told German Chancellor Kohl in July 1995 that he considered himself a 'coalition all of my own' (*Daily Telegraph*, 17 June 1995). Desperate for the support of the loyal middle ground, he equivocated. For instance, in a feature article in *The Economist* in September 1993, Major stressed his hostility to a single European currency but in a lecture in Leiden he declared he wanted Britain to be 'at the heart of Europe'.

Deadlock and the 1994 European community (finance) bill

Ratification of Maastricht wasn't the only battle in the war with Eurosceptics and it didn't represent 'the high water mark of European centralisation' as Major promised his party. In fact, the treaty's provisions soon provided rebels with retaliation opportunities. In November 1994, the *cassus belli* was the European Communities (Finance) Bill to extend the EU budget and Britain's contribution as agreed at an EU summit in December 1992 hosted by Major in Edinburgh since Britain held the EU rotating presidency.

Now the game, though, had a European dimension involving face saving for Major *vis-á-vis* his European counterparts. In terms of actors, preferences and strategies this game looks like a repeat of the Maastricht game except that the rebels had become more powerful since the government's majority had shrunk to 14 seats following by-election losses. Support of the nine Ulster Unionists MPs would give the government some wiggle room but these votes weren't guaranteed. If all opposition parties voted against the government, eight Conservative dissenting votes would be enough to wreck the bill. Conservative whips hauled into the House backbench MPs who were ill and Lord

James Douglas-Hamilton, Under-Secretary of State at the Scottish Office, surrendered his claim to an earldom in order to vote.

However, Major wasn't strong enough to impose his preferences unilaterally and to avoid a repeat of the Maastricht battle he put his retaliation in first. After the Queen's Speech on 16 November 1994, he declared in the House that he regarded the unamended passage of the bill a matter of confidence. Chancellor Kenneth Clarke and Chairman of the 1922 Committee Sir Marcus Fox confirmed a new 'suicide pact' had been made in the Conservative cabinet although it was the first time that most frontbenchers had heard of it (*Daily Telegraph*, 5 December 1994). According to Major, 'The cabinet were united in believing that the Bill was a matter of confidence' (Major, 1999: 600).

The players in this dyad are Conservative MPs loyal to Major against the Eurosceptic faction whose membership, albeit small and indeterminate, was likely to be decisive. However, Major's divide-and-rule strategy had disturbed factional tactics. The 'softliners' favoured conciliation, not wanting to waste energy blocking minor bills at the risk of losing the whole 'end game' on Europe as James Cran declared (*Independent*, 1 March 1995). 'Softliners' including Michael Spicer, James Cran, Christopher Gill, Sir Trevor Skeet, and Bill Walker wanted to influence the government's negotiating stance at the 1996 Intergovernmental Conference hoping to halt further European political and economic integration. But other Eurosceptic MPs such as Bill Cash, Iain Duncan-Smith, Bernard Jenkin, John Townend, John Whittingdale and Sir George Gardiner declared early in the game that, despite their strong disagreement, they would remain loyal and vote with the government (*Sunday Telegraph*, 18 November 1994).

Dispersion dynamics in the anti-Maastricht faction were counterbalanced by the pivotal power of 'hardliners' pledging that, this time, they wouldn't be intimidated by the party leadership's tactics. They included Tony Marlow, Teresa Gorman, Sir Teddy Taylor, John Wilkinson, Sir Richard Body, John Carlisle, Richard Shepherd, Christopher Gill and possibly Nicholas Budgen. Their first preference was a national referendum on a single currency. They emphatically disliked monetary union and thought the EU was a wasteful and fraudulent centralised government to whom no further concessions should be made. A European Court of Auditors' report published on the eve of the vote revealed 'endemic' fraud in the distribution of EU money amounting to £6 billion a year, prompting Bill Cash to say: 'We shouldn't increase payments to a Community that is riddled with fraud' (*The Economist*, 19 November 1994).

I have stood on the slogan 'value for money' – a great thing which the Conservative Party has held before the electorate of this country. Therefore it was impossible for me to agree to spend more money in Europe to help tobacco growers in Greece or mafiosi in Italy when money is needed in my own constituency.

(Conservative MP Michael Cartiss, *The Guardian*, 29 November 1994)

Seeking to capitalise on Conservative dissent, Labour whips tempted Conservative Eurosceptic MPs into another unholy alliance as during the Maastricht debate. A Labour amendment was drafted linking increased EU budget contributions to the curbing of EU fraud and reform of the Common Agricultural Policy (CAP).

Major's offensive strategy was more dangerous and less credible than in the Maastricht game. The government's wafer-thin majority made defeat and a Labour victory more likely. Voting intentions for the Conservatives had plummeted to an appalling 16.5 per cent. For Major, the face-saving cost was high. He would be ridiculed by the opposition even more than before for putting his government in danger by relying on the threat of a confidence vote to extract subordinates' compliance. Since 'executed threat is unsuccessful threat' (Swingle, 1970), Major tried to misrepresent the information to avoid suicide. His camp argued that the bill was central to the government's finances although it accounted for only the equivalent of 0.1 p in the pound on income tax (*The Economist*, 19 November 1994). Opponents were deceived into thinking that blocking the bill was equivalent to breaking a treaty obligation as Secretary of State for Foreign Affairs Douglas Hurd claimed.

The rebels' strategies were:

a) No Compromise: withdraw support from the government and risk triggering a confidence vote
b) Compromise: vote to increase Britain's EU budget contributions

Major's strategic choices depended on the strength of the rebellion (pivotality) generating two different scenarios and sub-strategies that don't affect outcomes and are therefore collapsed into single outcomes in the payoff matrix on Figure 4.4.

a) No Compromise: stand firm and punish disloyal MPs by either (i) calling for a confidence motion if the bill is defeated due to pivotal dissent or (ii) punishing rebels even if dissent is not pivotal.

John Major

	Compromise	Not compromise
Eurosceptic Rebels Compromise	(2, 2)	(1, 4)
Not compromise	(4, 1)	(3, 3)

Figure 4.4 European (finance) bill, November 1994 game between Major and Eurosceptic rebels pay-off matrix

b) Compromise: either (i) negotiate with Eurosceptic MPs to ensure the bill's passage or (ii) withhold punishment from those who vote against the bill to prevent the fall of the government.

The pay-offs and consequences associated with the ranks each player assigns to the four outcomes are as follows.

Rebels' pay-offs over outcomes

Best (4) Dissent is pivotal and the bill is blocked.

Major must either call a vote of confidence or work out a compromise thus strengthening the rebels' bargaining leverage.

Next best (3) Dissent is not pivotal and the bill is not blocked.

The rebels risk losing the whip or being deselected but the integrity and viability of Euroscepticism is preserved[24] and Major has to make the next move.

Next worse (2) Eurosceptic MPs support the bill conditionally: demanding a referendum.

To demand that Major negotiates fraud-curbing measures with EU partners is impossible since the Labour's amendment has a fraud-curbing clause forcing rebels to oppose a bill they agreed with.

Worse (1) Acquiescence means Major wins.

By caving in, the rebel faction and Eurosceptic cause looses all credibility.

Major's pay-offs over outcomes

Best (4) Major's offensive deterrence works. The bill is passed; the government survives and EU partners are kept happy.

The confidence threat remains a useful deterrent.

Next best (3) No 'suicide pact' needed since dissent is not pivotal. However, rebels must learn a lesson.

Withdrawing the whip may reassert his authority over the party (if not the country) although he may become leader of a minority government.

Rumours of a leadership challenge were in the air. Major's critics had tried to seduce Heseltine's left-wing supporters to gather the 34 names necessary to launch a leadership challenge. Lamont had made a 'stalking horse' speech in the House of Commons stressing the real cost of EU membership and Major's desperate tactics (*Guardian*, 29 November 1994).

At best a minority government may jeopardise government committee control blocking budget measures scheduled for the next day; at worst, the Queen may ask Tony Blair to form a new government (as in 1905 after Balfour's resignation).

Second worse (2) Compromise at the risk of losing face in the party, country and EU.

On the one hand, if Major signals his wish to negotiate before the vote rebels might demand a referendum on a single currency or an ironclad promise to preserve Britain's rebate at its current level thus tying his hands in the EU game. 'If Major spiked the Edinburgh deal he would face a Euro row' (*Economist*, 1 November 1994). On the other hand, having declared this 'is not an optional measure' Major will fail to discipline MPs in the future if he lets rebels off the hook.

Worse (1) If dissent is pivotal (and the whips estimated that up to 40 MPs might oppose the bill's second reading) but Major does not make good on his threat for fear of losing the confidence of the House he will be taunted for having wasted his deterrent weapon.

The outcome of this game was (3, 3) representing both actors' second-best preferences and a limited victory for Major. The government bill was approved with a majority of 285 votes thanks to Ulster Unionist support. Labour's amendment was defeated by 27 votes. Major, nevertheless, failed to discipline all his caucus. Eight Conservative MPs defied the whip by abstaining on the amendment vote leaving Major to decide whether to forgive or punish. Choosing the latter, Major withdrew the whip from the eight rebels and put his government in a minority position of 321 seats against opposition forces including the eight rebels of 325.

On the rebels' side, those who called Major's bluff included Budgen, Marlow, Taylor, Carttiss, Gorman, Shepherd, Wilksinson and Gill plus

Richard Body who resigned the whip in solidarity. This time, they had less to gain by cooperating than by defecting. The bill was not an EU treaty pushing European integration with a single currency. The faction's blocking cost was less than for the Maastricht bill and compromise would have been portrayed as capitulation. Anti-Maastricht Conservative MP Edward Leigh declared, 'I voted for the government with a heavy heart. Tony Marlow and the others did a brave thing.' Sir George Gardiner admitted, 'I supported the bill, but I have no pride in my government or in myself' (*The Guardian*, 29 November 1994). Rebel MP Teresa Gorman said, 'Those who voted for the government were cowards and had the spine of jellybeans.'

Despite second-best outcomes for both players, Figure 4.4 demonstrates that this game represents deadlock – a situation similar to the prisoners' dilemma featuring a dominant strategy (defection) – except that the order of penalty and reward for each player are reversed and the deadlock outcome delivers maximum joint pay-offs to both protagonists. 'Both players are better off with mutual defection than with mutual co-operation' (Tsebelis, 1990: 63). The rebels reasoned that Major could either compromise or not compromise. If Major compromised, rebels got 2 by also compromising but 4 by not compromising. If Major did not compromise, rebels got 1 by compromising and 3 by not compromising. In either case, the strategy of defection is dominant over the strategy of cooperation for each player.

However, Major miscalculated by being vindictive instead of magnanimous. His strategy intensified the desire of the vanquished for revenge. He later conceded that 'withdrawing the whip from the eight rebels had not worked' (Major, 1999: 614). Former Party Chairman Kenneth Baker called it 'an act of crass stupidity' (*Sunday Telegraph*, 4 December 1994). Nicholas Budgen said, 'We think the government escalated this quite unnecessarily' (*Daily Telegraph*, 29 November 1994).

The now 'whipless' Conservative MPs went on the offensive. They published their own manifesto setting out an alternative EU strategy and urged the government to argue for a 'substantial repatriation of decision making' at the upcoming 1996 Inter Governmental Conference. The faction's campaign of disobedience rattled the government on several occasions, notably on 6 December 1994, when it inflicted a humiliating defeat on government plans to increase VAT on domestic fuel, forcing Chancellor of the Exchequer Kenneth Clarke to introduce a mini-budget to recoup foregone revenues. Of the eight 'whipless' rebels, only one (Budgen) supported the government in this vote. Like the European (Finance) Bill, this bill was a matter of public finances but Major chose not to make this a vote of confidence, demonstrating an inconsistent strategy in dealing with dissidents.

Other votes provided opportunities for rebels to retaliate: a 14 December 1994 vote against the government on European fishing policy, a 1 March 1995 vote on a Labour motion of censure on the government's European policy and a 21 March1995 vote against a substantive motion congratulating the government on its 'robust negotiating stance' on the CAP.

Finally, on 26 April 1995 with looming local elections, the suspension of two Conservative MPs in a 'cash for questions' scandal and uncertainty about Ulster Unionist support, Major decided to break the deadlock[25] and restored the whip unconditionally to the eight MPs who, nevertheless, resolved to continue meeting as a group in pursuit of their fight against further European integration and a single currency.

'Back me or Sack Me': Major surrenders to his fate

The rebels' readmission didn't restore unity or consolidate Major's authority and rumours of a leadership challenge circulated ahead of the autumn leadership review's deadline. Already in June, Major had made another pre-emptive blunder after a disastrous meeting with the 'Fresh Start' group. Demanding that his opponents 'put up or shut up' and daring them to find someone better to fight the general election, Major took the unprecedented step of resigning as Conservative Leader and putting his name forward as a candidate in the race for his own job. John Redwood, one of the cabinet 'bastards', took up the challenge.

Major won the contest with 218 votes but not convincingly as 111 MPs (predominantly 'Fresh Starters' and anti-Maastricht rebels) voted against him including 89 for Redwood and 22 abstentions or spoilt ballots. The outcome was 'spinned' as a great triumph for the prime minister (Cowley, 1996) but, to insure against a run-off, Major had struck a deal with potential second-ballot challenger Michael Heseltine by later appointing him Deputy Prime Minister. Chairman of the 1922 Committee Sir Marcus Fox turned the contest into an open poll by asking Conservative MPs to sign their ballot papers in full view of party grandees (Peter Oborne, *The Spectator*, 24 February 2001) and then ruled out another leadership review before the general election.

Finally, in September 1996, the Eurosceptic rebels declared a ceasefire claiming that many of the internal arguments about Europe had been won. It was time to put aside internal squabbles and start attacking Labour.

Deprived of a majority, the Conservative government was teetering and MPs started breaking ranks and defecting. Paymaster General David Heathcoat-Amory resigned to speak out against a single currency. Former Party Chairman Lord Tebbit called for Eurosceptic MPs to form another political party. Sir James Goldsmith's Referendum Party threatened Conservative marginal seats and millionaire businessman Paul Sykes offered £3,000 campaign donations to Conservative candidates who ruled out a single currency – an offer accepted by 237 candidates.

Major began equivocating on the issue of Europe much like Thatcher during her last few months in office. The single currency 'wait and see' policy was relabelled 'negotiate and decide' although Major stubbornly refused to commit to a referendum. In March, 39 prominent Conservatives placed an ad in *The Times* calling on Britain to show its EU commitment and British Members of the European Parliament (MEPs) issued their own election manifesto.

By the fourth week of the campaign for the 1 May general election, Major threw in the towel allowing Conservative candidates to state their opposition to a single currency in their individual manifestos with a warning that 'if ministers dissent in any respect, they should not expect to remain in office'. Ministers and party officials voiced their scepticism in public notably Angela Browning, Angela Rumbold, Stephen Dorrell, Michael Rifkin and future Conservative Leader Michael Howard.

Major himself made a personal appeal to the nation in a televised broadcast and the next day declared he would offer his backbenchers a free vote on the single currency (Geddes, 1997). He may have made a tactical mistake by drawing attention to his party's divisions during the 1997 campaign (Geddes, 1997) but the opposition's stances on Europe weren't much different. Polls showed that Europe wasn't a priority issue for voters although a majority held Eurosceptic views. A January *Gallup Poll* for the *Daily Telegraph* revealed that almost 4 in 10 Britons wanted to leave the EU.

Conclusion

In majoritarian democracies, a heavy burden of party discipline falls on the party leader. This can be a source of strength or weakness depending on the leadership's conflict resolution capacity shaped by the state of the electoral market and intraparty opinion. This chapter has shown that, during the Conservatives' early years in office after 1979, factional conflict was kept under control thanks to a divided opposition. This allowed Thatcher to impose her neo-liberal preferences in cabinet and parliament despite intraparty and nationwide opposition.

My game theoretic analysis of the passage of the 1981 deflationary budget shows that Thatcher won that game against wet cabinet members because of the dries' dominant strategy. This victory was pivotal in kick-starting Britain's economic recovery leading to more victories for the Conservatives in 1983 and 1987.

However, Section 4.2 shows that Thatcher failed to significantly shift party opinion further towards neo-liberal values and struggled to retain the support of her party's 'pragmatic middle ground' – critical to her survival. Heseltine's 1986 cabinet defection was decisive in mobilising their support. However, Thatcher polarised party opinion by focusing on divisive issues like Europe and the poll tax, making enemies of former cabinet allies, ignoring warnings of leadership challenges and leading to her downfall in 1990. These internal divisions then reduced her successor's capacity to restore unity during the Conservatives' last parliament when its reduced majority in 1992 increased the bargaining power of a minority Eurosceptic faction. Contentious European legislation gave dissidents the opportunity to undermine Major's authority on numerous occasions including two legislative rebellions analysed with game theory.

Europe is an issue that has dominated Conservative politics for many years. After 13 years in opposition and within 18 months of returning to power in 2010, Conservative leader David Cameron suffered a record post-war legislative rebellion when more than half his caucus supported a motion calling for a referendum on Britain's EU membership. Cameron had imposed a heavy-handed three-line whip over this non-binding vote. A week later he wielded Britain's veto to block an EU fiscal compact to deal with the Eurozone crisis.

Looking at the fate of his predecessors, Cameron can only hope that the party won't continue to 'bang on about Europe'.

5
Case 2 – The Demise of Canadian Liberal Hegemony

Canada's 2011 national election was a humiliating disaster for the Liberal Party. Adding insult to their poor tally of just 34 seats, the Liberals were embarrassingly relegated to a third place showing. Since the turn of the twentieth century the Liberals have ruled Canada for a total of 81 years but that hegemony is becoming a distant memory.

The election in 1984 was also a disaster for the Liberals when they lost a century-old stranglehold on Quebec and were reduced to only 40 seats in the House of Commons. However, they bounced back to power nine years later to rule for another 13 years. A repeat of that bounce back looks like a tougher challenge now.

That 1984 defeat was the real watershed in the party's fortunes. It followed an acrimonious leadership change that clearly exposed rising factionalism in what had been a highly disciplined machine. According to Senator Michael Pitfield, 'The Liberal Party has no dogma. Its creed is unity – national unity and party unity' (quoted in McCall Newman, 1982: 356).

In that year, Pierre Trudeau finally stepped down as party leader after 16 years to be succeeded by his old rival John Turner. The transition unleashed a destructive cleavage in the Liberal Party that is still unresolved in the struggle for the soul of the party.

Power and fierce loyalty had always united the Liberals, unlike the then Progressive Conservatives. The latter were trapped in opposition by recurring factional leadership battles. Affective ties and antipathies towards a string of leaders resulted in a mutually reinforcing cycle of conflict and defeat described as a 'losing party syndrome'.[1] In contrast, the Liberals enjoyed a culture of cooperation fostered by long tenure of office and the ability to paper over internal disagreements (Thomas, 1989).

Post-Trudeau, the Liberals suffered organisational problems and split loyalties that fuelled bitter leadership battles. Nevertheless, the Liberals still managed a return to power in 1993–2006, winning three consecutive majorities under Jean Chrétien. However, this wasn't due to the restoration of Liberal hegemony and unity but mostly reflected the implosion of the Progressive Conservatives and their slow reconstruction as the Conservative Party of Canada.

Chrétien's authoritarian leadership concealed Liberal disunity for a while but intraparty conflict festered and an internal coup in 2003 dumped the sitting prime minister from office. Chrétien was replaced by Paul Martin, finance minister for most of the 1990s and a former leadership rival. This didn't end Liberal hostilities or stem voter disaffection. Four leadership changes in eight years was unusual for the Liberals with their history of long-lasting leaders[2] and the former 'natural party of government' now must redefine itself to avoid extinction.

Leadership rather than ideology drives party politics in Canada. Parties are generally loose organisations coming together for election campaigns. This doesn't mean they are free from ideology. The Liberals espouse federalism and Canadian unity coupled with the pan-Canadian values championed by Trudeau[3] (Chapter 3).

Liberal factional battles have revolved around the role of the federal government and its relationships with the provinces, particularly Quebec. Effective Liberal leaders integrated these competing views under a coherent popular brand. Institutional constraints have prevented this cleavage from creating formal factions with separate representational claims (Chapter 3). Nevertheless, the issue of national unity has split the contemporary Liberal Party into two broad wings. Such alignments can lie dormant for a long time but they can be quickly mobilised for party leadership contests, the primary mechanism for the Liberal Party's factionalism.

This chapter's five sections look at the factional politics of the Liberal Party of Canada, especially the two most recent periods of party dominance under Trudeau and Chrétien.

The Trudeau era alone takes up three distinct periods. The first started with Trudeau's initial election in1968 and ran into the mid-1970s, a period characterised by peaceful intraparty relations. The second from 1975 to 1979 was marked by internal dissent over Trudeau's centralising style of government, interventionist economics and polarising constitutional reforms. The third was Trudeau's final term from 1980 to 1984 when he was recalled to battle after the unexpected fall of a nine-month Conservative minority government. Trudeau's constitutional reforms and economic interventionism unleashed a cycle of instability and a long stretch in opposition for the increasingly factionalised Liberals.

John Turner's six-year interregnum (1984–90) is covered in the fourth section and kicks off with the Liberals' catastrophic loss of power in1984. His support for the constitutional Meech Lake Accord but opposition to the Canada–US Free Trade Agreement (FTA) – both negotiated by the Conservative Mulroney government – split his party into two rival leadership factions, 'business Liberals' and 'social Liberals'.

The latter group eventually drove out Turner in 1990, replacing him with Chrétien whose omnipotent leadership failed to restore party unity. Still, the Conservatives' implosion at the 1993 federal election allowed him to deliver three consecutive majority victories in snap elections from 1993 to 2003. This period, covered in the fifth section, focuses on the growing tensions and factional rivalry between Chrétien and Minister of Finance Martin who had the backing of 'business Liberals'.

5.1   Trudeaumania's inclusive politics (1968–75)

Trudeau was elected leader of the Liberal Party in 1968, only three years after joining it. He beat out nine other candidates to win on the fourth ballot with a slim 51 per cent majority of delegate votes. The extended voting process and narrow majority were partly due to Turner's refusal to release his delegates to speed up Trudeau's march to victory (Chapter 3). The result was far from a clear-cut mandate for Trudeau compared to the two previous leadership contests although it was still more decisive than that of most Conservative leaders.[4]

To consolidate power, Trudeau had to build an inclusive government since many Liberals regarded him as an 'outsider' with a complicated identity. His father was a *bleu* (a Catholic from French Canada who supported the Conservatives) and his mother was an *Anglo* (an English-speaking Quebecker with United Empire Loyalist roots). French-educated, Trudeau received a bilingual university education and was perfectly at ease with Canada's two official languages. In the early 1960s, he joined a Montreal leftist intellectual group writing pamphlets at *Cité Libre* and became a fervent federalist Quebecer during the 'Quiet Revolution', a period of social, political and cultural upheaval in Quebec where nationalism was mobilising against the minority English-speaking elite running business and finance. Some Liberals didn't think Trudeau was 'one of them' because of his intellectualism, academic background, frequent snubs at English Canada, lack of political acumen and obvious distaste for 'party politicking'.

Trudeau understood the need for government to reconcile competing regional claims and social divisions in Canada where political choices are shaped by regional, ethnic and linguistic differences. His first cabinet included leadership supporters and protagonists as well as various intellectual soulmates, including Marc Lalonde[5] who was appointed a special French Canadian lieutenant charged with maintaining peaceful relations with Quebec. The Liberals in the Quebec provincial government had already introduced policies to pacify nationalists by creating a provincial Department of Cultural Affairs, nationalising hydroelectric facilities and negotiating 'opt-outs' from federal government programmes such as the Canada Pension Plan.

Trudeau applied a constructive and conciliatory approach to government to his dynamic charisma that was fuelling a national euphoria labelled 'Trudeaumania'. It fed on a new national pride triggered by Canada's centennial celebration in 1967 and Montreal's popular international fair 'Expo 67'. Canada's six million baby boomers boosted the Liberals in the 1968 election to give them their first majority since 1953. Liberal sceptics could only rally behind Trudeau's sweeping but vague call to heal rifts between Canada's regions, especially Quebec (Meisel, 1981: 26).

This climate helped Trudeau deal with internal shocks during his first administration, particularly the 1970 October Crisis when the government proclaimed the War Measures Act to suppress a feared violent revolt after the *Front de Libération du Québec* (FLQ) abducted British trade commissioner James Cross and murdered Quebec Labour Minister Pierre Laporte.

Trudeau's inclusive strategy was also useful when the Liberals lost their legislative majority in 1972 due to an English backlash against French power and relied on legislative support from the leftist New Democratic Party (NDP). The hard slog of minority government led Trudeau to morph from a philosopher prime minister to a real politician. Intellectuals in both the cabinet and the Office of the Prime Minister (PMO) were replaced by technocrats and politicians closely linked to Liberal support groups. Notably, Trudeau promoted former leadership rival John Turner from the Justice Ministry to Finance to tap into Turner's business connections in Toronto. Trudeau also set up an electoral campaign group in Toronto under Liberal co-Chairman Keith Davey whose professional campaign team delivered the Liberals a clear majority in 1974.

5.2 Trudeau's seeding of Liberal disaffection (1975–79)

Bolstered by the renewed majority victory in 1974, Trudeau launched wide-ranging administrative and party reforms and radical policies that created enemies in many quarters: the civil service, cabinet, the Liberal caucus and extra-parliamentary party, business community, the Western provinces and French Canada.

Trudeau's government reforms fostered mistrust between civil servants and their political masters as well as within cabinet. The top civil servants were suspicious of a reformed cabinet system spearheaded by Michael Pitfield, Clerk of the Privy Council Office (PCO). They believed centralisation of federal power in Ottawa and creation of several new public agencies were an attempt by Trudeau's 'smart boys' to bring the Ottawa mandarinate under tighter political control. Meanwhile, cabinet members resented interference by the PCO and the Treasury Board, and by the proliferating bureaucracies of newly created public agencies such as Regional Economic Expansion, Consumer and Corporate Affairs, Urban Affairs and Science and Technology. The token placement of French Canadian appointees in government departments such as External Affairs and Finance only heightened hostility (McCall-Newman, 1982: 209–24).

Meanwhile, Trudeau antagonised the Liberal rank and file and party caucus by trying to rationalise the party organisation and transforming it into a participatory democracy. His proposed reforms included the election of the National Executive by party members instead of appointment by the party leadership. He also wanted regular two-year delegate conventions whereas previously the Liberals only had three such national gatherings in 1918, 1948 and 1958. Other proposals included the participation by the party's President and National Director in weekly political planning committees, the opening up of nomination meetings in the constituencies and the reform of fundraising practices.

Regional party chieftains saw these reforms as attacks on their autonomy and freedom to mobilise the vote according to local idiosyncrasies and preferences. The party was effectively a federation of 11 fairly autonomous provincial and territorial organisations with very different needs, traditions and memberships (Carty, 1992). Liberal support was based on accommodating the interests of an old alliance of societal groups, principally Quebec, the Western provinces and the English Canadian business establishment. This required targeted appeals and messy politicking by local powerbrokers to deliver the national Liberal vote in exchange for patronage. This 'brokerage politics' was built under

Mackenzie King and Louis St. Laurent during the Liberals' long tenure in office until the 1950s. It had already become a source of recurring corruption scandals but was difficult to dismantle. Regional barons were expected to rely on the party leader's ability to capture votes, using Toronto-based campaign strategists applying mass communication to capitalise on Trudeau's charisma and national appeal.

Trudeau had once called the party rank and file 'second-rate men of action' (Clarkson, 2005: 90) so they were now suspicious of a centralised hierarchy around the prime minister. The party caucus itself disliked the reform of the cabinet committee system and resented being cut off from political arguments since Trudeau had abandoned the consultation initiative originally set up in 1969.

Beyond party and government reforms, Trudeau's government policies themselves threatened the old Liberal support alliance. From the First World War to the 1960s, the Liberals' winning formula had been based on 'a partnership between the western prairies and French-speaking Quebec' (Carty, 2002: 49). But during the Liberals' years in opposition from 1957 to 1963, this coalition of divergent preferences and interests started to crumble as Pearson's model of 'cooperative federalism' failed to assuage the forces of nationalism in Quebec and anti-protectionism in the west.

The western provinces didn't like Trudeau's centralisation of power in Ottawa, his interventionist policies – especially in energy – and his indulgence of separatists in Quebec. This resentment was heightened by Trudeau's wish to constitutionally enshrine language rights for French Canada that would give Quebec a 'special status'. This was in line with the 1963 Royal Commission on Bilingualism and Biculturalism and the adoption of the 1969 Official Languages Act promoting equality between English and French communities. Some regions, especially in the west where there were few French speakers, resented the government imposing bilingualism on them.

Even French Canadians were critical of official bilingualism, seeing it as a threat to their identity and a capitulation to the English-speaking majority. They disagreed with Trudeau's pan-Canadian approach to federal–provincial relations and believed the creation of a bilingual community would deny Quebec a 'special status' within the federation. This eventually triggered the cabinet resignation of Trudeau's old Quebec ally Jean Marchand (Clarkson, 1981). In 1974, the Quebec National Assembly had already passed Bill 22 making French the sole official language of Quebec, prompting air traffic controllers to go on strike during the Montreal Olympic Games in the summer of 1976 over the issue of bilingualism. The strike was resolved through bargaining and blackmail but it triggered yet another cabinet resignation – Minister of National Defence James Richardson – that was taken in the west as further evidence of creeping French power. These cabinet defections undermined Trudeau's objective to firmly anchor Quebec into the Canadian federation and jeopardised the Liberals' electoral stronghold in Quebec.

Trudeau refused to establish a parliamentary committee to reflect on Canada's crisis of unity, provoking yet more acrimony. After a three-day parliamentary debate on the issue, Trudeau decided instead to create a special unit within the PCO and put government officials in charge of setting up a task force on Canadian unity. Meanwhile, the nation was stunned in November of 1976 when the *Parti Québécois* won the provincial election in Trudeau's native province under the charismatic leadership of René Lévesque. He had pledged to hold a referendum on Quebec's political independence, forcing this divisive issue to the top of Canada's political agenda.

As if alienation of the party establishment, westerners and Quebecers wasn't enough, Trudeau made more enemies in the business community and his own Ministry of Finance. 'Business' Liberals in English Canada were critical of government economic policies and resented Trudeau's failure to cultivate links with the Toronto business and financial community.

Under minority government, the Ministry of Finance had tolerated interventionist policies such as the creation of a Food Prices Review Board, passage of a Foreign Investment Review Act and the creation of the government-owned energy company Petro-Canada as the price for support from the left-wing NDP. However, the return of a Liberal majority in 1974 emboldened Trudeau's *protégés* in his office to begin encroaching on the Ministry of Finance by seeking advice from outsiders, not unlike the Thatcher–Lawson experience in the United Kingdom (see Chapter 4). A notable example was Trudeau's appointment to his office of a young government economist and author of the nationalist Gray Report on foreign investment that prompted the departure of five deputy ministers.

It all boiled over in mid-1975 when Trudeau refused to support the spending cuts and incomes policy proposed by Turner who resigned in protest. Trudeau swiftly accepted this resignation to the chagrin of the hapless Turner whose policies were introduced by the new Finance Minister uncontested by Trudeau. Wage and price controls were duly imposed and Trudeau seemed to be moving even further to the left when he questioned the viability of 'free market' economics in a televised interview in December 1975. This was too much for the business elites in English Canada who began to distance themselves from the government and coalesce around Turner, now perceived as a potential Liberal leader on the party's centre right and representing the anti-welfare coalition (Mulé, 2001).[6]

Turner's exit made Trudeau look weak but more importantly it factionalised the Liberal Party into two groups: the 'Trudeauite' left-leaning 'social' Liberals favouring welfare expansion and a centralised federalism and the 'Turnerite' right-leaning 'business' Liberals with a decentralised federalism. Now out of government, the ambitious Turner cultivated links with business and finance while practising corporate law in Toronto and maintained a distinctive power base within the Liberal Party with a view towards eventually making a leadership bid.

Within just a couple of years of the Liberals' 1974 majority victory, dissension was spreading from cabinet to party caucus to rank and file to the electorate. Experienced and loyalist cabinet ministers were dropping out from exhaustion or old age. The party caucus grew more rebellious and several times imposed policy reversals on the government (Clarkson, 1981: 163). The rank and file were becoming increasingly hostile to the small non-elected prime ministerial *coterie*. They had already voted against Keith Davey as party president at the 1975 autumn conference in protest at the manoeuvrings by Trudeau strategists to buy support from opposition ranks.[7] Out in the constituencies, Liberal activists were demoralised and potential candidates turned off by Trudeau's bitter divorce from his flaky young wife Margaret in July 1976.

By September of 1976, a Gallup poll put government popularity at 29 per cent, the lowest since 1947 and some 20 points behind the Conservatives. The poll found 36 per cent of respondents believing the newly chosen and largely unknown young Conservative leader, Joe Clark, would make a better prime minister as opposed to 28 per cent for Trudeau. Public trust was crippled by the government's seeming incompetence. The federal deficit ballooned once wage and price controls were lifted in 1978 leading Trudeau to cut $2 billion from federal expenditures without consulting ministers including his newly appointed Finance Minister (Chrétien, 1985: 177). Ministers refused to resign despite allegations of improprieties. Even the much cherished Royal Canadian Mounted Police had been found engaging in break-ins and other illegalities (Clarkson, 1981; Meisel, 1992).

By October 1978, some Liberal grass-roots members refused to work in 15 by-elections of which the Liberals lost 11 and, finally, in the May general election of the following year, the Liberals were thrown out of office after 16 years in power. However, it was an odd victory for Clark's Progressive Conservatives. They only took 35.9 per cent of the vote and 48.2 per cent of the seats compared to the Liberals' 40.1 per cent and 40.4 per cent, respectively. Their minority government lost a confidence vote on the budget after just 273 days in office. In response, the Liberals recalled Trudeau to battle again even though he had announced plans to leave politics after his election defeat.

5.3 Trudeau's last hurrah (1979–84)

The Liberals' nine months in opposition was marked by discord over party rebuilding. The party's national executive was divided and many anti-Trudeau party members from English Canada wanted a leadership convention as soon as possible. However, francophone Trudeau loyalists secured a delay until the autumn of 1980 when the expected Quebec referendum campaign would be under way and Trudeau could lead the charge against Lévesque's separatists.

Elsewhere, dissidents in the extra-parliamentary party wanted to use the opportunity of being out of office to discuss new policy ideas and regain control of the party from Trudeau's ruling clique. A group of former ministerial assistants and a few caucus members in a ginger group called 'The Grindstone Group[8]' organised a meeting in Winnipeg in the autumn of 1979 when eight policy papers were put forward for discussion. Trudeau and his staff boycotted the meeting in the knowledge that party rules mandated a membership convention and leadership review after an election defeat. To pre-empt a humiliating party rejection in November 1979, Trudeau announced his decision to retire from politics.

Back in parliament, though, Trudeau's Principal Secretary Coutts was engineering the fall of the Clark government in December over the Conservatives' tax-raising 'tough love' budget. This manoeuvre upset many Liberals who wanted the time for a proper party renewal (Wearing, 1980, 1989). However, with a new general election looming, the Liberals had no choice but to recall Trudeau to fight the early1980 contest.

Trudeau had become such a liability that campaign strategists kept him away from the public during the election campaign to avoid rekindling the animosity of the 1979 election (Wearing, 1989). Instead, brutally negative campaigning against Clark secured the Liberals a bare overall majority by winning most of the seats in Ontario and all but one in Quebec. However, there were no Liberal seats west of Manitoba, underscoring sharp geographical divide in the country's political allegiances.

Despite the unexpected return to power under Trudeau's continued leadership, the Liberals recognised the need for party unity. This looked easier now because of Trudeau's apparently renewed vigour and the defeat in Quebec of the 1980 referendum on 'sovereignty association' when Trudeau had backed the provincial Liberal leader Claude Ryan's 'no' campaign.[9] The referendum outcome seemed to align with Trudeau's vision of federalism but it also created a split in the federal and provincial Liberal organisations that would soon pose management difficulties and enduring problems for them.

Trudeau saw the Liberals' 1980 election victory as a golden opportunity to achieve his long-standing vision of promoting national unity through the repatriation of the Canadian constitution from Westminster and extending economic interventionism. The consequent introduction of controversial constitutional reforms and other government policies proved even more divisive than Trudeau's previous administration.

The repatriation of the constitution was quick and, by April 1982, Canada had its own constitution and Charter of Rights. However, the speed of repatriation had two major consequences: Quebec's refusal to sign the constitution and no agreement with provincial premiers on a formula to amend the constitution. The constitutional changes without Quebec's consent mobilised party and public opposition against Trudeau in his native province. Liberal members of Quebec's National Assembly rejected the constitutional deal and the provincial party refused to grant its usual support to its federal cousin (Clarkson, 1988). Quebec voters with nationalist sentiments switched allegiance from the Liberals to the separatist *Parti Québécois* who easily won re-election in 1981 despite having lost the referendum a year earlier.

On the policy front, Trudeau's interventionist economic strategy represented a frontal attack on big business, western farmers, provincial premiers and their governments. Most contentious was the 1980 National Energy Program (NEP) which unilaterally set prices for crude oil and natural gas and established Canadian ownership of the oil and gas industry. This enflamed relations with the western province of Alberta whose dominance of the oil and gas industry was under threat and angered the US government since the interests of multinational companies were at stake.

Elsewhere, Trudeau challenged farming interests in the western provinces by the decision to review the rail passenger service and grain transportation scheme and abolish the 1897 Crow's Nest Pass freight rate seen as the 'Magna Carta of the Prairies' (Meisel, 1988: 17–27).

The Atlantic fishery industry was angered by a government report recommending a comprehensive restructuring of the sector. Other controversial measures included an extension of welfare policies and a peace initiative which ran counter to the tough stances adopted by the governments of Thatcher in Britain and Reagan in the United States.

Despite that opposition, Trudeau's political agenda had been largely implemented by the autumn of 1982 but at much public disquiet that spread to the Liberal caucus, rank and file and grass roots. Already in October of 1980, the party caucus showed its potential for mutiny when Liberal MPs including some ministers committed 'one of the most unpardonable offences in the parliamentary system: they made their displeasure public' (Meisel, 1988: 22).

As for the rank and file, they were angry at the government's abuse of patronage and Trudeau's unilateral decision-making. They decided to hold a convention in the autumn of 1982 and to set up a reform commission to address the party's oligarchic tendencies, targeting members of Trudeau's *entourage*. Patronage appointments were strongly criticised and ministers reprimanded for conflict of interest guidelines and influence peddling (Meisel, 1988: 31–3).

Within a year of their unexpected return to power, the Liberals were already trailing the Conservatives in the polls and, by January 1984, a Gallup poll put the Liberals at 30 per cent compared to 53 per cent for the Conservatives under their new leader Brian Mulroney, born, raised and educated in Quebec. Worn out by years of confrontational politics, the Canadian public and the Liberals were ready for a change, and in March 1984 Trudeau announced his retirement from politics.

5.4 Turner's hapless interregnum (1984–90)

Trudeau's retirement left the Liberals in disarray in terms of leadership and policy outlook. There was no obvious candidate to succeed Trudeau. The party's tradition of alternating between francophone and anglophone leaders put the odds against Chrétien, an unsophisticated Quebecker but Trudeau's *protégé*, and in favour of someone appealing to the interests that Trudeau had alienated. That was obviously John Turner, Trudeau's former leadership rival and cabinet defector. He had been spending the previous eight years in political exile and didn't even have a seat in parliament when he became Liberal leader and Canadian Prime Minister by beating Chrétien on the convention's second ballot.

Turner failed to unify the Liberal Party, clarify its policy agenda and soothe Quebec's fears in time for the next election. Quebeckers needed reconciliation after the trauma of the referendum defeat and bitter constitutional battles under Trudeau. Turner, though, refused to defend the French language and culture during the leadership campaign and then miscalculated by rushing to call a general election only a month after replacing Trudeau as Prime Minister. This cleared the field for Conservative leader Brian Mulroney to capitalise on French Canadians' disaffection and destroy the Liberals' century-old stranglehold on Quebec. Already out of office in every Canadian province, the Liberals were crushed in the September 1984 election. Their national vote fell from 44 per cent to 28 per cent, leaving them with just 40 seats in the House of Commons. In Quebec their vote plummeted from 70 per cent to 35 per cent and their number of seats from 73 to 17. Of Quebec's 75 seats, an astonishing 58 fell to the Conservatives. Mulroney's promise of a new deal for Quebec, his native province, delivered the largest majority government in Canadian history. Eleven members of Turner's cabinet were defeated, leaving Liberals shattered and bewildered.

Turner's performance as Leader of the Opposition was lacklustre and he failed to meaningfully rebuild the party organisation. Still, Turner fended off a vote of confidence in his leadership at the Liberal Party's 1986 biennial convention when resentment between the Turner and Chrétien factions aggressively reignited. After ten months of factional warfare, two-thirds of delegates rejected a leadership review. Some 'old guard' members of the party elite blamed the bitter factionalism on old feuds caused by Turner's exit from Trudeau's cabinet in 1975 and the 1984 leadership contest when Chrétien's supporters were identified as Trudeau's acolytes (Jeffrey, 2010: 79–88).

Turner exacerbated party disunity by taking views opposed by his caucus and extra-parliamentary party on two major issues: the Meech Lake Accord on constitutional reform and the Canada–US FTA.

In 1987, Mulroney negotiated at great speed the Meech Lake Accord with the provincial premiers claiming it would bring Quebec 'into the constitutional fold with honour and dignity' by recognising Quebec as 'a distinct society' within Canada. The Accord was described by a Liberal MP as 'diametrically opposed to everything the Liberal Party had represented and worked for over the past twenty years' (Jeffrey, 2010: 92). However, Turner supported it, leading several MPs in his tiny caucus to start plotting against him. The Accord had a profound impact on Liberal intraparty politics and also on party competition nationwide since it fragmented the Canadian party system by triggering the formation of separatist federal parties such as Reform in the west and the Bloc in Quebec.

Liberal extra-parliamentary party opposition to the Accord complicated matters since it comprised a cross section of 'business Liberals' and 'social Liberals'. Trudeau himself launched a scathing attack on the Accord as a repudiation of his federalist legacy. The bill to ratify the Accord in the House of Commons and Senate provided several opportunities for intraparty dissidents to rebel against their leader and, in the final vote, a third of Liberal MPs failed to support the bill. The disgruntled Liberal MPs in 1987 had signed a letter calling for Turner to step down and renewed that call in April 1988. Twenty-two of the 39 Liberal MPs in the House of Commons signed a petition to get rid of Turner. This was ignored by party bigwigs but the aborted mutiny was just a sign of things to come.

Turner's opposition to the Canada–US FTA further divided and disaffected Liberal ranks. This trade deal negotiated by Mulroney transformed the 1988 general election into a single-issue referendum at a time when the Liberals were beginning to recover from their 1984 electoral debacle. Turner failed to convincingly defend his nationalist stance which was shared by many Canadians who feared the country becoming an American 'branch plant' economy.

Instead, Turner alienated his already fractured party caucus and deepened the divisions between the Liberal federal and provincial parties. Indeed, Quebec's Liberal Premier Robert Bourassa along with the major trade and farmers' unions in Quebec supported Mulroney and the FTA. This dismayed Turner who viewed his own support of the Meech Lake Accord the previous year as a concession to Quebec. More damaging to his leadership, Turner's opposition to the trade deal destroyed his support in western Canada and the business community. Big corporations withdrew donations from the Liberal Party and sent them to the free trade campaign and thus the Mulroney's Conservative government.

Organisationally, Turner's leadership was weak. He couldn't resolve personality clashes within his own office and campaign team and he failed to synthesise a coherent policy agenda from the numerous position papers from Liberal party activists and caucus members. Reforms to reassert power to provincial cadres were anachronistic and misdirected since Canadian parties had become publicly accountable organisations financed by the federal state and separated from their provincial party organisations. And Turner proved incapable of resolving local party nomination battles or countering the barrage of negative campaigning on his weak leadership from both the Conservatives and NDP.

To little surprise, even the scandal-ridden Progressive Conservative Party secured a handy re-election in 1988 with 43 per cent of the popular vote but a majority reduced by 42 seats. Turner had failed to capitalise on nationalist opposition to the Canada–US FTA shared by most Canadians and the other main opposition party, the NDP. The Liberals did manage to double their overall number of seats but, in Quebec, lost 5 of their 17 seats mainly due to Turner's support of the Meech Lake Accord.

Turner surrendered to factional pressures and resigned as Liberal leader in May 1989. The Meech Lake Accord proved Turner's undoing just as the 'poll tax' did for Thatcher and the Maastricht Treaty did for Major (Chapter 4). However, the Accord would continue to challenge Turner's successor, Jean Chrétien, with intraparty management. At the dawn of the new decade, the Liberals looked like victims of the 'losing party syndrome'.

5.5   Chrétien's battles of yesterday (1990–2003)

Turner's departure didn't restore party unity. Old rivalries festered and Chrétien's eventual delivery of three consecutive Liberal majorities was due more to the implosion of the Progressive Conservative Party and Chrétien's own authoritarian style of leadership than with the restoration of Liberal unity. The factional schism born during the bitter leadership battle in 1990 between Chrétien and Paul Martin defined intraparty relations for the next 15 years. It was kept underground for several years and had many parallels with the Trudeau–Turner struggle with Martin 'business Liberals' and Chrétien 'social Liberals'.

At the core of the schism was the Meech Lake Accord. This constitutional deal was a dilemma for leadership contenders since it transcended the usual Liberal left–right cleavage and the Accord dominated the 1990 leadership campaign because it was being ratified by Canada's provinces just as the Liberal leadership campaign got under way. For Chrétien, the most senior leadership candidate who had served in various Trudeau cabinets, the Accord was unacceptable because it went against Trudeau's federal and centralist vision which abhorred the Quebec 'distinct society' clause stubbornly rejected by Chrétien.

The other two leadership contenders, Sheila Copps and Paul Martin, were keen to garner French Canadian delegate votes so they supported Quebec distinctiveness in the mistaken belief that it represented the majority view within the Liberal Party. Copps, a dynamic and fully bilingual politician from the left of the party and a member of the 'Rat Pack[10]', was popular in Quebec but had entered the race late. Martin, son of a Mackenzie King-era minister of social reform, was the real rival to Chrétien. He put support for the Meech Lake Accord at the centre of his leadership bid and counted big business in Toronto and Montreal among his backers. Martin had been brought into the party by Turner's young new guard who subsequently provided him with a ready-made campaign team. Martin supporters shared a strong dislike of Trudeau, an emphasis on economic policy, a lack of interest in constitutional matters and a commitment to substantive party reform and democratisation (Jeffrey, 2010: 171–5). However, Martin had minimal support in the party caucus and his team was no match for Chrétien's in recruiting convention delegates.

Chrétien had left active politics after the Liberals' election disaster in 1984 to become a corporate lawyer and didn't have a seat in parliament. However, he could still rely on long-term party loyalists to select delegates, especially from minority groups, and so maximise personal support among delegates. Party reforms meant delegate selection was critical in choosing a new Liberal leader whereas, previously, party elites wielded the most influence (Chapter 3). Thanks to organisational superiority and claims he could deliver national unity, Chrétien, the 'little guy from Shawinigan', won the leadership on the first ballot with 57 per cent of delegate support.

However, Chrétien's victory was divisive. In his acceptance speech, the new Liberal leader praised his leadership rivals but angered Martin's Quebec supporters by hugging Newfoundland Premier Clyde Wells on the floor of the convention. Wells was responsible for killing the Meech Lake Accord by refusing to submit the deal to his provincial legislature and the accolade was a betrayal to Martin's loyalists who supported the Accord. They donned black armbands as a protest against Chrétien during the convention and a crowd of young Liberal delegates angry with Chrétien chanted '*Vendu*' (sell-out) and 'Judas'. Curiously, though, Martin still failed to gain the support of Quebec delegates.[11]

Appalled by Chrétien's election, defeated Martin supporters defected from the Liberal Party, including some policy activists and nationalist Quebec MPs.[12] Chrétien became a pariah in his native province and he subsequently tried to regain support in Quebec by allowing (if not engineering) irregularities in party funding there. (A sponsorship scandal known as Adscam was investigated by the Gomery Inquiry, appointed by Martin when he became Prime Minister in December 2003. It traced the first irregularities to the 1990 party leadership campaign in Quebec.)

Once at the helm of the Liberal Party, Chrétien took firm control of the organisation. For both the cabinet and his office, he appointed loyalists from both the 'social' and 'business' wings of the party but excluded hardcore Turnerites. He ruthlessly dismissed members of the old party executive who had supported Martin and Turner. However, without a seat in parliament, he didn't have the confidence of many caucus members for whom he was an unknown entity so he co-opted his two leadership rivals, Martin and Copps, in the shadow cabinet to deter any challenges to his authority.

His performance as Leader of the Opposition was unimpressive but Chrétien did have ample time to regroup and consolidate power before the 1993 election. He strengthened the party machinery, improved its finances and redefined party policies by organising a thinkers' conference. Critically, he was instrumental in nominating good candidates to fight the 1993 election by taking advantage of the increased powers of provincial campaign chairs.

However, factional preferences on the constitutional issue continued to bedevil party management. Reconciling the ideological preferences of the two Liberal wings created some muddles. The 'business Liberals' aligned behind Martin and offended by Turner's rejection of the free trade deal wanted a reduction of the ballooning federal deficit. Meanwhile, 'social Liberals' wanted to preserve universal welfare benefits while supporting Chrétien's attempts to clarify the constitutional question which would eventually become the Clarity Act of 1998.

In the end, luck was on Chrétien's side. He delivered a historic victory for the Liberals in 1993 due to a mix of factors: Mulroney's unpopularity and his sudden resignation and replacement by gaffe-prone Kim Campbell, the Canadian public's disenchantment with politicians and the Liberals' sleek media campaign as the party capable of solving Canada's unemployment while preserving the welfare state. The Progressive Conservatives were decimated at the polls and reduced to only two seats in the federal parliament. Some 40 per cent of voters shifted their support in one of the most volatile elections in western democracies.

Chrétien's victory, though, masked a more fundamental shift in Canadian politics. The surge in popularity for the western Reform Party led Canadian voters to abandon the Liberals in British Columbia and the Prairies while the newly created *Bloc Quebecois* took 54 of Quebec's 75 seats. This redrawing of the political map in Canada was heralded by academics as signalling the birth of a balkanised regional fourth party system (Carty, Cross and Young, 2000).

Divisive leaders eventually pay the price for failing to unite their parties. Chrétien stirred up backbench discontent by denying career advancement in his 1993 cabinet reshuffle to those MPs who didn't support him during the 1991 leadership (Chapter 3). Unlike Trudeau (and Blair in Britain), Chrétien didn't respect intraparty dissent and chose instead to assert authority by punishing disloyal MPs.

Nevertheless, luck continued to favour Chrétien and the Liberals. Over the next few years, internal disunity was kept behind closed doors and the opposition parties remained fragmented. The Conservatives' implosion in 1993 made the separatist *Bloc Québécois* (Bloc), a party with no national mandate, the Official Opposition, leaving the western Reform Party in third place with 50 seats.

This gave Chrétien a free hand to implement Liberal campaign promises in their famous election 'Red Book' that had been co-authored by Martin. Shrewdly, this manifesto excluded divisive constitutional reform which Canadians were sick of but emphasised reducing the ballooning national budget deficit which was officially costed and professionally packaged. Martin was appointed Finance Minister by Chrétien in 1993 and successfully delivered significant deficit reductions.

Feeling confident, Chrétien called an early general election in 1997 after only three years and four months when the right was still split and separatist forces at federal and provincial levels were in disarray.[13] In Quebec, a second referendum on sovereignty had been defeated in 1995 albeit by the slimmest of margins. The Liberals were re-elected by winning big in Ontario (101 out of 103 seats) where the Conservatives had failed to regroup. This second victory didn't signal a return to the old Liberal dominance of federal politics. With just 40 per cent of the popular vote, the Liberals only secured a four-seat majority.

As ever in Canada, constitutional issues continued to cross-cut partisanship and federal–provincial relations. Ontario's conservative premier Mike Harris opposed federal Conservative leader Jean Charest's support of Chrétien's position to enshrine Quebec's 'special status' in the constitution. Harris was siding with Preston Manning, the leader of the western Reform Party who replaced the Bloc as the Official Opposition in the federal parliament. And Quebec's sovereigntists kept everyone on their toes by defining the Liberals' ideological divide and shaping its internal politics.

Two successive electoral wins for the Liberals masked but didn't dissolve internal tensions. Anti-Chrétien forces mobilised around Martin whom Canadians considered the party's most popular politician thanks to his success in controlling the government's finances. Several of

Martin's supporters had declined to participate in Chrétien's re-election campaign and victory celebrations. Chrétien had won the support of 90 per cent of delegates at the obligatory leadership review following the 1997 election but that didn't stop party members from fretting about his succession. Chrétien himself was obfuscating about his future retirement.

Martin toiled as Chrétien's Minister of Finance for more than eight years but he maintained strong leadership aspirations and a virulent animosity towards the prime minister, even as they worked together in government. After the 1997 victory, Martin refused to satisfy pent-up desires of 'social Liberals' to use the fiscal dividend on new social initiatives. He eventually relented by directing his attention to productivity-raising policies in research and education leaving Chrétien to concentrate on health care, social housing and childcare (Jeffrey, 2010: 313). This was an alliance of convenience destined to break down.

Intraparty dissidence grew in response to Chrétien's leadership style and the career motivations of Martin's loyalists. The Liberal caucus was restless and the grass roots concerned about Chrétien's omnipotent power.[14] The balance of internal forces changed in 1999–2000 with the departure from cabinet and the PMO of many Chrétien loyalists. 'Business Liberals' started to flex their muscles. In 1999, several Martin supporters challenged cabinet ministers in parliamentary committees. Chrétien pleaded with disgruntled MPs against accusations of career deprivation but Martin's followers saw a change of leader as the only route towards career advancement.

The Liberals' tipping point came just two days before the party's 2000 biennial convention when the press revealed a failed plot to unseat the leader. A group of 25 known Liberal caucus members and Martin's supporters had apparently attended a meeting chaired by Martin's former executive assistant and attended by Martin's senior advisers.[15] With his public authority challenged, Chrétien went on the offensive and called another snap election in October 2000 to the dismay of many Liberal MPs who were nervous about having to face the electorate once more without having fulfilled their mandate.

In the event, this snap election turned out to be 'a masterstroke of political strategy' (Pammet and Dornan, 2001: 8) and a personal victory for Chrétien who delivered a third majority for the Liberals including 37 seats in Quebec (half of the province's MPs) leading to conclusions that the party's dominance was likely to continue for the foreseeable future (Doern, 2003: 3). 'Chrétien returned to Ottawa virtually impregnable' having won a 'resounding mandate for sticking to the status quo' and maintained the Liberals' quasi-monopoly in Ontario in a campaign marked by old-style patronage and clientelism especially in Quebec and the Atlantic provinces (Clarkson, 2005: 232–4). The opposition remained fragmented in four smaller parties. The Reform Party had been rebranded the Canadian Alliance under Stockwell Day who was soon replaced as party leader by the president of the National Citizens' Coalition, Stephen Harper, who eventually became Prime Minister in 2004.[16]

5.6 Chrétien–Martin: 'Scorpions in a bottle'[17]

Shortly after the third Liberal victory in 2000, battle lines were again drawn between the two feuding camps. Martin declined Chrétien's offer of a transfer to Foreign Affairs and retained the finance portfolio. Martin remained the most likely candidate to succeed Chrétien who gave the green light to two other possible leadership contenders (Sheila Copps and Allan Rock) to discreetly start organising for an eventual leadership race (Jeffrey, 2010: 359–63). Chrétien, seen by party dissidents 'as an albatross around the party's neck' (Jeffrey, 2010: 362–3), didn't want to be a lame duck and preferred delaying any leadership convention until late 2002. Martin supporters wanted it at the next biennial convention, as required by the party's new rules, hoping to force Chrétien's announcement of his retirement. The party plumped for February 2003 to the dismay of Martin's supporters who stepped up their call for Chrétien to resign.

Relations between Chrétien and Martin had soured so much that in June 2002, Martin was dismissed from cabinet.[18] In anticipation of a grass-roots revolt, Chrétien announced in August his decision to retire but not for another 18 months. With no cabinet responsibility and Chrétien a 'lame duck', Martin went on the offensive to oust Chrétien from office in an American-style leadership campaign. Since 1999, he had quietly taken over the extra-parliamentary organisation by capturing the presidencies of constituency associations during provincial conventions, enabling him to maximise delegate votes at the convention. Leadership rival Alan Rock described this organisational takeover as 'the Martin steamroller'.[19] Martin went on to easily knock out Sheila Copps for the leadership after two other candidates quit the race in protest against the seemingly rigged process (Clarkson, 2005: 239–41).

So, in November 2003, Martin finally avenged his father who had twice failed to win the party leadership against both Pearson and Trudeau in the 1960s. However, the dramatic removal of a popular sitting prime minister after nine years in power generated bad blood in a Liberal Party that knew Martin was no healer of divisions.

Martin's victory proved pyrrhic. His government became victim of the Adscam scandal investigated by the Gomery Inquiry which reminded the public of past Liberal infighting. Chrétien's loyalists were angry at Martin's intransigence towards them and worried about Martin's lack of commitment to Trudeau's vision of federalism. Quebec was outraged for being held responsible for Adscam which Martin's people associated with the province's 'tribalism' and 'culture of corruption'. Internal party morale was further damaged by nomination battles in candidate selections resulting from Martin's determination to get rid of dissenters before the next general election. His refusal to endorse sitting MPs from the other camp drove 36 Liberal MPs (including Copps) to quit parliament in 2004.

Liberal MPs were apprehensive about another snap election called by the party leadership two years ahead of time. In June 2004, after a campaign marked by party dissension, the Liberals were re-elected with 36.7 per cent of the popular vote against a united right but were denied a majority. They lost seats in all provinces especially Quebec, reminding many Liberals of Turner's electoral debacle in 1984.

Martin's minority government was marred by continued controversy over the Gomery Inquiry revelations, the prime minister's deteriorating relationship with the public service and his vision of 'asymmetric federalism' whose fiscal implications offended the 'social Liberals' commitment to pan-Canadian solidarity. Critically, the issue of national unity on which the Liberals had had a quasi-monopoly for so long was now hijacked by the Conservatives. Harper's decentralist version labelled 'open federalism' promised to redress the federal–provincial fiscal imbalance and allow Quebec representation on international bodies such as the United Nations Educational, Scientific and Cultural Organization (UNESCO).

Throw in the Liberals' organisational and financial difficulties and prolonged infighting, and the Liberal minority government was ripe for overthrow. Within 18 months, the Martin government was brought down in a straight no-confidence motion. After near oblivion in 1993 and a decade-long reconstruction, the Conservatives won the federal election in January 2006 to form a minority government led by Harper. He delivered another minority victory in 2008 before finally winning a majority in the 2011 election that clobbered the Liberals in their worst-ever defeat.

Conclusion

The Liberal Party of Canada since the 1960s shows that the lack of formal institutionalised factions due to majoritarian constraints (Chapter 3) didn't free the party from factional politics. Political scientist Kenneth Carty has argued that there are no enduring and organised factions in the Liberal Party of Canada because there is no organised party in which factions can become embedded, the party consisting mainly of loose networks of ambivalent partisans (Carty, 2010). 'What can appear to be vigorous leadership-centred personal factions in the Liberal Party are essentially personal campaign organisations that arise when the party's leadership is in question' (Carty, 2010: 149).

That said, since the departure of Trudeau in 1984, intraparty relations have been marked by centrifugal forces between two enduring although not institutionalised ideological alignments led by rivals engaged in adversarial competition for party control. While faction membership may be fluid given the high turnover of MPs in each parliament (45% on average according to Docherty (1997)) new cohorts have tended to identify either with the 'social Liberals' or with 'business Liberals' although not always in a linear way.

In Canada, the 'national question' has constituted the primary line of division between these two Liberal wings. However, it has created management dilemmas for the party leadership because the constitutional issue cross-cuts the economic policy cleavage[20] and is nested in provincial politics and federal–provincial diplomacy resulting in a separation between the federal and provincial party organisation especially in Quebec. The issue of national unity has transformed with the evolving debate about Canadian federalism. Under Trudeau, it became ensnared with the role of the state in the economy which polarised party opinion and mobilised 'business Liberals' against Trudeau during the late 1970s.

The fumbling of these issues by the leadership during the 1980s represented by Turner's support of the Meech Lake Accord and opposition to the US–Canada FTA had a long-lasting impact on Liberal unity. It factionalised the party by encouraging the left-leaning 'social Liberals' to align behind Chrétien and against the right-leaning 'business Liberals' behind Turner and then Martin.

This ideological factionalisation hastened the break-up of the already crumbling Liberal alliance of interests spawned by the Liberals' crushing defeat in 1984 and it caused factional rivalries to endure under subsequent leaders. Chrétien failed to heal party wounds even though he restored the Liberals' dominance of national politics after the earth-quake election in 1993 which fragmented the party system and facilitated three Liberal re-elections (1997, 2000 and 2004). While intraparty dissidence remained potent, it stayed underground during much of the 1990s but Martin eventually re-energised 'business Liberals' and mobilised dissidents against Chrétien.

For 30 years, the Liberals were obsessed with the issue of national unity. This caused the party to become divided and introverted and out of touch with voters, especially since the late 1990s when the constitutional issue of Quebec's distinctiveness lost its saliency. The Conservatives' majority victory in 2011 showed that the centre of gravity of Canadian politics has shifted westwards and away from Quebec. If federalism and constitutional issues are of little interest to voters, the Liberals face a concerted period of redefining themselves to regain power.

6
Non-Majoritarian Democracies: Centrifugal Italy and Consensual Japan

Non-majoritarian institutions – typical of consensus democracies (Lijphart, 1999) – put less of a premium on party unity and fewer constraints on factionalism than majoritarian institutions typical of Westminster systems (Chapter 3). According to the theory of representative government, elections primarily allow voters to signal their preferences or opinions; choosing a particular government is secondary. Indeed, majoritarian governance and government–opposition politics, typical of Westminster systems, are seen as exclusive and defective in heterogeneous societies divided by cleavages.

Instead of concentrating power with the majority and its leaders, the consensus model of democracy seeks to share, disperse and restrain power in different ways[1] (Lijphart, 1999). However, maximising representativeness through consensual arrangements discourages strong leadership and makes majority failures more likely due to the fragmentation of political power.

This chapter examines institutional incentives and disincentives on factionalism in political parties competing in non-majoritarian democracies using Italy and Japan for empirical comparison. Italy is more fragmented and less consensual than Japan and both lack some features of Liphhart's ideal type. Moreover, the new mixed-member voting systems adopted in both countries in the 1990s introduced a more majoritarian logic of party competition and reduced the role of factions.

The chapter's first three sections examine the impact of systemic institutions such as permissive voting systems, coalition government and legislative procedures. The final part, divided into two sections, examines party institutional incentives concentrating on the rules used by Italy's Christian Democrats (DC) and Japan's Liberal Democrats (LDP) to select candidates, leaders and policies. A temporal analysis of the factional politics and internal struggles of the DC is further studied in Chapter 7 and of the LDP in Chapter 8.

6.1 Permissive electoral systems

Academics seeking to explain the presence of factions inside the LDP and DC have focused, sometimes exclusively, on the effects of electoral systems (for a summary, see Boucek, 2009). For sure, the different mechanical and psychological effects of the old multi-preference voting system in pre-1992 Italy and the single non-transferable vote in multi-member districts (SNTV) in pre-1994 Japan were instrumental in institutionalising early leadership groups into power-oriented factions. However, factions weren't simply a product of the electoral system. LDP factions have survived (albeit in a different form) in Japan after SNTV was replaced in 1994 by a majoritarian mixed-member system (Krauss and Pekkanen, 2011). In Italy, despite several reforms of the electoral system, factions still exist within left parties (Giannetti and Laver, 2009).

The Duvergerian logic claims that by lowering barriers to entry the simple majority system with second ballot and proportional representation in multi-member districts favours multiparty competition (Duverger, 1964). However, the latter may result as much from social forces nationwide than the voting system's opportunities to split without penalty. A secondary consequence of multi-seat voting systems is co-partisan competition at the district level which promotes fractionalisation in parties that allow multiple district nominations.

Preference voting incentives in Italy

Before the 1992 introduction of the single preference vote,[2] Italy's Chamber of Deputies was elected by a multiple preference open-list voting system. There were 31 multi-member constituencies (ranging from 4 to more than 50 candidates) using the Imperiali quota, the 'least proportional among quota systems' (Lijphart, 1994: 23). Each voter cast a single ballot for one party but could state between three or four preferences (depending on district size) for individual candidates on the party list for the district. After a quota of seats had been allocated to a party based on its proportion of list (party) votes, candidates were assigned seats based on the rank ordering of the preference votes cast by party supporters (Wildgen, 1985). The winners were those who gathered the highest number of preference votes on the list prepared by the party for each district. List voting in Italy is regarded as semi-compulsory.

Co-partisan competition for preference votes, similar to American primaries, could be fierce since the number of candidates a party nominated in each district tended to exceed the number of seats it could reasonably expect to win, narrowing the margin of victory between winners and losers in individual districts (Katz and Bardi, 1980).

In districts where most voters stated their preferences for individual candidates on ballot papers, party nominees simply tried to maximise their total number of personal votes. However, in districts where voters didn't indicate their preferred candidates' names or numbers on ballot papers,[3] the composition of party lists became a powerful source of intraparty competition, factional rivalries and manipulation. In Southern Italy, 70 per cent of the electorate cast single-party votes. The key to election and re-election lay in being chosen head of list (*capolista*) or named near the top of the party list (Katz and Bardi, 1980). This was advantageous to the DC given its high levels of preference vote usage and intraparty competition compared to the Communists (PCI). Communist voters chose the PCI first and cast a preference vote 'as an afterthought' whereas DC voters choose a candidate first and cast a DC list vote 'only as a mechanical prerequisite to casting the preference vote' (Wildgen, 1985: 955).

However, the number of district seats won by each party was determined before the preference votes were examined (Katz and Bardi, 1980). This had implications for nomination strategies for large parties like the DC who stood to gain more than one seat in many districts. It gave local party bosses and faction leaders a stranglehold on nomination and they bargained hard inside the DC national executive committee (NEC) for the final composition of party lists to build local reputations and power in the party organisation (Section 6.4). Allum explains how by first joining a faction and then using its support to gain office a politician could build up his own position independent of the faction enabling him to then quit that faction to form his own (Allum, 1973: 90).

By promoting the personal vote and the proliferation of clientelist networks, these nomination strategies encouraged 'machine politics'. As noted in Chapter 1, the DC harnessed public-sector resources for partisan purposes (Chubb, 1982)[4] especially under Fanfani who embedded the clientele networks into the DC transforming it into a 'capillary organisation' (Leonardi and Wertman, 1989: 108). These complex networks were often controlled by party 'bosses' affiliated with a particular DC faction or who worked directly for a national faction leader like Giovanni Gioia, Fanfani's representative in Palermo, Sicily. The 1970s decentralisation programme multiplied the number and complexity of transacting units between national and local governments. The adoption of single preference voting by referendum in 1991which eliminated co-partisan competition for list placement weakened the factional system that had sustained clientelism in Italy (Sani and Radaelli, 1993).

SNTV incentives in Japan

In 1994, six months after the LDP lost power for the first time in 39 years, the Japanese Diet replaced SNTV with a mixed-member majoritarian system[5] to elect members of the lower house and changed the rules governing campaign finance. SNTV was blamed for encouraging intraparty competition and persistent factionalism in the ruling party and for personalising politics and widespread political corruption (Reed and Thies, 2001).

While factions predated the introduction of SNTV the latter contributed to the institutionalisation of factions in the LDP. By allowing co-partisans to compete for local votes, SNTV promoted competition between different cliques of politicians (*habatsu*) supported by *köenkai* often corresponding to electoral district lines. *Köenkai* were purely instrumental vote-gathering networks that mobilised committed voters for individual politicians by providing services to constituents. Predating LDP formation, *köenkai* grew to mesh with LDP factions and blocked party centralisation although a rise in floating voters and television influence has reduced their electoral importance (Krauss and Pekkanen, 2011: 63).

Under SNTV until 1994, each citizen had one vote to elect one candidate on a categorical ballot but constituencies returned between three to five members to the lower chamber of the Diet without run-off contests. Votes couldn't be pooled with those of intraparty colleagues nor transferred to lower-scoring candidates within the same party. Hence, candidates needed a bloc of committed voters in order to win the elections.

To win a legislative majority under SNTV, parties had to nominate several candidates in each district. Trying to match the number of candidates to their total district vote could be tricky. A party might be able to win three seats in a five-member district if it ran three candidates but could only win two seats if it ran four (Reed, 2009). The LDP was initially more successful than its rivals at minimising wasted votes although opposition parties had some successes in striking electoral agreements in 1971 and 1989 (Christensen, 2000). Matching its expected vote share against district magnitude meant the LDP had to refrain from contesting the third or fourth seat in the bigger districts (Cox, 1997: 238–50). An LDP candidate could secure a seat with 15 per cent or less of the popular vote in the largest districts or constituencies. Cox argued that the LDP resolved past problems of over-endorsement and dilution of the party vote by optimising its local nomination and vote division strategies through its factions (Cox, 1997). However, Reed counters that the underlying nomination mechanism was the strategic behaviour of candidates, not the LDP's rational nomination strategy which couldn't be enforced (Reed, 2009).

The evidence supports Reed's trial-and-error approach. In the 1970s and 1980s, an average 15 per cent of districts continued to run multiple candidates supported by the same faction including conservative independent candidates who promised to join an LDP faction if elected in exchange for aid and support from that faction's leader (Krauss and Pekkanen, 2011: 118–23). Factions with strong contenders for party president and prime minister were also more likely to run multiple candidates in a single district especially where other ambitious factions had strongholds leading to the conclusion that 'factional competition drove electoral district competition rather than the other way around'(Krauss and Pekkanen, 2011: 120). Reed argues that the LDP nomination policy under the mixed-member system is still guided by the rule 'if you win, you are LDP' (Reed, 2009: 312).

Faction leaders controlled the distribution of campaign resources so nominees competing for the same pool of votes in districts where the LDP stood to gain more than one seat rationalised that joining a resourceful faction was the best way to maximise electoral advantage. In time, aspiring politicians joined the most resourceful LDP factions and abandoned those with fewer claims on partisan resources. This rationalisation brought down the effective number of LDP factions to moderate levels (Kohno, 1992; Boucek, 2010b; and Chapter 8). Crucially, nomination strategies were also constrained by the high number of inherited Diet seats (*nisei giin*) going from fathers to sons in districts with strong *köenkai*.

Since the 1994 electoral reform, the district nomination and money advantages of faction membership have been almost eliminated although the expected involvement of factions in ranking candidates on PR lists remains unclear (Krauss and Pekkanen, 2011). Moreover, the introduction of election manifestos in 2003 has made party competition more policy-driven and existing factions slightly more policy-oriented.

The mechanics of preference voting in Italy had a major impact on intraparty competition for electoral stakes among the DC. The electoral system promoted the development of the personal vote and the multiplication of factions (Chapter 7).

In both Italy and Japan, the partisan competition for electoral stakes generated by permissive voting systems provided the right conditions for factions to become major players in the mobilisation of the personal vote and distribution of partisan advantages to candidates. By channelling funds directly to factions and *köenkai* instead of the central party organisation, interest groups and clientele networks enabled LDP and DC faction leaders to build local power bases and stake claims in the party organisation. Faction leaders acted as brokers on behalf of individual candidates or slates of candidates between local interests and supporters. In Italy, sponsors even provided organisational endorsements, funds and newspaper support beyond those available from the party[6] (Katz and Bardi, 1980: 109). In the DC the accumulation of preference votes by senior politicians became a symbol of virility and a harbinger of personal power similar to the building of large campaign war chests by LDP faction leaders (Cox and Rosenbluth, 1993).

All else being equal, permissive voting systems provide good conditions for intraparty competition, weak partisanship, faction entrenchment and machine politics. Although these patterns aren't intrinsic properties of voting systems, electoral reform in Italy and Japan came to be seen as the solution to eradicate them.

6.2 Coalition government

Permissive electoral systems promote multiparty competition and the formation of coalition governments. In multiparty systems, political parties are normally smaller, more homogenous and ideologically coherent than in systems of bipolar competition where parties are broad churches. This lessens competitive pressures inside parties making dissent less likely although defection costs are also lower. A narrow range of ideological divisions means, in theory, fewer opportunities for factions to emerge and stake separate policy and leadership claims. However, defection is less costly if there are closely connected niche parties that dissidents can join and if start-up costs for new parties are relatively low, unlike Westminster systems (Chapter 3).

Coalition parties must be flexible to facilitate interparty bargaining in government formation. Intraparty differences expressed through factions may provide avenues for building broad coalitions unlike in

Westminster systems where factions are an obstacle to majority rule under the 'responsible party' model.

In coalition government, factions offer bargaining advantages and flexibility to potential coalition partners when governments are being formed or dissolved (Laver and Shepsle, 1996, 1999; Maor, 1998). Assuming that parties care about policy and factions are distinct groups with distinct preferences, factions can provide parties with strategic advantages in coalition bargaining so long as political competition is not one-dimensional (Laver and Shepsle, 1996, 1999). The portfolio allocation model shows that senior politicians within parties containing two or three factions have more flexibility than those in less diverse parties because they can change the party's overall policy profile by nominating different politicians as spokespersons for particular areas (Laver and Shepsle, 1996: 249). As semi-autonomous decentralised units of authority, factions also provide mechanisms for the diffusion of dissent which can be useful to political leaders in forming multiparty governments (Maor, 1998).

Italy

In Italy, coalition strategies used the DC's bargaining leverage in forming winning coalitions with surplus majorities to neutralise cooperation threats between rival parties and intraparty dissidents (Chapter 1). However, inter-factional bargaining was even more central to coalition building and government instability. 'It was factionalism, rather than multi-party government, which was responsible for the instability of Italian politics' (Clark, 1984: 332).

The construction of Italian cabinets has been described as the 'dance of Party Secretaries'[7] and the DC government as 'a committee of delegates of factions' (Dogan, 1989: 125). They controlled the *lottizzazione* attributing ministerial posts to each coalition party and intraparty faction according to their parliamentary and intraparty strength. The DC established 'squatter' rights especially in patronage-rich ministries (Furlong, 1994).

DC rules for carving out government appointments were set out in the *Manuale Cencelli* which assigned points to each government post. A full ministerial portfolio was worth three points but the presidency of the Council of Ministers (the PM) was only worth two points and an under-secretary of state just one (Dogan, 1989).

Under-secretaries distributed ministerial patronage to their constituents in their own name rather than in the name of the minister in charge, enabling them to set up separate factions (Allum, 1973).

By combining power in the national government (as under-secretaries) with regional power (exercised through control of a large provincial DC federation or positions as mayors or local councillors) senior politicians such as Andreotti, Colombo and Rumor set up their own factions. This interparty and intraparty factional division contributed to the transformation of the DC into a federation of independently organised fiefdoms (Tables 6.1 and 6.2).

Japan

There were no coalition governments in Japan during the first 38 years of LDP rule from 1955 to 1993. Under the '55 system', coalition building took place between the party factions. However, defection threats by intraparty dissidents forming coalitions with rival parties were a constant danger. The LDP's factional structure reflected the diverse political formations that coalesced during the 1950s and led to the 1955 merger between the Liberals and the Democrats. It followed protracted bargaining between Japan's major post-war political parties after the Liberals lost their parliamentary majority in 1953. Conclusion to the merger talks was hastened by the decision of left-wing and right-wing Socialists to reunite.[8]

Intraparty coalitions revolved around LDP leadership selection. Faction leaders were the key actors in coalition bargaining for office-seeking (vote-seeking was controlled by MPs and the *köenkai* and policy-seeking was delegated to the Policy Affairs Research Council (PARC), see below). Under the second generation of LDP leaders, the 1955 component factions of the merged party lost their policy orientation and became mere vehicles in distributing office perks and political patronage. As explained later, the LDP presidential elections institutionalised this factional apportionment of cabinet, government and party posts through the formation of minimum winning coalitions of 'mainstream' and 'non-mainstream' factions during presidential campaigns.

After electoral reform in 1994, Japan experimented with different types of government coalitions with and without the LDP and minority governments. Many of these governments have been made and broken by factional and party splits (Chapter 8). But after a decade of political realignment, the strongly majoritarian mixed-member system had generated single-party governments giving landslide majorities to the winning party: the LDP in 2005–09 and the Democratic Party of Japan (DPJ) in 2009. The new voting system has also weakened the role of factions and *köenkai* especially under Koizumi (Chapter 8).

Table 6.1 Italy's DC – factional representation on intraparty organs and in government in 1971

Faction name	Faction leaders	DC National Congress (per cent)	DC National Executive Council seats (per cent)	Government ministries seats (per cent)	Under-secretaries seats (per cent)
Iniziativa Popolare	Rumor Piccoli	20.4	6 (17)	3 (19)	6 (18)
Impegno Democratico	Andreotti Colombo	15.1	3 (9)	3 (19)	6 (18)
Nuove Cronache	Fanfani Forlani	17.4	6 (17)	2 (12.5)	5 (15)
Tavianei	Taviani	10.5	4 (11)	2 (12.5)	5 (15)
Morotei	Moro	13.4	4 (11)	1 (6)	4 (12)
Base	De Mita Misasi	11.0	4 (11)	2 (12.5)	2 (6)
Forze Nuove	Donat-Cattin	7.0	5 (14)	2 (12.5)	3 (9)
Forze Libere	Scalforo Scelba	3.5	2 (6)	1 (6)	1 (3)
Nuova Sinistra	Sullo	1.7	1 (4)	0	1 (3)

Source: Adapted from Sartori (1971), 'Proporzionalismo, frazionismo e crisi dei partiti', in Rivista Italiana di Scienza Politica August 1971: 629–55.

Table 6.2 DC – factional representation on intraparty organs and in government in 1986–87

Faction	Faction leaders	DC National Congress 1986 (per cent)	DC National Council 1986 (per cent)	DC National Executive 1986 (per cent)	Government ministries 1987 (per cent)
Left (*Base* and ex-*Morotei**)	Zaccagnini	34	37	43	40
Centrist Group±		26	24	23	27
Forlaniani	Forlani	11	10	10	13
Fanfaniani	Fanfani	5	5	3	7
Andreottiani	Andreotti	16	16	13	7
Forze Nuove	Donat-Cattin	8	8	7	7

Cabinet seats in the Goria government formed in July 1987.
*Includes some members of *Forze Nuove* who split from the Donat-Cattin faction in 1980 and some of some followers of de Mita.
±Includes the two *Dorotei* splinter groups followers of Bisaglia/Piccoli, and Scotti/Colombo.
Source: Leonardi and Wertman (1989) *Italian Christian Democracy: The Politics of Dominance.*

6.3 Legislative incentives

By de-emphasising partisanship, non-majoritarian rules dampen the competition for policy claims between and within parties. This relaxes the need for legislative discipline unlike Westminster systems where party cohesion is necessary for majority government. Under one-party dominance in Italy and Japan, the real struggle for political power took place between factions inside the ruling parties, transforming national elections into intraparty primaries.

Italy

In Italy before the 1990s, party discipline was slack due to a weak and reactive parliament and a decentralised legislative process where parties didn't act as legislative blocs. Party incohesion was due to several factors. First, the Italian Prime Minister (officially the President of the Council of Ministers) didn't have any sticks or carrots to gain the compliance of subordinates. Faction leaders controlled the composition of cabinets and MPs' careers and the confidence vote wasn't a tool of internal discipline (Boucek, 2001: 183–9).

Second, the unusual but widely used 'secret ballot' for votes on bills in the Italian Chamber of Deputies (limited after 1988) made rebelling against the party's position relatively easy (Wertman, 1988). Irrationally, a formal vote on a bill had to occur after the vote of confidence.[9] Moreover, deputies could vote against their own party without detection when decree laws were transformed into ordinary laws and thus not subject to open roll calls (Di Palma: 1977; Hine, 1993: 191–3; Katz, 1997). Snipers (*franchi tiratori*) tended to fall into line for confidence motions although government defeats were usually caused not by legislative dissent but by extra-parliamentary and factional disagreements. Factional defections were a common source of government break-ups (Pridham, 1988).

Third, rebel politicians could evade punishment by voting against their parties in specialised permanent parliamentary commissions which had law-making powers acting as 'mini parliaments' but didn't publish voting records (Della Sala, 1993; Furlong, 1994). During the pre-1992 so-called 'First Republic', approximately two-thirds of legislation was enacted through these parliamentary commissions, decreasing the capacity for socialisation and agenda control (Di Palma, 1977). Fourth, since legislative convergence between political parties in the Chamber of Deputies produced surplus majorities for key votes (Chapter 1), legislators weren't pressured to toe the party line.

Free of the shackles of party discipline, Italian deputies could focus on their electoral role instead of their legislative careers. Re-election depended on servicing the needs of constituents. 'Logrolling' took the form of private member bills (*leggini*) granting favours to small groups of people, four times more numerous than in the British House of Commons and half of which were submitted by the DC (Di Palma, 1977). Unsurprisingly, the dispersion of power produced by consociational politics in the legislature created disincentives to cohesion resulting in undisciplined parties, policy gridlock, unaccountable governments and policy incoherence. MPs perceived themselves as party functionaries first and as parliamentarians second (Di Palma, 1977; Spotts and Wiener, 1986).

Japan

In Japan, unlike most parliamentary democracies, there was no whipping system to administer discipline in the legislature. Japanese prime ministers (who were simultaneously LDP presidents) had little power over legislators apart from the power to call snap elections. LDP factional politics determined their selection and the composition of their cabinets.

National political debate was practically non-existent in Japan until constitutional reform became politicised in the late 1980s. Policy was determined by the state bureaucracy inside the ministries and particularly in the notorious 'iron triangles' of the special interests, the bureaucracy and the LDP policy tribes (*zoku giin*). Moreover, the LDP and the opposition could reach compromises through consultative bodies such as the House Management Committee and the Diet Countermeasure Committee (Kohno, 1997: 118)

PARC, the key LDP's policymaking body, substituted for the parliamentary committees and government bureaucracies in conventional parliamentary democracies. This extra-parliamentary body had facilitated the fusion of the Liberal and Democratic Parties during the 1950s. In the LDP, it became the disciplinary mechanism for the management of government–backbencher conflict and MPs' careers, at least until electoral reform opened it up to non-LDP members (Krauss and Pekkanen, 2004, 2011). This intricate system of functional divisions and specialised committees examined all legislation to be sent to the Diet as cabinet-sponsored legislation and it acted as a forum for politicians to develop their policy expertise and gain careers and electoral advantages (Thayer, 1969; Krauss and Pekkanen, 2011).

The risk of legislative dissent and rebellion was low since LDP factions became indistinguishable on policy grounds and public policy was made outside of parliament through opaque corporatist arrangements. Consequently, party voting became the norm in committees and on the floor of the Diet (Fukui, 1970: 65). In any case, dissidents faced high exit costs given the LDP's strong grip on government and high start-up costs for new parties under Japan's uncompetitive party system. In 1976, a dissenting group of MPs formed a separate (albeit temporary) parliamentary group – the New Liberal Club – to voice their disenchantment with LDP corruption but they did not formally defect (Chapter 8).

6.4 Party organisational incentives and faction institutionalisation

The proportional rules and procedures used by the LDP and DC were key determinants of faction institutionalisation. Faction leaders weren't only decisive players in candidate selection as explained earlier but also in controlling leadership selection and the internal distribution of career benefits and partisan resources.

Italy's Christian Democrats

Candidate selection was dominated by faction leaders working through the different tiers of the DC organisation: provincial, regional and national (Wertman, 1988: 159). In the NEC, faction leaders controlled the selection of candidates through the powerful provincial party organisations responsible for blocking the Zaccagini 1976 and De Mita 1983 reforms to deselect long-term incumbents (Chapter 7). In 1953–86, more than 90 per cent of DC incumbents were renominated, except in two elections. (Wertman, 1988)[10]

From 1964, intraparty power was allocated by proportional representation giving factions stakes in various party organs in proportion to their size. Delegates to various deliberative assemblies were selected by PR among contending lists of candidates sponsored by factions in a bottom-up process. The sectional assemblies selected delegates to attend the provincial assemblies which, in turn, selected delegates to the regional pre-congresses who elected the delegates to the national congress who then selected the members of the national council (NC) who in turn selected the members of the NEC – the key decision-making organ setting the broad policy outline and strategy of the DC along with the Party Secretary.

Before 1964, however, the members of the NC were selected according to a disproportional majority system resulting from a leadership decision in 1952 to award the dominant faction of Prime Minister De Gasperi four-fifths of the seats on the NC. In 1956, this seat quota was reduced to two-thirds by Fanfani who simultaneously increased the total number of executive seats from 40 to 60 (Leonardi and Wertman, 1989). This still penalised minority factions and failed to conceal the dominant faction's decreasing pivotality (Chapter 7). The majority seat quota was awarded to the faction receiving a plurality of preference votes in a final round of voting at the party's biennial national congress. The remaining seats were split according to the number of preference votes received by all the minority candidates[11] (Leonardi and Wertman, 1989).

This reinforced majority rule was unfair to minority factions on the left of the party who wanted to have a say over the formulation of DC strategy and government programme. So, after two failed attempts, the DC leadership agreed to their demands. At the 1964 national congress, proportionalism was introduced as a general principle of internal representation shortly after the formation of a centre-left coalition government that included the Socialists (Chapter 1). This procedural change effectively forced all delegates in local, regional and national DC congresses to affiliate with rival factions from the ground up.

Under the new rules, only motion-lists (factional motions with lists of supporting candidates attached) could be submitted to the Central Directorate. NC nominees had to attach their names to one of the motions submitted by the regional assemblies to the Central Directorate and presented to the national congress. But motions had to be submitted to the Central Directorate prior to the convening of provincial assemblies, which institutionalised factionalism at the grass roots. Factions were forced to decentralise their operations in order to compete against other factions to recruit local delegates and run election campaigns.

Factional motion-lists regulated the choice of the DC majority platform, the NC leaders and the Party Secretary (except for 1976–82). At all the provincial congresses, each faction presented a national programme covering its thoughts on government and party policies. The number of provincial delegates from each faction was determined by the percentage of votes received by each programme. These factional programmes were then presented by an official spokesman for each faction to the delegates at the national congress who debated the motions before voting. The distribution of factional support in these congressional votes is used to calculate the effective number of factions and the power of individual factions in Chapter 7.

For individual national congress votes, factions behaved as unitary actors. However, between votes, there was much behind-the-scene bargaining among faction leaders who struck inter-factional alliances. The leader of the faction winning the factional bargaining game usually became the Political Secretary (although not Prime Minister except rarely and temporarily) subject to approval by the NEC where all the top factional leaders were represented.

Inter-factional bargaining was also reflected in the selection of DC candidates for presidential elections. These contests were notorious for degenerating into protracted factional battles when factions would deploy their blackmail potential to block the candidates of rival factions. It took 21 ballots to elect Saragat as President of the Republic in 1964, 23 ballots (and 16 days) to elect Leone in 1971 and 16 ballots to elect Scalfaro in 1992.

To illustrate how party fractionalisation affects the bargaining power of individual factions let's look at three different scenarios. Table 6.3 outlines the DC factional configuration and bargaining structure in 1949, 1969 and 1982 using the measures explained in Chapter 2: the effective number of factions and faction bargaining power.

1. In 1949, the DC was relatively concentrated with a 2.2 effective number of factions (N_f) and one dominant faction (de Gasperi) that had a majority of NC seats and thus held all the pivotal power (NBP_{f1}). Hence, in coalition terms, all the other factions were dummies and this faction had the capacity to dictate the party agenda.

2. In 1969, the situation changes significantly as a result of institutional incentives. The DC was moderately fragmented ($N_f = 5$) even though seven observable factions competed for the support of congressional delegates. No faction held majority control over the congress although the plurality faction (Faction 3: *Impegno Democratico*) enjoyed bargaining power disproportional to its strength. Its 38 per cent share of delegate support translated into a 57 per cent share of voting power. In other words, it was pivotal in 57 per cent of all possible internal winning coalitions.

3. Finally in 1982, the DC had become an extremely fractionalised party. There were 10 effective factions ($N_f = 10$) although 12 different factions actually competed for delegate support and no faction enjoyed more than a 15 per cent share of support. Under this fragmented configuration, factional shares of normalised Banzhaf power are almost proportional to factional strength (columns 8 and 9). This was an unstable situation that offered strategic opportunities for minority factions to create mischief and destabilise the DC.

The effect of this rule change on party fragmentation points to two separate intraparty electoral regimes: before 1964 when the system of

Table 6.3 Factions' shares of delegate votes and of normalised Banzhaf power DC national congresses of 1949, 1969 and 1982

1949			1969			1982		
Faction	Seats*	NBP±	Faction	per cent votes	NBP±	Faction	per cent votes	NBP±
1	14.0	0.000	1	18.0	.106	1	9.0	.091
2	23.0	0.000	2	16.0	.106	2	10.0	.102
3	63.0	1.000	3	38.0	.574	3	9.0	.015
			4	13.0	.106	4	4.0	.037
			5	10.0	.064	5	8.0	.0819
			6	3.0	.0213	6	14.0	.147
			7	3.0	.0213	7	7.0	.072
						8	2.0	.019
						9	13.0	.136
						10	9.0	.091
						11	10.0	.102
						12	3.0	.028

*Estimated strength on the NC.
±NBP: factional share of total normalised Banzhaf power.
Source: For 1949 figures: Adapted from Chasseriaud J.P. (1965) Le Parti Démocratique Chrétien en Italie (Librairie Arman Colin: Paris) p. 335. For 1969 and 1982 figures: Leonardi and Wertman (1989) Italian Christian Democracy: The Politics of Dominance pp. 114–5.

'reinforced majority' prevailed and the effective number of DC factions (N_f) was relatively moderate and after 1964 when the adoption of a proportional system of internal representation triggered a significant growth in N_f (see Figure 7.1). As expected, a more fragmented party causes the most powerful faction (NBP_{f1}) to lose coalition power since it is less pivotal in making or breaking intraparty coalitions.

Unsurprisingly, the frequency of party congresses and expanding number of factions created a lot of churn at the top of the DC organisation resulting in majority failures and decisional stalemate (Chapter 7). Senior politicians were incentivised to set up new factions and split existing ones to strengthen their personal position within the party. By 1982, no less than 12 separate intraparty factions competed for the support of congress delegates. The appointments of career administrators in the DC central party bureaucracy and in the regional and provincial bodies were also allocated along factional lines. 'The adoption of proportional representation for the election of collective organs within the party facilitated the power and proliferation of the factions, but the factionalisation of the DC had already begun before this change of rules' (Leonardi and Wertman, 1989: 145).

Japan's Liberal Democrats (LDP)

'Faction leaders help members win party endorsement, rise through party ranks, and gain access to funding – in short, to improve their re-election chances. To promote their faction leaders' ability to perform these services for them, faction members support their leaders in the prime ministerial races'(Ramseyer and McCall Rosenbluth, 1997: 59).

To assess the impact of institutions on factionalism in the LDP it is important to differentiate between the political norms and party procedures that prevailed under the '55 system'[12] and under the new institutional regime (post-1994 electoral reform).

Under the '55 system', LDP leadership selection, controlled by factions, determined the internal division of office spoils creating incentives for factions to become institutionalised. Like the DC, the LDP started out as a heterogeneous group of separate political alignments following the 1955 party merger. The factions (*habatsu*) were fluid, looser, more informal and internally diverse before the adoption of competitive elections for the party presidency (Krauss and Pekkanen; 2011: 110). However, the selection of the LDP president through elections (1958) and membership primaries (1978) made the factions the main players in these biennial contests,[13] transforming them into competitive factions of patronage. '*Habatsu* politics does not correspond to any form of pluralism. It is a power game, entirely bereft of meaningful political discussion, and one over which the voters exercise no influence at all' (van Wolferen, 1989: 139).

LDP presidential elections were high-stake games since they determined which faction leader would become prime minister and which faction or factional alliance would receive the lion's share of cabinet posts: the 'mainstream' factions. The factions backing presidential losers ('anti-mainstream') were originally excluded from the cabinet. In 1956–78, the leadership winner was the candidate gaining a majority of votes, cast by all members of both houses of the Diet plus one representative from each of the 47 prefectural chapters of the party. However, until Sato's retirement in1972, prime ministers tended to pick their own successors[14] without recourse to elections although the largest faction's leader was usually chosen.

In 1978 against the background of the Lockheed scandal, the LDP tried to introduce more intraparty democracy. It adopted membership primaries hoping to weaken the factions' power and mitigate voters' disenchantment with their corrupt leaders. Any registered party member could vote in the primaries although LDP Diet members retained the final vote in the run-off race between the top two contenders. In 1981, following a battle for party control and yet more corruption, presidential election rules were amended again to deter intra-elite conflicts (Chapter 8). At least four candidatures were required for primaries to be held and each candidate needed the endorsement of at least 50 Diet members.

Presidential primaries didn't dampen factional rivalries. On the contrary, this well-intended reform by Takeo Miki to counter the fallout from the Tanaka scandal provided more scope for manipulation through membership 'padding' by self-serving leaders and for the decentralisation of factional activities (Chapter 8). Presidential races remained dominated by backroom negotiations between party bosses (Cox and Rosenbluth, 1993).

Like the DC motion-lists system, LDP presidential primaries forced factions to become active in local districts where large sums of money were channelled to recruit supporters expected to back the faction's favourite contender during the primaries. The search for votes intensified so much that in 1978 membership numbers tripled from 0.5 million to 1.5 million and hit 3 million in 1980 when Kakuei Tanaka engaged in an aggressive recruitment drive to increase the power of his own faction (Chapter 8).

In 1998, election rules for the party presidency were changed to give more voting power to the LDP prefectural chapters. Although Diet members still had the most votes, they would now know the results of prefectural votes before casting their own votes. Hence, 'they could be swayed if a candidate won the prefectures instead of faction leaders completely controlling the process' (Kabashima and Steel, 2007: 101).

In 2011, Koizumi took advantage of this change to bypass the party elite and appeal directly to the rank and file (Chapter 8). With his win of 90 per cent of the prefectural votes in the local primaries, the party leadership couldn't reject the rank-and-file preferences. Afterwards, 'factions still counted in influencing who becomes prime minister, but they were no longer the whole game' (Krauss and Pekkanen 2011: 141).

As in Italy, the allocation of cabinet, non-cabinet and top party posts was controlled by LDP faction leaders. Factions received office pay-offs in proportion to their size (the number of MPs belonging to each faction) and status (mainstream or non-mainstream). Nominees for top positions such as Party President, Secretary General, Chairman of the Executive Council and Chairman of PARC were customarily chosen from the four main factions. And the Director of the party's Treasury Bureau was usually nominated from a faction other than that of the President or the Secretary General (Kohno, 1992, 1997). Non-mainstream factions weren't totally excluded since their support might be required to form a winning coalition during the next presidential race. The LDP president allocated appointments to factions according to their future coalition potential and reshuffled cabinets regularly. Ministers rarely spent more than a year in a particular ministry leaving civil servants to provide continuity.

Factional promotion determined by rank and seniority raised barriers to exit. The number of portfolios and party posts was limited, making career advancement slow and frustrating. Kohno (1997) calculated that, on average, an LDP Diet member needed to be re-elected at least six times to be considered for a cabinet post and four times for a non-cabinet post in PARC for instance (Table 6.4) and promotional barriers were raised over time.[15] Consequently, dissidents were loath to leave their faction for fear of starting at the bottom of a new faction's career ladder.

Careerist politicians responded to incentives by joining factions with presidential potential and abandoning those without. In 1972–88, the number of MPs not affiliated with factions decreased from 25 per cent to less than 5 per cent. Presidential primaries consolidated factions rather

Table 6.4   The LDP seniority system

Ladder of public roles	Number of re-elections required for advancement
House Committee Member or Vice-Chair of a PARC Committee	2
Vice-Minister	3
Chair of a PARC Committee	4
House Committee Chair	5
Minister	6 or more

Source: Kohno (1997), Table 6.1, p. 95.

than multiplied them. Factions decreased in number but increased in size (Chapter 8).

Since SNTV was abandoned in 1994, the electoral incentives for faction affiliation have declined. Under Koizumi who vowed to destroy factions, a quarter of Diet members were unattached to factions and by 2009 that number had climbed to 40 per cent. However, until the LDP lost power in 2009, factions were still important in post allocation and career advancement although at the cabinet level the factional proportionality norm across all post-reform prime ministers had consistently weakened (Cox, Rosenbluth and Thies, 1999; Reed and Thies, 2001, Krauss and Pekkanen, 2011).

Conclusion

The DC and LDP started as coalitions of disparate and loose political groupings who coalesced into large 'catch-all' parties after the Second World War. At the beginning, a factional structure facilitated party integration and power-sharing between these sub-party components resulting in a form of 'cooperative factionalism' (Boucek, 2009). Factional power-sharing and proportionality enabled factions to become the key representative units in these dominant parties and the channels to power for their politicians.

Non-majoritarian electoral systems provided ideal conditions for the development of the personal vote and transformation of factions. By allowing co-partisans to compete for local votes, Italy's multi-preference voting system and Japan's SNTV promoted clientelism through factions and the Japanese *köenkai*. The original DC and LDP leadership groups quickly became factions of patronage. Faction leaders rather than party leaders controlled the allocation of private benefits to office seekers (such as candidate nominations, campaign funding and 'pork') and career benefits to office holders. This redirected politicians' loyalties from the party towards factions and weakened partisanship.

Permissive electoral systems fractionalise party systems and political parties. They tend to produce multiparty coalition governments where factions can be instrumental in coalition building. However, they can also be a source of coalition break-up as in Italy. The factional division of government posts contributed to the persistence and proliferation of factions in both countries. In Japan the persistence of single-party government internalised coalition politics inside the LDP where defection threats were a constant risk.

In both countries, legislative incentives failed to discourage factionalism. The Italian and Japanese prime ministers lacked policy-making authority and statutory powers to bind cabinets or discipline representatives whose careers depended on factional affiliation rather than loyalty to the party leader. In the Italian legislature, parliamentary procedures allowed dissenting MPs to escape the consequences of their actions. In the Japanese non-partisan Diet, members toed the party line without compulsion since legislative careers and appointments were determined by extra-parliamentary organisations such as PARC and the factions.

The proportional rules and procedures of the LDP and DC were key determinants of faction institutionalisation. In both parties, leadership selection was dominated by inter-factional bargaining. The DC factional motion-lists system and LDP presidential primaries pushed the factions to decentralise their operations and become embedded in the party grass roots.

Non-majoritarian institutions enabled the DC and LDP to contain competitive pressures and internalise conflict resolution. However, the next two chapters will show that, in the long run, containment strategies have unintended consequences and negative trade-offs.

7
Case 3 – Italy's Christian Democrats: How Factional Capture Bred Self-Destruction

In 1994, the Christian Democratic Party of Italy (DC) was tossed out of power after almost five decades, crashing to just 46 seats from 207 in the lower house. It had been the senior member of 51 coalition governments even though it only had an absolute parliamentary majority once. Mired in corruption and disoriented by the break-up of the Communist Party, the Christian Democrats had been losing support for many years.

In 1976, the Communists' vote jumped from 27.2 per cent to 34.4 per cent – only 4.3 per cent behind the DC – triggering a 'historic compromise' between the two parties for a government of national unity until 1979 when the Communists withdrew their support. During the 1980s, the DC's power-sharing with Craxi's equally corrupt and factionalised Socialists was the road to perdition.

The 1992 election proved seminal as the Christian Democrats started losing support at an alarming rate to new anti-establishment parties changing trade-offs between voice and exit for dissidents and reformist DC politicians.

This chapter charts the DC's factional politics from its birth in 1945 to its dramatic implosion in 1994 which ended Italy's 'First Republic'. Institutional incentives had played a big part in the maintenance, growth and transformation of DC factions. However, a salient line of factional division – the governing formula determining which parties to include in DC-led coalitions – shaped the party's internal politics throughout its period of dominance.

The first section looks at centre-right coalitions in 1945–64 when factionalism was cooperative and a dominant faction existed. The second looks at 1964–76 when institutional fragmentation and the formation of centre-left coalitions made factionalism more competitive and harmful. The co-opting of the Communists and the 'historic compromise' in 1976–79 shifted the internal balance of power towards left factions. The final section looks at the DC's decline and collapse in 1980–94 and the consequences of factional capture.

7.1   Cooperative factionalism and centre-right coalitions (1945–64)

The original factions in the DC resulted from various political groups coalescing in 1945 around Alcide de Gasperi, former leader of the pre-war Popular Party of Italy (*Partito Popolare Italiano*; PPI). De Gasperi, Prime Minister in 1945–54 in eight consecutive governments, eased Italy's delicate transition from fascism to democracy by creating a broadly based interclass centrist mass party with strong Catholic roots (Leonardi and Wertman, 1989: 21–46). However, there was no articulate vision of society, neither capitalist nor anti-capitalist, and Italians were seen 'not merely as the faithful but as the sum of various cultural groups' (McCarthy, 1997: 34). De Gasperi's 'masterpiece consisted in fusing the logic of the secular parliamentary party as an instrument of government with that of the religious mass party as an electoral machine, without one harming the other' (Allum, 1995: 123). A centrist position enabled the DC to dominate every government in Italy in 1945–93 through Communist delegitimation (Section 1.5).

Initially, cooperative factionalism allowed factions to maintain their identity, personal followings and links with 'flanking organisations' through separate study groups even though Article 91 of DC statutes expressly disallowed factions (*correnti*). However, a major line of cleavage soon emerged between the DC right wing and the centre and centre-left factions around the governing formula – which parties to include in DC-led coalition governments. Left factions wanted to include the Socialists but, in 1958–63, the DC was pivotal in forming centre-right coalitions with the Social Democrats (PSDI), the Republicans (PRI) and the Liberals (PLI) (Chapter 1).

When the DC was created in 1945, it had four observable factions or study groups although the 'effective number of factions' (N_f) was 2.8 (Figure 7.1) since the weighting process discounts factions with small vote shares. However, by 1962 this number doubled. Eight factions competed for delegate support at the DC national congress although (N_f) was only 4.1.

Ideologically, factions were on each side of the dominant centrist faction led by de Gasperi known as the *centristi* or *degasperini*. It held a

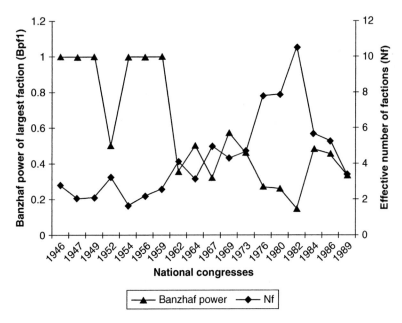

Figure 7.1 Effective number of factions and factional power Italian Christian Democratic Party

majority of seats on the party's national council (NC) and incorporated office-seeking *notables* seeking to form a broad centre party to buttress democracy against both Communists and post-fascists. At the end of Italy's constituent assembly, the former monarchists on the DC right set up a separate parliamentary group of deputies and *notables* called the *Vespa*[1] mainly to fight the government's agrarian reforms.

To the left of de Gasperi's *centristi* were three factions on the DC executive. One was led by Giovanni Gronchi, a former trade unionist, who articulated ideas in the review *Politica Sociale* (Social Policy). They backed de Gasperi's centrist governments despite Gronchi's support for a Socialist *rapprochement* and softening of the government's anti-communist stance. At the start of the Cold War, the American government had linked the distribution of Marshall Aid to fighting Communism. Italy then had the largest communist party in Europe and, for the next quarter century, Communist delegitimation became the linchpin of the DC's coalition strategies. Gronchi also opposed the government's foreign policies on the 1949 Atlantic Pact, the 1950 Korean War and the United Nations' (UN's) refusal to recognise Franco's Spain and Mao Tse Tung's China.

The second-largest leftist faction *Cronache Sociali*, named after the journal *Social Chronicles* and led by Professor Guiseppe Dossetti, comprised progressive intellectuals from Catholic Action including future DC leaders Fanfani and Aldo Moro. Guided by 'Christian Socialist' principles they resented the DC becoming subordinate to the Catholic Church and disliked parliament's manoeuvrings reminiscent of the 1920s' Liberals. As regards the governing formula, they favoured the maintenance of DC-led tripartite governments including the Communists (PCI) and Socialists (PSI) but excluding the small centre parties, leftovers from the pre-Mussolini Liberal regime. They favoured progressive *dirigisme* with cooperatives replacing nationalised industries and worried about the social costs of an unconditional defence of the Italian lira. A third left faction, *Forze Sociali* led by Giulio Pastore, represented trade union interests (*sindacalisti*) in the Confederation of Worker's Unions (CISL).

Conflict over the governing formula and economic policy emerged during the DC's third national congress in Venice in June 1949. Delegates from the Gronchi and Dossetti factions gained 35 per cent of national council seats by forming an alliance for extensive social reforms. However, they weren't a real threat to de Gasperi's faction which had a 65 per cent control of the executive making all other factions 'coalition dummies' (Table 7.1).[2]

A government crisis in April 1951 was the first of many factional splits as Dossetti and de Gasperi clashed over the Social Democrats'[3] withdrawal from the government coalition. This triggered Dossetti's exit and the resignations of the prime minister and minister of finances although de Gasperi retained his Treasury position. Taking advantage of the disruption, Fanfani defected from the Dossetti faction to set up his own faction *Iniziativa Democratica* and take with him key defectors from Dossetti's faction (including Moro, Zaccagnini and Gui) and from the *degasperini* (including Rumor and Taviani).

With the party in disarray, de Gasperi unilaterally changed party rules and grabbed four fifths of executive seats for his faction (Chapter 6). He was an old hand at this game, having already tampered with electoral laws at the 1951/52 municipal elections[4] and nearly succeeding in doing the same for parliamentary elections[5] (Leonardi and Wertman, 1989: 104). Without this manipulation, the DC could have split in two: a conservative Catholic party and a more progressive secular party which would have bipolarised Italy's party system four decades earlier than it did.

In the event, though, the DC's balance of power shifted towards minority factions and away from the dominant centrist faction.

Fanfani's split threatened the *degasperini* dominance and so, backed by only 43 per cent of delegates at the 1952 congress, de Gasperi gave Fanfani a cabinet post in exchange for his delegates' support and stripped all the other factions of any bargaining power (see Table 7.1). Despite its much smaller size, *Vespa* was as pivotal a coalition player as Fanfani's faction (*Iniziativa Democratica*) with three times as many seats.

Table 7.1   Christian Democratic Party of Italy, factional strength and pivotal power, 1946–62

DC National Congress	DC factions	National Council strength* (%)		Normalised Banzhaf power$^\pm$	
1946	*Politica Sociale (Gronchi)*	12		0.00	
$N_f = 2.8$	*Cronache Sociali (Dossetti)*	25		0.00	
	Popolari (De Gasperi)	53		1.00	
	Destra (Jacini, Reggio d'Aci)	10		0.00	
1947	*Politica Sociale/Sindacalisti*	22		0.00	
$N_f = 2.1$	*Cronache Sociali (Dossetti)*	13		0.00	
	Centristi (De Gasperi)	65		1.00	
1949	*Politica Sociale/Sindacalisti*	14		0.00	
$N_f = 2.1$	*Cronache Sociali (Dossetti)*	23		0.00	
	Centristi (De Gasperi)	63		1.00	
1952	*Politica Sociale/Forze Sociali*	16		0.17	0.00
$N_f = 3.2$	*Iniziativa Democratica (Fanfani)*	30		0.17	
	De Gasperi	43	73	0.50	1.00
	Vespa	11		0.17	0.00
1954	*Sindacalisti*	11		0.00	
$N_f = 1.7$	*Iniziativa Democratica*	76		1.00	
	De Gasperi	12		0.00	
	Primavera (Andreotti)	1		0.00	
1956	*Base*	8		0.00	
$N_f = 2.2$	*Forze Sociali/Sindacalisti*	8		0.00	
	Iniziativa Democratica	65		1.00	
	Destra & notabili	13		0.00	
	Primavera	6		0.00	
1959	*Base*	3		0.00	
$N_f = 2.6$	*Rinnovamento*	5		0.00	
	Fanfaniani	30		0.00	
	Dorotei	54		1.00	
	Notabili & Centrismo Popolare	5		0.00	
	Primavera	3		0.00	

1962	Base	3	0.03
$N_i = 4.1$	*Rinnovamento (Pastore, Donat Cattin)*	5	0.05
	Fanfaniani (Nuove Cronache)	27	0.23
	Morotei	17	0.23
	Dorotei	37	0.35
	Notabili & Centrismo Popolare	5	0.05
	Friends of Tambroni	3	0.03
	Primavera	3	0.03

*Figures derived from J.P. Chasseriaud (1965) *Le Parti Démocratique Chrétien en Italie* (Librairie Armand Colin: Paris), Table XXXII, p. 335. He notes that this repartition of NC strength after the national congresses was approximate because memberships to particular tendencies were unofficial and tended to shift.
±NBP Banzhaf power measures computed with the software programme developed by Thomas Bräuninger and Thomas Köenig (Mannheim Centre for European Social Research, University of Mannheim, Germany).

However, ideologically *Vespa* was located well to the right of Fanfani's faction whose economic interventionism it vehemently opposed. The effective number of factions increased from 2.1 to 3.2 because the trade unionist faction (later called *Forze Sociali*) put forward a separate list of candidates at the 1952 congress.

The 1953 general election was a turning point for the DC which lost its parliamentary majority as their popular vote fell to 40.1 per cent from 48.5 per cent. Much of this was due to big losses in the South (Table 7.2) where the pseudo-fascist Social Movement (MSI) welcomed many southern *notables* who defected from the DC in protest against land reform, reducing the DC's patronage control in the *sottogoverno* (subterranean government). Unable to form a new government, de Gasperi was replaced as prime minister by Finance Minister Pella although he remained Political Secretary – party leader. However, de Gasperi died in 1954 when the leadership passed to Fanfani whose faction (*Iniziativa Democratica*) controlled three quarters of party executive seats. Mario Scelba took control of the *degasperini* faction now renamed *Centrismo Popolare*.

By the mid-1950s, conflict over internal democracy and the governing formula resurfaced as a new generation of leaders shifted the centre of gravity to the left. At the 1954 DC congress, the left minority factions rallied behind Gronchi to launch a campaign to change the DC's rules of representation (Section 6.4). Fanfani – a polarising figure unlike de

Table 7.2   Southern vote shares for Christian Democrats and Right Parties, general elections 1948 and 1953 (per cent)

Regions	Right-wing parties*		Christian Democrats	
	1948	1953	1948	1953
Lazio	6.6	19.1	51.7	37.0
Campania	16.4	28.4	50.4	36.1
Puglia	7.9	22.4	48.6	38.4
Basilicata	8.0	17.3	48.4	41.3
Calabria	6.9	16.5	48.8	40.6
Sicilia	12.1	23.3	47.9	36.4
Sardegna	4.4	18.3	51.2	41.7

*Popular Monarchist Party and MSI (Social Movement). Data from Galli G. (1978) *Storia della Democrazia Cristiana*.

Gasperi – did not control the parliamentary party and wanted to delay the rule change but, luckily for him, Gronchi's congress motion was narrowly defeated. As a compromise, Fanfani agreed to lower the dominant faction's executive seat bonus but also raise total seats from 40 to 60 giving his faction 40 seats and the minority bloc (*Primavera, Base* and *Forze Sociali*) 20 seats. However, this stalling tactic didn't prevent dissident attacks from all sides.

On the governing formula, the centre-left factions were united in their desire for a Socialist alliance in opposition to the DC's right-wing and coalition partners. Socialist leader Pietro Nenni declared they were available for an 'opening to the left' and Fanfani favoured such a move against the views of his faction's senior members (Rumor, Russo, Colombo and Taviani). At a DC national council meeting in Vallombrosa in July 1957 a factional split over this issue was avoided on technicalities[6] but it was only a matter of time.

The DC improved its performance at the 1958 general election with 42.4 per cent of the popular vote but this didn't hide a widening fault line over Fanfani's authoritarian leadership and 'opening to the left'. Left-wing Christian Democrats and Socialist 'autonomists' were the main beneficiaries of this electoral victory resulting from a strong economy, internal preference vote shifts and declining support for southern monarchists. Fanfani, back in office after four years, dropped the Liberals (PLI) in favour of Social Democrats (PSDI) but antagonised DC and PSDI members for backing Silvio Milazzo's party eviction in Sicily. Milazzo had formed a coalition in the regional government with the Socialists, Communists and MSI and then set up a splinter Catholic party called the Sicilian Christian Social Union.

Meanwhile, the right-wing *Primavera* faction (backed by the Catholic Church and *Confindustria*) thought Fanfani was moving too quickly towards an opening to the left unlike the left faction *Base* which demanded the immediate inclusion of the PSI. Moderates were suspicious of Fanfani's anti-capitalist tendencies and pre-war dabbling with the fascist regime's corporatism and racism causing the faction to split in 1959. Moderates within Fanfani's faction (such as Moro, Rumor, Colombo, Taviani and Piccoli) recognised the need for centre-left coalition governments but felt the DC wasn't yet ready. Elsewhere, trade unionists within *Forze Sociali* were worried about divisions in the Catholic working class and CISL whose young members (such as Carlo Donat-Cattin and Livio Labor) yearned for a Socialist–Christian Democratic alliance through social and economic reforms.

The party condemned Fanfani's shady tactics such as using DC funds to build his faction's grass-roots support, grabbing three key posts (President of the Council of Ministers, Political Secretary – hence party leader – and Minister of Foreign Affairs), rebuking *Base* members for attending the 1956 communist-sponsored Helsinki Conference and expelling the editor of their journal (*Prospettive*) for criticising Fanfani's leadership (Irving, 1979: 80). Prime minister of four different governments at different times, Fanfani 'seemed to be the master of Italy'(Ottone, 1966: 110).[7] Meanwhile, in parliament, 'snipers' from the *Primavera* and *Centrismo Popolare* factions and southern *notables* were using their secret vote to defeat cabinet-sponsored legislation.

In 1959–62, the DC started fragmenting. The number of competing factions increased from six to eight although the effective number of factions remained relatively low ($N_f = 4.1$ in 1962) as five factions had 5 per cent or less representation. No single faction had absolute control of the party executive and factions' coalition potential was now commensurate with their individual party strength (Table 7.1).

Some Fanfani loyalists set up a separate group around the journal *Nuove Cronache* while others clustered around the young and ambitious Aldo Moro. His new faction *Dorotei*[8] became dominant thanks to the support of *Coldiretti*, the Catholic Association of Peasant Proprietors (Leonardi and Wertman, 1989: 112–3). Moro's 54 per cent delegate support at the 1959 congress translated into two-thirds of executive seats. In June 1963, the fourth Fanfani government fell after a Social

Democrat's cabinet exit forced Fanfani's resignation from his three posts allowing Moro to become party leader.

Moro's leadership coincided with the conclusion of his three-year preparation for centre-left government. In 1962, a majority of congress delegates approved a PSI alliance on an experimental basis. This was backed by left-wing factions *Rinnovamento* and *Base* (who had supported Moro in the leadership race) and by members from the Gronchi and Fanfani factions. However, it was vehemently opposed by the DC right-wing and business particularly *Confindustria* which rallied around Mario Scelba, former leader of the *degasperini*.

Such an eclectic coalition that included regional chieftains like Colombo, Rumor, Taviani and Piccoli with personal followings and ambitions of their own created intense pressures. By 1960 the ideological shadings and strategic conceptions distinguishing factions were difficult to define. DC congresses had become a 'confusing melange of mutually overlapping factions gravitating around coalitions of leading personalities' and many leaders were unpredictable and volatile in their policy stands (Zariski, 1965). In 1962, Moro defected from the *Dorotei* to form his own faction *Morotei* to push the 'opening to the left' agenda. Tambroni also formed a separate faction and disunity worsened after the 1963 general election when DC support dropped to 41.3 per cent against the Communists' 26.3 per cent. Moro had to consolidate his left flank to block an alliance between the Communists and the divided Socialists so he co-opted PSI 'autonomists' by making Nenni deputy prime minister in the new government.[9] In the spirit of Catholic unity, Moro's internal opponents supported his government during the investiture vote which Moro repaid by resigning from the party leadership (unlike Fanfani) in favour of Rumor, a senior faction member.

7.2   Competitive factionalism and centre-left coalitions (1964–76)

In the 1960s and 1970s, DC factional competition intensified as a result of two shifts. A shift in preference from centrist to centre-left governments changed the balance of internal power in favour of the left while an institutional change from reinforced majority to proportional representation created centrifugal forces in the DC, transforming factions into veto players. Minor factions gained bargaining power disproportionate to their size, providing incentives for new factions to emerge and disincentives for careerist politicians to exit. Dissidents and reformists would face an uphill battle to change the *status quo*.

DC dominance was boosted by the Socialists' split in July 1969 which reduced the risk of a third force arising between Catholicism and Communism. DC patronage powers grew on the back of the 1960s economic boom and 1970s decentralisation. Regions became large depositories of economic power, enabling the DC to convert incumbency advantages into partisan resources (Section 1.6). By the mid-1960s, the DC had morphed into a federation of oligarchies and factions (Galli, 1993: 190). 'The years of the centre-left could be called the golden years of state clientelization and party factionalism' (Di Palma, 1977: 130).

In 1959–76, N_f increased by two-thirds, causing a significant drop in the dominant faction's coalition potential. Its pivotality (NBP_{f1}) declined in line with the growth in fragmentation shown by the steady rise in N_f in 1964–80 and the dramatic fall of NBP_{f1} after 1964 (Figure 7.1). By the mid-1980s, this asymmetry diminished due to factional coordination. The slight reduction in N_f from 5 to 4.3 in 1969 reflects increasing support for moderates within the *Dorotei* and Andreotti factions and the entry of a new faction – *Nova Sinistra* – under Florentine Sully.

In 1964, the DC's configuration lined up as follows:

- Two left factions: *Base* and trade unionist *Forze Sociali* (renamed *Rinnovamento* in 1959 and *Forze Nuove* in 1964)
- Two moderate centre-left factions: *Dorotei* and Fanfani's faction (renamed *Nuove Cronache*)
- One centre-right faction *Primavera* (renamed *Centrismo Popolare* and then *Forze Libere* in 1969)

Inevitably, DC biennial witnessed majority failures and gridlock. At the 1964 national congress, delegates were presented with four motion-lists. The majority factional block *Impegno Democratico* containing primarily the fissiparous *Dorotei* and Andreotti's faction lost their absolute majority to the benefit of three minority factions including tiny *Impegno Democratico* (see Table 7.3). Despite their unequal party strength, *Forze Nuove* (20.7 per cent), *Nuove Cronache* (21.3 per cent) and *Centrismo Popolare* (11.5 per cent) were equally pivotal in making or breaking internal coalitions. Hence, when the DC national council met to elect the executive committee, the dominant block *Impegno Democratico* formed a 'minimum winning' coalition with the smallest faction *Centrismo Popolare*, dividing key executive posts between them.

Table 7.3 Christian Democratic Party of Italy, factional strength and pivotal power, 1964–73

DC National Congress	DC factions	Congress support (per cent)	Share of normalised Banzhaf power
1964 $N_f = 3.2$	Left* *Forze Nuove* and *Base*	20.7	0.17
	Nuove Cronache (Fanfani's Group)	21.3	0.17
	Impegno Democratico$^{\pm}$	46.5	0.50
	Centrismo Popolare	11.5	0.17
1967 $N_f = 5$	Left* *Forze Nuove* and *Base*	23.8	0.25
	Nuove Cronache (Fanfani's Group)	17.5	0.18
	Impegno Democratico$^{\pm}$	28.3	0.32
	Morotei (Moro's Group)	11.7	0.11
	Centrismo Popolare (Scelba, Restivo)	7.5	0.04
	Ponte (Taviani's Group)	12.0	0.11
1969 $N_f = 4.3$	Left* *Forze Nuove* and *Base*	18.2	0.11
	Nuova Sinistra (*Sullo*)	2.6	0.02
	Nuove Cronache (Fanfani, Forlani)	15.9	0.11
	Impegno Democratico$^{\pm}$	38.3	0.57
	Morotei (Moro's Group)	12.7	0.11
	Forze Libere (ex *Centrismo Popolare*)	2.9	0.02
	Ponte (Taviani's Group)	9.5	0.06
1973 $N_f = 4.7$	*Forze Nuove* (Donat-Cattin)	10.0	0.08
	Base (De Mita, Granelli)	10.8	0.11
	Nuove Cronache (Fanfani, Forlani)	19.8	0.14
	Iniziativa Popolare (Rumor, Piccoli, Taviani)	34.2	0.46
	Impegno Democratico$^{\pm}$ (Andreotti, Colombo)	16.5	0.14
	Morotei (Moro, Zacagnini)	8.7	0.08

Total Banzhaf Power Index might add up to more than 1.00 because of the rounding-off process.
*For 1964, 1967 and 1969, the left includes *Forze Nuove* and *Base* combined.
$^{\pm}$*Impegno Democratico* includes mainly the *Dorotei* and Andreotti faction at least until 1973 when Piccoli and Rumor split to form their own group.
Source: Based on data gathered by Leonardi and Wertman (1989) *Italian Christian Democracy: The Politics of Dominance*, 114–5.

Left factions were quick to recognise that factional coordination was crucial to extract majorities. At the 1967 national congress, *Forze Nuove* and *Base* joined forces to present party delegates with a common programme and single slate of candidates. Although their combined 973,600 delegate votes delivered 78 of the 120 national council seats, the alliance lacked cohesion. Meanwhile, the centre and centre-right factions presented a joint motion and supporters of Taviani (DC leader in Liguria and head of both Defence and Interior Ministries) tabled a third motion-list. The plurality factional bloc included *Morotei* (Moro's left-leaning followers who defected from the *Dorotei* in 1968), the small Fanfani faction (*Nuove Cronache*) and moderates from *Impegno Democratico* (*Dorotei* and Andreotti's faction) and the right-wing *Centrismo Popolare* (followers of Scelba and Restivo). By 1969, the DC contained seven observable factions (Table 7.3). The centre couldn't hold.

With no dominant faction controlling the agenda, decision-making in the party and political system became complicated. For instance, the 1962 election by parliament of Italy's President of the Republic was so protracted by factional games that it took nine ballots to produce a winner. Moro failed to impose his preferred candidate Antonio Segni on the DC. Segni's choice was a side payment to *Dorotei*'s conservative members for backing Moro's 'opening to the left' experiment. However, Gronchi, Piccioni and Fanfani backed other candidates. The lay parties rallied behind Guiseppe Saragat leader of the PSDI. Only Moro's threat of a government crisis finally convinced Fanfani to release his supporters (Kogan, 1983: 173) allowing Segni to win on the ninth round. Worse, when Segni resigned due to illness in 1964, factional infighting reignited during the DC national congress. This time it took 21 ballots to elect Italy's president. By the end of the tenth round, three DC candidates (Fanfani, Pastore and Leone) were still competing against each other.

Centrifugal forces operated within the DC and inside its centrist faction. *Dorotei* relied for its majority and survival on the personal followings of senior politicians like Moro, Andreotti and Colombo who insisted on maintaining separate ideological and organisational identities (Leonardi and Wertman, 1989: 118). Taviani defected first from the *Dorotei* despite lack of ideological distinction. He had built a fief in Liguria with the backing of large interest groups allowing him to gain an organisational foothold in the DC. Taviani's *Ponte* (bridge) aimed to bring factions closer together although the opposite seemed obvious. It gained 12 per cent delegate support at the 1967 congress.

Moro also established a separate current to protest against the conservatism of new leader Piccoli elected with a simple plurality of votes after the 1968 election when Rumor became prime minister. Piccoli and Rumor were suspicious of Moro's flirtations with Marxism and criticised his *strategia dell' attenzione*: a more attentive, active and reformist style of centre-left government (Irving, 1979: 85). They wanted to control the

Dorotei's left-wing which no longer contained the 'median voter', now located within the left factional bloc (*Base* and *Forze Nuove*) rather than the centre-left (Boucek, 2001).

Incredibly, in 1969, congress delegates were presented with eight separate factional motion-lists preselected by the new regional conventions.[10] Unsurprisingly, no faction controlled a majority of delegate votes although the plurality faction (*Impegno Democratico*) maintained disproportional bargaining power. With 38 per cent support, it was pivotal in 57 per cent of all internal winning coalitions. However, without an absolute majority in the party executive, it failed to block Fanfani's manoeuvrings in this disorderly congress. Having got his lieutenant Forlani endorsed by unanimity as Political Secretary (party leader), Fanfani freed himself for the Italian presidential race which he then lost.

By the early 1970s, third-generation reformists within the DC left started mobilising against entrenched interest-oriented faction leaders by taking command of senior party posts. De Mita became Vice-Secretary and Zaccagnini, a reform-minded leading member of *Morotei*, replaced Scelba as President of the DC national council. Following the 1969 fractious congress and the DC's poor performance at the 1972 general election, De Mita, Forlani and Ciccardini made a pact – the Pact of San Ginesio – to narrow the widening gap between left and right factions and restore the DC's public image.

However, this pact was counterproductive as it splintered the centrist *Dorotei*. At the 1973 national congress, the Rumor–Piccoli alignment joined forces with Taviani to form a separate faction *Iniziativa Popolare* gaining plurality support (34.2 per cent) and enabling Rumor to become prime minister and Fanfani party leader for a second time. Meanwhile, the Colombo–Andreotti alignment also defected to form *Impegno Democratico* gaining 16.5 per cent delegate support. Keen to maintain control of the DC, these centre-right faction leaders wanted a return to centrist multiparty governments (*quadripartite*) rather than a DC–Socialist alliance. However, the previous year, this strategy had driven snipers to threaten government survival by pushing the DC to readmit the Socialists in government.[11]

Desperate to restore value to the DC brand against the backdrop of a bribery scandal involving Fanfani, the leadership engaged in absurd institutional tinkering (Chapter 6). Forlani and Scalfaro even campaigned for the restoration of 'reinforced' majority in the party.[12] However, measures to dampen factional competition were either defeated by countermeasures or blocked by rival factions.

De Mita, leader of *Base*, decided with Moro's support that the time was right to relaunch the idea of a constitutional pact with the Communists backed by a unified national executive except for *Forze Nuove* (Leonardi and Wertman, 1989: 117). However, this show of unity was mere posturing as factions proceeded to parcel out power between them in the usual manner (Galli, 1978: 315).

7.3   Communist co-optation and the 'historic compromise' (1976–79)

In the mid-1970s, Italian politics were so disastrous that, when the government fell in March 1974, none of the key DC leaders (Fanfani, Moro and Andreotti) wanted to replace Rumor as prime minister (Kogan, 1983: 285). Moro eventually agreed to form a government – his fourth. Italy at this time was marred by social unrest, terrorist kidnappings, neo-fascist violence, bribery scandals and economic mismanagement. High oil prices from the 1973 OPEC (Organisation of Petroleum Exporting Countries) oil embargo were compounded by double-digit inflation, alarming public-sector deficits, growing unemployment and political scandals.[13] After a dismal performance at the 1974–75 local elections,[14] DC leader Antonio Bisaglia declared 'the country is tired of us' (quoted in McCarthy, 1997: 104).

Christian Democrats squabbled about resolving the national crisis and reforming their party. Some favoured expanding the economy while others preferred deflationary policies with the International Monetary Fund (IMF) intervention if necessary. Excessive intraparty democracy created gridlock in the party and instability in government – 31 different governments had come and gone in 29 years. Secularisation had eroded the DC's traditional Catholic base. At the 1974 referendum on divorce, 59 per cent voted against repeal and 40.9 per cent in favour. The DC was no longer '*the* party of *all* Catholics' (Pasquino, 1983). Interest factions had become 'empty shells' (Di Palma, 1977: 133). Clientele networks were threatened by declining local public and semi-public resources. After peaking at 1,879,429 subscribed members in 1973, DC membership had dropped to just over one million members in 1977 with the largest decline in the South (Rossi, 1979: 17).

Euro-communism was growing across the continent and DC dominance was threatened by Communist–Socialist government coalitions in Emilia-Romagna, Tuscany and Umbria and in new local administrations in Lombardy, Piedmont, Liguria and Lazio. Milan, Naples, Turin, Genoa, Florence, Venice and eventually Rome had Communist mayors.

Electoral pressures and the DC's loss of pivotal power in government coalitions (Chapter 1) made a Communist *rapprochement* inevitable but at the cost of greater party disunity. In November 1974, Moro headed a DC–PRI government supported by the PSI, PLI and PSDI. This followed covert discussions with Communist leader Enrico Berlinger about a 'historical compromise' and the formation of 'emergency governments' that would include the Communists in the majority if not in cabinet. 'Berlinguer saw this as the meeting of the Communist and Catholic cultures, the twin forces that were shaping modern Italy' (McCarthy, 1997: 106). After the party executive withdrew its confidence from Fanfani, Moro put forward Benigno Zaccagnini (a member of his own faction) as provisional Political Secretary endorsed by unanimity.

Labelled 'honest Zac', Zaccagnini wasn't a 'faction man' but a reformist politician, follower of the *Partito Popolare*'s founding fathers: Don Sturzo and De Gasperi.[15] His reforms were designed to increase elite turnover in the party, parliament and government to encourage generational change. Incumbency rates were particularly high in the government's parastate, local politics and in the DC (Di Palma, 1977). Zaccagnini wanted to open up the party to outside forces and forbid elected politicians from holding party posts. He presented his programme to the party's thirteenth national congress in 1976 but failed to get a mandate due to the party's multi-factional character and narrow victory for the leadership now the responsibility of national council members voting in congress instead of through the wheeling–dealing of tribal chieftains. In the leadership race, Zaccagnini received 885,500 votes (51.6 per cent) against Forlani with 831,500 delegates (48.4 per cent).

Excessive factionalism made inter-factional alliances mandatory for reaching decisions. However, fickle alliances generated majority failures due to three factors: excessive fragmentation and lack of a dominant faction, non-concurrent majorities in separate decisional bodies and cross-cutting factional cleavages.

First, factional splits had produced nine observable factions raising N_f from 4.7 to 7.8 since the last national congress (Table 7.4). Fanfani's faction had split again with some defectors joining Arnaud and Prandini into a new faction while others aligned behind Forlani who condemned Fanfani's newfound enthusiasm for centre-left coalitions. If the power of the Political Secretary was 'conditional' on the strength and stability of the 'dominant faction' (Pridham, 1988: 270), this was bad news. A dominant faction[16] had emerged at all the previous 12 congresses except in 1967. However, by 1976, no faction controlled the agenda as

Table 7.4 Christian Democratic Party of Italy, factional strength and pivotal power, 1976 national congress

Congress (thirteenth)	List	Factions	Support (per cent)	Banzhaf power
1976 $N_f = 7.8$	2	Pro-Zaccagnini factions: *(Rifondazione Del Partito)*		
		Forze Nuove: Donat-Cattin	13	0.13
		Base (De Mita)	10	0.10
		Morotei	10	0.10
		Rumor, Gullotti	9	0.09
		Colombo	7	0.07
	1	Pro-Forlani factions: '*Unita e rinnovamento*' (Daf)		
		Dorotei	23	0.27
		Andreotti	9	0.09
		Fanfani	12	0.12
	3	Dissident fanfaniani: '*Autonomia per il rinnovamento*' (Arnaud, Prandini, Becciu)	6	0.04

Source: Data from Leonardi and Wertman (1989) as before, and Galli (1993) *Mezzo secolo di Dc.*

their coalition potential was now roughly commensurate to their party strength (delegate support).

Consequently, to avoid gridlock at the 1976 DC congress, factions coalesced into three main blocs offering delegates three separate programmes arranged into three separate motion-lists: List 1 sponsored by the pro-Forlani factional block, List 2 sponsored by the pro-Zaccagnini factional block and List 3 supported by the defectors of Fanfani's faction.

Calling for a party re-foundation, Zaccagnini's *rinovatori* (renovators) gained 49 per cent of delegate support (Table 7.4). However, this block itself was fractious, bringing together left faction leaders such as Donat-Cattin, De Mita and Aldo Moro, old party stalwarts such as Rumor, Colombo and Cossiga and reformists such as Bassetti, Gorrieri[17] and Borruso leader of integralist splinter group *Comunione e Liberazione*.

The pro-Forlani bloc headed by chief power-brokers Fanfani and Andreotti called itself '*Unita e rinnovamento*' (unity and renewal) and included former *Dorotei* leaders such as Piccoli and Bisaglia, and southern 'notables' Gava and Gioia (suspected of links with organised crime).

The third group '*Autonomia per il rinnovamento*' (autonomy for renewal) containing mainly dissidents from Fanfani's faction only gained 6 per cent support but could be pivotal in a less complicated configuration.

Second, non-concurrent majorities in two executive bodies made intraparty deadlock even more likely. The 'renovators' had plurality support in the national congress but the 'moderates' had a slim margin in the national executive committee. In the national council, the 'renovators' gained a slim majority of national council seats (62) compared to the 'moderates' (52) and dissidents from Fanfani's faction (6). However, once non-elected council members (including former DC leader Forlani) were added to the lists, the two factional blocs had roughly equal national council representation.

Third, the factional blocks' cross-cutting memberships muddied the picture even more. Factional allegiances differed in the votes for congressional motion and for the leadership now directly elected by secret vote in congress. Leaders of the *Dorotei* breakaway groups (*Iniziativa Popolare* under Rumor and Piccoli and *Impegno Democratico* under Colombo and Andreotti) backed different candidates for the leadership with Rumor and Colombo backing Zaccagnini and Piccoli and Andreotti backing Forlani. Non-coincidental majorities and cross-cutting memberships can act as a check against the tyranny of the majority but risk creating gridlock.

In 1976, Italy's dominant party desperately lacked clear majorities to produce decisive outcomes. To implement his ambitious party renewal and win over factional leaders, Zaccagnini needed more than a bare majority of support.

This fragile balance was a bad omen for Christian Democrats and forced a premature general election in June 1976 when the Socialists withdrew from the government. Despite Zaccagnini's attempt to reach out beyond the Catholic subcultures, the election campaign was divisive. Catholic collateral organisations (CISL and Associazioni Christiane Lavoratori Italiani (ACLI)) were keen to dissociate themselves from the corrupt Christian Democrats and let their members decide which party to support. Half a dozen prominent Catholics ran as independents on Communist lists, prompting the Italian Episcopal Conference's intervention despite the Pope's ambivalence (Di Palma, 1977). Seeking to recapture Catholic votes, a new group *Communione e Liberazione* rooted in the 1960s student movement mobilised 100,000 members attracting much media attention during the campaign.

Zaccagnini's reforms included the deselection of long-term parliamentary incumbents which would bar 36 per cent of DC deputies including long-serving 'notables' from seeking re-election since they had already spent a minimum of four terms or 20 years in office. Chairmen of parliamentary groups were asked to provide local federations with attendance and participation reports on the legislative activities of each senator and deputy. National headquarters tried to claw back power from local federations by reserving the right to nominate candidates in 23 senate seats and one candidate in each district for lower house seats and insisting on having the final say in controversial cases (Wertman, 1987). However, nomination battles prompted revolts in Lombardy, repeals in Emilia-Romagna, mass resignations of provincial electoral committees in Rome and national executive intervention in Turin. In the end, 99 of 401 deputies and senators were dropped from final lists (41 per cent of senators and 17 per cent of deputies).

The 1976 election was seismic. For the first time since 1948, the ruling Christian Democrats lost the 'median' voter to the small PRI and the Communists became the decisive players in government formation. Their popular vote jumped from 27.2 per cent to 34.4 per cent, 4.3 per cent behind the DC, translating into 36 per cent of the seats in the Chamber of Deputies. Although the DC regained their 1972 overall level of support (38.7 per cent), factional leaders such as Moro, Andreotti, Rumor and Donat-Cattin were outperformed by newcomers in district-level preference votes.

Numerically, neither the DC nor the PCI could govern alone. The smaller centre parties had less than eight per cent of the vote. The Socialists, just as pivotal as the PCI in coalition terms despite 27 per cent fewer seats, couldn't be included as they had engineered the fall of the previous government when their leader resigned in favour of Bettino Craxi. Communist leader Berlinger had long claimed that profound changes in Italian society would only come about if serious political polarisation was avoided. He argued strongly in favour of a 'historic compromise' and the formation of a government of 'national solidarity' to combat terrorism (Maor, 1998: 37).

Three-time Prime Minister Andreotti formed a minority (*monocolore*) cabinet by getting all the parties in the 'constitutional arch' to bargain over parliamentary offices. He gave all the DC factions representation in his bloated 69-member cabinet raising the number of under-secretaries from 39 to 47 to ensure full factional representation. He also made sure that Fanfani was re-elected President of the Senate. This government of *non-sfiducia* ('not no-confidence') relied on opposition parties' support or abstention in the investiture vote and then for the passage of legislative bills and emergency economic measures and, ultimately, for government survival. In the party organisation, Zaccagnini became Political Secretary and Moro President of the NC.

The alliance with the Communists was formalised in July 1977 when the DC and PCI reached a programmatic agreement despite 100 out of the 263 DC deputies dissenting on the vote through no votes, abstentions and 'no-shows' (Wertman, 1981). However, government's fragile unity was shaken by student unrest and violence requiring increased police powers. In November 1977 after returning from Moscow, Berlinguer triggered a cabinet crisis and Andreotti's resignation by threatening to withdraw his party's abstention if the Communists remained excluded from cabinet. In the face of strong opposition by the United States Carter administration, Berlinguer retreated and Andreotti was called back and Moro, the *grande tessitore*[18] (master weaver) perceived as the effective DC leader, stepped in to negotiate a compromise (Maor, 1998). Berlinguer saw the DC as made up of two souls – Moro a 'good' DC and Fanfani as the incarnation of a 'bad' DC (McCarthy, 1997: 107).

Many Christian Democrats opposed PCI inclusion in the national government so Moro spent several weeks mediating with DC elites and the rank and file. On his way to parliament for the debate on the new government's investiture vote, Moro was kidnapped by the Red Brigades who savagely killed five of his bodyguards. After 54 days, Moro's body was found in Rome in the trunk of an abandoned car. These Marxist revolutionaries, strongly denounced by the Communists but not by Craxi's Socialists, included offspring of the bourgeoisie, reflecting the *embourgeoisement* of Italian society and reaction to Italy's non-ideological politics and *consociativismo* (Burnett and Mantovani, 1998). *Consociativismo* has been likened to an 'underground railway linking the two great postwar opposing forces, Communism and Christian Democracy ... sharing the spoils of power, consulting on anything that affected the other's interests, approving without question, in parliamentary committee, each other's budgets' (Burnett and Mantovani, 1998).

The DC stuck to its agreed formula for PCI inclusion in the parliamentary majority, enabling the minority government to introduce wage restraints and other deflationary measures to address a ballooning trade deficit from high oil prices and high wage costs in a rigid labour market. The alliance lasted until March 1979 when the PCI returned to opposition after withdrawing support in protest at Italy's membership of the European Monetary System and nominations to state industries. Nevertheless, 'During the historic compromise the PCI rendered Italy two major services. It helped defeat the terrorist onslaught and it left the economy in better shape than it found it' (McCarthy, 1997: 115). However, the electoral price for the PCI was high. At partial local elections in May 1979, their vote dropped from 35.5 per cent in 1976 to 26.4 compared to the DC's increase from 39 to 42.6 per cent.

The historic compromise had created discontent within DC ranks but no outright defection. Conflict had been contained through Communist co-optation creating disincentives to exit for intraparty dissidents and by the presence of factions and other groupings providing channels for anti-Communist voices. They included *Iniziativa Democratica* (a lay-oriented but conservative group led by Massimo De Carolis and Luigi Rossi di Montelera), *Proposta* (a parliamentary group of dissenting MPs who had abstained in the programmatic agreement's vote) and technocrats associated with new Rome Senator Agnelli. In early 1978, dissidents signed a letter to Zaccagnini stating their opposition to Communist entry into the majority. However, they were small and loosely organised so they had limited impact (although *Proposta* got 4 per cent support at the 1980 national congress) and dispersed after the 1979 break-up of the DC–PCI alliance.

Critically, in protest at the DC's factional politics and Italy's political inertia, several reformist politicians including Gerardo Bianco, Vito Scalia, Roberto Mazzotta and Mario Segni quit their factions to start campaigning for institutional reform. In the late 1980s, Segni would galvanise support for a referendum movement on electoral reform. Disenchantment with the DC was reflected in anti-establishment parties gaining representation in the Chamber of Deputies including the Radical Party and Proletarian Democracy in 1976 and the civil rights movement in 1979.

7.4 Degenerative factionalism and DC collapse (1980–94)

Early elections called in 1979 were the third time in a decade that the legislature had failed to complete its full term. The DC's national vote declined marginally from 38.7 to 38.3 per cent but for the first time the Communists lost many votes. Their national share dropped from 34.4 per cent to 30.4 per cent, giving new strength to minor parties. The DC was also losing control locally. At the 1980 regional and local elections, many popular front alliances were reinstated and at the 1982 local elections the DC registered losses in most of Italy. The 1981 referendum on abortion exposed the erosion of the Catholic vote when 68 per cent of voted against repealing abortion laws.

Caretaker governments came and went – the average duration of Italian governments since 1945 was just under nine months. In 1979, Andreotti resigned as prime minister of his fifth cabinet (albeit not his last). As unrest and violence spread to the extreme right,[19] faction leaders squabbled over strategy involving Communist inclusion in local government and centre-left coalitions in the national government with Craxi's pushy and unreliable Socialists.

Meanwhile, more corruption further undermined the government's moral authority. In June 1981, the Masonic Lodge P-2 (Propaganda 2) scandal involving illegal shares dealings by the Vatican's bank Banco Ambrosiano triggered the fall of Forlani's government and the mysterious death of Ambrosiano executive Roberto Calvi.[20] In Sicily, mafia wars led to the murder in 1982 of anti-terrorist General Carlo Alberto Dalla Chiesa and an assassination attempt on magistrate Carlo Palermo in 1985 leading to extensive anti-mafia police operations.

Factional capture in cahoots with the Socialists

The end of the 'historic compromise' provided Socialist leader Craxi an opportunity to force his way into government, grabbing nine ministries in the second Cossiga cabinet in 1980 including Finance, Public Sector and Defence. The Socialists became breakers of government causing four of the five subsequent crises. Back in 1978, parliament had already elected the Socialist Alessandro Pertini as President of the Republic and in 1981 the office of prime minister went to Republican Party leader Giovanni Spadolini, replacing Forlani. In August 1983, Craxi became prime minister and was in office for almost four years at the head of an equally corrupt and factionalised party devoid of any reformist credentials.

Christian Democrats continued to play factional games. At the 1980 congress, 11 DC factions (some extremely small) put six separate candidate motions before delegates (Table 7.5). Donat Cattin, a fervent opponent of Communist collaboration, caused a split in *Forze Nuove* with the remaining group renamed *Nuove Forze*. United behind Zaccagnini, the left factions backed a single list of candidates for NC elections despite congress' divisions on the DC's coalition strategy.

To narrow down the options, delegates were presented with two final documents. The 'pro-solidarity' Zaccagnini bloc (supported by Andreotti's faction) recommended a cautious opening to the PCI (possibly through DC–PCI alliances in local areas) and got 42 per cent of delegate votes. All the other factions (Fanfani, Forlani, Piccoli, Bisaglia, Donat Cattin, Colombo and Rumor) rallied behind Donat Cattin under

Table 7.5 Christian Democratic Party of Italy, factional strength and pivotal power, 1980 and 1982 national congresses

Congress	List	Factions	Support (per cent)	Banzhaf power
1980	2	Zaccagnini factions: *Base*	13	0.13
(fourteenth)		*Nuove Forze*	7	0.07
6 motions		Ex-*Morotei*	6	0.06
$N_f = 8$		Gullotti	3	0.03
	6	*Forze Nuove*: Donat-Cattin	9	0.09
	1	*Dorotei*: Piccoli, Bisaglia	23	0.27
	3	Fanfani	13	0.12
	4	Andreotti	13	0.12
	5	*Proposta*: Prandini, Mazzotta	4	0.04
		Colombo	5	0.05
		Rumor	4	0.04
1982	1	List 1: (56 National Council seats)		
(fifteenth)		Piccoli	13	0.14
3 motions		Andreotti	14	0.15
$N_f = 10.5$		Fanfani	8	0.08
	2	List 2: (56 National Council seats)		
		Bisaglia	10	0.10
		Forze Nuove (Donat Cattin)	9	0.09
		Forlani	9	0.09
		Colombo	4	0.04
		Rumor	2	0.02
	3	List 3: pro-Zaccagnini (48 NC seats)		
		Base	9	0.09
		Nuove Forze	7	0.07
		Ex-*Morotei*	10	0.10
		Gullotti	3	0.03

Source: Data from Leonardi and Wertman (1989) and Galli (1993) as before.

the '*Preambolo*' banner and got 57 per cent support for their document's preamble rejecting further Communist cooperation in favour of closer relations with the Socialists. The DC suspended the party leadership election by secret ballot appointing Piccoli as Political Secretary to replace Zaccagnini and Donat Cattin briefly as Vice-Secretary.[21]

The DC had become captive of its factions. Cycling majorities from excessive factionalism created even more decisional dilemmas and majority failures blocking leadership attempts to rejuvenate the party.

Fragmentation peaked at the 1982 congress where 12 factions competed for delegate support with N_f reaching its highest level at 10.5. The largest but still small faction of Andreotti was pivotal in only 14 per cent of all possible winning intraparty coalitions, providing plenty of scope for Andreotti's factional machinations (Table 7.5). Inter-factional coalitions generated three equally powerful blocs (each holding 33.3 per cent of total normalised Banzhaf power). Hence, to produce winners in DC executive and leadership elections two of the three factional blocs would have to coalesce and present delegates with common motions. Since Italy's National Assembly demanded that the DC reinstate the direct election by secret vote of its Political Secretary, each leadership candidate was required to make a 'declaration of intention' in a new type of congressional motion meant to facilitate debate.

In 1982, three broad coalitions backed three different motion-lists for NC elections (see Table 7.5, bottom section). List 1 (Piccoli, Andreotti and Fanfani) obtained 35 per cent of congress votes and 56 NC seats. List 2 (Bisaglia, *Forze Nuove*, Forlani, Columbo and Rumor) obtained 34 per cent of the vote and 56 seats. List 3 (the Pro-Zaccagnini factions: *Base*, *Nuove Forze*, Ex-*Morotei* and Gullotti) gained 29 per cent of the vote and 48 NC seats. For the leadership election, List 1 factions (Piccoli, Andreotti and Fanfani) joined the pro-Zaccagnini bloc to back Ciriaco De Mita[22] leader of *Base* already endorsed by prominent industrialists thanks to Agnelli's campaign. Having won the leadership with a majority of 55.2 per cent against Forlani with 42.2 per cent, De Mita became the longest-serving Political Secretary briefly combining it with the prime minister's post in 1988–89.

However, the leadership's mandate was weakened by the same factional allegiances that obstructed Zaccagnini in 1976. The Fanfani–Forlani group and the former *Dorotei* had split their votes in the leadership election. By backing De Mita, Fanfani abandoned Forlani, his loyal lieutenant since the birth of the DC. Meanwhile, within the former *Dorotei*, Bisaglia's followers backed Forlani whereas Piccoli's followers supported De Mita. No mechanism could prevent De Mita's 'kingmakers' Andreotti and Fanfani from changing sides later on. De Mita's reforms were likely to alarm their clientele-based factions.

Like Zaccagnini in 1976, De Mita came into office pledging a party renewal agenda. He wanted to transform the DC from a federation of oligarchs into a responsible governing party with renewed Christian values. He hoped to change the logic of party competition by creating an alternative pole to the Communists which could facilitate government alternation while blocking Craxi's command and control tactics. Policies would involve austerity measures to curb government spending and reform of the welfare state. Organisationally, De Mita aimed to replace incumbents with *esterni* (independents) in senatorial seats, put professionals at the head of state industries and DC organisation and rebuild party strength in the major cities (Wertman, 1987). Fanfani and Andreotti feared that De Mita's 'soft' approach towards the Communists would alienate core DC voters. His organisational reforms were sure to jeopardise their own power base.

However, the DC's disastrous 1983 general election dampened De Mita's reform zeal. The party's share of the national vote plummeted to an all-time low of 32.9 per cent compared to the PCI's 29.9 per cent and PSI's 11.5 per cent. There were substantial losses in the largest cities where the average level of DC support dropped to 24.7 per cent (Wertman, 1987). DC losses in the South were blamed on De Mita's attempt to purge the region of its clientele networks (Chubb, 1986: 69–86).The DC was still the largest electoral and government party but no longer an anti-Communists bulwark. Crucially, the 'median' voter was now located to its left inside the small Republican Party (Boucek, 2001). Taking advantage of DC disarray and leadership alternation in multiparty government, Craxi muscled in as prime minister grabbing a disproportionate share of ministerial posts in the five-party coalition government. This gave the Socialists an advantage ratio of 2 and allowed the DC to resume its traditional factional division of government posts.

During the 1980s, anti-Communism lost its saliency and the degree of Socialist involvement in government became the polarising issue for Christian Democrats. De Mita's anti-socialism and party reforms alienated tribal chieftains and long-standing faction leaders such as Forlani, Donat-Cattin, Piccoli and Andreotti who had a stranglehold on the regions, the DC congress and its national executive. They had no qualms about making deals with Craxi.

In the mid-1980s, the structure of intraparty bargaining altered. In 1982–89, N_f dropped by two-thirds (Figure 7.1 and Table 7.5). Although 10 and 9 observable factions competed for DC delegate support at the 1984 and 1986 congress, left factions had gained bargaining leverage by endorsing common motion-lists for NC elections reflected in the downward sloping lines for both N_f and BP_{fl} in Figure 7.1. Their 34 per cent congress support (Area Zaccagnini) in both 1984 and 1986 translated into 48.3 per cent and 45.6 per cent of pivotal power.

However, factional coordination failed to boost De Mita's authority. In 1984, his unified list for NC elections got 88 per cent delegate support although he himself only got 57 per cent support in the leadership re-election against Scotti, leader of a tiny faction who gained 32 per cent. De Mita's 1986 re-election as Political Secretary by three quarters of DC delegates including all faction leaders except for Andreotti and Donat Cattin was a shallow victory – an act of defiance against Craxi rather than a genuine attempt to seek Christian Democratic unity. There was no natural challenger (Galli, 1993: 355).

After three years of political manoeuvrings, Prime Minister Craxi didn't want to be a mere supporting actor on the political stage but to transform the Socialists into a key protagonist like Mitterrand's Socialists in France or the Social Democratic Party (SPD) in Germany. The 1987 election for the Chamber of Deputies widened the gap between the DC and PCI to the benefit of the Socialists whose national vote climbed from 11.5 to 14.3 per cent giving them 21 extra seats. The Greens gained 13 seats.

However, after four years as prime minister, Craxi had completely failed to sort out Italy's budget deficit and ballooning national debt (110 per cent of the gross domestic product (GDP) by 1991) and ignored demands for constitutional reform. Hence, after the 1987 election, De Mita engineered Craxi's exit (Bibes and Besson, 1989). He was briefly replaced by Fanfani in a caretaker government (his sixth) followed by two five-party governments, first under Goria (July 1987–April 1988) and then under De Mita who retained the post of Political Secretary while prime minister in April 1988–August 1989 when Andreotti displaced him from the Prime Minister's Office.

Organisationally, De Mita tried 'to cut power in a different way in the DC, that is, regionally, rather than by faction' (Wertman, 1988). To gain autonomy from faction leaders, he needed to change congress delegate selection from the traditional 'bottom-up' proportional system introduced in 1964 to regional lists. Prior to the 1986 national congress, he tried with limited success to construct a unified list of supporters in as many regions as possible hoping to replace faction leaders and sub-leaders with regional secretaries and lieutenants loyal to him. But, somehow, factional leaders still managed to manipulate the process, ensuring that regional lists and the unified congress list reflected each region's factional strength (Wertman, 1988). Moreover, national faction leaders remained key players in the national executive committee.

De Mita had more success in improving parliamentary turnover. At the 1983 general election, 17 per cent of incumbents weren't renominated. Incumbency rates also declined at the 1985 regional and local elections and Sicily's regional elections in 1986 when candidates accused of corruption were dropped (Wertman, 1988). De Mita also managed to bring in high-profile independents such as *Confindustria* CEO Guido Carli although grass-roots revitalisation was defeated by local apathy (Wertman, 1988). However, by the end of De Mita's third term in office in 1989, party membership remained sluggish and structurally unchanged (Caciagli, 1990).

Nevertheless, by their eighteenth national congress in 1989 Christian Democrats seemed on the rebound. They had regained the Presidency of the Republic in 1985 with Francesco Cossiga's election. They had performed well at the 1985 local elections and recouped some losses at the 1987 general election. Academics even claimed that 'the DC's unparalleled record among parties in Western democracies of remaining in power for the entire post-war period is very likely to be extended well beyond the late 1980s...and would remain the plurality party in Italy for a considerable time' (Leonardi and Wertman, 1989).

However, in the late 1980s, dissidents' exit costs declined, changing the trade-offs between voice and exit. A more competitive electoral market created by new parties offered refuge for disaffected voters and reformist politicians. The regional leagues (Liga Veneta, Lega Lombarda) contested local and European elections making a breakthrough in 1992 with 8.7 per cent support for the Chamber of Deputies and 55 seats (Katz, 2001). In the South, another DC defector Leoluca Orlando set up *La Rete* (the 'network'), an anti-Mafia movement campaigning for 'clean government', and contested the 1991 regional elections in Sicily. Exit costs also declined as the pool of partisan resources to purchase consent had shrunk through privatisations, the dissolution of state agencies such as the Ministries of State Participation, Agriculture and Tourism Office and the disappearance of selective benefits such as the political appointment of savings banks' chairs and other positions in the parastate.

Against this backdrop, Christian Democrats were having an existential crisis. De Mita was assailed from all sides for his lack of credible commitment to reform. He couldn't offer a new political vision after triggering Craxi's departure. During the 1987 electoral campaign, the Catholic right-wing *Communione and Liberazione* had signed a document criticising De Mita's secularism and President Cossiga even held exploratory talks with the Communists. In 1988, old party stalwarts like Forlani, Donat-Cattin, Piccoli and Andreotti had threatened De Mita's government by encouraging followers to join 'snipers' in a secret vote on party policy. The left factions were outraged by his surrender to the factional division of spoils when he became prime minister and his association with the corrupt 'Bay of Naples' leaders Vincenzo Scotti and Antonio Gava. They were 'the most powerful "lords of the card carrying members" of all Christian Democrat leaders' (Caciagli, 1990: 14) and suspected of Mafia connections and accused of bribery in 1993.

At its 1989 congress, the DC was in a critical state. Factional plots against De Mita (Caciagli, 1990) allowed Andreotti 'Alcide De Gasperi's heir' (McCarthy, 1997: 5) to gain the upper hand. The former centrist Dorotei had regrouped under the aegis of *Azione Popolare* after organising a convention in Padua in November 1987. The followers of Colombo, Piccoli, Fanfani and even Forlani (who until then stood above factional politics) joined Gava in an unholy un-programmatic 'Grand Centre' alliance gaining 61 per cent delegate support. Tactical alliances brought N_f down to 3.4. This changed the bargaining structure giving centre factions an equal third of pivotal power and neutralising the left bloc's previous bargaining advantage. 'Andreotti was the real winner at the Congress' (Caciagli, 1990: 9). With half the support of the other two blocs, his faction was as pivotal a coalition player (with an equal 33.3 of NBP, third column bottom section of Table 7.6) leaving Fanfani and *Forza Nuova* as 'dummies' although they gained representation on the national executive committee when the NC met a month after the congress.

Andreotti used this victory to retaliate against De Mita by backing Forlani as leader. De Mita had previously refused to back Andreotti's bid for President of the Republic and twice as Prime Minister. With no guaranteed support from the left, De Mita appealed to the plurality bloc *Azione Popolare* that included the shifty 'Bay of Naples' Gava and Scotti who ended up backing Forlani after making a pact with Andreotti. In a last stand before delegates, De Mita defended his record as if to secure his place in history. Forlani argued that, in view of De Mita's failed 'bipolar hypothesis', the DC needed to improve relations with the Socialists but kept left factions sweet by recognising their help in securing De Mita's government achievements. After DC national council elections, Forlani and De Mita merely swapped seats – Forlani became DC Political Secretary with the support of 61 per cent of councillors and De Mita became President of the DC national council.

The 1989 DC congress was the apotheosis of factional degeneration. The delegate assembly was reduced to a competition for applause. Andreotti won with 26 minutes although Mino Martinazzoli (nominated by a regional congress in Lombardy) got a standing ovation and 19-minute applause indicating the Left's bitterness towards the victors (Caciagli, 1990). Afterwards, Andreotti sidelined the left by giving covert support to a power-sharing deal between Forlani and Craxi made in a trailer during the Socialists' congress in May. They agreed that the Prime Minister's Office would go to Andreotti and divided the spoils between them including appointments to public bodies,

Table 7.6 Christian Democratic Party of Italy, factional strength and pivotal power national congresses (1984, 1986 and 1989)

Congress	List	Factions	Support (per cent)	Banzhaf power
1984	2	Left (Area Zaccagnini)	34.0	0.48
(sixteenth)	2	*Dorotei* of Piccoli	12.8	0.10
2 motions	2	*Dorotei* of Bisaglia	7.8	0.07
$N_f = 5.7$	2	Colombo	3.3	0.02
	2	Forlani	9.9	0.08
	2	Fanfani	6.7	0.06
	2	Andreotti	12.2	0.09
	1	*Forze Nuove* (Donat-Cattin)	8.0	0.07
	1	Scotti	2.3	0.02
		Others	2.7	0.02
1986		Left (Area Zaccagnini)	34.0	0.46
(seventeenth)		*Centristi: Dorotei* of Piccoli	15.0	0.12
3 motions		*Dorotei* of Bisaglia	6.0	0.05
$N_l = 5.3$		Scotti	2.0	0.02
		Colombo	3.0	0.03
		Forlani	11.0	0.10
		Fanfani	5	0.04
		Andreotti	16.3	0.13
		Forze Nuove: Donat-Cattin	7.5	0.05
1989		Left (Area *del Confronto*): Zaccagnini, De Mita, Martinazzoli, Bodrato, Goria	35.0	0.33
(eighteenth)		*Azione Popolare* (anti-De Mita *Grand Centre* Headed by Gava and Including *Dorotei*, Forlani, Scotti, Colombo)	37.0	0.33
$N_l = 3.4$		Andreotti	17.8	0.33
		Fanfani	3.2	0.00
		Forze Nuove (Donat-Cattin)	7.0	0.00

Sources: Data from Leonardi and Wertman (1989) as before pp. 114–5; Galli (1993) *Mezzo Secolo di DC*; Galli (1978) *Storia Della Demcrazia Cristiana*; Magri (Volumes 1 & 2); Giovagnoli (1996) *Il Partito Italiano: La Democrazia Cristiana dal 1942 al 1994.*

control of major media outlets and alliances with large industrial groups. Ostracised from Andreotti's sixth government (followed by a seventh), DC left factions had their representatives ejected from major public bodies such as Radiotelevisione Italiana (RAI) and the Institute for Industrial Reconstruction (IRI). Outraged, De Mita refused the foreign affairs portfolio and threatened to resign as NC President.

Changing voice and exit trade-offs in a competitive market

By the turn of the new decade, the electoral market had become more competitive due to the entry of new parties and the drop in market value of the DC which changed DC dissenters' trade-offs between voice and exit.

According to Hirschman, the mixture of exit and voice of customers' responses depends on the sensitivity of demand to declines in an organisation's performance or quality (Hirschman, 1970). Using Hirschman's representation of voice and exit (Hirschman, 1970: 129–31; see also Dunleavy, 1991: 16–18), Figures 7.2 and 7.3 show the quality/performance of Christian Democracy along the vertical axis with distance from the origin increasing the poorer the brand's quality. The horizontal axis shows the DC's levels of support by voters and intraparty actors. Figure 7.2 represents in the abstract DC dominance until the mid-1970s when party support was relatively stable and resistant to quality deterioration. Since exit was virtually ruled out in Italy's blocked democracy – mainly due to Communist co-optation in sub-national and national government culminating with the 'historic compromise' – discontent with the ruling parties was articulated through civil unrest and declining voter turnout and reflected by unstable governments and early elections. A plurality of voters 'held their noses' and continued to vote for the corrupt Christian Democrats.

The shaded ABCD rectangle on the top graphs of both Figures 7.2 and 7.3 represents voice. According to Hirschman, its size depends on the number of non-exiting customers and on the degree of quality deterioration from A to B. For any drop in quality, exit and voice somehow combine to exert influence on the organisation's management. The sensitivity of demand to drops in quality is what determines the relative influence of voice or exit on management. Before the 1980s, demand was relatively inelastic and DC support quite unresponsive to changes in quality. *Consociativismo* and factionalism lowered the risk of exit blocking management efforts (notably under Zaccagnini and De Mita) to respond to electoral changes thus allowing further deterioration of the DC brand.

In contrast, Figure 7.3 illustrates the post-Craxi era in the late 1980s– early 1990s when the political market had become more competitive with the entry of new parties (flatter demand), making DC support much more sensitive to quality deterioration. As the quality of the DC brand deteriorates from A to B, the extent of support declines from Q_0

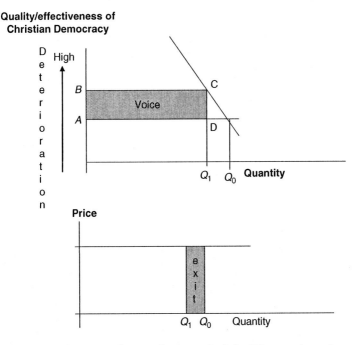

Figure 7.2   The relative significance of voice and exit for DC supporters – demand inelastic for political consent with respect to quality

to Q_1. The degree to which this change affects the DC is shown in the bottom graph where support is displayed against the price (cost to DC supporters). The shaded rectangle in the bottom graph of each figure shows the amount of exit (levels of defection) the extent of which, according to Hirschman, may wipe out the organisation's profits.

Hence, in Figure 7.3 because a rather small decline in quality triggers a large loss of party support, exit responses are more important than voice protests compared to in Figure 7.2 where the relative size of the exit and voice rectangles indicate that exit is less influential than voice because demand is quite inelastic. As the rate of substitution is low (few viable alternatives to the DC), voters continued to support the DC and intraparty dissidents remained inside the organisation voicing their discontent to elicit reforms by the party leadership. A flatter demand curve on Figure 7.3 indicates that the extent of support supplied to the DC declines more rapidly (from Q_0 to Q_1) in response to quality deterioration (from A to B) triggering more exit reactions. This time, the size of the exit rectangle is disproportionately larger than the

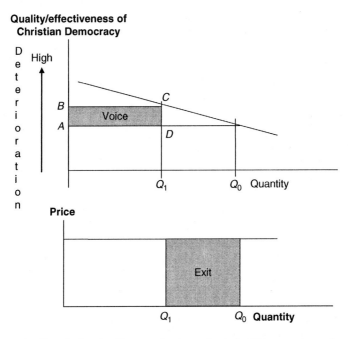

Figure 7.3   The relative significance of voice and exit for DC supporters – demand elastic with respect to quality
Sources: Adapted from Hirschman (1970) 129–31 and Dunleavy (1991) 18.

voice rectangle since more actors are prepared to defect. Voters support and join other parties and reformist politicians leave the DC to mobilise reform movements and set up new organisations.

Up until the late 1980s, the costs of voice had been relatively low on the DC. Citizens' unrest had been managed through Communist co-optation. The financing of the exchange vote managed by factions had been shifted unto society through high budget deficits and enormous public debt. Given that elite responses to electoral changes were internally blocked, effectiveness continued to deteriorate. Had the demand for political consent remained relatively inelastic, the scale of voice reactions might have continued to surpass exit responses for much longer.

However, in the early 1990s, a confluence of endogenous and exogenous factors tipped the balance of forces against the DC, reducing dissidents' exit costs. DC defection gathered pace. Several left-wing ministers withdrew from Andreotti's seventh cabinet (April 1991–June

1992). De Mita left in 1992 to head the bicameral committee on constitutional reform (COREL) although he was soon forced to resign due to his brother's implication in the Irpinia earthquake relief funds scandal. President of the Republic Cossiga accused the DC of blocking institutional reform and of fiscal irresponsibility stating that 'if an individual managed his personal financial affairs the way the government is running those of the nation, he would soon end up in prison' (Follini, 1993; Galli, 1993: 391). Cossiga tore up his party membership card on television and finally resigned from the DC in January 1992. In a letter published in the DC official newspaper *Il Popolo*, he declared he was no longer part of the DC because 'I no longer understand it, and because I have been not very quietly expelled from it'. Other defectors included Sardinian politician Mario Segni, son of former President Antonio Segni and Massimo Severo Gianini (former minister for administrative reform). Segni co-founded the 1988 Movement for Electoral Reform (MRE) that eliminated the corruption-induced multi-preference vote in an overwhelming 'yes' vote in a 1991 referendum (Chapter 6). After De Mita's forced resignation, he took over as President of COREL before finally quitting the DC in 1993 to concentrate on institutional reforms.

In 1991, the DC's major rival – the PCI – split following the demise of Communism at the end of the Cold War. Achille Occhetto, PCI leader since 1988, took two-thirds of party members with him and formed the Democratic Party of the Left (PDS). The rest formed the Communist Refoundation Party (PRC) under Armando Cossutta. Meanwhile, the resources to purchase consent had shrunk. The government's struggle to meet Maastricht Treaty criteria for the European Monetary Union first bounced the lira out of the Exchange Rate Mechanism in 1992 before subsequently re-entering, with the net result that money for political disbursement grew increasingly scarce. Meanwhile, the Mafia ended their complicity with the DC and declared war on the state. Four weeks before the March 1992 general election, it assassinated Salvo Lima, ex-mayor of Palermo and head of Andreotti's faction in Sicily.

As a consequence, electoral reform through referenda became the catalyst for political change as in Japan. Social change through referenda had already occurred on divorce in 1974 and abortion in 1981 and between 1990 and 1999, some 30 other referenda were held. However, the DC leadership lacked the vision for constitutional reform that could end the politics of bargained pluralism and bring about single-party government and alternation in power. Some members suggested that majority single-party governments could be engineered under the new single preference voting system by giving a 12 per cent premium to the party winning a plurality of seats in the Chamber of Deputies (Follini, 1993). This option was rejected by Segni who instead proposed a bill to adopt single-member plurality (SMP) rule for both houses of parliament. The party merely agreed to set up 'a constituent legislature' after the upcoming general election.

That general election in April 1992 came against the backdrop of massive corruption scandals and broke the traditional pattern of governing alliances by making exit more attractive to DC supporters and dissidents. For the first time since 1948, the four-party coalition failed to get a majority of the votes cast. The DC's national vote fell below 30 per cent (Table 7.7, Election 1) as anti-establishment parties made major breakthroughs. The Northern League (Lega Lombarda) won 55 seats with 8.7 per cent of the national vote and 40 per cent of the northern vote while *La Rete* got 12 seats with just under 2 per cent of the national vote. The DC still had nearly twice the support and number of seats (206) as its nearest rival, the newly formed PDS (107) but its main electoral plank – the 'red threat' – would no longer rally support. The Socialists who only lost two seats would, nevertheless, see their vote progressively diminished by the 1994 dealigning election. Giuliano Amato formed a four-party government.

Two weeks later, Cossiga resigned as President of the Republic two months ahead of schedule. However, this may have been a pre-emptive strike against the Gladio investigation of alleged American Central Intelligence Agency (CIA)-sponsored Secret Services suspected of right-wing plots (McCarthy, 1997: 135). A month later, proclaiming that he 'was not a man for all seasons', Forlani resigned as DC leader to run for president, leaving the leaderless Christian Democrats to squabble endlessly over their choice of presidential candidate and forcing Forlani to withdraw after the seventh round. However, two days before the sixteenth and final round of voting, anti-Mafia judge Giovanni Falcone was assassinated. As the national mood turned sour, parliamentarians settled on compromise candidate Oscar Luigi Scalfaro as President but, in July, Falcone's celebrated partner Paolo Borsellino was also assassinated and the Italian state looked on the brink of self-destruction.

After much argument about Forlani's leadership replacement, left-wing Senator Mino Martinazzoli was chosen by acclamation with the backing of moderates within *Movimento Popolare* who had abandoned Andreotti (under investigation and left out of Amato's cabinet).

Table 7.7 Italian national, regional, provincial and communal elections, April 1992–November 1993

Party	April 1992	2	3	4	5	6	7	8
RC	5.6	6.7	6.3	5.5	5.1	8.0	1.3	5.3
PDS	16.1	17.8	11.4	9.9	7.7	19.8	4.6	12.1
PSI	13.6	7.2	9.9	4.7	2.5	0.6	0.6	1.2
PSDI	2.7	0.8	4.9	1.6	0.8	0.4	0.9	0.9
PRI	4.4	1.5	3.6	1.7	0.7	0.2	0.5	0.2
DC	29.7	14.0	24.3	22.3	18.7	12.1	14.3	10.7
PLI	2.8	1.2	2.9	1.3	0.2			0.1
Greens	2.8	2.4	1.6	5.4	1	3.4	3.4	3.5
Rete	1.9	2.7	4	1.8	2	1.8	5.2	3.1
Pannella	1.2		0.8					
LN	8.7		13.7	26.7	11.7	30.5	9.6	6.2
MSI	5.4	3.2	7.2	8.3	4	5.3	7.4	12
Others	5.1	8.6	9.4	10.8	45.6	17.9	52.2	43.8

(1) General Election, 5 and 6 April 1992.
(2) Provincial elections: Mantua, 28 September 1992.
(3) Communal elections: 55 communes, 14 December 1992.
(4) Regional elections: Friuli Venezia Giulia, 6 June 1993.
(5) Partial communal elections (1,192 communes) 6 June 1993.
(6) Provincial elections (Gorizia, Ravenna, Viterbo, Mantova, Pavia, Trieste, Varese, Genova, La Spezia) 6 June 1993.
(7) Regional elections: Trentino, Alto Adige, 21 November 1993.
(8) Partial communal elections (424 communes), 21 November 1993.
Source: Adapted from Bull and Rhodes (1997), pp. 1–13; and Newell and Bull (1997), pp. 81–109.

Education Minister Rosa Russo Jervolino was endorsed as President of the DC national council – the first woman appointed to this post. Appealing to DC unity, Martinazzoli declared it important to break with the past to save the party's moral credibility (Follini, 1993: 94). Borrowing Andreotti's famous phrase, he said the DC was no longer 'condemned to govern' but needed to redefine its Catholic identity in the tradition of Sturzo and De Gasperi and to make Europe rather than Atlanticism the core of its foreign policy (Giovagnoli, 1996: 268).

Amid this political disarray, Milan magistrates launched investigations into political bribery that had been going on for years in what became known as *tangentopoli* (Bribesville) leading to the collapse of Italy's post-war political establishment in less than two years. The day after the February presidential election, the opening act of Operation Clean Hands (*mani pulite*) saw the arrest by judge Antonio Di Pietro in PSI stronghold of Socialist Mario Chiesa, Director of a major Milan charity, for taking kickbacks on maintenance contracts. His revelations prompted more massive investigation of party financing. For a long time, politicians had extracted ever bigger bribes (*tangenti*) from business whose pay-offs were now shrinking fast. Once Di Pietro made his first move in February, business promptly abandoned their partners in crime (Bufacchi, 1996) and corrupt politicians were now 'portrayed as awful Genghis Khans bent on destroying the economy whereas for years they were depicted as Robin Hoods' (Sidoti, 1993).

The ruling parties' plunder of state resources motivated actors to denunciate their political accomplices in patronage-rich state agencies including ENEL (National Electrical Energy Agency), ENI (National Hydrocarbons Agency), ANAS (National Road Agency), the Ministry of Public Works, the trade unions (CISL and Italian Labour Union (UIL)) and the private sector (Fiat and Olivetti). After nearly three years of investigation, the magistrates reported that 2,150 individuals were under investigation with the government nearly collapsing as ministers, parliamentarians, mid-level party officials and businessmen felt vulnerable to the intimidating tactics of Di Pietro's team.

The crisis led voters to abandon the DC in droves (Table 7.7). In April 1993, Amato's cabinet was replaced by Carlo Azeglio Ciampi's 'government of technocrats'. Martinazzoli defended the government's economic reforms and due process of law in bringing to justice DC politicians implicated in the *Tangentopoli* scandals. However, he was too slow in withdrawing support from Craxi in his fight against the 'clean hands' judges.[23] In June, he had to carry the blame for the

DC's disastrous performance in regional and communal elections when the Northern League gained 32 per cent of the northern vote for directly elected mayors and the DC's northern vote plummeted from 22.7 per cent to 10.4 per cent winning only 11 out of 143 mayorships (Table 7.7, election 4). In the autumn, TV magnate Silvio Berlusconi started mobilising cross-country support by setting up around 4,000 *Forza Italia* clubs.

Meanwhile, Segni had launched the Democratic Alliance in October 1992 hoping to provide a broadly based alternative to the existing parties. Describing the DC as 'a rotten apple with a healthy core', he wanted to build on existing cross-party support and media backing for constitutional reform. His cross-party supporters made a pact to unite in the next legislature and vote for a single-district voting system. At the April 1991 referendum, 82.7 per cent of voters who turned out (75 per cent of the electorate) voted 'yes' to change the electoral law to a 'mixed' system (Chapter 1). The Bicameral Committee for Institutional Reform started deliberating once parliament reconvened in the autumn.

Believing the DC could remain the pivotal player in forming government coalitions with the PDS or as a minority government with Northern League's support, Martinazzoli and his parliamentary supporters argued for a mixed-member system rather than a French-style majority two-ballot system. However, the South viewed his muddled proposals as a takeover by the party's left wing in the North where Rosy Bindi, new regional secretary in the Veneto, launched '*Cosa Bianca*' – a party renewal project supported by the Catholic left. Martinazzoli made tactical errors missing his chance of an alliance with Segni in a local election in March 1993.

In the summer of 1993, the collapse of the DC was imminent. Martinazzoli was told the DC faced dissolution at its next party meeting. A constituent assembly which excluded the elite under investigation such as Andreotti, Gava, Goria, Scotti and many others proposed renaming the DC *Partito Popolare Italiano* (PPI), which the party membership approved by referendum. However, a membership drive to undercut the power of party bosses who still controlled pockets of memberships revealed mass defection by the rank and file and grass roots. DC membership was cut in half when only 600,000 members renewed their membership (Wertman, 1995: 141). Although newcomers were brought into the political office including Romano Prodi, long-standing party leaders, former political secretaries and veterans from party headquarters couldn't be kicked off the party national executive council.

Hoping to provide clarity, Prime Minister Ciampi announced a general election would be held in April 1994. Forced to reassess their alliance strategies under the new mixed-member electoral system approved by parliament in August 1993, Martinazzoli stated the PPI wouldn't cooperate with the Northern League at the election as relations with Segni had improved. In September, Segni agreed to officially abandon the Democratic Alliance and refused any agreement with the PDS.

However, the centre had disappeared from Italian politics. The flight of voters from the DC and from all mainstream parties was unstoppable. At the November regional and communal elections, half the vote went to the non-mainstream parties (see elections 7 and 8, Table 7.7) and a major party dealignment was under way. Former alliances collapsed when Berlusconi decided to enter the race under the *Forza Italia* banner forcing major protagonists including Segni and Umberto Bossi (head of the Northern League) to review their positions and in some cases start discussions with Berlusconi.

When the DC finally held its long-postponed national congress in January 1994 to officially approve its new name, the party splintered into four groupings: the PPI under Martinazzoli, Segni's *Patto per l'Italia* (Pact for Italy), *Centro Cristiano Democratico* (CCD) and *Cristiano Sociali* (Social Christians). Some right-wing elites joined the neo-fascist National Alliance and others *La Rete* or *Forza Italia*. The Christian Democrats had come full circle through disaggregation. For the parliamentary elections under the new mixed-member electoral system, alliances were made between CCD and Berlusconi and the PPI and Segni. In the event, the former Christian Democrats saw their number of deputies reduced from 207 to 46 – only three of which were elected in the single-member constituencies.

While Berlusconi's entry was the immediate factor breaking the dominance of Christian Democracy in 1994, the judicial investigations, more competitive party system and institutional reforms significantly contributed to changing the trade-offs between voice and exit for disaffected voters and reformist politicians. Under a more bipolar logic of party competition and three separate Berlusconi reigns, the former Christian Democrats continued to divide, split and coalesce into different coalition blocks.

Conclusion

After nearly 50 years of continuous rule, the Christian Democrats were brought down by the centrifugal pull of their factions. Despite frequent corruption scandals and economic mismanagement, the DC kept power thanks to its centrist position in a system of 'polarised pluralism' (Sartori, 1976) sustained through a corrupt form of consociationalism. The DC maintained party competition in equilibrium by conniving with the opposition to blend a *de jure* anti-communist electoral strategy with *de facto* communist co-optation, first in the 'parastate' and then in the national government culminating with the 1970s 'historical compromise' (see also Chapter 1).

A similar equilibrium of competing forces operated inside the dominant party. Once the party adopted a proportional system of internal representation in 1964, most of the factions aggregated by De Gasperi after the Second World War lost their ideological character especially in the party's centre and centre-right. Adding to the effects of the multi-preference voting system (Chapter 6), these internal rules incentivised power-brokers to split from existing factions and set up new ones to maximise their organisational power producing fractionalisation and centrifugal forces inside the DC.

By transforming factions into veto players, these perverse incentives created a leadership vacuum and collective action dilemmas adding to the diffusion of power created by intricate local networks run by self-serving regional oligarchs. Inter-factional alliances, mandatory to extract majorities, produced tactical opportunities for power-brokers in the national organisation to use their minority factions' blackmail potential to block much-needed party reforms.

Obsessed with finding the centre of gravity inside the DC, power-brokers became unpredictable coalition players, producing cycling majorities and gridlock while hampering party renewal by left-leaning leaders Zaccagnini in the 1970s and De Mita in the 1980s. These organisational dilemmas coincided with shrinking partisan resources to sustain clientelism during the 1980s' power-sharing with Craxi's Socialists creating further pressures for careerist politicians relying on a personal vote.

It took major changes in the electoral market to break this paralysing equilibrium and expose the costs of Christian Democratic rule. The 1991 Communist Party's split broke the mould of party competition but the gradual deterioration in the quality of the DC brand had already created opportunities for anti-establishment parties in the late 1980s and early 1990s to shift the trade-offs between voice and exit for DC supporters and reformist politicians in the face of a value-destroying brand.

The realigning election of 1992 opened a window of opportunity for a small group of left-leaning Milan magistrates to finally expose the extent of political corruption produced by five decades of Christian Democratic rule. When the centre of gravity of Italian politics disappeared, the DC imploded.

8
Case 4 – The Liberal Democratic Party of Japan (1955–2009): End of Hegemony

In 2009, Japan's Liberal Democratic Party (LDP) was tossed out by voters after almost half a century of continuous rule and two decades of economic stagnation. Yet, in the previous election in 2005, the party had won a landslide victory under maverick leader Koizumi who had enraged his party by putting forward fresh candidates to unseat LDP rebels opposed to his postal reform.

The breakdown in LDP hegemony and unity began in 1993 when factional dissent first sent the party into opposition for ten months. Ichirō Ozawa, a key LDP faction leader and party secretary-general but never a prime minister, had defected with other LDP rebels and joined the opposition to defeat the government in a no-confidence vote. This provided a brief opportunity for a new multiparty government to introduce electoral reform. However, by 1996 the LDP was back in office after coaxing two parties to defect from the government coalition.

Party splits were a constant threat for the LDP in 38 years of continuous rule. Recurring corruption scandals incentivised reformist politicians to mobilise against the leadership but, until 1993, collective action by dissident forces failed. Threats of defection lacked credibility because the costs of exit for LDP careerists were too high. They figured that joining the opposition wouldn't deprive the LDP of its majority as opposition forces were too weak, fragmented or ideologically distant to form an alternative government. The LDP further locked in Diet members by making their access to partisan resources and career benefits conditional upon seniority and factional loyalty (Chapter 6).

Explanations for the persistence of LDP factions initially focused on cultural factors (Thayer, 1969; Nakane, 1967; Ishida, 1971; Ike, 1978; Baerwald, 1986; Pempel, 1986, 1990; Curtis, 1988). More recently, institutional explanations notably the effects of the SNTV voting system, bicameralism and party rules and procedures on LDP career incentives have been cited (Kohno, 1992, 1997; Cox and Rosenbluth, 1993, 1995; Ramseyer and Rosenbluth, 1997; Cox, Rosenbluth, and Thies, 1999). More recently, a study of the LDP guided by historical institutionalism claims that electoral system explanations are overdeterministic since factions predated the birth of the LDP[1] and the adoption of SNTV and have survived (albeit weakened) after the 1994 electoral reform (Krauss and Pekkanen, 2011).

This chapter examines the factional politics of the LDP by focusing on two processes: (a) how systemic and party-specific institutions regulated inter-factional competition and transformed the consensus-oriented leadership factions of the 1960s into a moderate number of exclusive, power-oriented and fully institutionalised factions in the 1980s and (b) how a changing electoral market and better coordinated opposition incentivised reform-minded dissidents to defect in 1993, triggering the first LDP defeat.

The chapter's five sections further examine how LDP politicians adapted to political norms and party procedures under the '55 system' and the post-1994 institutional regime. Internal conflict mostly arose during the LDP presidential elections that were marked by intense competition and interfactional bargaining. These high-stake games between 'mainstream' and 'non-mainstream' factional blocs determined the prime minister's selection and distribution of office perks which generated power struggles inside the LDP.

However, recurring corruption scandals entangled political reform with LDP factional politics, motivating reformists to instigate collective action from within and without. This finally succeeded in 1993 by boosting the ranks of the opposition defectors and causing LDP dominance to break down. The messy and drawn-out political realignment produced by the 1994 electoral reform didn't prevent the LDP from returning to power and ruling for another 15 years but it did transform political incentives and enabled government alternation.

8.1 Party realignment and cooperative factionalism (1955–74)

LDP factionalism is rooted in the 1955 merger of Liberals and Democrats which brought together eight different leadership groups with clearly separate memberships. After the Liberals lost their parliamentary majority in 1953, prolonged bargaining between all post-war Japanese parties was suddenly transformed by the reunification of left- and right-wing

Socialists, prompting the Liberals and Democrats to merge (Kohno, 1992, 1997; Cox and Rosenbluth, 1995). The 'catch-all' nature of the LDP reflects the amalgamation of components from the Liberal and Democratic parties and pre-war bureaucrats such as Hayato Ikeda and Eisaku Satō who became LDP faction leaders and Japanese prime ministers in 1960–72.

The LDP merger had reduced the number of parties, skewing party competition in favour of the Liberal Democrats and creating disincentives to exit for careerist politicians until the 1980s (Chapter 1). In 1958, the LDP took 58 per cent of the vote and 61.5 per cent of the seats (298 out of 467 seats) in the House of Representatives, with the Socialists holding the remaining seats (167) but two. The popular expectation was that 'the Japanese party system was moving into an Anglo-American type of two-party system' (Kohno, 1997: 117). However, by the end of the 1960s, two new parties emerged – the Clean Government Party at the centre and the Japan Communist Party on the left. Political realignment remained a live issue thereafter but the LDP managed to stay in office, thanks to disproportional elections and ineffective interparty coordination on its left (Chapter 1).

As in the party system change in Italy in the early 1990s, there was no viable alternative that could defeat the dominant Japanese party where the factional structure was no impediment to hegemony. On the contrary, factions (*habatsu*) helped blur the lines between the pre-merger cleavages[2] and also regulated the competition for the party leadership. Complemented by the *köenkai*, factions provided ready-made structures for electoral coordination under SNTV and LDP elite circulation (Chapter 6).

Committed to free enterprise, the development of an export-led economy and an independent foreign policy in close association with the United States following their 1960 joint security treaty,[3] LDP governments delivered average growth rates of 10 per cent until the 1973 recession triggered by the oil crisis. This was helped by political clientelism (through the *Koenkaï* and factions), weak partisanship and failures of the Socialists and Communists to form alliances (Christensen, 2000), enabling the LDP to retain a majority of voters and parliamentarians despite occasional electoral setbacks in local assemblies and prefectural governorships. However, the party's electoral predominance ended in 1967 when the LDP's vote share in the lower house first dropped below the 50 per cent mark.

During its first 15 years in power, the LDP represented a coalition of seven or eight observable factions. However, as shown in Figure 8.1, the

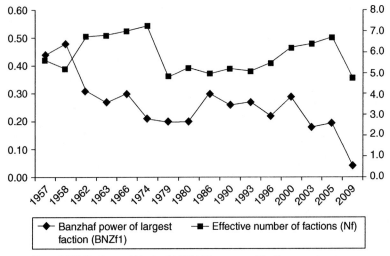

From 2003 the largest block of LDP MPs were not faction members

Figure 8.1 Effective number of factions and factional power Japanese Liberal Democratic Party

effective number of factions (N_f) ranged from 5.2 (1958) to 7 (1966) because of the weighting effect of N_f on small factions. The integration of the original eight groups from the Liberal and Democratic party camps was facilitated by deciding to alternate the leadership between the founding political leaders: Democratic Hatoyama and Liberal Ogata. Ogata's sudden death in 1956 prolonged Hatoyama's term in office and helped cement party unity as the remaining leaders formed cross-party alliances at the 1956 party convention to elect the first LDP president (Kohno, 1992: 89).

The selection of the LDP president (hence, the Japanese prime minister) by election blurred the old party allegiances but also changed the factions' character and the LDP's factional politics. The factional coalitions emerging from the 1956 leadership race were 'not institutionalised along previous party lines', as Ishibashi, a former Democrat, was backed by Ishii, a former Liberal, who himself became leader in 1957, backed by a mixed coalition of former Liberals and Democrats (Krauss and Pekkanen, 2011: 110). After 1956, factions became less consensual and more exclusive and opportunistic in response to electoral and career incentives pushing Diet members to affiliate with factions (Chapter 6).

Party presidential elections transformed the face of LDP factionalism – from cooperative to competitive – and altered the internal balance of power (Boucek, 2009). Intraparty competition intensified in line with the decrease in size and power of the dominant faction. As Figure 8.1 shows, during the 1960s, the increase in the effective number of LDP factions (N_f) was accompanied by a decrease in the pivotal power of the largest faction (BNZ_{f1}). In 1958, the Kishi-Sato faction represented 35 per cent of the LDP caucus in the House of Representatives (the Diet's lower house), giving the faction almost half (48 per cent) the pivotal power. However, by the end of Satō's three terms as prime minister in 1972, the dominant faction's pivotality in making and breaking coalitions had fallen due to its declining size and a more equally distributed balance of internal power. This change reflected a shift in the prime minister's power of appointment in relation to faction leaders.

By the 1970s, LDP factions had become the decisive players in the competition for the party presidency (hence, prime minister) and the allocation of career benefits and partisan resources. In 1974, the LDP had nine factions that were represented in the Diet. Each of the five medium-sized factions (Fukuda, Ikeda, Kono, Ono and Miki) held between 15 per cent and 20 per cent of Diet seats, and only 4 per cent of the party's MPs weren't members of factions. Two or three mainstream factions would form a minimum winning coalition to produce a prime minister[4] and divide most cabinet and party executive posts, leaving lower-tier positions to non-mainstream factions (Leiserson, 1968). Minority factions with memberships of 5 per cent or less[5] acted as potential junior partners in future presidential coalitions.

> It is in the race for the prime ministership that factional competition is at its rawest and most intense.
>
> (Ramseyer and Rosenbluth, 1997: 63)

This new factional balance took away bargaining power from the dominant faction and destabilised the leadership. In 1958, the dominant faction had been pivotal in 44 per cent of all possible interfactional coalitions but by 1974 its power had dropped to 18 per cent, making all the major LDP factions equally pivotal in coalition terms. LDP presidential elections generated intense rivalries between the majority 'mainstream' factional block (that elected the president) and the minority 'non-mainstream' factional bloc. Given that the LDP leader was elected for only two years (renewable once), these interfactional games created a lot of churning. In 1960–72, the LDP presidency had changed only twice but over the next decade the party changed its leader five times.

LDP factional coalitions became unstable for three main reasons. First, no faction controlled a majority (or near majority) of Diet seats, so a 'mainstream' alliance was needed to win presidential races and create majority cabinets. However, the alliance was always fragile because factions in the 'non-mainstream' block were constantly seeking to redress their under-representation by trying to join the 'mainstream' bloc. Second, minimum winning factional alliances had to be cohesive to survive, so there was a constant risk that factional splits would cause coalition break-ups. Such power struggles occurred in 1961 when the Kishi faction split and in 1964 when members of the Ikeda faction defected to back Satō instead of Ichiro Kōno. Third, the fear of an LDP split was heightened by the opposition's readiness to cooperate with LDP defectors, as in the 1971 election of the House of Councillors Speaker and several times afterwards (Christensen, 2000: 143–6). However, disagreements in the opposition combined with the LDP's career structure (based on seniority and rigid factional memberships) deterred factions from breaking away (Chapter 6).

8.2   Rebellion and the struggle for party control (1975–80)

As argued in Chapter 2 the dual conditions of a competitive electoral market and a factionalised ruling party give intraparty dissidents strategic opportunities to change the *status quo* by mobilising and threatening defection.

By the mid-1970s, the dominant party in Japan (as in Italy) faced increased competition from the left and disunity within its own ranks. The party failed to get a parliamentary majority in three of the four general elections in 1976–83. The ranks of disaffected voters were growing as a result of corruption in the ruling party and the economic decline triggered by the oil shocks.[6] LDP governments had to introduce austerity in a country totally dependent on foreign oil, putting pressure on the incumbent's resource advantages.

In 1974, the LDP barely retained its majority in the House of Councillors, causing the resignation of some ministers, including Prime Minister Tanaka who was charged with personal and financial irregularities. This scandal involving America's Lockheed Aircraft Corporation determined the outcome of the 1974 LDP presidential race. Miki Takeo won after a protracted battle involving defection plots and counterplots by faction leaders Fukuda, Nakasone and Miki in separate talks with opposition parties about forming a new party. Although Miki's defection threat was the most credible, given his historical ties with the opposition and his genuine desire for political reform, Miki didn't get a second mandate in 1976 (Christensen, 2000: 143–6). He had made too many internal enemies by relentlessly investigating the Lockheed scandal.

The Lockheed scandal was decisive in mobilising dissidents and rebels behind a 'clean government' campaign to restore public confidence. In 1976, Tanaka was arrested on charges of foreign exchange abuses and of taking $1.6 million in bribes from Lockheed. Wishing to distance themselves from their corrupt party, six young LDP mavericks led by Yōhei Kōno (son of Ichiro Kōno) formed a breakaway group in the Diet called the New Liberal Club (NLC). An opinion poll put their support at 13 per cent but in the 1976 election the group only took 4.2 per cent of the popular vote and 17 Diet seats. In that election, voters denied the Liberal Democrats a majority. LDP support had been declining since 1958 when the party had won 58 per cent of the popular vote. Support dropped to just below 42 per cent in 1976, forcing the LDP to rely on minor parties and on conservative independent MPs to pass legislation.

However, the NLC faction lacked bargaining power due to its lack of cohesion and pivotal power. NLC leaders were divided on strategy: Kōno wanted alliances with the centrist parties (the Komeito and the Social Democratic League) but the group's more conservative General Secretary Nishioka Takeo merely wanted to reform conservative politics, hoping to recruit around 50 Diet members with a view to rejoining the LDP as reformers (Curtis, 1988: 33). Crucially, the dissidents weren't pivotal to government survival because the LDP could usually count on independent MPs for a working legislative majority (Baerwald, 1986).

Nevertheless, the rebels were decisive in two-party leadership contests. In 1978, in the first presidential election under membership primaries (Chapter 6), two mainstream factions (Ohira and Tanaka) and three non-mainstream factions (Fukuda, Nakasone and Miki) fielded candidates. Thanks to the pivotal support of the NLC, Ohira won the run-off against the incumbent Fukuda. So, to buy the peace in an increasingly factionalised party (in 1974 N_f was 7.3 but there were nine observable LDP factions in the Diet) and to signal his desire for party renewal, Ohira didn't reappoint previous cabinet members. Only five of the new members had any cabinet experience and Ohira gave 'non-mainstream' factions a disproportionate share of appointments as chairs and vice-chairs (Cox and Rosenbluth, 1993: 588).

The rebels' support was also critical in the 1979 leadership race after the 1979 snap election called by Ohira to capitalise on LDP victories in local and regional elections. However, Ohira miscalculated. While the LDP's overall vote share increased to 44.6 per cent, the party failed to get an absolute majority of seats (48.5 per cent), leaving independent MPs to make up the nine-seat shortfall as before. However, the NLC's four Diet seats were pivotal to Ohira's survival in the decisive first ballot of the leadership race. To ward off Fukuda, Ohira promised the NLC a cabinet seat in exchange for their support but he reneged on his promise. Adding insult to injury, Kōno was forced to resign as leader of the dissident group because, by backing Ohira in the presidential election, he had become associated with the corrupt Tanaka faction and thus renounced his group's reformist principles.

Fukuda went on the offensive and prolonged the rebellion by joining the opposition in defeating the LDP government in a no-confidence motion (the first since 1953) tabled by the Socialist Party. Fukuda led 69 MPs from the 'non-mainstream' factional bloc (Fukuda, Miki and Nakagawa) who abstained from voting on the motion and so defeated his own government by 56 votes. However, instead of resigning in favour of an intraparty opponent, Ohira called an unprecedented 'double election' for both houses of the Diet to be held in June. Ohira's sudden death from a heart condition ten days before the election transformed that election's context.

At Ohira's wake, the acting president, Chief Cabinet Secretary Masoyoshi Ito, appealed to party members to close ranks. For the second time, the fortuitous death of its leader had unified the ruling LDP. Thanks to the 'sympathy' vote, a high voter turnout, an improving economy (triggered by the Tokyo land boom) and opposition disunity, the LDP scored a resounding victory, its greatest in terms of the popular vote since 1967, and won comfortable majorities in both houses. Despite the number of cooperation agreements, the 1980 double election was 'one of the worst opposition defeats in the entire post-war period' and destroyed 'the facade of opposition unity' (Christensen, 2000: 69, 103). After protracted negotiations, the LDP decided to choose a new leader by consensus. Suzuki was nominated after Nakasone and Komoto withdrew from the race. At the end of his two-year term, Suzuki didn't seek re-election.

The rebels' defection had been a 'win–win' situation. The breakaway group provided the LDP with a safety valve by preventing opposition parties from cashing in on the antagonism of Japanese voters towards their corrupt political leaders. The rebels who rejoined the LDP in 1986 gained a voice without closing the door on their party. NLC leader Kōno actually enhanced his career prospects.[7] Fukuda could bury the hatchet with honour after ending the 'Kaku-Fuku War' and taking a stand against Tanaka, his old party rival. Tanaka's power and reputation were in tatters after receiving a four-year prison sentence in the Lockheed trial that had concluded a seven-year investigation.

8.3   Faction institutionalisation and Nakasone's leadership (1982–89)

> The combined effect for LDP members of Japan's economic recovery and the chilling of US–Soviet relations was both to increase the value of the LDP's majority status and to decrease the size of any escape hatch.
>
> (Cox and Rosenbluth, 1995: 366)

In 1982, Yasuhiro Nakasone became the prime minister after a decisive victory in the party presidential election, thanks to the support of the Tanaka and Ohira factions. This race was held under the amended rule for presidential primaries requiring a minimum of four contestants, each supported by at least 50 Diet members (Chapter 6). Since only two other candidates[8] had sufficient endorsements, Fukuda decided it was time to put in his retaliation against Tanaka and Ohira for having forced him in 1978 to withdraw from the run-off presidential race. Fukuda 'lent' enough members from his faction to enable a fourth candidate (Nakagawa Ichiro) to enter the race (Curtis, 1988: 102–3).

Tanaka's conviction cast a shadow over Nakasone's victory and dominated the 1983 general election campaign. After withdrawing from the LDP, Tanaka insisted on remaining in the Diet as an independent MP and filed an appeal against his conviction. This posed a dilemma for Nakasone who owed his leadership victory to the 108-member-strong Tanaka faction. Nakasone's faction only had 49 members spread over both the Diet houses. Opposition forces wanted to break the LDP majority by tabling a resolution demanding Tanaka's Diet resignation. After nudging the party executive, Nakasone succeeded in extracting Tanaka's resignation by transforming the context of this internal row. Rather than appeal to reason, Nakasone appealed to emotions – he shed some tears and recast Tanaka's resignation as a non-party affair.[9]

Nakasone's conciliatory style of leadership and international image made him popular with voters and foreigners if not with the LDP elite. Nakasone had a history of plotting against his party. In the 1966 LDP presidential race, Nakasone had worked against incumbent Prime Minister Satō Eisaku who retaliated by relegating Nakasone to the anti-mainstream group after his re-election. This rejection apparently prompted Nakasone to scheme with a Democratic Socialist official to form a new centrist coalition to bring down the LDP government and force an election (Christensen, 2000: 137–45). As already mentioned,

Nakasone had already plotted in 1974 with members of the Fukuda and Miki factions to leave the LDP and form a new party

Despite losing its parliamentary majority in the 1983 general election for the third time in seven years, the LDP renewed its leader's mandate. In 1984, Nakasone became the first LDP president in 20 years to be re-elected. Unlike his grey and anonymous predecessors, Nakasone had a high-profile international image. He was close to US President Ronald Reagan and other G7 leaders. Thanks to the growing power of television, he developed an international image that drew attention to Japan's phenomenal economic performance.[10]

In government, Nakasone shifted power back to the prime minister's office and away from the factions and the PARC. He adopted a top-down policymaking approach, using his office's advisory councils (*shingikai*) to open up foreign trade and introduce administrative reforms (Krauss and Pekkanen, 2011).

In 1986, Nakasone timed a lower house election to coincide with elections for the upper house and delivered LDP majorities in both chambers. With a 58.1 per cent majority, the LDP seized control of the House of Representatives, and Nakasone declared that all factions were now 'mainstream' factions. He formed an inclusive cabinet which represented a careful balancing of factional strength. Nakasone invited the eight rebels in the NLC to rejoin the LDP in exchange for a cabinet post.[11] This was a magnanimous gesture since the rebels' pivotal power had been cancelled out by the LDP's 1986 landslide victory. They were officially reunited in 1987 when Kōno unilaterally dissolved the group even though the NLC secretary wanted it to remain independent. Nakasone was so popular that his second term was extended by one year in 1986.

By the late 1980s, LDP factions had become fully institutionalised, balanced and controlling. In 1986, only 5 per cent of the LDP members in the House of Representatives and only two of the 144 members of the House of Councillors weren't members of a faction. The LDP was evenly factionalised into four major factions (Tanaka, Miyazawa, Nakasone and Abe), each controlling between 18 per cent and 28 per cent of the LDP's lower house seats, and one smaller faction (Komoto). This internal balance of power translated into almost proportional shares of pivotal power for each faction. Simultaneously, the factions' electoral successes became closely tied to the size of their war chests, compared to the previous 20 years when the mainstream factions had consistently outperformed their non-mainstream rivals (Cox and Rosenbluth, 1993). Nevertheless, the post-Lockheed reforms of party finance changed Diet members' motivations. Instead of relying on the variable fundraising successes of faction bosses, MPs started raising their own money (Cox and Rosenbluth, 1993).

When Nakasone left office in November 1987, intraparty relations seemed peaceful – internal conflict had been skilfully managed and party fractiousness concealed, if not eliminated. Electoral performance had been improved, if not stabilised.

However, a new political storm was brewing. Tanaka's faction controlled nearly a third of pivotal power and had claims on the party leadership but was tarnished by scandal. Tanaka's chief fundraiser, Noboru Takeshita, was the natural heir to Nakasone but he broke the peace by taking over the faction's leadership without Tanaka's blessing.

In the summer of 1988, the stock-for-favours Recruit scandal, involving Takeshita and most of the political establishment. broke out. Forty-three senior politicians, apart from Takeshita, were accused of having taken bribes from real estate firm Recruit/Cosmos in 1984–86 through cut-price unlisted shares. Those implicated included Nakasone, Finance Minister Miyazawa Kiichi, the chairmen of the *Komei* (the 'Clean Government' party), members of the Democratic Socialist Party, businessmen and party officials. Accused of making profits in excess of $1 million, Takeshita was forced to resign in 1989 although he kept a strong grip on the LDP. His short-lived successor, Sōsuke Uno from the small Komoto faction, was an obscure politician untainted by the Recruit scandal who also had to resign after 53 days in office over a sex scandal. He was replaced by Toshiki Kaifu.

8.4 The struggle for electoral reform and loss of power (1990–94)

By the early 1990s, LDP dominance was under threat from centrifugal forces in the party system and inside the dominant party. Despite the LDP's 1990 general election victory, opposition forces were closing in. A more competitive electoral market made exit threats by intraparty dissidents more credible to the leadership and to opposition forces looking for defectors. Christensen (2000: 184) explains that 'the path to power for the opposition in the 1970s and 1980s and for the Democratic Party in the 1990s was to encourage defection and recombine existing units to create a new majority party'.

Frustrated young LDP reformers began to mobilise and campaign for electoral reform. As with Italy's DC, the LDP's internal politics and power struggles became embroiled with the issue of electoral reform.

The end of the Cold War depolarised party politics. The lines between left and right had been blurred, making anti-communism obsolete in party competition (as in Italy) and increasing pressure on the LDP from the centre–left. The growth in young, educated and urban voters benefited the non-communist left at the expense of the LDP whose core vote remained concentrated in over-represented rural districts (Chapter 1). Furthermore, the economic downturn significantly reduced the LDP's capacity to service its clients and factions. Big trade deficits with the United States and deflating asset prices from the collapse of the Tokyo land market and banks' bad debts shrank government resources. On top of this, recurring corruption scandals made organisations and business cautious about giving money to politicians.[12] All these created fertile conditions for opposition parties and LDP reformists to coalesce and campaign for electoral reform.

Voter disaffection with the LDP was underscored by the 1989 Tokyo municipal election when the party barely got a third of the vote. Three weeks later, the LDP lost its overall majority in the House of Councillors for the first time since 1955, a defeat that would complicate government. Without a two-thirds majority in the lower house, the LDP would have to rely on other parties to get its bills passed.[13] Luckily, thanks to Kaifu's 'clean government' agenda, the LDP preserved its majority in the House of Representatives election in 1990 despite a 5 per cent drop in popular support. However, the Socialists were the real winners. Their 25 per cent support translated into 136 seats (an increase of 51 seats) – half the LDP's seat share – partly due to their successful nominations of female candidates (the 'Madonna strategy') which appealed to young urban floating voters.

In Japan (as in Italy) in the early 1990s, there was intense public pressure to cleanse the country of money politics. Reform of the voting system came to symbolise a commitment to real political change endorsed by all the political parties, the media and academics. However, the idea wasn't new. Twice in the past in 1956 and 1973, the LDP leadership had put electoral reform on its agenda, hoping to win more seats under a system of single-seat districts, only to drop the issue when election results improved[14] (Sakamoto, 1999). LDP incumbents who relied on a strong personal vote didn't want electoral rules that would reduce the influence and fundraising abilities of their personal networks (*köenkai*).

However, blocks of reformists campaigning for political change had emerged regularly, usually in the face of political scandals. Back in 1962, Prime Minister Ikeda had set up an electoral reform committee to end corrupt campaign practices and this project was revived in the 1970s. In the summer of 1988, a dozen junior reform-minded LDP Diet members set up the 'Utopia Political Study Group' under freshman Takemura Masayoshi in protest at the LDP's sluggish response to the Recruit scandal. They recommended the adoption of a 'mixed' single-member district ballot system and state-subsidised political parties (Otake, 1996; Sakamoto, 1999).

After the Recruit stock-for-favours scandal, the LDP leadership recognised that political reform was necessary for survival but it disagreed about its extent and timing.[15] In response to voters who expected individual politicians to make their reform commitments explicit, Prime Minister Takeshita set up the LDP Political Reform Committee, proposing a consumption tax and electoral reform. However, factional intrigue stalled the project which ended up on Kaifu's desk when he took office after two quick prime ministerial resignations over scandals. Keen to signal his reform commitment, Kaifu appointed to cabinet only scandal-free politicians (reappointing only the foreign and finance ministers). In1990, he received the report of the reform commission set up under Takeshita, which recommended the adoption of a new 'mixed' system for the lower house that involved 300 single-member districts and 200 proportional representation (PR) seats in 11 regional PR districts.

Without a power base inside the LDP, though, Kaifu failed to get enough support for the reform bill. He had the backing of Ozawa (the 'shadow shogun' and former LDP General Secretary) but Kaifu was opposed by anti-reformers who used the bill to block his re-election as the LDP president, forcing him to stand down at the end of his term in October 1991. Miyazawa,[16] won the presidential three-way race by 285 votes against Watanabe (120) and Mitsuzuka (87), thanks to the backing of the dominant Takeshita faction (formerly Tanaka) to which Ozawa belonged and the small Komoto faction.

Already beset by scandals and resignations including that of Finance Minister Ryutaro Hashimoto,[17] the LDP was shaken to its roots in January 1992 by another financial scandal, much larger than Lockheed or Recruit. Sagawa Kyubin, Japan's second-largest trucking company, had been caught paying some ¥70 billion ($56 million) to more than 200 politicians.[18] Shin Kanemaru (the leader of the dominant Takeshita faction) had to resign from the LDP vice-presidency and from the Diet for violating political finance regulations and income tax law. He was arrested in March 1993 on charges of tax evasion when massive amounts of securities, gold and cash were discovered in his home.

Kanemaru's conviction had important repercussions for the dominant Takeshita faction, the LDP's internal politics and government survival. It motivated Ozawa to mobilise dissent, triggering a chain of events leading to the LDP's downfall and party realignment. Morihiro Hosokawa, a former prefectural governor, was the first to defect from the LDP after the 1992 Kyubin scandal. He formed the Japan New Party (JNP) by using the media to expand his support base and mobilise the masses.

Prime Minister Miyazawa was publicly committed to electoral reform but faced resistance from his own ranks. Disliking Kaifu's plan, he decided to put off reform until after the upper house elections scheduled for 1995, hoping that if the LDP regained its majority, it could stay in power by adopting a single-member plurality (SMP) voting system. However, opponents saw this as a clear attempt to reassert LDP dominance and intensified their campaign for reform in the hope of attracting LDP defectors.

Electoral reform became mixed up with the LDP's factional politics and leadership rivalries. Young reformists in vulnerable seats were frustrated by Miyazawa's slow response and by their exclusion from party policy decisions (Otake, 1996: 276). Many junior and some senior LDP politicians eventually sided with Ozawa. They wanted a 'mixed' system of single-member districts and PR seats rather than pure SMP (Ozawa's initial preference). SMP would threaten the re-election of members with only one or two terms in office. Long-term incumbents backed by *köenkai* with vested interests were more likely to hang on to single seats. Statistics show that Diet members who eventually defected with Ozawa were more junior than those who stayed loyal to Obuchi (Kohno, 1997: 147). However, many junior reformers weren't careerist politicians but *'nisei'* – MPs with nothing to lose by campaigning for reform. Many had abandoned business careers to reluctantly take over their fathers' Diet seats (with *köenkai* backing) or had inherited large fortunes (Otake, 1996: 276).

Ozawa, a powerful force within the LDP, was a key mobiliser of internal dissent.[19] A seasoned politician with extensive cabinet experience, he was considered '*de facto* prime minister in the Kaifu's cabinet often called a "double government" for that reason' (Otake, 1996: 16). With neo-conservative ideas and a desire to transform Japan, Ozawa was also a backroom operator whose motivations were sometimes ambiguous, explaining why his role in splitting the LDP has had different interpretations. After the resignation of his mentor Kanemaru, Ozawa had failed to gain the Takeshita faction's leadership against Obuchi, so he appealed to the faction's reformists to follow him rather than Obuchi. He was supported by young Diet members whose election he had facilitated as LDP Secretary General, but Obuchi garnered more support from upper house members (Otake, 1996: 287).

The breakaway faction was headed by Tsutomu Hata, the agriculture minister and a consensus leader committed to electoral reform but unconnected to factional intrigue unlike Ozawa. Reform presented a dilemma for members of the Takeshita faction since reform was a response to their former leader's misbehaviour. But Ozawa got around this problem by portraying anti-reform LDP members as 'reactionaries'. This turned public opinion in his favour and convinced 43 members of the Takeshita faction to form a breakaway study group under Hata, leaving 62 faction members aligned behind Obuchi (Kohno, 1997).

Senior LDP hardliners viewed this faction split as Ozawa's attempt to trigger a party realignment (Sakamoto, 1999). Supporters saw Ozawa's endorsement of SMP as the key to policy-driven two-party competition that would enable government alternation to replace a regime dominated by LDP factions. Others saw the Ozawa/Hata split as a strategic move in an internal power struggle – the consequence of an abortive bid for power in a changing institutional environment (Cox and Rosenbluth, 1995; Kohno, 1997).[20] Things were changing by the day but it appears that Ozawa may have calculated that if a motion of 'no confidence' against the government was tabled and lost, Miyazawa wouldn't call an election but would instead be replaced by someone who could reinstate the LDP, probably Masaharu Gotoda from the Tanaka faction. Miyazawa did indeed try to co-opt dissidents and prolong the Diet session by offering Hata the foreign affairs portfolio. However, by then, Ozawa was already in talks with the opposition.

On 18 June 1993, the balance of internal forces tipped in favour of exit. Thirty-eight members of the Hata–Ozawa faction joined the opposition in a 'no-confidence' vote won by 255 votes against 220 votes and 18 LDP abstentions. Miyazawa dissolved the lower house and called a snap election for 18 July. Having triggered the government's downfall, LDP dissenters defected as two separate groups which joined Hosokawa's JNP in a reformist alliance. Pro-reform defectors, mainly junior members of the Mitsuzuka faction, formed the New Party Harbinger (Sakigake). Two days later, Ozawa's followers formed the Renewal Party (Shinseito) although their policies weren't different from those of the Sakigake.

These defections triggered an electoral earthquake – the defeat of the LDP after 38 years of continuous rule. In the 1993 general election, the

LDP got less than 37 per cent of the popular vote. This presented an opportunity for the new multiparty coalition government to introduce electoral reform under Hosokawa (Chapter 6).

8.5   Return to power and the Koizumi phenomenon

Internal defection was the catalyst for the breakdown in LDP dominance in 1993, even though the party's electoral vulnerability had become apparent since the 1970s. The tipping point came in 1993 when the anti-LDP alliance reached critical mass, enabling opposition forces boosted by LDP defectors to deprive the LDP of its House of Representatives majority. Thereafter, electoral reform introduced by the multiparty coalition government in 1994 transformed the dynamics of party competition in Japan, leading to the formation of various coalition governments with and without the LDP.

The eight-party coalition that dislodged the LDP from office in 1993 was fragile and fissiparous. Once their unifying cause – the electoral reform bill – had been passed, the alliance's internal tensions became apparent. The Sakigake and Socialists disliked Ozawa's coalition manoeuvrings, abrasive personality and autocratic leadership. For example, he concocted a proposal for a 'national welfare tax' with the Ministry of Finance bureaucrats without consulting his coalition partners (Otake, 1996). In the summer of 1994, these parties withdrew from the government, leaving Hata (Hosokawa's replacement) in charge of a minority government for 63 days.

In 1994, the LDP pounced on a split in the coalition government to outbid Ozawa. They invited the Sakigake and Socialists to form a three-party coalition with them under a Socialist prime minister (Muyarama). The first LDP government not led by a Liberal Democratic prime minister stayed in office until the 1996 general election. This election for the 500-seat House of Representatives, held under the new mixed-member electoral system, was inconclusive. The LDP's share of the vote was poor and the party was 12 seats short of a bare majority. The LDP leader Hashimoto formed a minority government with legislative support from the diminished Socialist Party and Sakigake but kept them out of cabinet. Many of their members had already joined the newly formed Democratic Party (DPJ).

For the next few years, the LDP was vulnerable and unstable. After a setback in the 1998 House of Councillors election, LDP Prime Minister Hashimoto was replaced by Obuchi who died in 2000 after a stroke. Obuchi was followed by the gaffe-prone and unpopular Yoshirō Mori, the head of the former Fukuda faction, who was pressured to step down before the 2001 upper house election. By dumping two leaders in quick succession, the LDP recognised the growing importance of the leader's television image (Krauss and Pekkanen, 2011: 238).

Meanwhile, in the opposition, LDP defectors regrouped under the banner of the New Frontier Party (NFP) led by Ozawa, whose divisive leadership failed to hold the merged party together.[21] In December 1997, the NFP disbanded, leaving Ozawa in charge of a small breakaway group, the Liberal Party. The DPJ was now the second-largest party behind the LDP. It boosted its ranks even more by absorbing Ozawa's Liberal Party. In the 2003 general election, the DPJ surpassed the LDP in votes and seats in the PR tier (37.4 versus 35 per cent) and increased its district seats from 27.6 to 36.7 per cent (from 80 to 105 seats).

In sum, the second half of the 1990s was marked by instability which had resulted from a realignment of Japanese politics which had been triggered by LDP defections, electoral reform and the repositioning of left parties towards the centre. Electoral reform had increased volatility, made different types of coalitions possible and significantly altered the LDP's internal politics. When Koizumi became the LDP leader and prime minister in 2001, Japan had suffered a decade of political turmoil. Nine prime ministers and more than ten new parties had come and gone since 1989, when Akihito had become Emperor of Japan after the death of his father Hirohito.

The new mixed-member voting system has eroded the electoral value of factional membership. Paradoxically, in 1996–2009, the number of observable factions in the LDP more than doubled, from five to eleven. However, their relative size shrank significantly, as indicated by the effective number of factions (N_f). This weighted measure of factionalisation is 5.5 in 1996 and 4.8 in 2009. As Figure 8.1 shows, the proportion of LDP members in the lower house of the Diet who weren't affiliated with a faction dropped to 9 per cent in 2000 from 15 per cent in 1996, when the consequences of electoral reform had been still unclear. In 2003 and 2005, this proportion climbed to 25 per cent under Koizumi, who vowed to destroy the factions. By 2009 when the LDP was thrown out of office after losing nearly two-thirds of its seats, only 40 per cent of its 119 MPs were members of factions and only one of the 11 LDP factions had more than 7 per cent representation in the party caucus. While faction membership was still valuable in the allocation of posts, faction leaders ceased to control their members' votes and the bargaining deals that used to determine candidate selection (Krauss and Pekkanen, 2011: 141).

Koizumi burst on the political scene in 2001 after winning a landslide victory in the LDP presidential election with about 90 per cent of the prefectural votes in the local primaries. Having been defeated twice in the past, Koizumi wasn't expected to win. Considered a maverick and outsider, he took advantage of the 1998 changes in the LDP presidential selection rules which increased the voting power of the prefectural votes and gave Diet members prior knowledge of the prefectural results before casting their votes (Chapter 6). Instead of relying on faction leaders for cues, parliamentarians could now be swayed by a candidate's prefectural results, making it difficult for the party elite to reject the rank-and-file preferences.

Determined to destroy the factions, Koizumi bypassed the party network and appealed directly to the rank and file (Kabashima and Steel, 2007). He communicated directly with the public through the media with the slogan: 'Change the LDP! Change Japan!' He provided the media with a human interest angle: 'the outsider battling with entrenched interests' (Park, 2001) and took advantage of coverage in television news to develop a public image (Kabashima and Steel, 2007). Referring to himself as the 'Lionheart', Koizumi campaigned for structural reforms, notably the privatisation of the postal service, which he claimed was necessary even if it meant short-term economic costs. Combining populism and neo-liberalism, Koizumi used slogans like 'pain for gain' and 'reforms sparing no sacred cows', which the media reported verbatim (Park, 2001: 106).

Koizumi's bold message and 'outsider' status resonated with the rank and file and the electorate, especially young urban voters. A study of the impact of prime ministerial popularity on the changing electoral fortunes of the LDP in 1958–2005 indicates that Koizumi's approval ratings influenced voting behaviour in 2001. The LDP's vote share with independent voters surged from 14 per cent in 2000 (lower house election) to 25 per cent in 2001(upper house election), mainly due to Koizumi's positive ratings which were reinforced by opposition supporters (Patterson and Maeda, 2007). After his leadership re-election in 2003, Koizumi's approval ratings surged from around 50 per cent to 65 per cent before returning to 50 per cent after the 2003 lower house election. That was still higher than the approval ratings of most previous prime ministers.

However, Prime Minister Koizumi had a troubled relationship with his party. His star quality and strong leadership style were in stark contrast with those of his predecessors, except Yoshida and Nakasone. He capitalised on the public's loathing of the LDP by using his popularity to get what he wanted. He attacked powerful vested interests and disregarded the factions when making cabinet appointments. He even urged the new intake of MPs not to join factions (Krauss and Pekkanen, 2011: 146). He shifted policymaking power away from PARC and the policy tribes (*zoku giin*), and towards the Cabinet Office and prime ministerial councils. He created a Council on Economic and Fiscal Policy (CEFP) to introduce economic reforms and chaired its meetings.

Strategically, Koizumi was a gambler. He put his leadership and government position on the line by introducing divisive legislation. First, he risked being removed from office by calling a snap election in 2005, two years ahead of time, when his party had a majority in both houses of the Diet. Then, during the 2005 election campaign he enraged the party elite by putting forward fresh candidates to unseat the 32 LDP rebels who had voted against his pet project – postal reform.

Postal privatisation was Koizumi's make-or-break issue, not unlike the Maastricht bill for John Major (Chapter 4). Denationalising the Japanese Postal Savings System – the world's largest savings bank – meant attacking 'a major sacred cow in the Japanese political–economic system' and undermining the powerful interests which mobilised the LDP vote. Disregarding the LDP Executive Council's unanimity rule, Koizumi got a simple majority for his postal privatisation bill which was introduced in the House of Representatives on 5 July 2005. The bill was passed by only five votes, as 37 LDP members voted with the opposition who disagreed with the bill's details rather than its intention.

Getting the postal bill passed in the House of Councillors would have been much harder, so Koizumi took pre-emptive action. He threatened to dissolve the lower house and call a general election if the bill didn't pass. But Koizumi's plan failed and the vote was lost by 125 to 108 votes. Twenty-two LDP Councillors voted against the bill and eight abstained or were absent. Making good on his threat, Koizumi immediately dissolved the house and called a general election. He used the election as a referendum on his reform programme, revealing the underlying power relationship between himself and his LDP opponents (Christensen, 2006: 503). Koizumi expelled the 32 postal rebels from the party by nominating other candidates known as 'assassins' and notably women to contest their seats.

Koizumi's gamble paid off. In the 2005 lower house election, the LDP achieved its greatest parliamentary majority in a quarter century with the highest turnout since 1990. A huge swing among urban voters, including in the single-seat districts, gave the party 296 out of 480 seats (219 single-member district seats and 77 list seats in the PR tier). The DPJ was the clear loser. It lost 53 of the 105 single-member seats gained in 2003 and nine of the 70 PR seats. Having achieved a two-thirds majority with its coalition partner the New Kōmeitō, the LDP government reintroduced its postal bill which became law after the upper house granted approval.

As the third-longest serving post-war Japanese prime minister who led the LDP to its biggest victory in 2005, Koizumi was undeniably a successful political leader. But was his leadership transformative? He certainly declared war on the LDP factions and patronage networks that had sustained the party vote-getting machine for so long, especially in the rural areas. Koizumi also used institutional changes and tactics to introduce economic reforms and cut public works programmes opposed by his party. However, 'it was not the "shock therapy" that Margaret Thatcher deployed in Britain in the 1980s'.[22]

In the end, the LDP's two-thirds majority was wasted. As soon as Koizumi retired in 2006, the LDP's decline resumed in earnest. The bad old days of faction-driven politics and revolving-door prime ministers were back. Three prime ministers followed over three years (Shinzō Abe, Yasuo Fukuda and Taro Aso). Abe's hapless government was dogged by financial scandals and ended in a crushing defeat in the 2007 upper house election when, for the first since its formation, the LDP was no longer the largest party. The DPJ under Ozawa was the clear winner, having succeeded in wooing voters who had been marginalised by Koizumi's pro-market policies. Fukuda's leadership selection and chaotic government looked like a return to backroom factional intrigue as Ozawa even tried to use the DPJ's upper house victory to engineer a 'grand coalition' with his former party.

In 2009, Also led the Liberal Democrats to their crushing defeat. In the general election, the LDP ended up with a dismal 119 out of 480 seats in the House of Representatives. Its district seats plummeted to 64 from 219 in 2005 and its list seats fell to 55 from 77 in 2005. For the second time in four years, the majoritarian bias of the voting system had produced seismic elections which exaggerated the parliamentary majority of the plurality electoral party. The long-term ambition of the LDP destroyer Ozawa – to replace single-party dominance with two-party dynamics – was finally realised 16 years after his defection from the LDP.

Conclusion

As with the other dominant parties covered in this book, the Japanese LDP was eventually brought down from within.

So long as opposition forces remained weak, fragmented uncoordinated and internal dissent lacked cohesion and critical mass, the collective action needed to unseat the LDP was bound to fail. LDP defection plots foundered on three occasions: in 1960 following the Socialist Party's split and Kishi's resignation as the LDP's leader; in 1966 when Nakasone hatched a plan with a Democratic Socialist official to form a new centrist coalition; and in 1974 when he plotted with the Fukuda and Miki factions to leave the LDP and form a new party (Christensen, 2000: 137–45).

Under the '55 system', reformist politicians faced disincentives to mobilise from within since their defection threats wouldn't be credible. When the LDP's parliamentary majority was vulnerable due to scandals, the party relied on the legislative support of independent MPs to get its government bills passed. This provided the LDP with insurance against exit from its own ranks. Defection plots usually vanished once the LDP secured a majority, explaining why the breakaway Liberal Club rejoined the LDP in 1986.

These strategic exit barriers were reinforced through institutions which provided the LDP with further insurance against defection. Careerist politicians faced disincentives to break away from the party and individual factions because their political careers depended on rank and seniority linked to faction membership and their re-election on the basis of patronage by faction leaders and *köenkai* who controlled selective resources.

This crisis containment had unintended consequences: intraparty churning and political inertia due to lack of leadership. The interfactional bargaining leading to the selection of the LDP president created leaders without clear mandates and revolving-door prime ministers. The only strong LDP leaders under the '55 system' (Nakasone and Koizumi) were the ones who were prepared to split their party.

The turning point came in the early 1990s when party vulnerability and internal dissidence reached critical levels. The competitive playing field had gradually expanded. Political scandals boosted the ranks of floating voters, providing the right conditions for collective action by opposition forces and LDP dissidents to coalesce and deprive the LDP of its majority and unseat it from power after 38 years of continuous rule.

The 1994 electoral reform introduced by the multiparty coalition government that replaced the LDP produced more fluid patterns of party competition and transformed political incentives. Different coalition and minority governments have resulted from party system reconfiguration, reducing the likelihood of a return to long periods of single-party dominance in Japan.

However, government alternation has come about by convulsions. The bipolar logic of the majoritarian mixed-member voting system produced two landslide elections in four years, giving the LDP an overwhelming victory in 2005 and a crushing defeat in 2009. Whether the DPJ is capable of using its stunning victory to provide the political leadership that Japan needs remains in doubt. Two years after coming to power, the fractious DPJ had already changed its leader three times.

The consequences of electoral reform on the LDP organisation have been profound if not always clear-cut. The party has found it difficult to adapt to the new environment. Despite Koizumi's attempts to destroy the factions and *köenkai* that sustained LDP power for so long, these institutions have survived, although weakened. It is far from clear whether the LDP's shocking defeat in 2009 will be the catharsis leading to the party's rejuvenation.

Conclusion: How Parties Succeed or Fail to Manage Factionalism and Stay in Power

Some dominant parties degenerate into fatal factionalism while others keep factionalism in check and cling to power. In this book's survey of Japan, Canada, Britain and Italy, particular circumstances may have differed but internal dissent and disorder were common to all. In Japan and Canada, warning signs of internal discord emerged before the final collapse and only weak opposition parties forestalled the inevitable. In Italy, the collapse of the Christian Democrats (DC) dragged on for years while the end to 18 years of Conservative rule in Britain was brutally quick.

In all cases, though, it's clear that party unity is a necessary but insufficient condition for party dominance. Such unity proves difficult to maintain in the long run as factional pressures increase due to rising internal competition for electoral, policy and career claims.

Japan's Liberal Democratic Party (LDP) was finally tossed out by voters in 2009 after almost half a century of continuous rule and just four years after its landslide victory under maverick leader Koizumi who then enraged his party by putting forward fresh candidates to unseat the LDP rebels.

In Canada, the Liberals had ruled for 81 years since the turn of the twentieth century but were almost wiped out in the 2011 elections. Their hegemony began to fade in 1984 when Pierre Trudeau stepped down as party leader after 16 years to be succeeded by his old rival John Turner. This acrimonious transition exposed rising factionalism over the 'national question' in a highly disciplined party machine, unleashing a destructive cleavage and bitter leadership battles. While the Liberals bounced back into power from 1993 to 2006 under Jean Chrétien, this was largely due to an even more fatal implosion of the Progressive Conservatives and their slow reconstruction as the Conservative Party of Canada.

Italy's DC imploded in 1994 after five decades in power, crashing to just 46 seats from 207 in the lower house. It had been the senior member of 51 coalition governments despite winning an absolute parliamentary majority only once. Its centrifugal pluralism was sustained by a corrupt form of consociationalism through which it connived with the opposition by blending a *de jure* anti-communist electoral strategy with *de facto* communist co-optation. During the 1980s, power-sharing with Craxi's equally corrupt and factionalised Socialists proved to be the road to perdition – following 1992 when the break-up of the Communist Party was a tipping point that enabled Milan magistrates to finally expose the massive political corruption engendered by five decades of Christian Democratic rule.

For Britain's Conservatives, big election defeats had always been caused by party splits and proved to be their undoing again in their huge loss to Tony Blair's New Labour in 1997 – their worst electoral result since 1832. This humiliating defeat under John Major concluded an internal war of attrition over Europe that had started under Margaret Thatcher. Despite three successive majority elections, she was dumped after 15 years as party leader after her neo-liberal policies, authoritarian leadership and anti-Europe views had polarised the Conservatives. Like Canada's Liberals, a big part of their success had been due to an even more fractured Labour Party. The Conservatives won a reprieve in their fourth electoral victory in 1992 due to their leadership change and the still unfinished modernisation of Labour under Neil Kinnock.

That party unity is a necessary but insufficient condition for party dominance reveals a paradox. Factionalism can become destabilising and dangerous if factions wield a veto but it can also prolong office tenure by containing conflict to prevent exit. In the long run, though, using factions to regulate the division of the spoils has perverse consequences that lead to bad governance and brand devaluation. Failing to manage factional conflict creates intraparty disequilibrium, prompting insurgencies and collective action by dissidents who mobilise against the leadership to bring about change and, in a worst-case scenario, trading off voice for exit.

Intraparty politics: the neglected variable in explaining one-party dominance

Intraparty competition is critical in explaining the emergence, persistence and decline of dominant parties. In competitive democracies, dominant parties endure because their vote-seeking, office-seeking and policy-seeking strategies skew party competition in their favour, which Chapter 1 explains from sociological, institutional and strategic theoretical perspectives. However, by transforming incumbency advantages into partisan resources, prolonged office tenure can encourage self-serving behaviour and risks, subtracting value from a recognised party brand in the long run. As quality deteriorates, reformist politicians and voters abandon long-term incumbents in favour of opposition parties and break down single-party dominance.

By questioning the unitary actor assumption of political parties, this book offers more complete causal explanations of single-party dominance and its breakdown than conventional studies which have focused mainly on party competition to explain dominant parties' competitive strategies or opposition parties' failures to compete. Overlooking intraparty politics may lead to premature conclusions about dominant parties' resilience and underestimate the potential for disunity.

The book's case studies show that disunity and factional splits were the immediate reasons for breakdowns of dominant party rule (Japan in 1993) or major contributors to dominant parties' implosion (Italy) or had an effect on their scale of defeat (Britain and Canada). The hypotheses found in Chapter 2 about why long office tenure is likely to result in internal competition and disunity are also borne out by the case studies. The capacity of dominant parties to maintain unity over time declines as growth in the internal competition for election and ideological/policy and career claims push dissidents and the deprived to challenge the leadership through collective action and defection. The effectiveness of this collective action is determined by the size of a government's majority which affects bargaining leverage and exit costs. However, the ideological location, size and cohesion of dissident factions also determine the credibility of their exit threats.

By conceptualising factionalism as a process of sub-group partitioning, this study avoids the trap of static categorisation and allows the analysis of the internal dynamics of differently organised parties with different types of sub-party groups. A variety of methods, including strategic games and bargaining, analyses conflict resolution inside political parties with weighted measures of the effective number of factions and their pivotal power. Factionalism turns out to be a multifaceted phenomenon that changes over time and leads to shifting patterns of factional competition and cooperation over the life of a party. Italy's DC suffered the full range of conditions leading to factional capture and the transformation of factionalism from a process of cooperation to one of competition and then to degeneration.

Majoritarian constraints on and non-majoritarian incentives for factionalism

The 'most similar/most different systems' design reveals contrasting incentive structures between dominant parties operating in majoritarian/Westminster democracies (United Kingdom and Canada) and non-majoritarian/consensus democracies (Italy and Japan). However, the key differences in each type of democracy (such as federalism and more power-sharing in Canada than in the United Kingdom's unitary state and more centripetal forces and consensus in Japan than in Italy's centrifugal polity) allow a finely grained qualitative analysis of how political institutions shape partisanship and factional behaviour. In addition, by integrating the analysis of systemic institutions with organisational arrangements, the general contours of party conflict regulation emerge.

Chapter 3 explains how the majoritarian prerequisites of single-member plurality (SMP) rule incentivise electoral and legislative parties to behave as unitary actors shaping voters' expectations of 'strong' parties and perceptions of disunited parties as unfit to govern. This raises exit barriers for intraparty dissidents who face high start-up costs for new parties. Bipolar competition reinforced by a top-down 'responsible' party model of government directs MPs' loyalty towards the party leader who controls career advancement. This explains why parliamentary parties are highly disciplined and legislative rebellions rare but meaningful in Westminster systems. Prime ministers also have a mighty but blunt weapon to enforce legislative cohesion: the confidence vote. However, this is a dangerous way to restore order since the use of deterrent force involves a unilateral threat but bilateral punishment. Chapter 4 uses game theory analysis of John Major's battles with Conservative Eurosceptic MPs to demonstrate this.

The pressures for party unity remain strong in hybrid systems such as Canada where power-sharing and federalism dampen partisanship and relax the constraints of bipolar competition. However, despite more multiparty competition in Canada than in Britain, single-party rule and minority governments persist. Moreover, federalism linked to national unity has been a source of factional division for the Liberals. In Canada, 'prime ministerial government' gives the prime minister even more disciplinary control over MPs' careers than in Britain, explaining the absence of legislative factions in the federal parliament and of party leaders' capacity to withhold selective benefits from disloyal MPs in leadership selection (Chapter 5).

These majoritarian constraints put a heavy burden of discipline on the party leader. This can be a source of strength by providing leaders with opportunities to introduce radical programmes without a strong party mandate – for example Thatcher's deflationary policies and Trudeau's constitutional reforms. However, it can also be a source of weakness by stifling debate and making leaders feel invincible and prone to unilateral decisions and polarisation as with Thatcher's 'poll tax' and Trudeau's Quebec's constitutional status. The case studies show that, in the long run, party leaders must rely on discipline and social norms to thwart dissent and maintain trust in a caucus whose members hold the key to their survival. Otherwise, dissidents' collective action risks destabilising parties and triggering the overthrow of sitting incumbents as in the case of Thatcher and Chrétien and nearly so in the case of Major. Leaders' willingness to compromise with dissidents and avoid threats to power can be decisive in maintaining unity in ruling parties, especially in competitive electoral markets where dissidents have bargaining leverage.

In contrast, non-majoritarian institutions – typical of consensus democracies – put less of a premium on party unity and fewer constraints on factionalism. Sharing, dispersing and restraining power in different ways, consensual arrangements maximise representativeness. However, the resulting fragmentation of political power weakens the leadership, making majority failures and organisational dilemmas more likely.

As Chapter 6 explains, lower entry barriers and co-partisan competition under Italy's old multi-preference open-list voting system and Japan's SNTV in multi-member districts were disincentives to party unity. By fragmenting party systems and political parties, these permissive voting systems produced unstable multiparty coalition governments under the DC in Italy and fragile minimum-winning factional alliances under the Liberal Democrats in Japan (under the '55 system').

Co-partisan competition for district votes pushed factions to become major players in the mobilisation of the personal vote and in the distribution of partisan advantages to candidates. This redirected politicians' loyalties from the party towards factions and provided ideal conditions for clientelism, machine politics and factional capture. Intraparty ideological groups were transformed into factions of patronage whose members became rent seekers operating within intricate local networks run by self-serving regional oligarchs in Italy and faction-linked *köenkai* in Japan.

In post-1994 Japan, the bipolar logic of the new majoritarian mixed-member voting system has transformed political incentives and reduced the likelihood of a return to long periods of single-party dominance. However, government alternation has been convulsive. The LDP experienced both overwhelming victory in 2005 and crushing defeat in 2009. Moreover, weakened factions continue in both mainstream parties: within two years of coming to power, the fractious Democratic Party (DPJ) has already changed its leader three times.

By de-emphasising partisanship, non-majoritarian institutions dampen the competition for policy claims, relaxing the need for legislative discipline. The Italian and Japanese prime ministers lacked policy-making authority and statutory powers to bind cabinets or discipline representatives whose careers depended on factional affiliation rather than on loyalty to the party leader. Disincentives to legislative cohesion in Italy's reactive parliament generated by perverse procedural and consociational arrangements allowed rebels to escape the consequences of their actions, producing gridlock, incoherent policies and unaccountable governments. In the Japanese non-partisan Diet, dissent was a non-issue. Members toed the party line without compulsion since public policy was made outside of parliament within 'iron triangles' and other institutions and legislative careers and advancement were determined by extra-parliamentary organisations such as the Policy Affairs Research Council (PARC) and LDP factions.

Unintended consequences of organisational incentives

The organisational arrangements of parties can offset systemic constraints and reduce conflict. However, striking the right balance of incentives isn't easy.

If we accept that '*intra*- and *inter*party competition are inversely related' (Gerring and Thacker, 2008: 35) then organisational arrangements that counterbalance rather than reinforce the effects of systemic institutions should be more conducive to conflict resolution and good governance. For example, in concentrated executive-dominant majoritarian regimes, parties should privilege inclusive rules to decentralise power and promote debate. Conversely, parties operating in non-majoritarian pluralist systems should adopt arrangements promoting centripetal competition.

However, there is nothing predetermined about these patterns. Firstly, political parties use a variety of different rules and procedures to carry out separate activities such as the selection of candidates, party leaders and policies that determine internal power distribution and shape leader–follower relationships in different ways. Secondly, rules and procedures are prone to elite manipulation, particularly when the incumbent is in power for a long time.

This book's case studies show that tinkering with organisational arrangements to increase party democratisation and pre-empt conflict can have unintended consequences. In 1997, British Conservatives adopted a parliamentary mass-membership hybrid system to protect future leaders and sitting prime ministers from any messy coups like the one suffered by Thatcher in 1990. However, the 2001 party membership run-off race between the two front runners selected by MPs produced majority failure which cost the Conservatives dearly (Section 3.8). The Canadian Liberals' adoption of an automatic leadership review after general elections motivated the incumbent Jean Chrétien to call snap elections to pre-empt challenges by grass-roots revolts. However, this also enabled his challenger Paul Martin to capture the extra-parliamentary organisation and launch a leadership bid (Chapter 5).

The proportional rules and procedures adopted by the LDP and DC to give factions organisational stakes produced their own negative trade-offs which were not conducive to good governance: party fragmentation, high leadership turnover, government churning and gridlock and accountability losses. As faction leaders rather than the party leadership controlled office seekers' campaign benefits and office holders' career benefits, politicians switched their loyalty from the party and towards factions, thus weakening partisanship and cohesion, which are characteristics of 'strong' parties. To maximise their organisational clout, DC power brokers were incentivised to split from existing factions and set up new ones. As factions became veto players, collective action dilemmas and decisional stalemates emerged inside the DC. Faction leaders used their veto power in the national organisation to block much-needed party reforms under Zaccagnini in the 1970s and De Mita in the 1980s. Fragmentation of the LDP was moderated by district magnitude under SNTV and the seniority system regulating career advancement. In both parties, leadership selection resulted from factional bargaining in fragile *ad hoc* factional alliances generated by the DC's congressional motion-lists system and the LDP's presidential primaries. Apart from pushing factions to decentralise their operations and become embedded in the party grass roots, these factionalised contests produced party leaders without clear mandates and revolving-door prime ministers. Paradoxically, the only strong LDP leaders (Nakasone and Koizumi) were those prepared to split their party.

Electoral market conditions

This book's case studies show that electoral market conditions affect dominant parties' exposure to factionalism and defections. Single-party dominance breaks down when changes in the electoral market increase the vulnerability of ruling parties shifting dissidents' trade-offs between voice and exit. The leadership's failed responses to deterioration in the quality of governance may trigger critical defections and the loss of power.

Chapter 2 illustrates the market for political consent under two opposite demand scenarios affecting dissidents' bargaining leverage and exit costs. In a sub-competitive electoral market such as in a dominant party system where the governing party or coalition has a large working majority and the demand for voter consent is elastic, defection threats by dissidents and disgruntled office holders wouldn't be credible. Their support would be unlikely to be pivotal to government survival although they might still organise as a faction to voice discontent. However, in a competitive market of elastic demand, these actors would gain bargaining leverage because their support would be more critical to government survival, making their exit threats more credible and creating opportunities for dissident collective action.

Chapter 4 showed that the British Conservatives' reduced majority in 1992 increased the bargaining leverage of a minority Eurosceptic faction whose legislative rebellions undermined Major's authority over party and country. Similar conditions prevailed in Italy and Japan in the early 1990s when the competitive playing field expanded with the entry of new parties and old parties' splits. These conditions made exit more attractive for members disgruntled by their corrupt political masters and by the LDP and DC leaderships' failures to effectively respond to brand deterioration. In Italy, the 1992 realigning election was the tipping point that pushed voters and reformists to abandon this value-destroying brand, leading to the DC's implosion in 1994 after a two-year investigation of political corruption.

In Japan, reformist politicians faced strong disincentives to mobilise because their defection threats wouldn't be credible. When the LDP's parliamentary majority was vulnerable due to scandals, the party relied on independent MPs to get its government bills passed. So long as opposition forces remained weak, fragmented and uncoordinated, the collective action needed to unseat the LDP was bound to fail, explaining why defection plots foundered in 1960, 1966 and 1974 and why the breakaway Liberal Club rejoined the LDP in 1986. However, in the early

1990s, political scandals boosted the ranks of floating voters and provided the right conditions for collective action by opposition forces and LDP dissidents to coalesce. Trading off voice for exit, defectors joined the opposition, deprived the LDP of its majority and drove it from power after 38 years of continuous rule.

The key to retaining dominance is to design suitable incentives which align factions with overall party interests and to maintain an effective overall party leadership at the service of the public interest.

Notes

1 The Theory of One-Party Dominance

1. Combining the degree of party system fragmentation and polarisation in a two-dimensional format, Sartori indicates that centrifugal forces are pulling the system towards its two extreme ideological poles: in post-war Italy towards the left under the influence of the Communists and towards the right under the influence of the neo-Fascists.
2. To characterise a party as dominant scholars tend to use either a party's share of the vote or a party's share of seats, although some definitions use a plurality of votes/seats as a benchmark and others require an absolute majority or even a qualified majority of seats.
3. After the 2012 French presidential and legislative elections, the French Socialist Party controlled the presidency, both houses of the legislature, all but one French region and most of the country's departments, big towns and communes.
4. During the period 2003–08, United Russia controlled two-thirds of the seats in the Duma and a majority of seats in all regional legislatures and 78 of Russia's 83 regional administrations were headed by party members (Reuter, 2009).
5. The Republicans were strongly dominant in 2002–06 and less so after the mid-term elections in 2010 when they regained control of the House of Representatives and controlled 25 state legislatures, leaving the Democrats in control of the presidency and nominally in control of the senate under its arcane supermajority rules.
6. For Sauger incumbents are in a dominant position if their individual chance of staying in office after the next election is superior to a predetermined threshold (set at 90 per cent), meaning that they are likely (with less than 10 per cent chances of error) to keep their dominant position after the next election. Sauger argues that this definition corresponds to classical definitions of dominance that posit the necessity to hold an office for at least three consecutive terms to be acknowledged as dominant (Sauger, 2010: 110).
7. In his study of Mexico's PRI Greene defines dominance as 'continuous executive and legislative rule by a single party for at least 20 years or at least four consecutive elections' (Greene, 2007: 12).
8. However, quirks of majoritarian voting systems can occasionally deliver more seats to a party with a smaller aggregate share of the popular vote than the best-placed party (as in the United Kingdom in 1974), but this is rare even under biased electoral systems, such as SMP rule.
9. Under Wilfrid Laurier the Liberals' national appeal was based on 'a nationwide coalition of supporters, an expansionary role for government, an intimate connection with business, and an accommodation between the

French and the English' (Clarkson, 2005: 8). But a puzzling survey suggests that Liberal electoral dominance has rested on a significant religious cleavage in English-speaking central and eastern Canada, where the Liberals receive a disproportional share of the Catholic vote without which their dominance 'would disappear' (Blais, 2005).

10. The sale of council housing at a huge discount triggered rising property prices and helped fuel a property boom and credit crisis two decades later and reduced significantly the stock of social housing at the disposal of local councils.

11. One of the most notable examples was British Telecom (BT). Two million people applied for BT shares in its 1984 sell-off, including two Conservative MPs who made multiple applications and had to resign.

12. This study includes four dominant party systems using majoritarian voting systems (Britain and Canada under SMP, France under two-ballot plurality and Japan under the old single non-transferable voting system) and three types of PR (Sweden, Ireland and Italy under the old preference voting system).

13. Recent research shows that Labour's advantage is less a function of malapportionment (soon to be addressed in a review of constituency boundaries) and more a function of vote distribution and to a lesser extent abstention resulting from Labour's ability to win relatively small inner-city seats and constituencies with lower turnouts (Borisyuk, Thrasher, Johnston, and Rallings, 2010a, 2010b).

14. In contrast the 1922 election launched two-party politics in Britain. The Conservatives and Labour won between them 68 per cent of the popular vote. By 1951 only nine MPs did not follow the Labour or Conservative whips. This number rose to 12 MPs in 1970, 27 MPs in 1979 and 85 MPs in 2010. After the 2010 general election 57 British MPs were taking the Liberal Democrat whip; 28 MPs from minority parties gained an aggregate 9.7 per cent share of the popular vote.

15. The Conservatives won big in 1983 because the Labour Party split. Labour and the Alliance (the Liberals and the new SDP, now Lib Dems) each received a little over a quarter of the national vote, but Labour won 209 seats and the Alliance a mere 23 seats.

16. In 2010, 298 of the 306 seats won by the Conservatives were in England. Labour won 26 of the 37 Welsh seats with only 36 per cent of the popular vote in Wales.

17. A compelling study of the Canadian party system as a case of 'polarized pluralism' shows that outside Quebec the Liberals have dominated district-level three-party competition on a left–right ordering while on the national question they control a pole within each segment: the pro-Quebec pole outside Quebec and the pro-Canada pole inside Quebec (Johnston, 2008).

18. There were 32 electoral colleges for 630 members of the Chamber of Deputies, with a magnitude ranging from 1 to 36 members per college except for the Valle d'Aosta constituency which had a single seat.

19. Clause VI committed the Labour Party to the nationalisation of the means of production, distribution and exchange. In 1960 Hugh Gaitskell had tried unsuccessfully to remove it from the Labour Party's constitution.

20. In Italy a quasi-monopoly of state television existed under Prime Minister Berlusconi due to his private ownership of TV channels (his brother owns the newspaper *il Giornale*).

21. Alistair Campbell, frenetically feeding the ravenous British press with news fodder to try and capture the headlines, was the inspiration behind the satirical television series 'The Thick of It', where the key character, Malcolm Tucker, bears a distinct resemblance to Campbell, as acknowledged by him.

22. Subsequently the SAP became more vulnerable as the field of competition expanded with the entry in the Riksdag of the Greens in 1988, two new parties in 1991 (the Christian Democrats and the right-wing New Democracy) and a new far-right anti-immigrant party (Sweden Democrats) in 2010, which enabled a governing centre–right coalition to be re-elected for the first time (under Prime Minister Fredrik Reinfeldt) with Sweden Democrats holding the balance of power with their 20 seats.

23. Craxi was a corrupt politician, an ineffective chief executive and a very poor party leader. He failed to sort out Italy's deficit, ignored demands for constitutional reform and presided over a very factionalised and corrupt Socialist Party that became the target of Milan's investigating magistrates who brought down the political establishment in the mid-1990s.

24. For example, Andreotti's 1976 government of solidarity had the support of only 258 out of 630 deputies, but the minority government gained office comfortably due to the high level of abstentions in the investiture vote (Strom, Budge, and Laver, 1994).

25. In France top mandarins trained in the *grandes écoles* played a key modernising role producing *trentes glorieuses*, 30 glorious years of high economic growth.

26. The financial institution Monte dei Paschi di Siena was for many years controlled by Fanfani's faction. State radio and television RAI, controlled by Fanfani's *protégé* Ettore Berabei, was in 1975 fought over by faction leaders Piccoli and Zaccagnini and was then split into three networks as rewards to PSI and PCI for their cooperation in previous governments (Zucherman, 1979: 123).

27. The IRI president was arrested in May 1993 for corruption and violation of party finance laws related to the construction of the Rome metro and power stations in Brindisi. He was replaced by Romano Prodi, who was head of IRI in 1982–89 and 1993–94 and was investigated but acquitted of conflict-of-interest charges. Prodi was the prime minister of Italy in 1996–98 and 2006–08 and the president of the European Commission in 1999–2004.

28. The Arezzo section of the Rome–Florence *autostrada* was associated with Fanfani and the one near Avellino with De Mita, a highway south of Rome with Andreotti and the *autostrada* from Rome to L'Aquila with Lorenzo Natali. The partially constructed *autostrada* in the North was named 'PiRuBi', based on the names of its factional sponsors Piccoli, Rumor and Bisaglia. In the late 1960s the DC set up four state-funded chemical groups, each associated with a DC faction (Spotts and Wieser, 1986).

29. Karel van Wolferen (1989: 115–9) reported that Japan's Ministry of Construction had the authority to issue licences to the entire construction industry. This accounted for between 15 per cent and 16 per cent of Japan's gross

domestic product (GDP) each year and involved maintaining 232 offices in construction, maintenance and research and 655 smaller area offices as well as 162 extra-departmental institutions and more than half a million public works projects (in 1986).

30. Canadian Crown corporations are instrumentally linked to the formation of the Canadian state (at federal and provincial levels). They are involved in distributing, using and pricing all sorts of goods and services, including energy development, resource extraction, public transport, the promotion of the arts and culture and property management.

31. This ADSCAM scandal involved the Liberal government making illicit contributions to Quebec industries, especially in advertising in order to counteract the actions of the separatist *Parti Québécois* when the Liberals were in power under Jean Chretien in 1993–03.

2 Why Does One-Party Dominance End in Factionalism?

1. In 2000, the PRI lost the presidency for the first time after 71 years of political dominance although previous internal conflicts and state-level splits had increased the party's vulnerability since 1987.

2. Blair exonerated Labour MPs who rebelled over key government legislation on university top-up fees, foundation hospitals, fox hunting and UK involvement in the Iraq war.

3. These elections delivered large parliamentary majorities for the Conservatives thanks to a split in the Labour Party which facilitated the Conservatives' introduction in 1981 of a radical deflationary budget in the middle of a recession (see Chapter 4) and subsequently a vast privatisation programme without full cabinet and parliamentary backing.

4. While the two indices are slightly different, they deliver comparable results with differences occurring only in the second or third decimal places.

5. Intraparty competition in the DC was based more on political patronage than on ideology although DC factions tended to align themselves on the basis of the party's alliance strategy in government formation which from the early 1960s led to a *rapprochement* with left parties first, the Socialists and then the Communists.

3 Majoritarian Democracies: Executive-Dominated Britain and Decentralised Canada

1. Critics contest the unity of Lijphart's model noting that features are endogenous to other features of the polity (Gerring and Thacker, 2008).

2. Lijphart identifies ten interrelated elements of the Westminster or majoritarian model: concentration of executive power in one-party and bare-majority cabinets, cabinet dominance, two-party system, majoritarian or disproportional system of elections, interest group pluralism, unitary and centralised government, concentration of legislative power in a unicameral legislature, constitutional flexibility, absence of judicial review and a central bank controlled by the executive (Lijphart 1999).

3. Under the 1832 Reform Act there were 153 single-member constituencies, 240 double-member constituencies, 7 three-member constituencies, and 1 four-member constituency.

4. During the early Reagan presidency Liberal Republicans set up the Ripon Society, the Wednesday Group and the 92 Group to moderate the 'New Right' and, after the 1994 midterm elections, two informal caucus factions formed to counter Newt Gingrich's conservatism: the 'Tuesday Group' among liberal and moderate Republicans and the 'Blue Dog' coalition among moderate and conservative Democrats (Kolodny, 1999).

5. This times-series analysis uses historical data of political attitudes from Gallup surveys now discontinued.

6. John Smith was Leader of the Labour Party from July 1992 until his sudden death from a heart attack in May 1994.

7. I thank Lawrence LeDuc for confirming that the absence of continuous polling data on party unity in Canada indicates its lack of saliency to Canadian voters until recently. Survey data in the early 1990s shows that 81 per cent of Canadians thought there was too much party squabbling for good government and 78 per cent said they were opposed to political parties disciplining their MPs (Blais and Gidengil, 1991).

8. In fact, recent research shows that 'MPs reap electoral rewards for taking a stand against their parties' (Kam, 2009: 19) indicating that voters value party unity in the aggregate much more than at the individual level.

9. Lord Hailsham, 1976 BBC Richard Dimbleby Lecture.

10. Matthew Shugart calculated that roughly one eighth of Westminster prime ministers leave due to intraparty conflict, compared to well over a quarter of non-Westminster prime ministers (as reported in his academic blog 'Fruits and Votes' on 3 September 2010).

11. The Conservative 1959–64 parliament had a 12 per cent rate of dissent but this was mostly accounted for by dissenting votes on the Resale Price bill.

12. In the 1983–87 parliament (Conservative majority of 144 seats) Conservative backbench MPs broke ranks in 17 per cent of parliamentary divisions almost as much as under the allegedly rebellious minority Labour government of 1974–79 (Norton, 1990b).

13. Massive anti-war protests were held in February 2003 involving hundreds of thousands of people in the streets of London, Glasgow and Belfast.

14. In the US Congress incentives differ due to the separation of powers. Politicians owe their nomination not to the party leader or president but to local voters who select candidates in direct primaries and local interests who finance campaigns.

15. The so-called 'payroll vote' almost doubled during the twentieth century. It includes cabinet and non-cabinet posts, whips, law officers and party parliamentary secretaries (the latter are not paid). The Ministerial and Other Salaries Act of 1975 set a limit of 110 paid office holders but in 1999 Blair got around this restriction by appointing ministers who did not draw a salary. His first administration included 113 government posts including 64 non-cabinet ministers (Theakston, 1999).

16. The coalition government proposes to reduce the British House of Commons to 600 seats.

17. Additional research on ministerial selection in the British Parliament between 1987 and 2005 shows that party backbenchers have considerable

influence over ministerial appointments regardless of the formal and informal powers of party leaders (Kam, Bianco, Sened and Smyth, 2010).

18. The Reform Party of Canada was created in 1987 as a populist western protest party advocating the break-up of Canada into its two founding regions. It then became the Conservative Canadian Alliance and eventually merged with the federal Progressive Conservative Party to form the new Conservative Party of Canada.

19. Major royal commissions include the 1940 Rowell–Sirois Commission on dominion–provincial relations, the 1956 Royal Commission on Canada's Economic Prospects, the 1963 task force on Bilingualism and Biculturalism and the 1976 task force on Canadian Unity.

20. For example, only 26 of the 84 Conservative MPs who signed a motion calling for a 'Fresh Start' on Europe voted against the 'paving motion' to pass the bill and 41 of the early day motion signatories failed to cast a single dissenting vote on any part of the Maastricht Treaty legislation. On European Monetary Union (EMU) and Central Bank legislation only 9 per cent of Conservative backbench MPs defied the party whip in the division lobbies even though an attitude survey had revealed that more than 60 per cent had declared they were against such developments (Baker, Gamble, Ludlam, 1993a; Baker, Gamble, Ludlam and Seawright, 1999).

21. Reforms in 1993 divided the college vote equally between Labour MPs, party members and trade unions, each controlling one-third of the vote. But when college was created in 1981, 70 per cent of the vote was controlled by those annual conference delegates representing local party branches and corporately affiliated organisations such as trade unions and socialist societies (Webb, 1995).

22. New Zealand, another of Lijphart's three majoritarian prototypes, no longer approximates this model since the country ditched its SMP electoral system in a referendum in 1993.

4 Case 1 – The Thatcher–Major Factional Wars over Europe

1. They include the Conservatives' split over the Corn Laws in 1846, the Liberals' split over Irish Home Rule in 1886, the Conservatives' split over Tariff Reform in 1906, the Liberals' quarrel between Asquith and Lloyd George over coalition politics during the First World War and Labour's failure in 1931 under Ramsay Macdonald to carry his party into the National Government.

2. At the 2002 Conservative annual conference Party Chairman Theresa May described them as 'the nasty party' urging a change of 'behaviour and attitudes'.

3. John Major's speech to the 1993 Conservative Annual Conference.

4. Thatcher won by146 votes against Whitelaw (79), Geoffrey Howe (19), Jim Prior (19), John Peyton (12) and 2 abstentions.

5. Comments made by the late Lord Joseph in an interview with the author in May 1991.

6. In his memoirs, Nigel Lawson explains that Thatcher borrowed the term 'wet' from English public schools (independent schools) to designate 'those Tories who had no stomach for the fight ahead' (Lawson, 1992: 26). The label 'dry' attached to those with opposite characteristics.

7. Ian Gow was killed by a car bomb in 1990 claimed by the Irish Republican paramilitaries.

8. In many European coalition governments such government defeats often cause government break-ups but at Westminster they are unusual although possible.

9. Potential Treasury concessions were managing sterling down, introducing an economic forum on wages, delaying reductions in the annual Public Sector Borrowing Requirement (PSBR) as a percentage of gross domestic product (GDP) and extra spending to curb unemployment (Middlemas, 1991: 242).

10. Named after John Nash, this is a stable collective outcome produced by the decisions of certain actors from which no actor has an incentive to depart since neither player would gain by unilaterally changing his or her strategy.

11. Applying the rules set out by Steven Brams in his *Theory of Moves* (1994) shows the outcome to be stable whatever the initial states of the move–countermove process.

12. In 2008 Gordon Brown's government made the same mistake with proposals to abolish the 10 p tax rate and the 90-day detention, splitting the parliamentary Labour Party and triggering legislative rebellions.

13. Howe became Leader of the House and Deputy Prime Minister (a mostly honorific title then).

14. A similar row between Prime Minister Gordon Brown and Chancellor of the Exchequer broke out in August 2008 when Alistair Darling was forced by No. 10 to lift the stamp duty threshold in a desperate attempt to alleviate a crashing housing market, which thus highlighted fundamentally opposed views on the economy between the Treasury and No. 10.

15. Heseltine was made Secretary of State for the Environment in charge of sorting out the poll tax.

16. Richard Shepherd had introduced a Private Member's Bill in December 1991 requiring a national referendum as a precondition to the ratification of certain treaties. Bill Cash, a lawyer with impressive skills in exploiting loopholes and parliamentary grey areas to delay legislation, had been demoted as Chairman of the Conservative backbench European Affairs Committee.

17. This comment was made to Independent Television News (ITN) Political Editor Michael Brunson at the end of a television interview which Major apparently thought to be 'off air' (*The Observer*, 25 July 1993).

18. Opposition to the Maastricht bill consumed more than 200 hours of debate, 23 days in committee and produced 600 amendments (Baker, Gamble, Ludlam; 1994: 39).

19. *Ex post* the Social Chapter 'opt-out' turned out to be a pyrrhic victory. The European Court of Justice decided in November 1996 that the directive on the 48-hour working week fell under EU Health & Safety regulations rather than under the provisions of the Social Chapter. Hence, it applied to the United Kingdom.

20. In his memoirs, Major says this 'triumphalist crowing' erroneously attributed to him was made in private by a member of his press staff (Major, 1999: 288).

21. Major claims that what he meant was that if the electorate disagreed with what he had done, they could toss him out at the next election (Major, 1999: 364).

22. Rebel MP Teddy Taylor declared, 'There is a solution here – have a referendum and the rebellion ends tomorrow' (Baker, Gamble, Ludlam; 1994: 39).
23. However, an error the next morning revealed that the government had won by one vote.
24. Rebel MP Teddy Taylor admitted he could not have lived with himself if he'd agreed to dispense more money to a wasteful organisation (*Newsnight*, 29 November 1994).
25. At local elections in April and May, the Conservatives lost control of 60 councils and 2,042 seats across England and Wales.

5 Case 2 – The Demise of Canadian Liberal Hegemony

1. This idea was developed by George C. Perlin in his book *The Tory Syndrome: Leadership Politics in the Progressive Conservative Party* (1990) claiming that the Conservatives' 'persistence of internal conflict helped create an enduring image of a party unable to manage its own internal affairs and therefore not to be trusted with managing public affairs' (Perlin, 1980, 1990: 301, 1991; Blake, 1987).
2. Wilfried Laurier was Liberal leader for 32 years (1887–1919); William Lyon Mackenzie King for 29 years (1919–48); Louis St. Laurent and Lester Pearson for 10 years each (1948–58 and 1958–68, respectively); Pierre Trudeau for 16 years (1968–84); and Jean Chretien for 13 years (1990–2003).
3. During the post-confederation period and the early part of the twentieth century, Canada's 'national question' revolved around anti-imperialism particularly in French-speaking Quebec. But after the Second World War the issue became inward-looking focusing mainly on Quebec's place within Canada and its status as a distinct society.
4. Trudeau's predecessor Lester B. Pearson won the leadership in 1958 on the first ballot with 87.5 per cent of the vote and in 1948 Louis St. Laurent won on the first ballot with 61.4 of delegate votes. In contrast, at the Conservative leadership elections of 1967 and 1976 when Robert Stanfield and Joe Clark were elected they each had to face 11 contenders at the first round. After resigning and resubmitting his candidature in 1983, Clark faced eight challengers in a four-ballot race which he lost to Brian Mulroney.
5. Lalonde had been Trudeau's Quebec campaign strategist and was later promoted to Principal Secretary.
6. Rosa Mulé explains Trudeau's switch to restrictive redistributive policies in the second half of the 1970s as power plays in the executive and legislative arenas (Mulé, 2001, chapter 2).
7. The Prime Minister Principal Secretary Jim Coutts tried to entice a redneck Conservative MP from Alberta (Jack Horner) to cross the floor with a promise of a cabinet post or a senate seat if the Liberals lost the election (Meisel, 1992) and a seat held by a Liberal MP was purposefully vacated to allow Coutts to contest it (Wearing, 1989).
8. The group took its name from Grindstone Island, near Kingston, where they assemble to discuss party reforms.
9. The result of the referendum to allow the Quebec government to negotiate a new agreement on 'sovereignty association' with Canada showed

that 85 per cent of eligible voters turned out to vote but that 60 per cent voted 'no'.

10. This nickname was attributed to a group of young (albeit unknown) Liberals on the party's left who gained prominence after the Liberals' shattering defeat in1984 by mounting an effective attack against the Mulroney government.

11. Party insider Brooke Jeffrey claims that 'Martin forces learned the wrong lesson from their defeat in 1990' believing that Chrétien's grab of 800 Quebec delegate votes was due to his control of the 'old boys' elite network whereas anti-Meech Lake Liberals believed it was due to Martin's view of the Accord which was popular strictly among the small provincial Liberal elite (like Bourassa) who, crucially, were also nationalists (Jeffrey, 2010: 195).

12. Quebec MP Gilles Rocheleau sat as an Independent and Martin's campaign chair Jean Lapierre went on to form the separatist Bloc Québécois with Lucien Bouchard – former minister in the Mulroney's government.

13. Lucien Bouchard, the Bloc's leader, had recently left federal politics to become Premier of Quebec.

14. For example, the Liberal Party Office in Toronto was kept completely in the dark about the timing of the election until ten days before the writs were served (Clarkson, 2005: 219).

15. There are different accounts of this meeting held at the Constellation Hotel near Toronto airport summarised by Brooke Jeffrey in her chronicles of the Liberal Party in 1984–2008 (Jeffrey, 2010: 337–40).

16. In May 2002 Harper won a parliamentary seat in Preston Manning's former constituency in Calgary.

17. As described by journalist Jeffrey Simpson in *The Globe and Mail*, 23 April 2000.

18. Different interpretations of this exit from each side are summarised by Brooke Jeffrey (2010, 372–4).

19. It was reported that Martin had the backing of more than 100 MPs, 259 of the 301 riding (constituency) presidents, all provincial presidents, the presidents of the Young Liberals and all members of the national women's commission (*Toronto Star*, 7 March 2003).

20. A compelling study of the Canadian party system as a case of 'polarized pluralism' shows that outside Quebec the Liberals have dominated district-level three-party competition on a left–right ordering while on the national question they control a pole within each segment: the pro-Quebec pole outside Quebec and the pro-Canada pole inside Quebec. (Johnston, 2008).

6   Non-Majoritarian Democracies: Centrifugal Italy and Consensual Japan

1. Lijphart identifies ten interrelated elements of the consensus model: executive power-sharing in broad coalition cabinets, executive–legislative balance of power, multiparty system, proportional representation, interest group corporatism, federal and decentralised government, strong bicameralism, constitutional rigidity, judicial review, central bank independence.

2. In a 1991 referendum 95.6 per cent of voters voted to reduce the number of preference votes to one following a campaign headed by DC reformer Mario Segni to reduce corruption.
3. Not allowed to take the list of candidate names into the polling booth voters had to memorise the names or numbers of candidates they wished to support. This created opportunities for elite ballot manipulation afterwards when names or list numbers of individual candidates could be added on ballot papers.
4. Judith Chubb provides an insightful and empirical analysis of this phenomenon in the cities of Palermo and Naples (Chubb, 1982).
5. The new system, first used in 1996, combined 300 single-member plurality seats and 200 PR seats (later changed to 180) elected from 11 regional districts.
6. According to Katz access to and support by the press was 'controlled by a limited number of leaders with direct partisan interests'. Many DC factions had their own newspapers and press agencies and DC leaders controlled periodicals or press agencies such as *Politico*, *Forze Libere* or *RADAR* while interest or business groups controlled such dailies as *Il Giorno* or the Vatican's *Ossevatore Romano*.
7. The Council of Ministers described by Prime Minister Emilio Colombo in *The Economist* (26 June 1993).
8. Kohno provides a detailed analysis of the interparty bargaining leading to the merger of the Liberals and the Democrats (Kohno, 1997: Chapter 5).
9. The Standing Orders were changed in 1988 to avoid members of the legislature (safeguarded by the secret ballot) defeating government policy after supporting the government in the confidence vote (Huber, 1996: 195).
10. The average of newly elected DC deputies for all post-war elections after 1953 was 28 per cent, compared to 36.1 per cent for the Socialists and 41.3 per cent for the Communists (Guadagnini, 1984: 138) and half the DC's turnover was due to losses in intraparty battles for preference votes (Wertman, 1988: 151).
11. *Panachage* allowed small quota of seats to be shared among members of several small factions (Leonardi and Wertman, 1989).
12. The '55 system' is a 'catch all' label used to describe Japanese politics and policy under LDP single-party rule prior to the 1994 electoral reform.
13. In 2002, the LDP president's term of office was increased from two to three years.
14. Kishi handed the job to Ikeda, who in turn passed it to Sato. But Sato didn't appoint anyone on retirement (van Wolferen, 1989: 139).
15. Percentage figures of 'leap-frog' promotions to all first-time ministerial promotions indicate that there were no 'leap-frog' promotions during the 1980s. However, this ratio was as high as 31 per cent during the 1950s (Kohno, 1997: 98–9).

7 Case 3 – Italy's Christian Democrats: How Factional Capture Bred Self-Destruction

1. The faction was named after the Vespa motor scooter Club in Rome where they first met.

2. The distribution of factional strength on the NC is based on data from J.P. Chasseriaud (1965), *Le Parti Démocratique Chrétien en Italie* (Cahiers de la Fondation Nationale des Sciences Politiques – Partis et Elections), p. 335. These scores are estimates as faction membership was very fluid and unofficial before the party officially adopted a proportional system of representation in 1964.

3. The PSDI had split from the PSI in 1947.

4. In councils of communes with more than 10,000 people, the party alliance holding a plurality of votes was awarded two-thirds of the seats allowing the DC to capture left-controlled cities such as Turin, Florence, Venice, Milan and Genoa. In provincial councils, two-thirds of the seats were awarded to the list gaining a simple majority of votes.

5. According to the Electoral Reform Law ('swindle law'), violently opposed by both Communists and Socialists, only 57,000 more votes were needed to award the party or group of parties on a single list winning 50 per cent $+1$ of total votes, 2/3 of the seats in the Chamber.

6. Senior politicians Segni, Colombo, Taviani and Cossiga did not defect because, in the vote for the new Party Directorate, Rumor who was Vice-Secretary had no choice but to back Fanfani. Moro was absent due to illness and a number of councillors had decided to cast blank votes (Giovagnoli, 1996: 85–6).

7. In July 1960 Fanfani returned to office for the third time as prime minister heading two consecutive governments in July 1960–June 1963 and briefly for a fifth time in 1982.

8. It was named after the Convent of St. Dorothea where the DC national council met in March 1959 to discuss governing formula which split the Fanfani faction.

9. PSI dissidents formed a third socialist party – the Italian Socialist Party of Proletarian Unity (PSIUP).

10. In 1969, a regional congress inserted between the provincial and national congresses gained responsibility for electing national congress delegates. The preferential vote (banned in 1966) was reinstated allowing preference votes to be cast within factional lists.

11. Prime Minister Andreotti briefly reinstated the centrist formula to appease neo-fascist MSI after they won 8.7 per cent of the popular vote at the 1972 general election.

12. Minimum thresholds would prevent factions with less than 10 per cent support (later raised to 15 per cent) from gaining representation at provincial and regional congresses. The NC also tried to reintroduce the majority premium for National Congress delegate selection giving any faction or factional block with 54 per cent delegate support 64 per cent of NC seats.

13. One scandal involved the US government's financing of the DC. Another involved the payment of bribes by American aircraft company Lockheed to Italian and Japanese politicians implicating DC leaders Rumor and Luigi Gui and Social Democrat Mario Tanassi.

14. At the 1975 regional and local government elections the Left polled 47 per cent of the votes. The Communists' popular vote increased by 5.1 per cent since 1972 putting them 2 per cent behind the DC.

15. First elected MP in Italy's Constituent Assembly, Zaccagnini held many key posts including Minister of Labour and Public Works, President of the DC national council and DC parliamentary group in the National Assembly during the 'opening to the left'.

16. Applying the concept of a 'dominant' party in interparty coalitions (Laver and Shepsle, 1996 and Laver and Kato, 1998) to the intraparty arena, a dominant faction exists if the second- and third-largest factions are each large enough to form a majority coalition with the largest faction, but are too small to form a majority coalition with each other. The second and third-largest factions can then be played off against each other by the dominant faction in bargaining games. Alternatively, a 'dominant' faction can be identified by looking for the largest faction and then for the smallest of the remaining factions with which the largest faction can form a majority. If the second-largest faction cannot form a winning coalition with this smaller faction, then the largest faction is a 'dominant' faction.

17. Gorrieri was the author of '*la giungla retributiva*' – a critique of civil service fragmentation.

18. There is no English equivalent of the *tessitore*, the politician who knows how to weave together a political alliance, because British and American parties dissolve less easily into factions.' (McCarthy, 1997: 10).

19. The extreme right were held responsible for explosions at Bologna station in August 1980 causing 85 deaths and on the Naples–Milan express train in December 1984 causing 15 deaths and 116 injuries.

20. In May 1982 Roberto Calvi was found hanging from the scaffolding of London's Blackfriars Bridge. Investigations leading to a final trial in March 1985 revealed hundreds of prominent figures were involved including cabinet ministers, MPs and politicians from all parties (except PCI and Radical Party), army personnel, industrialists (including Silvio Berlusconi), bankers, magistrates, editors, civil servants and the Secret Services.

21. However, shortly after, Donat-Cattin was forced to resign due to a scandal involving his son who had flown the country to avoid arrest for terrorism.

22. De Mita epitomised best-selling American author Tom Wolff's 'radical chic' (Galli; 1993: 337).

23. In February Craxi finally resigned as PSI leader after 17 years later escaping to his Tunisian villa to evade the law.

8 Case 4 – The Liberal Democratic Party of Japan (1955–2009): End of Hegemony

1. Pre-war political parties contained factions under both SNTV (1918–25) and the single-member district system (1900–17 and 1925–38) and in the early post-war years, but they differed in fundamental ways (Krauss and Pekkanen, 2011: 106–7).

2. There were four leaders from each camp: former Democrats Nobusuke Kishi, Ichiro Kohno, Takeo Miki and Tanzan Ishibashi, and former Liberals Hayato Ikeda, Eisaku Sato, Banboku Kohno and Mitsujiro Ishii.

3. Up until the 1980s Japan relied on the United States for its economic prosperity and military security. Managing Japan's relationship with the United States was the prime minister's responsibility, explaining why in 1960 Prime Minister Nobusuke Kishi stepped down (in favour of Hayato Ikeda) following mass riots against the signature of the US–Japan Security Treaty.

4. Democratic leader Ishibashi was the only prime minister who was not from the largest faction.

5. In 1957–74 the negative relationship between N_f and BNZ_{f1} was strong as the two variables moved in opposite directions ($R = -0.98$ and $R_2 = 0.96$) compared to 1957–2000 when the correlation coefficient was -0.07 ($R_2 = 0.005$). In 1979–2000 only 33 per cent of the variation in the dominant faction's pivotal power could be explained by the change in the number of factions.

6. In 1973–91 economic growth rates in Japan were half what they had been in 1955–73.

7. Yōhei Kōno was Chief Cabinet Secretary in 1992–93, president of the LDP (in opposition) in 1993–95, Deputy Prime Minister in 1994–95, Minister of Foreign Affairs in 1994–96 and 1999–2000 as well as Speaker of the House of Representatives in 2003–09.

8. They were Abe Shintaro, heir apparent to the Fukuda faction, and Komoto Toshio, the leader of the Miki faction.

9. For a compelling account of Tanaka's resignation, see Takako Kishima (1991) *Political Life in Japan: Democracy in a Reversible World* (Princeton, NJ: Princeton University Press) 57–76.

10. In 1950–90, Japan's gross national product (GNP) rates per head (at 1990 prices) averaged 7.7 per cent compared to 1.9 per cent in the United States and 1 per cent in the United Kingdom.

11. Yamaguchi Toshio got the labour portfolio. Kōno who had been reappointed NLC leader in 1984 was put in charge of the Science Technology Agency.

12. Rengō (Japanese Trade Union Confederation) and particularly Keidanren (Japan Federation of Economic Organizations) refused to provide funds to the party factions (Otake, 1996: 272).

13. A bill is blocked if the House of Councillors rejects it unless the House of Representatives passes it again by a two-thirds majority (this rule doesn't apply to the budget and prime ministerial investiture).

14. In 1956, the Hatoyama government proposed a single-member system involving 455 single-seat districts and 21 two-member districts. In 1973, the Tanaka government proposed a mixed system involving 310 single-member districts and 210 PR seats.

15. Otake (1996) provides a comprehensive account of the internal forces pushing reform from 1988 to 1993, including the setting up by young reformers of various organisations and committees.

16. A couple of years earlier Miyasawa had resigned as finance minister in the wake of the Recruit scandal.

17. Hashimoto's resignation followed revelations that tax evasion had enabled securities dealers to cover up reimbursements to favoured clients who had suffered investment losses.

18. In his book *Shadow Shoguns: The Rise And Fall Of Japan's Post-War Political Machine* (Simon & Schuster), Jacob Schlesinger recounts that Tanaka didn't even bother to arrange dummy Kyubin stock deals, taking delivery through his front door of a trolley cart containing ¥500 (then worth $3.5 million).

19. First appointed to cabinet by Nakasone in 1985 Ozawa served as vice secretary of the Takeshita faction and became LDP General Secretary in 1989 at the age of 47. He was regarded as a future prime minister but had to resign in 1991 after the LDP's defeat in the Tokyo gubernatorial election when the LDP incumbent lost by a 2–1 margin.

20. Kato (1998) explains the split through Hirschman's 'exit and voice' model analysing the behaviour of LDP and SDP Diet members during the parliamentary debates over corruption, political reform, policies and party management.

21. The NFP was split between the Ozawa faction, the Hata/Hosokawa faction and Diet members linked to the Soka Gakkai (a Buddhist movement with deep pockets). Fifty-four NFP members quit to form the DPJ.

22. 'The sun also rises' by Bill Emmott (*The Economist*, 6 October 2005).

Bibliography

Allum P.A. (1973) *Italy – Republic without Government* (New York and London: W.W. Norton and Company).

Allum P.A. (1995) 'The Changing Face of Christian Democracy', in Duggan C. and C. Wagstaff, eds., *Italy in the Cold War: Politics, Culture and Society 1948–58* (Oxford, Washington: Berg).

Allum P.A. (1997) 'From Two into One: The Faces of the Italian Christian Democratic Party', *Party Politics* 3(1): 23–52.

Almond G. and Verba S. (1963) *The Civic Culture* (Princeton: Princeton University Press).

Alt J. and Shepsle K. eds. (1990) *Perspectives on Positive Political Economy* (Cambridge MA: Cambridge University Press).

Anderson G.E. (2004) 'Lionheart or Paper Tiger? A First-Term Koizumi Retrospective', *Asian Perspective* 28(1): 149–82.

Andrews J. T. (2002) *When Majorities Fail: The Russian Parliament 1990–1993* (Cambridge MA: Cambridge University Press).

Arian A. and Barnes S.H. (1974) 'The Dominant Party System: A Neglected Model of Democratic Stability', *The Journal of Politics* 36: 592–614.

Ashford N. (1980) 'The European Economic Community' in Layton-Henry Z., ed., *Conservative Party Politics*, pp. 95–125 (London, Basingstoke, Delhi, Dublin, Hong Kong, Johannesburg, Lagos, Melbourne, New York, Singapore, Tokyo: Macmillan).

Aucoin P. ed. (1985) *Party Government and Regional Representation in Canada* (Toronto: University of Toronto Press).

Aughey A. (1996) Chapters 5 'Philosophy and faction' and 13 'The party and foreign policy', in Norton P. ed., *The Conservative Party* (London, NY Toronto, Sydney, Tokyo, Singapore, Madrid, Mexico City, Munich: Prentice Hall Harvester Wheatsheaf).

Austen-Smith D. and Banks J.S. (1988) 'Elections, Coalitions, and Legislative Outcomes', *American Political Science Review* 82: 405–22.

Axelrod R. (1984) *The Evolution of Cooperation* (New York: Basic Books, Inc. Publishers).

Axworthy T. (1991) 'The Government Party in Opposition: Is the Liberal Century Over?', in Thorburn H. ed., *Party Politics in Canada* (Scarborough, ON: Prentice Hall Canada).

Baerwald H.H. (1986) *Party Politics in Japan* (Boston: Allen & Unwin).

Baget B.G. (1974) Il partito cristiano al potere: la DC di De Gasperi e di Dossetti, 1945–54 Vols. 1 and 2 (Firenze: Valleschi).

Baget B. G. (1977) *Il partito cristiano e l'apertura a sinistra* (Florence: Valleschi).

Baker D., Gamble A. and Ludlam S. (1993a) 'Whips or Scorpions? The Maastricht Vote and the Conservative Party', *Parliamentary Affairs* 46(2): 151–66.

Baker D., Gamble A. and Ludlam S. (1993b) '1846...1906...1996? Conservative Splits and European Integration', *Parliamentary Affairs* 46(2): 151–66.

Baker D., Gamble A. and Ludlam S. (1994) 'The Parliamentary Siege of Maastricht 1993: Conservative Divisions and British Ratification', *Parliamentary Affairs* 47(1): 37–60.

Baker D., Gamble A. and Ludlam S. (1995) 'Sovereignty – The San Andreas Fault of Conservative Ideology?' paper given at the *Political Science Association of the UK* Annual Conference in York.

Baker D., Gamble A., Ludlam S. and Seawright D. (1999), 'Backbenchers with Attitude: A Seismic Study of the Conservative Party and Dissent on Europe', in Bowler S., Farrell D. and Katz R., eds., *Party Discipline and Parliamentary Government* (Michigan: Ohio State University).

Banks J.S. (1991) *Signalling Games in Political Science* (London: Harwood).

Banzhaf J. (1965) 'Weighted Voting Doesn't Work: A Mathematical Analysis', *Rutgers Law Review* 19: 317–43.

Barnes J. (1994) 'Ideology and Factions', in Seldon A. and Ball S., eds., *Conservative Century: The Conservative Party Since 1900* (Oxford: Oxford University Press).

Barnes S. and Sani G. (1974) 'Mediterranean Political Culture and Italian Politics: and Interpretation', *British Journal of Political Science* July 1974: 289–303.

Barzini L. (1984) *The Europeans* (London: Penguin Books).

Beattie A. (1995) 'Ministerial Responsibility and the Theory of the British State', in Rhodes R.A.W. and Dunleavy P., eds., *Prime Ministers, Cabinet and Core Executive*, pp. 158–78 (New York: St. Martin's Press).

Beer S.H. (1965) *Modern British Politics: A Study of Parties and Pressure Groups* (London: Faber and Faber).

Belloni F. and Beller D. (1978) *Faction Politics: Political Parties and Factionalism in Comparative Perspectives* (Santa Barbara, Oxford: ABC-Clio Inc.).

Berrington H. (1980) 'The Common Market and the British Parliamentary Parties, 1971: Tendencies, Issue Groups...and Factionalism', Paper presented at *ECPR workshop* on Factionalism, Florence, March 25–29, 1980.

Berrington H. (1985) 'MPs and Their Constituents in Britain: The History of the Relationship' in Bogdanor V., ed., *Representatives of the People? Parliamentarians and Constituents in Western Democracies* (Gower: Cambridge).

Berrington H. (1998) 'Britain in the Nineties: The Politics of Paradox', *West European Politics* 21(1): 1–27.

Berrington H. and Hague Rod R. (1995) 'A Treaty Too Far? Opinion, Rebellion and the Maastricht Treaty in the Backbench Conservative Party 1992–94; Paper presented at the *Political Studies Association* Annual Conference, York University, England, April 18–20, 1995.

Berringon H. and Hague R. (1998) 'Europe, Thatcherism and Traditionalism: Opinion, Rebellion, and the Maastricht Treaty in the Backbench Conservative Party, 1992–94, *West European Politics* 21(1): 44–71.

Bibes G. and Besson J. (1989) 'The Resurgence of Christian Democracy and the Search for "New Rules of the Game"', *Italian Politics: A Review* 3, pp. 92–106 (London: Pinter).

Biffen J. (1989) *Inside the House of Commons* (London: Grafton).

Birch A.H. (1975) 'Economic Models in Political Science: The Case of Exit, Voice, and Loyalty', *British Journal of Political Science* 5(1): 69–82.

Blair T. (2010) *A Journey* (London: Hutchinson).

Blais A. (2005) 'Accounting for the Electoral Success of the Liberal Party in Canada', *Canadian Journal of Political Science* 38(4): 821–40.

Blais A. and Carty R.K. (1987) 'The Impact of Electoral Formulae on the Creation of Majority Governments', *Electoral Studies* 6(3): 209–18.

Blais A. and Carty R.K. (1991) 'The Psychological Impact of Electoral Laws: Measuring Duverger's Elusive Factor', *British Journal of Political Science* 21(1): 79–93.

Blais A. and Gidengil E. (1991) *Making Representative Government Work: The Views of Canadians* (Toronto: Dundurn Press).

Blake D.E. (1985) *Two Political Worlds: Parties and Voting in British Columbia* (Vancouver: UBC Press).

Blake D. (1987a) 'Division and Cohesion: The Major Parties', in Perlin G., ed., *Party Democracy in Canada: The Politics of National Party Conventions*, pp. 32–53 (Scarborough, ON: Prentice Hall).

Blake D. (1987b) 'Division and Cohesion: The Major Parties', in Perlin G., ed., *Party Democracy in Canada: The Politics of National Party Conventions* (Scarborough, ON: Prentice Hall).

Blake R. (1998) *The Conservative Party from Peel to Major* (Arrow Books).

Blick A. and George J. (2010) *Premiership: The Development, Nature and Power of the Office of the British Prime Minister* (Exeter: Imprint Academic and Charlottesville USA; Societas Imprint Academic).

Blondel J. (1968) 'Party Systems and Patterns of Government in Western Democracies', *Canadian Journal of Political Science* 1/2: 180–203.

Blondel J. (1973) *Comparative Legislatures* (Englewood Cliffs: Prentice Hall).

Blondel J. and Rommel M. eds. (1993), *Governing Together: The Extent and Limits of Joint Decision-Making in Western European Cabinets* (New York: St. Martin's Press).

Bogaards M. and Boucek F. eds. (2010) *Dominant Political Parties and Democracy: Concepts, Measures, Cases and Comparisons* (Abingdon, NY: Routledge).

Boissevain J. (1966) 'Patronage in Sicily' *Man* Oct. 1966: 18–33.

Borisyuk G., Johnston R., Rallings C. and Thrasher M. (2010a) 'Parliamentary Constituency Boundary Reviews and Electoral Bias: How Important Are Variations in Constituency Size?', *Parliamentary Affairs* 63(1): 4–21.

Borisyuk G., Johnston R., Thrasher M. and Rallings C. (2010b) 'A method for measuring and decomposing electoral bias for the three-party case, illustrated by the British case', *Electoral Studies* 29(4) 733–745.

Boucek F. (1991), 'Party Adaptation, Ideological Groups and Policy-Formulation by the British Conservative Party in the 1980s' Unpublished MSc. dissertation London School of Economics and Political Science.

Boucek F. (1993) 'Developments in Postwar French Political Economy: The Continuing Decline of Dirigisme?' in Sheldrake J. and Webb P., eds., *State And Market: Aspects of Modern European Development* (Aldershot, Brookfield USA, Hong Kong, Singapore, Sydney: Darmouth).

Boucek F. (1998) 'Electoral and Parliamentary Aspects of Dominant Party Systems', in Pennings P. and Erik Lane Jan., eds., *Comparing Party System Change*, pp. 103–24 (London and New York: Routledge).

Boucek F. (2001) *The Growth and Management of Factionalism in Long-Lived Dominant Parties: Comparing Britain, Italy, Canada and Japan* (Unpublished PhD Thesis, London School of Economics and Political Science).

Boucek F. (2002) 'The Structure and Dynamics of Intra-Party Politics in Europe' in Lewis P. and Webb P., eds., *Pan-European Perspectives on Party Politics*, pp. 55–95 (Brill: Leiden, Boston, Köln).

Boucek F. (2003) 'Managing Factional Conflict under Severe Constraints: John Major and British Conservatives 1992–1997', Paper presented at the Political Studies Association Annual Conference, Leicester, England April 16, 2003.

Boucek F. (2009) 'Rethinking Factionalism: Typologies, Intra-Party Dynamics and Three Faces of Factionalism' *Party Politics* 15(4): 455–85.

Boucek F. (2010a) 'The Intra-Party Dimension of Dominance' in Bogaards M. and Boucek F., eds., *Dominant Parties and Democracy: Concepts, Measures, Cases and Comparisons*, pp. 109–15 (Abingdon, NY: Routledge).

Boucek F. (2010b) 'The Factional Politics of Dominant Parties: Evidence from Britain, Italy and Japan' in Bogaards M. and Boucek F., eds., *Dominant Political Parties and Democracy: Concepts, Measures, Cases and Comparisons*, pp. 117–39 (Abingdon, NY: Routledge).

Boucek F. (2010c), 'The Least Worst Option? The Pros and Cons of Coalition Government', *Political Insight*, pp. 48–51 (Oxford: Blackwell Publishing).

Boucek F. and Dunleavy P. (2003) 'Constructing the Number of Parties', *Party Politics* 9(3): 291–315.

Bowler S., Farrell D. and Katz R. eds. (1999) *Party Discipline and Parliamentary Government* (Columbus: Ohio State University).

Brady D. and Bullock C. (1985) 'Party and Factions within Legislatures', in Lovenberg G., Patterson S., and Jewell M.E., eds., *Handbook of Legislative Research* (Cambridge MA: Harvard University Press).

Brady D., Cooper J. and Hurley P. (1979) 'The Decline of Party in the House?', *Journal of Politics* 42: 549–59.

Brams S. (1985) *Rational Politics: Decisions, Games, and Strategy* (Boston: Harcourt Brace Jovanovich).

Brams S. (1994) *Theory of Moves* (New York, Melbourne: Cambridge University Press).

Brand J. (1989) 'Faction as Its Own Reward: Groups in the British Parliament 1945 to 1985', *Parliamentary Affairs* 42/2: 148–65.

Breton A. and Galeotti G. (1985) 'Is Proportional Representation Always the Best Rule?', *Public Finance* 10(1): 1–16.

Brodie M.J. and J. Jenson (1989) 'Piercing the Smokescreen: Brokerage Parties and Class Politics' in Gagnon A.G. and Tanguay A.B., eds., *Canadian Parties in Transition: Discourse, Organization and Representation* (Scarborough, ON: Nelson Canada).

Brooke J. (2010) *Divided Loyalties: The Liberal Party of Canada, 1984–2008* (Toronto, Buffalo, London: University of Toronto Press).

Broughton D. and Donovan M. eds. (1999) *Changing Party Systems in Western Europe* (London and New York: Pinter).

Buchanan J.M. and Tullock G. (1962) *Calculus of Consent* (Ann Arbor: University of Michigan Press).

Budge I. (1985) 'Party Factions and Government Reshuffles: A General Hypothesis Tested Against Data from 20 Post-war Democracies', *European Journal of Political Research* 13: 327–34.

Budge I. (1998) 'Great Britain: A Stable but Fragile Party System?' in Pennings P. and Lane J-E., eds., *Comparing Party System Change*, pp. 125–36 (London and New York: Routledge).

Budge I. and Farlie D.J. (1977) *Voting and Party Competition* (London and New York: Wiley).

Budge I. and Keman H. (1990) *Parties and Democracy: Coalition Formation and Government Functioning in 20 States* (New York: Oxford University Press).

Budge I., Robertson D. and Hearl D. eds. (1987) *Ideology, Strategy and Party Change: Spatial Analyses of Post-War Election Programmes in 19 Democracies* (Cambridge: Cambridge University Press).

Bufacchi V. (1996) 'The Success of "Mani Pulite": Luck or Skill?', in Leonardi R. and Nanetti R.Y., eds., *Italy: Politics and Policy* Vol. 1, pp. 189–210 (Dartmouth: Aldershot, Brookfield USA, Singapore, Sydney).

Bull M. and Rhodes M. (1997a) *Crisis and Transition in Italian Politics*, a special issue of *West European Politics* 20 (London: Frank Cass).

Bull M. and Rhodes M. (1997b) 'Between Crisis and Transition. Italian Politics in the 1990s', in Bull M. and Rhodes M., eds., *Crisis and Transition in Italian Politics,* a special issue of *West European Politics*, Vol. 20, pp. 1–13 (London: Frank Cass).

Burch M. (1980) 'Approaches to Leadership in Opposition: Edward Heath and Margaret Thatcher' in Layton-Henry Z., ed., *Conservative Party Politics* (London & Basingstoke: Macmillan).

Burnett S.H. and Mantovani L. (1998) *The Italian Guillotine: Operation Clean Hands and the Overthrow of Italy's First* Republic (Lanham, Boulder, New York, Oxford: Rowman and Littlefield Publishers, Inc.).

Busteed M.A. (1990), *Voting Behaviour in the Republic of Ireland: A Geographical Perspective* (Oxford: Clarendon Press).

Butler, D. and Butler G. (994) *British Political Facts 1900–1994*, 7th ed. (Macmillan: London).

Caciagli M. (1990) 'The 18th DC Congress: from De Mita to Forlani and the Victory of "Neodoroteism" ', in Cattaneo I., Sabetti F. and Catanzano R. eds. *Italian Politics: A Review*, Vol. 5, pp. 8–22 (London, New York: Pinter Publishers).

Caciagli M. and Spreafico A. (1975) *Un systema politico all a prova, Studi sulle elezioni politiche del 1972* (Bologna: Il Mulino).

Caciagli M. and Spreafico A. (1990), A *cura di, Vent'anni di elezioni in Italia 1968– 1987* (Padova: Liviana Editrice).

Campaign Information Ltd. (1987–91 and 1992–93), *Conservative Dissent and Labour Party Dissent* (Campaign Information Ltd. Minard House, 20 Norhill Road, Ickwell Green, Biggleswade, Bedforshire, SG18 9ED).

Campbell J.(2000), *Margaret Thatcher: The Grocer's Daughter* (London: Jonathan Cape).

Carty R.K. (1991) 'Three Canadian Party Systems: An Interpretation of the Development of National Politics', in Carty R.K., ed., *Party Politics in Canada* (Scarborough, ON: Prentice-Hall Canada).

Carty R.K. ed. (1992) *Canadian Political Party Systems: A Reader* (Peterborough, Ont.: Broadview Press).

Carty R.K. (2002) 'Canada's Nineteenth-Century Cadre Parties at the Millennium', in Webb P., Farrell D. and Holliday I., eds., *Political Parties in Advanced Industrial Democracies* (Oxford: Oxford University Press).

Carty R.K. (2010) 'Dominance without Factions: The Liberal Party of Canada', in Bogaards M. and Boucek F., eds., *Dominant Political Parties and Democracy: Concepts, Measures, Cases and Comparisons*, pp. 140–52 (Abingdon, NY: Routledge).

Carty R.k. and Blake D. (1999) 'The Adoption of Membership Votes for Choosing Party Leaders: The Experience of Canadian Parties, *Party Politics* 5(2): 211–24.

Carty R.K., Cross W. and Young L. (2000) *Rebuilding Canadian Party Politics* (Vancouver: UBC Press).

Cazzola F. (1972a) 'Partiti, correnti e Voto di preferenza', in Caciagli M. and Spreafico A., eds., *Un sistema politico alla prova* (studi sulle elezioni politiche italiane del 1972 pp. 127–51 (Bologna: Societa Editrice Il Mulino).

Cazzola F. (1972b), 'Consenso e Opposizione nel Parlamento Italiano. Il Ruolo del PCI dall I alla IV Legislatura', *Rivista Italiana di Scienza Politica* 2 (1972).

Cazzola F. (1974), *Governo e opposizione nel parlamento italiano* (Milano: Giuffrè).

Ceccanti S. (1993) 'Nessuna Falcidia: I giovani, le donne e l'elettora razionale' in Pasquino G., ed., *Votare Un Solo Candidato: Le Consequenze politiche della preferenza unica* (Bologna: Il Mulino).

Chasseriaud J.P. (1965), *Le Parti Démocratique Chrétien en Italie*, Cahiers de la Fondation Nationale des Sciences Politiques (Paris: Librairie Armand Colin).

Cheng T-j (2008) 'Embracing defeat: The KMT and the PRI after 2000' in Friedman E. and Wong J., eds., *Political Transitions in Dominant Party Systems: Learning to Lose* pp. 127–47 (Abingdon, UK, and New York, USA: Routledge).

Chong D. (1991) *Collective Action and the Civil Rights Movement* (Chicago: The University of Chicago Press).

Chrétien J. (1985) *Straight from the Heart* (Toronto: Key Porter Books).

Christenden R. (1996) 'Strategic Imperatives of Japan's SNTV Electoral System and the Cooperative Innovations of the Former Opposition Parties', *Comparative Political Studies* 29(3): 312–34.

Christensen R. (2000) *Ending the LDP Hegemony: Party Cooperation in Japan* (Honolulu: University of Hawaï Press).

Christensen R. (2006) 'An Analysis of the 2005 Japanese General Election: Will Koizumi's Political Reforms Endure?' *Asian Survey* 46(4): 497–516.

Chubb J. (1982) *Patronage, Power, and Poverty in Southern Italy – A Tale of Two Cities* (Cambridge, New York, New Rochelle, Melbourne and Sydney: Cambridge University Press).

Chubb J. (1986) 'The Christian Democratic Party: Reviving or Surviving?', in Leonardi R. and Nanetti R.Y., eds., *Italy: Politics and Policy* Vol. 1 (Aldershot, Brookfield USA, Singapore, Sydney: Dartmouth).

Clark A. (1993) *Diaries* (London: Phoenix).

Clark M. (1984) *Modern Italy 1971–1982* (Harlow UK: Longman Group Ltd).

Clark P. and Wilson J.Q. (1961), 'Incentive Systems: A Theory of Organisations', *Administrative Science Quarterly* 6: 129–66.

Clarke H., Jenson J., LeDuc L. and Pammett J. (1996) *Absent Mandate: Canadian Electoral Politics in an Era of Restructuring*, 3rd ed. (Vancouver: Gage).

Clarkson S. (1981) 'The Defeat of the Government, the Decline of the Liberal Party and the (Temporary) Fall of Pierre Trudeau', in Penniman H., ed., *Canada at the Polls, 1979 and 1980: A Study of the General Elections*, pp. 152–89 (Washington and London: American Enterprise Institute for Public Policy Research).

Clarkson S. (1988), 'The Dauphin and the Doomed: John Turner and the Liberal Party Debacle', in Penniman H.R., ed., *Canada at the Polls, 1984: A Study of the Federal General Elections*, pp. 97–120 (Washington and London: American Enterprise Institute for Public Policy Research).

Clarkson S. (2005) *The Big Red Machine: How the Liberal Party Dominates Canadian Politics* (Vancouver, Toronto: UBC Press).

Clokie H. (1950) *Canadian Government and Politics* (Toronto: Longmans).

Coase R. (1960) 'The Problem of Social Cost', *Journal of Law and Economics* 3: 1–44.

Colomer J.M. (1995) *Game Theory and the Transition to Democracy: The Spanish Model* (Aldershot, UK, and Brookfield, Vermont, USA: Edward Elgar).

Colomer J.M. (1996a) 'Measuring Parliamentary Deviation', *European Journal of Political Research* 30(1): 87–101.

Colomer J.M. ed. (1996b) *Political Institutions in Europe* (London and New York: Routledge).

Colomer J. and Martinez F. (1995) 'The Paradox of Coalition Trading', *Journal of Theoretical Politics* 7(1): 477–501.

Courtney J. (1988) 'Reinventing the Brokerage Wheel: The Tory Success in 1984' in Penniman H.R., ed., *Canada at the Polls, 1984: A Study of the Federal General Elections*, pp. 190–208 (Washington and London: American Enterprise Institute for Public Policy Research).

Cowley P. (1996a) 'How Did he Do That? The Second Round of the 1990 Conservative Leadership Election' *British Elections and Parties Yearbook* (London: Frank Cass).

Cowley P. (1996b) '111 Not Out: The Press and the 1995 Conservative Leadership Contest', *Talking Politics* 8: 187–90.

Cowley P. (1999) 'The Absence of War? New Labour in Parliament', in Fisher J., Cowley P., Denver D. and Russell A., eds., *British Elections and Parties Review* 9: 154–69 (London and Portland Oregon: F. Cass).

Cowley P. (2002) *Revolts and Rebellions: Parliamentary Voting under Blair* (London: Politico's).

Cowley P. (2005) *The Rebels: How Blair Mislaid His Majority* (London: Politico's).

Cowley P. and Norton P. (1996), *Are Conservative MPs Revolting?* (Hull: University of Hull Centre for Legislative Studies).

Cowley P. and Stuart M. (1997) 'Sodomy, Slaughter, Sunday Shopping and Seatbelts; Free Votes in the House of Commons' *Party Politics* 3(1): 119–30.

Cox G. (1987) *The Efficient Secret: The Cabinet and the Development of Political Parties in Victorian England* (Cambridge: Cambridge University Press).

Cox G. (1997) *Making Votes Count: Strategic Coordination in the World's Electoral Systems* (Cambridge, New York, Melbourne: Cambridge University Press).

Cox G. and McCubbins M. (1993) *Legislative Leviathan: Party Government in the House* (Berkeley: University of California Press).

Cox G. and Niou E. (1994) 'Seat Bonuses Under the Single Non-Transferable Vote System: Evidence from Japan and Taiwan', *Comparative Politics* 26: 221–36.

Cox G. and Rosenbluth F. (1993) 'The Electoral Fortunes of Legislative Factions in Japan' *American Political Science Review* 87(3): 577–89.

Cox G. and Rosenbluth F. (1995) 'Anatomy of a Split: the Liberal Democrats of Japan', *Electoral Studies* 14(4): 355–76.

Cox G., Rosenbluth F. and Thies M.F. (1999), 'Electoral Reform and the Fate of Factions: The Case of Japan's Liberal Democratic Party', *British Journal of Political Science* 29(1): 33–56.

Cox G. and Shugart M. (1991) 'Comment on Gallagher's 'Proportionality, Disproportionality and Electoral Systems', in *Electoral Studies* No.10/1, pp. 348–52.

Curtice J. (1994) 'Why Do Conservatives Keep on Winning?' in Margetts H. and Smyth G., eds., *Turning Japanese? Britain with a Permanent Party of Government* (London: Lawrence & Wishart).

Curtice J. and Semetko H. (1994) 'Does It Matter What the Papers Say? in Heath A., Jowell R. and Curtice J., eds., *Labour's Last Chance? The 1992 Election and Beyond*, pp. 43–64 (Aldershot: Dartmouth).

Curtis G. (1988) *The Japanese Way of Politics* (New York: Columbia University Press).

Curtis G. (1999) *The Logic of Japanese Politics: Leaders, Institutions and the Limits of Change* (New York: Columbia University Press).

Cyert R.M. and J.G. March (1963) *Behavioral Theory of the Firm* (Englewood Cliffs, NJ: Prentice Hall Inc.).

Czada R. (1993) 'Institutional Difference, Concepts of Actors, and the Rationality of Politics', in Keman H., ed., *Comparative Politics: New Directions in Theory and Method* (Amsterdam: VU University Press).

Dahl R. (1966) *Political Oppositions in Western Democracies* (New Haven: Yale University Press)

D'Alimonte R. (1977) 'Sulla Teori della Democrazio Competitiva', *Rivista Italiana di Scienza Politica* 7: 3–26.

D'Alimonte R. and Mair P. (1998) 'The Italian Parliamentary Elections of 1996 – Competition and Transition', *The European Journal of Political Research,* Special issue (August 1998).

D'Amato L. (1964) *Il voto di preferenza in Italia* (Milan: Gruiffe).

D'Amato L. (1966) *L'equilibro in un sistema di partiti di correnti* (Rome: Edizioni di Scienza Sociali).

D'Amico R. (1990)'La fisionaomia dei partiti nel voto di preferenza' in Caciagli M. and Spreafico A., eds., *A cura di, Vent'anni di elezioni in Italia 1968*–1987 (Padova: Liviana Editrice).

Daniels P. (1999) 'Italy: Rupture or Regeneration?', in Broughton D. and Donovan M., eds., *Changing Party Systems in Western Europe*, pp. 71–95 (London and New York: Pinter).

D'Aquino T., Doern B. and Blair C. (1983) *Parliamentary Democracy in Canada: Issues for Reform* (Toronto, New York, London, Sydney, Auckland: Methuen).

Davidson R.H. (1969) *The Role of the Congressman* (Indianapolis: Bobbs-Merrill).

De Mesquita B. (1979) 'Parties Short Term and Long Term Utilities', *Comparative Political Studies* 12: 61–81.

Della Porta D. (1995) 'The Vicious Circle of Political Corruption in Italy', in della Porta D. and Mény Y., eds., *Political Corruption and Democracy* (London: Pinter).

Della Porta D. (1996) 'The System of Corrupt Exchange in Local Government', in Gundle S. and Parker S., eds., *The New Italian Republic: From the Fall of the Berlin Wall to Berlusconi* (London: Routledge).

Della Sala V. (1993) 'The Permanent Committees of the Italian Chamber of Deputies: Parliament at Work?' *Legislative Studies Quarterly* 18(2): 157–83.

De Micheli C. (1997) 'L'attività legislativa dei governi al tramonto della prima republica', *Rivista Italiana di Scienza Politica* XXVII(1): 151–87.

Denver D. (1988) 'Britain: Centralized Parties with Decentralized Selection', in Gallagher M. and Marsh D., eds., *Candidate Selection in Comparative Perspective: The Secret Garden of Politics* (London, Newbury Park, Beverly Hills, New Delhi: Sage Publications).

Diamanti I. and Mannheimer R. (1994) Milano a Roma: Guida all'Italia Elletorale del 1994 (XXX).

Di Palma G. (1977a) *Surviving without Governing: The Italian Parties in Parliament* (Berkeley, Los Angeles, London: University of California Press).

Di Palma G. (1977b) 'Christian Democracy: The End of Hegemony?', in Penninman H.R., ed., *Italy at the Polls: The Parliamentary Elections of 1976* (Washington DC: The American Enterprise Institute).

Di Palma G. (1990) 'Establishing Party Dominance: It Ain't Easy', in Pempel T.J., ed., *Uncommon Democracies: The One-Party Dominant Regimes* (Ithaca & London: Cornell University Press).

Docherty D. C. (1997) *Mr Smith Goes To Ottawa: Life in the House of Commons* (Vancouver: UBC Press)

Doern B.G. (2003) 'The Chrétien Liberals' Third Mandate', in *How Ottawa Spends: 2002–2003*, 3rd ed. (Don Mills: Oxford University Press).

Dogan M. ed. (1989a) *Pathways to Power: Selecting Rules in Pluralist Democracies* (Boulder, San Francisco and London: Westview Press).

Dogan M. (1989b) 'How to Become a Minister in Italy: Unwritten Rules of the Political Game', in Dogan M., ed., *Pathways to Power: Selecting Rules in Pluralist Democracies* (San Francisco and London: Westview Press).

Dogan M. and Kazanugil A. eds. (1994) *Comparing Nations: Concepts, Strategies, Substance* (Oxford: Blackwell).

Donovan M. (1991) 'Centre Domination and Party Competition: Christian Democratic Strategy in Italy 1943–89', (Doctoral Thesis submitted to the London School of Economics and Political Science).

Donovan M. (1995) 'The Politics of Electoral Reform in Italy', *International Political Science Review* 16: 47–64.

Donovan M. and Broughton D. (1999) 'Party System Change in Western Europe: Positively Political', in Broughton D. and Donovan M., eds., *Changing Party Systems in Western Europe*, pp. 255–74 (London, New York: Pinter).

Döring H. ed. (1995) *Parliaments and Majority Rule in Western Europe* (New York and Rankfurt: St. Martin's Press).

Dowding K. and Kimber R. (1987) 'Political Stability and the Science of Comparative Politics', *European Journal of Political Research* 15(1): 103–22.

Dowding K. (1991) *Rational Choice and Political Power* (Aldershot: Edward Elgar).

Dowding K. (1994a) 'Policy Networks: Don't Stretch a Good Idea Too Far', in Dunleavy P. and Stanyer J., eds., *Contemporary Political Studies 1994*, Vol. 1, pp. 59–78 (Belfast: Political Studies Association of the UK).

Dowding K. (1994b) 'The Compatibility of Behaviouralism, Rational Choice and New Institutionalism', *Journal of Theoretical Politics* 6(1): 105–17.

Dowding K., John P., Mergoupis T. and Van Vugt M. (2000) 'Exit, Voice and Loyalty: Analytic and Empirical Developments', *European Journal of Political Research* 37: 469–95.

Downs A. (1957) *An Economic Theory of Democracy* (New York: Harper and Row).

Draper D. (1997) *Blair's Hundred Days* (London: Faber and Faber).

Druckman J. (1996) 'Party Factionalism and Cabinet Durability', *Party Politics* 2(3): 397–407.

Dunleavy, P. (1991) *Democracy, Bureaucracy, and Public Choice* (New York, London, Toronto, Sydney, Tokyo, Singapore: Harvester Wheatsheaf).

Dunleavy P. (1994) 'The Core Executive Analytic Approaches to Developments Under Major', *Contemporary Political Studies* 1: 359–382 (Newcastle-upon-Tyne: Political Studies Association).

Dunleavy P. (1995) 'Reinterpreting the Westland Affair: Theories of the State and Core Executive Decision Making', in Rhodes M. and Dunleavy P., eds., *Prime Minister, Cabinet and Core Executive* (Basingstoke and London: St. Martin's Press).

Dunleavy P. (1996) 'Political Behaviour: Institutional and Experiential Approaches', in Goodin G. and Klingemann H.D., eds., *A New Handbook of Political Science*, pp. 276–93 (Oxford: Oxford University Press).

Dunleavy P. (2010) 'Rethinking Dominant Party Systems', in Bogaards M. and Boucek F., eds., *Dominant Political Parties and Democracy: Concepts, Measures, Cases and Comparisons*, pp. 23–44 (Abingdon, NY: Routledge).

Dunleavy P. and Boucek F. (2003) 'Constructing the Number of Parties', *Party Politics* 9(3): 291–315.

Dunleavy P., Gamble A. and Peele G. (1990) *Developments in British Politics* No 3 (Basingstoke and London: Macmillan).

Dunleavy P., Gamble A. and Peele G. (2000) *Developments in British Politics* No 6 (Basingstoke and London: Macmillan).

Dunleavy P. and Husbands C. (1985) *British Democracy at the Crossroads: Voting and Party Competition in the 1980s* (London: Allen and Unwin).

Dunleavy P. and Margetts H. (1993) 'Disaggregating Indices of Democracy: Deviation From Proportionality and Relative Reduction In Parties', Paper presented at the *ECPR Annual Workshops*; University of Leiden, 2–8 April, 1993.

Dunleavy P. and Margetts H. (1997) 'The Electoral System', *Britain Votes 1997* (New York: Oxford University Press).

Duverger M. (1964) *Political Parties: Their Organisation and Activity in the Modern State* (London: Methuen).

Eldersveld S.J. (1964) *Political Parties: A Behavioural Analysis* (Chicago: Ran McNally & Co.).

Eldersveld S.J. and Hardin R. (1982) *Collective Action* (Baltimore & London: The Johns Hopkins University Press – Resources for the Future).

Epstein L. (1980) *Political Parties in Western Democracies* (New York: Praeger).

Esping-Andersen G. ed. (1990) *The Three Worlds of Welfare Capitalism* (Cambridge: Polity).

Estévez Federico A.D.-C. and Magaloni B. (2008) 'A House Divided against Itself: The PRI's Survival Strategy after Hegemony' in Edward F. and Wong J., eds., *Political Transitions in Dominant Party Systems: Learning to Lose*, pp. 42–56 (Abingdon, UK, and New York, USA: Routledge).

Fabbrini S. (1994), *Quale democrazia* (Bologna: Il Mulino).

Farrell D.M. (1987) 'Campaign Strategies: The Selling of the Parties', in Laver M., Mair P. and Sinnot R., eds., *How Ireland Voted: The Irish General Election 1987* (Dublin: Poolbeg).

Farrell D.M. (1994) 'Ireland: Centralization, Professionalization and Competitive Pressures' in Katz R. and Mair P., eds., *How Parties Organize: Change and Adaptation in Party Organizations in Western Democracies*, pp. 216–41 (London, Southern Oaks, CA, New Delhi: Sage).

Farrell D.M. (1996) 'Campaign Strategies and Tactics', in Leduc L., Niemi P.R. and Norris P., eds., *Comparing Democracies: Elections and Voting in Global Perspective*, pp. 160–83 (Thousand Oaks, London, Delhi: Sage Publications).

Ferrero M. and Brosio G. (1997) 'Nomenklatura Rule Under Democracy: Solving the Italian Political Puzzle', *Journal of Theoretical Politics* 9(4): 445–75.

Ferrero M. and Brosio G. (1998) 'Rejoinder to Martelli', *Journal of Theoretical Politics* 10(2): 245–9.

Finkel S.E., Muller E. and Opp K.D. (1989) 'Personal Influence, Collective Rationality, and Mass Political Action', *American Political Science Review* 83: 885–903.

Flanagan T. (1998) *Game Theory and Canadian Politics* (Toronto, Buffalo, London: University of Toronto Press).

Follini M. (1990) *L'arcipelaga democrastiano* (Bari: Laterza).

Follini M. (1993) 'Christian Democracy: Extreme Remedies for Extreme Problems?', in Hellman S., Pasquino, eds., *Italian Politics: A Review*, Vol. 8, Istituto Cattaneo (London and New York: Pinter Publishers).

Franklin M., Baxter A. and Jordan M. (1986) 'Who Were the Rebels? Dissent in the House of Commons 1970–74', *Legislative Studies Quarterly* 11(2): 143–59.

Franks C.E.S. (1987) *The Parliament of Canada* (Toronto: University of Toronto Press).

Friedman E. and Wong J. eds. (2008) *Political Transitions in Dominant Party Systems: Learning to Lose* (Abingdon, UK, and New York, USA: Routledge).

Fukui H. (1970) *Party in Power: The Japanese Liberal Democrats and Policy Making* (Berkeley and Los Angeles: University of California Press).

Fukui H. (1985) *Political Parties in Asia and the Pacific* (The Greenwood Historical Encyclopedia of the world's political parties).

Furlong P. (1994) *Modern Italy: Representation and Reform* (London and New York: Routledge).

Gagnon A. and Tanguay A. eds. (1989) *Canadian Parties in Transition: Discourse, Organization and Representation* (Scarborough, ON: Nelson Canada).

Gagnon A. and Tanguay A. eds. (1996) *Canadian Parties in Transition*, 2nd ed. (Scarborough, ON: Nelson Canada).

Gallagher M. (1975) 'Disproportionality in a Proportional Representation System: The Irish Experience', *Political Studies* 23: 501–13.

Gallagher M. (1985) *Political Parties in the Republic of Ireland* (Manchester: Manchester University Press).

Gallagher M. (1988) 'Ireland, the Increasing Role of the Centre', in Gallagher M. and Marsh M., eds., *Candidate Selection in Comparative Perspective: The Secret Garden of Politics*, pp. 119–44 (London and Newbury Park: Sage).

Gallagher M. (1991) 'Proportionality, Disproportionality and Electoral Systems' *Electoral Studies* 1: 33–51.

Gallagher M. (1998) 'The Political Impact of Electoral System Change in Japan and New Zealand, 1996', *Party Politics* 4(2): 203–28.

Gallagher M., Laver M. and Mair P. eds. (1995) *Representative Government in Modern Europe*, 2nd ed. (New York, St. Louis, San Francisco, Auckland, Bogota, Caracas, Lisbon, London, Madrid, Mexico City, Milan, Montreal, New Delhi, San Juan, Singapore, Sydney, Tokyo, Toronto: McGraw-Hill Inc.).

Gallagher M. and Marsh M. eds. (1988) *Candidate Selection in Comparative Perspective: The Secret Garden of Politics* (London and Newbury Park: Sage).

Galli G. (1967) *Il bipartitismo imperfetto: Communisti e democrastiani in Italia* (Bologna: Il Mulino).

Galli G. (1968) *Il comportamento elettorale in Italia* (Bologna: Il Mulino).

Galli G. (1975a) *Dal bipartitismo imperfetto alla possibile alternativa* (Bologna: Il Mulino).

Galli G. (1975b) *Fanfani* (Milan: Feltrinelli).

Galli G. (1978) *Storia della Democrazia Cristiana* (Roma Bari: Editori Laterza).

Galli G. (1993) *Mezzo secolo di Dc* (Milano: Rizzoli).

Galli G. and Facchi P. (1962) *La Sinistra Democristiana: Storia e ideologice* (Milano: Feltrinelli).

Galli G. and Prandi A. (1970) *Patterns of Political Participation in Italy* (New Haven, CT: Yale University Press).

Gamble A. (1974) *The Conservative Nation* (London: Routledge).

Gamble A. (1988) *The Free Economy and the Strong State. The Politics of Thatcherism* (London: Macmillan).

Garret G., McLean I. and Machover M. (1995) 'Power, Power Indices and Blocking Power: A Comment on Johnston' *British Journal of Political Science* 25: 563–8.

Garry J. (1995) 'The British Conservative Party: Divisions over European Policy' *West European Politics* 18: 170–89.

Geddes A. (1997), 'Europe: Major's Nemesis?', in Geddes A. and Tongue J., eds., *Labour's Landslide: The British General Election of 1997* (Manchester: Manchester University Press).

Gerring J. and Thacker S.C. (2008) *A Centripetal Theory of Democratic Governance* (Cambridge, New York, Melbourne, Madrid, Cape Town, Singapore, São Paulo, Delhi: Cambridge University Press).

Giannetti D. and Laver M. (2009), 'Party cohesion, party discipline and party factions in Italy', 146-168 Gianetti D. and Benoit K. eds. *Intra-Party Politics and Coalition Governments* (Abingdon UK and New York USA: Routledge)

Gillespie R., Waller M. and Lopez-Nieto L. eds. (1995) 'Factional Politics and Democratisation, *Democratisation* special issue, Spring 1995, Vol. 2(1).

Gilmour I. (1971) *The Body Politic* (London: Hutchinson).

Gilmour I. (1977) *Inside Right* (London: Hutchinson).

Gilmour I. (1992) *Dancing with Dogma: Britain under Thatcherism* (London: Simon and Schuster).

Ginsborg P. (1990) *A History of Contemporary Italy: Society and Politics 1943–1988* (London: Penguin Books).

Ginsborg P. (1996) 'Explaining Italy's Crisis', in Gundle S. and Parker S., eds., *The New Italian Republic: From the Fall of the Berlin Wall to Berlusconi* (London and New York: Routledge).

Giovagnoli A. (1996) *Il Partito Italiano: La Democraxia Cristiana dal 1942 al 1994* (Editori Laterza: Roma-Bari).

Godechot T. (1964) *Le Parti Démocrate Italien* (Paris: Pichon et Durand-Auzias).

Goldfarb M. and Axworthy T. (1988) *Marching to a Different Drummer: An Essay on the Liberals and Conservatives in Convention* (Toronto: Stoddart).

Goldman R.M. (1993) 'The Nominating Process: Factionalism as a Force for Democratization', in Wekkin G.D., Wistler D.E., Kelly M.A., and Maggiotto M.A., eds., *Building Democracy in One-Party Systems: Theoretical Problems and Cross-National Experiences* (Westport, CT and London: Praeger).

Golombiewski R. (1958) 'A Taxonomic Approach to State Political Party Strength', *Western Political Quarterly* 11: 390–420.

Goodart P. and Branston U. (1973) *The 1922: The Story of the Conservative Backbenchers' Parliamentary Committee* (London: Macmillan).

Graham B.D. (1993) *Representation and Party Politics: A Comparative Perspective* (Oxford, UK, and Cambridge, USA: Blackwell).

Greene Kenneth F. (2007) *Why Dominant Parties Lose: Mexico's Democratization in Comparative Perspective* (Cambridge, New York, Melbourne, Madrid, Cape Town, Singapore, Sao Paulo, Delhi: Cambridge University Press).

Grofman B., Lee S.C., Winckler E. and Woodall B. eds. (1999) *Elections in Japan, Korea and Taiwan under the Single Non-Transferable Vote: The Comparative Study of an Embedded Institution* (Ann Arbor: University of Michigan Press).

Grotty W.J. (1968) *Approaches to the Study of Party Organisation* (Boston: Allyn and Bacon Inc.).

Guadagnini M. (1984) 'Il personale politico parlamentari dagli anni '70 agli anni '80: Problemi di ricerca e di analisi e alcuni dati empirici' in Bonanate L., ed., *Il Sistema Politico Italiano tra Crisi e Innovazione*, pp. 131–52 (Franco Angeli Editore: Milan).

Gundle S. and Parker S. eds. *The New Italian Republic: From the Fall of the Berlin Wall to Berlusconi* (London and New York: Routledge).

Hall P. (1986) *Governing the Economy: The Politics of State Intervention in Britain and France* (New York: Oxford University Press).

Hardin R. (1982) *Collective Action* (Baltimore: Resources for the Future by Johns Hopkins University Press).

Hardin R. (1995) *The Logic of Group Conflict* (Princeton, NJ: Princeton University Press).

Harmel R., Heo U.K., Tan A. and Janda K. (1995) 'Performance, Leadership, Factions and Party Change: An Empirical Analysis', *West European Politics* 18(1): 1–33.

Hazan R.Y. and Rahat G. (2010) *Democracy within Parties: Candidate Selection Methods and their Political Consequences* (New York and Oxford: Oxford University Press).

Heath A. and Jowell R. (1994)'Labour's Policy Review' in Heath A., Jowell R. and Curtice J., eds., *Labour's Last Chance? The 1992 Election and Beyond*, pp. 191–212 (Aldershot: Dartmouth).

Heath A., Jowell R. and Curtice J. eds. *Labour's Last Chance? The 1992 Election and Beyond*, pp. 43–64 (Aldershot: Dartmouth).

Heath A., Jowell R. and Curtice J. eds. (1994) *Labour's Last Chance? The 1992 Election and Beyond* (Aldershot: Dartmouth).

Hine D. (1982) 'Factionalism in West European Parties: A Framework for Analysis', *West European Politics* 5: 36–53.

Hine D. (1993) *Governing Italy: The Politics of Bargained Pluralism* (Oxford: Clarendon Press).

Hirschman A. (1970) *Exit, Voice, and Loyalty: Responses to Decline in Firms, Organizations, and States* (Cambridge, MA, and London: Harvard University Press).

Hirschman A. (1982) *Shifting Involvements: Private Interests and Public Affairs* (Princeton: Princeton University Press).

Hix S. (2000), 'Britain, the EU and the Euro', in Dunleavy P., Gamble A., Holliday I. and Peel G., eds. *Developments in British Politics 6*, pp. 47–67 (New York: St. Martin's Press Inc.).

Hix, S., A. G. Noury and G. Roland (2007) *Democratic Politics in the European Parliament* (Cambridge, New York, Melbourne, Madrid, Cape Town, Singapore, Sao Paulo: Cambridge University Press).

Hoffman J. (1964) *The Conservatives in Opposition* (London: MacGibbon and Kee).

Holcombe R.G. (1991) 'Barriers to Entry and Political Competition', *Journal of Theoretical Politics* 3(2): 231–40.

Holler M. ed. (1982) *Power, Voting, and Voting Power* (Würzburg: Physica-Verlag).

Holler M. ed. (1984) *Coalitions and Collective Action* (Würzburg: Physica-Verlag).

Holler M. ed. (1987) *The Logic of Multiparty Systems* (Dordrecht and Boston: Kluwer).

Holmes M. (1985) *The First Thatcher Government 1979*–83 (Brighton: Wheatsheaf).

Holmes M. (1989) *Thatcherism: Scope and Limits 1983*–87 (London: Macmillan).

Horn M. (1995) *The Political Economy of Public Administration: Institutional Choice in the Public Sector* (Cambridge: Cambridge University Press).

Howe G. (1994) *Conflict of Loyalty* (London: Pan).

Hrebenar R.J. (1986) *The Japanese Party System from One-Party Rule to Coalition Government* (Boulder and London: Westview).

Huber J.D. (1996) *Rationalizing Parliament: Legislative Institutions and Party Politics in France* (Cambridge, New York, Melbourne: Cambridge University Press).

Ike N. (1978) *A Theory of Japanese Democracy* (Boulder: Westview Press).

Inoguchi T. (1990) 'The Political Economy of Conservative Resurgence under Recesion: Public Policies and Political Support in Japan', in Pempel T.J., ed., *Uncommon Democracies: The One-Party Dominant Regimes*, pp. 128–61 (Ithaca & London: Cornell University Press).

Inoguchi T. (1991) 'The Nature and Functioning of Japanese Politics', *Government and Opposition* 26(2): 185–98.

Inoguchi T. (1993a) 'Japanese Politics in Transition: A Theoretical Review', *Government and Opposition* 28(4): 443–55.

Inoguchi T. (1993b) 'Factional Dynamics of the Liberal Democratic Party', *Asian Journal of Political Science* 1(1): 76–84.

Irving, R. (1979) *The Christian Democratic Parties of Western Europe* (London: Allen and Unwin).

Ishida T. (1971) *Japanese Society* (New York: Random House).

Ishiyama J. (2008) 'Learning to lose (and sometimes win): The neocommunist parties in post-Soviet politics, Friedman E. and Wong J., eds., *Political Transitions in Dominant Party Systems: Learning to Lose* pp. 148-168 (Abingdon, UK, and New York, USA: Routledge)

Janda K. (1979) *Comparative Political Parties Data 1950*–1962 (Ann Arbor: Inter-University Consortium for Political and Social Research, study 7534).

Janda K. (1980a) 'A Comparative Analysis of Party Organization: The United States, Europe, and the World', in Crotty W., ed., *The Party Symbol: Readings on Political Parties* (San Francisco: W.H. Freeman).

Janda K. (1980b) *Political Parties: A Cross National Survey* (New York: The Free Press).

Janda K. (1993) 'Comparative Political Parties: Research and Theory, *Political Science: The State of the Discipline* II, Chapter 7 (Washington, D.C: American Political Science Association).

Jesse N.G. (1996) 'Thatcher's Rise and Fall: An Institutional Analysis of the Tory Leadership Selection Process', *Electoral Studies* 15(2): 183–202.

Johnson C. (1986) 'Tanaka Kakuei, Structural Corruption and the Advent of Machine Politics in Japan', *Journal of Japanese Studies* 12(1): 1–28.

Johnson C.A. ed. (1994) *Japan: Who Governs? – The Rise of the Developmental State* (New York, London: W. W. Norton & Company).

Johnston R. (2008) 'Polarized Pluralism in the Canadian Party System: Presidential Address to the Canadian Political Science Association, June 5, 2008', *Canadian Journal of Political Science/Revue canadienne de science politique* (December 2008): 815–834.

Johnston R., Blais A., Brady H. and Crete J. (1989) 'Free Trade and the Dynamics of the 1988 Canadian Election'; paper presented at the *Canadian Political Science Association*, June 1989.

Jones G.W. (1987), 'Cabinet Government and Mrs. Thatcher', *Contemporary Record*, 1(3): 8–12.

Jones G.W. (1990), 'Mrs. Thatcher and the Power of the Prime Minister', *Contemporary Record* 3(4): 2–6.

Jones G.W. (1995), 'The Downfall of Mrs. Thatcher', in Rhodes R.A.W. and Dunleavy P., eds., *Prime Minister, Cabinet and Core Executive*, pp. 87–107 (New York: St. Martin's Press).

Judge D. (1983) (ed.) *The Politics of Parliamentary Reform* (London: Heinemann).

Kabashima I. and Steel G. (2007) 'How Junichiro Koizumi Seized the Leadership of Japan's Liberal Democratic Party', *Japanese Journal of Political Science* 8(1): 95–114.

Kam C. (2009) *Party Discipline and Parliamentary Politics* (Cambridge University Press).

Kam C., Bianco W.T., Sened I. and Smyth R. (2010) 'Ministerial Selection and Intraparty Organization in the Contemporary British Parliament', *American Political Science Review* 104(2): 289–306.

Kang W.T. (1997) *Support for Third Parties under Plurality Rule Electoral Systems: A Public Choice Analysis of Britain, Canada, New Zealand and South Korea* (Unpublished PhD Thesis, London School of Economics and Political Science).

Kang W.T. (2004) 'Protest Voting and Abstention under Plurality Rule Elections: An Alternative Public Choice Approach', *Journal of Theoretical Politics* 16(1): 79–102.

Kato J. (1998) 'When the Party Breaks Up: Exit and Voice among Japanese Legislators', *American Political Science Review* 98: 857–70.

Katz R. (1980a) *A Theory of Parties and Electoral Systems* (Baltimore and London: The Johns Hopkins University Press).

Katz R. (1980b) 'Preference Voting and Turnover in Italian Parliamentary Elections', *American Journal of Political Science* 24(1) 97–114.

Katz R. ed. (1987) *Party Government: European and American Experiences* (Berlin: de Gruyer).

Katz R. (1995) 'The 1993 Parliamentary Electoral Reform, the 1994 Parliamentary Election, and Party Politics in Italy', prepared for the conference *'Party Politics in the Year 2000'* (University of Manchester, 13–15 January 1995).

Katz R. (1997) *Democracy and Elections* (Oxford and New York: Oxford University Press).

Katz R.S. (2001) 'Reforming the Italian Electoral Law, 1993', in Soberg Shugart M. and Wattenberg M.P., eds., *Mixed-Member Electoral Systems: The Best of Both Worlds?* (New York: Oxford University Press).

Katz R. and Bardi L. (1980) 'Preference Voting and Turnover in Italian Parliamentary Elections, *American Journal of Political Science* 24(1): 97–114.

Katz R. and Mair P. (1994) *How Parties Organize: Change and Adaptation in Party Organizations in Western Democracies* (London and Southern Oaks, CA, New Delhi: Sage).

Kavka G.S. (1991), 'Rational Maximizing in Economic Theories of Politics', Chapter 15 in Renwick –Monroe K., ed., *The Economic Approach to Politics: A Critical Reassessment of the Theory of Rational Action* (New York: HarperCollins).

Keesings' UK Records (London: Keesings Publications) Vol. 1 (1988)–Vol. 10 (1997) ceased publication.

Kellner P. (1997), 'Why the Tories were Trounced', *Britain Votes 1997*, in Norros P. and Gavin N.T., eds., (Oxford: Oxford University Press).

Kelly R. (1989) *Conservative Party Conferences: The Hidden System* (Manchester: Manchester University Press).

Kelly R. (1992) 'Power in the Conservative Party', *Politics Review* 1(4): 26–9.

Kerbel M.R. (2002) 'Political Parties in the Media: Where Elephants and Donkeys are Pigs', in Maisel L.S., ed., *The Parties Respond: Changes in American Parties and Campaigns* (Boulder, CO, and Oxford, UK: Westview Press).

Key V.O. (1949) *Southern Politics* (New York: Knopf).

Kilgour D.M. (1974) 'A Shapley Value for Co-Operative Games with Quarrelling', in Rapoport A., ed., *Game Theory as a Theory of Conflict Resolution*, pp. 193–206 (Dordrecht, Holland: D. Reidel Publishing Co.).

Kilmuir Earl of (1964) *Political Adventure* (London: Weidenfeld).

King A. (1976) 'Modes of Executive-Legislative Relations: Great Britain, France and West Germany', *Legislative Studies Quarterly* Vol 1 No 1 (Feb 1976) 11–36.

King A. (1981) 'The Rise of the Career Politician in Britain – and Its Consequences', *British Journal of Political Science* 11(3): 249–85.

King A. (1993) 'The Implications of One-Party Government' in King A., Crewe I., Denver D., Newton K., Norton P., Sanders D. and Seyd P., eds., *Britain at the Polls 1992*, pp. 223–48 (Chatham, NJ: Chatham House).

Kirchheimer O. (1966) 'The Transformation of the Western European Party Systems', in LaPalombara J. and Weiner M., eds., *Political Parties and Political Development* (Princeton, NJ: Princeton University Press).

Kishima T. (1991) *Political Life in Japan: Democracy in a Reversible World* (Princeton, NJ: Princeton University Press).

Kogan N. (1983) *A Political History of Italy: The Postwar Years* (New York: Praeger).

Kohno M. (1992) 'Rational Foundations for the Organisation of the Liberal Democratic Party of Japan' *World Politics* 44: 369–97.

Kohno M. (1997) *Japan's Postwar Party Politics* (Princeton, NJ: Princeton University Press).

Kolodny R. (1999), 'Moderate Party Factions in the U.S. House of Representatives', in Green J.C. and Shea D.M., eds., *The State of the Parties: The Changing Role of Contemporary American Parties,* 3rd ed. (Lanham, Boulder, New York, Oxford: Rowman and Littlefield Publishers Inc.).

Krause S. (1989) 'The Liberals: Disoriented in Defeat', in Frizzell A., Pammett J.H. and Westell A., eds., *The Canadian General Election of 1988*, pp. 27–41 (Ottawa: Carleton University Press).

Krauss E. and Pekkanen R. (2004) 'Explaining Party Adaptation to Electoral Reform: The Discreet Charm of the LDP?', *Journal of Japanese Studies* 30(1): 1–34.

Krauss E. and Pekkanen R. (2011) *The Rise and Fall of Japan's LDP: Political Party Organizations as Historical Institutions* (Ithaca and London: Cornell University Press).

Krauss E. and Pierre J. (1990) 'The Decline of Dominant Parties: Parliamentary Politics in Sweden and Japan in the 1970s', in Pempel T.J., ed., *Uncommon Democracies: The One-Party Dominant Regimes*, pp. 226–59 (Ithaca & London: Cornell University Press).

Lane E. and Ersson S. (1991) *Politics and Society in Western Europe*, 2nd ed. (London, Newbury Park, New Delhi: Sage Publications).

Lane E. and Ersson S. (1996) 'The Nordic Countries: Contention, Compromise and Corporatism', in J. Colomer, ed., *Political Institutions in Europe* (London and New York: Routledge).

Lange P. and Tarrow S. eds. (1980) *Italy in Transition* (London: Cass).

LaPalombara J. (1964) *Interest Groups in Italian Politics* (Princeton: Princeton University Press).

LaPalombara J. (1987) *Democracy, Italian Style* (New Haven & London: Yale University Press).

LaPalombara J. and Weiner M. eds. (1968) *Political Parties and Political Development* (Princeton: Princeton University Press).

Laver M. (1981), *The Politics of Private Desires* (Harmondsworth: Penguin Books).

Laver M. (1983) *Invitation to Politics* (Oxford: Martin Robertson & Co. Ltd.).

Laver M. and Hunt B. (1992) *Policy and Party Competition* (New York and London: Routledge).

Laver M. and Kato J. (1998), Theories of Government Formation and the 1996 General Election in Japan', *Party Politics* 4(2): 229–52.

Laver M. and Schofield N. (1990) *Multiparty Government: The Politics of Coalition in Europe* (New York: Oxford University Press).

Laver M. and Shepsle K. (1996) *Making and Breaking Governments: Cabinets and Legislatures in Parliamentary Democracies* (Cambridge, New York, Melbourne: Cambridge University Press).

Laver M. and Shepsle K. (1999) 'Government Formation and Survival: A Rejoinder to Warwick's Reply', *British Journal of Political Science* 29(2): 412–15.

Lawson N. (1992) *The View from No. 11: Memoirs of a Tory Radical* (London: Gorgi Books).

Layton-Henry Z. ed. (1980) *Conservative Party Politics* (London & Basingstoke: Macmillan).

Leduc L. (1999) 'New Challenges Demand New Thinking about Our Antiquated Electoral System', in Milner H., ed., *Making Every Vote Count: Reassessing Canada's Electoral System* (Peterborough, ON: Broadview Press).

Leduc L., Niemi P.R. and Norris P. eds. (1996) *Comparing Democracies: Elections and Voting in Global Perspective* (Thousand Oaks, London, Delhi: Sage Publications).

Leiserson M. (1968), 'Factions and Coalitions in One-Party Japan: An Interpretation Based on the Theory of Games', *American Political Science Review* 68: 770–87.

Leonardi R. (1973) *The Politics of Choice: An Inquiry into the Causes of Factionalism in the Christian Democratic Party*. Unpublished Ph.D. dissertation, University of Illinois at Urbana-Champaign.

Leonardi R., Nanetti R.Y. and Fedele M. (1996) *Italy: Politics and Policy*, Vol. 1 (Aldershot, Brookfield, USA, Singapore, Sydney: Dartmouth).

Leonardi R. and Wertman D. (1989) *Italian Christian Democracy: The Politics of Dominance* (Basingstoke and London: Macmillan).

Levite A. and Tarrow S. (1983) 'The Legitimation of Excluded Parties in Dominant Party Systems: A Comparison of Israel and Italy', *Comparative Politics* April 1983: 295–327.

Lijphart A. (1979) 'Consociation and Federation: Conceptual and Empirical Links', *Canadian Journal of Political Science* 12: 499–515.

Lijphart A. (1984) *Democracies: Patterns of Majoritarian and Consensus Government in Twenty-One Democracies* (New Haven & London: Yale University Press).

Lijphart A. (1994) *Electoral Systems and Party Systems – A Study of Twenty-Seven Democracies, 1945–1990* (New York: Oxford University Press).

Lijphart A. (1999) *Patterns of Democracy: Government Forms and Performance in Thirty-Six Countries* (New Haven & London: Yale University Press).

Lipset S.M. and Rokkan S. (1967) Party Systems and Voter Alignments: Cross National Perspectives (New York: Free Press).

Loewenstein G. and Elster J. eds. (1992) *Choice over Time* (New York: Russell Sage Foundation).

Lombardo A. (1976) 'Sistema di Correnti e Deperimento dei Partiti in Italia', *Rivista Italiana di Scienza Politica* April 1976: 139–62.

Loomis B.A. (1981) 'Congressional Caucuses and the Politics of Representation', in Dodd L.C. and Oppenheimer B.I., eds. *Congress Reconsidered*, 2nd ed. *Congressional Quarterly*, pp. 204–20.

Loveday P. and Martin A. (1966) *Parliaments, Factions and Parties: The First Thirty Years of Responsible Government in New South Wales, 1856–1889* (Melbourne, Australia: Melbourne University Press).

Lovenberg G., Patterson S. and Jewell M. eds. (1985) *Handbook of Legislative Research* (Cambridge, MA: Harvard University Press).

Lowell L. (1902) 'The Influence of Party upon Legislation in England and America', *Annual Report of the American Historical Association* for 1901 Vol. 1, pp. 321–544.

Luebbert G. (1986) *Comparative Democracy: Policy Making and Government Coalitions in Europe and Israel* (New York: Columbia University Press).

MacIvor H. (1995) 'Leadership Selection in Canada: Is Constitutional Government Being Perverted Into Democracy?' Paper presented at the *'Party Politics in the Year 2000'* Conference in Manchester, UK, on 14 January 1995.

MacIvor H. (1999) 'A Brief Introduction to Electoral Reform', in Milner H., ed., *Making Every Vote Count: Reassessing Canada's Electoral System* (Peterborough, ON: Broadview Press).

Mackie T. and Rose R. (1991) *The International Almanac of Electoral History,* 3rd ed. (London: Macmillan).

Magri F. *La Democrazia Cristiana in Italia* Vols 1 and 2 (Editrice La Fiaccola: Milano).

Mair P. (1987) *The Changing Irish Party System: Organisation, Ideology and Electoral Competition* (London: Pinter).

Mair P. ed (1989) 'Understanding Party System Change in Western Europe', *West European Politics,* Vol. 12, No. 4 (London: Frank Cass).

Mair P. ed (1990) *The West European Party System* (Oxford: Oxford University Press).

Mair P. and Sakano T. (1998) 'Japanese Political Realignment in Perspective: Change or Restoration? *Party Politics* 4(2): 177–201.

Major J. (1999) *John Major: The Autobiography* (London: HarperCollins Publishers).

Manzer R. (1985) *Public Policies and Political Development in Canada* (Toronto, Buffalo, London: University of Toronto Press).

Maor M. (1995) 'Intra-Party Determinants of Coalition Bargaining', *Journal of Theoretical Politics* 7(1): 65–91.

Maor M. (1997) *Political Parties and Party Systems. Comparative Approaches and the British Experience* (London: Routledge).

Maor M. (1998) *Parties, Conflicts and Coalitions in Western Europe: Organisational Determinants of Coalition Bargaining* (London and New York: Routledge).

Margetts H. and Smyth G. (1994) *Turning Japanese? Britain with a Permanent Party of Government* (London: Lawrence & Wishart).

Margolis H. (1982), *Selfishness, Altruism and Rationality: A Theory of Social Choice* (Cambridge: Cambridge University Press).

Marsh D. and Stoker G. eds. (1995) *Theory and Methods in Political Science* (Basingstoke and London: Macmillan).

Martelli P. (1998) 'Is Nomenklatura Rule the Clue to the Riddle of Italian Politics? A Comment on Ferrero and Brosio', *Journal of Theoretical Politics* 10(2): 237–44.

McAllister I. (1991), 'Party Adaptation and Factionalism within the Australian Party System.' *American Journal of Political Science* 35: 206–27.

McCall-Newman C. (1982) *Grits: An Intimate Portrait of the Liberal Party* (Toronto: Macmillan of Canada).

McCarthy P. (1995) *The Crisis of the Italian State: From the Origins of the Cold War to the Fall of Berlusconi and Beyond* (Basingstoke and London: Macmillan).

McGann A.J. (2002) 'The Advantages of Ideological Cohesion: A Model of Constituency Representation and Electoral Competition in Multi-Party Democracies', *Journal of Theoretical Politics* 14(1): 37–70.

McKelvey R.D. (1976) 'Intransitivities in Multidimensional Voting Models, and Some Applications for Agenda Control', *Journal of Economic Theory* 2: 472–82.

McKelvey R.D. (1986) 'Dominance and Institution-Free Properties of Social Choice', *American Journal of Political Science* 9: 283–311.

McKenzie R.T. (1955) *Political Parties* (London: Heineman).

McLean I. (1987) *Public Choice – An Introduction* (Cambridge, MA: Basil Blackwell).

McNaught K. (1982) *The Pelican History of Canada* (Harmondsworth UK., New York, Victoria Aus., Markham Ont., Auckland N.Z: Penguin Books).

Meisel J. (1981) 'The Larger Context: The Period Preceding the 1979 Election', in Penniman H., ed., *Canada at the Polls, 1979 and 1980: A Study of the General Elections* (Washington and London: American Enterprise Institute).

Meisel J. (1988) 'Introduction' in Penniman H., ed., *Canada at the Polls 1984: A Study of the Federal General Elections* (Washington and London: American Enterprise Institute for Public Policy Research).

Meisel J. (1991) 'The Dysfunctions of Canadian Parties: An Exploratory Mapping', in Thorburn H., eds., *Party Politics in Canada,* pp. 234–54 (Scarborough, ON: Prentice-Hall Canada).

Meisel J. (1992) 'The Stalled Omnibus and the Decline of Party', in Carty R.K., ed., *Canadian Political Party Systems: A Reader,* pp. 328–50 (Broadview Press).

Merkl P. ed. (1980) *Western European Party Systems: Trends and Prospects* (New York: Free Press).

Michels R. (1915/1962) *Political Parties: A Sociological Study of the Oligarchical Tendencies in Modern Democracy* (New York: Free Press).

Middlemas K. (1991), *Power, Competition and the State – The End of the Post-War Era: Britain Since 1974,* Vol. 3 (Houndsmills, Basingstoke, London: Macmillan).

Miller G.J. (1992) *Managerial Dilemmas: The Political Economy of Hierarchy* (New York, Melbourne: Cambridge University Press).

Milner H. ed. (1999) *Making Every Vote Count: Reassessing Canada's Electoral System* (Peterborough, Ont: Broadview Press).

Misgeld K., Molin K. and Åmark K. (1992) *Creating Social Democracy. A Century of the Social Democratic Labor Party in Sweden* (Pennsylvania: The Pennsylvania State University Press).

Moe T.M. (1980) *The Organisation of Interests* (Chicago: University of Chicago Press).

Moe T.M. (1984) 'The New Economics of Organization', *American Journal of Political Science* 28: 739–77.

Molinar J. (1991) 'Counting the Number of Parties: An Alternative Index' *American Political Science Review* 85(4): 1383–91.

Morris R. (1991) *Tories -: From Village Hall to Westminster: A Political Sketch* (Edinburgh: Mainstream).

Mount F. (1992) *The British Constitution Now* (London, Auckland, Melbourne, Singapore, Toronto: Mandarin).

Mulé R. (2001) *Political Parties, Games and Redistribution* (Cambridge, New York, Melbourne, Madrid: Cambridge University Press).

Muller E.N. (1979) *Aggressive Political Participation* (Princeton, NJ: Princeton University Press).

Muller E.N. and Opp K.D. (1986) 'Rational Choice and Rebellious Collective Action',; *American Political Science Review* 80(2): 471–87.

Müller Wolfgang C. (1994) 'The Development of Austrian Party Organizations in the Post-war Period', in Katz R. and Mair P., eds., *How Parties Organize: Change and Adaptation in Party Organizations in Western Democracies,* pp. 51–79 (London, Southern Oaks Calif., New Delhi: Sage).

Nakane C. (1967) *Tate-Shakai no Ningen Kanakei* (Human Relations of Vertical Society) (Tokyo: Kodan-sha).

Nanetti R., Leonardi R. and Corbetta P. eds. (1988) *Italian Politics: A Review* Vol. 2 (London: Pinter).

Newell J. and Bull M. (1997) 'Party Organisations and Alliances in Italy in the 1990s: A Revolution of Sorts', in Bull M. and Rhodes M., eds., *Crisis and Transition in Italian Politics,* a special issue of *West European Politics,* Vol. 20, pp. 81–109 (London: Frank Cass).

Nicholson N.K. (1962) 'The Factional Model and the Study of Politics', *Comparative Political Studies* 5(3): 292–94.

Noel S. (1991) 'Dividing the Spoils: The Old and New Rules of Patronage in Canadian Politics', in Thorburn H., ed., *Party Politics in Canada,* 6th ed. (Scarborough, ON: Prentice-Hall Canada).

Norris P. (1997) 'Anatomy of a Labour Landslide' in Norris P. and Gavin N., eds., *Britain votes 1997* (Oxford: Oxford University Press).

North D. (1984) 'Government and the Cost of Exchange', *Journal of Economic History* 44: 255–64.

North Douglas C. (1990a) *Institutions, Institutional Change and Economic Performance* (Cambridge, New York and Melbourne: Cambridge University Press).

North Douglas C. (1990b) 'Institutions and a Transaction-Cost Theory of Exchange', Alt J.E. and Shepsle K.A., eds., *Perspectives on Positive Political Economy Performance* (Cambridge, New York and Melbourne: Cambridge University Press).

Norton P. (1978a) *Dissension in the House of Commons: Intra-Party Dissent in the House of Commons Division Lobbies, 1945–1974* (London: Macmillan).

Norton P. (1978b) *Conservative Dissidents: Dissent within the Parliamentary Conservative Party* 1970–74 (London: Macmillan).

Norton P. (1978b) 'Party Organisation in the House of Commons', *Parliamentary Affairs* 31(4): 406–23.

Norton P. (1980) *Dissension in the House of Commons 1945–79* (Oxford: Clarendon Press).

Norton P. (1985) 'Behavioural Changes: Backbench Independence in the 1980s', in Norton P., ed., *Parliament in the 1980s* (Oxford and New York: Basil Blackwell).

Norton P. (1987) "Mrs. Thatcher and the Conservative Party: Another Institution 'Handbagged'?", in Minogue K. and Biddis M., eds., *Thatcherism* (Basingstoke: Macmillan).

Norton P. (1990a) "The Lady's Not for Turning' But What about the Rest? Margaret Thatcher and the Conservative Party 1979–80, *Parliamentary Affairs* 43(1): 41–58.

Norton P. (1990b), 'Parliament in the UK', *West European Politics* 13: 3.

Norton P. (1990c) 'Choosing a Leader: Margaret Thatcher and the Parliamentary Conservative Party 1989–90', *Parliamentary Affairs* 43: 249–59.

Norton P. ed. (1990d) 'Parliaments in Western Europe', a special issue of *West European Politics.*

Norton P. (1994a) 'Factions and Tendencies in the Conservative Party', in Margetts H. and Smyth G., eds. (1994) *Turning Japanese? Britain with a Permanent Party of Government* (London: Lawrence & Wishart) 93–104.

Norton P. (1994b) 'The Parties in Parliament' in Robins L., Blackmore H. and Pyper R., eds., *Britain's Changing Party System,* pp. 57–74 (London: Leicester University Press).

Norton P. ed. (1996) *The Conservative Party* (London, New York, Toronto, Sydney, Tokyo, Singapore, Madrid, Mexico City, Munich: Prentice Hall Harvester Wheatsheaf).

Norton P. and Aughey A. (1981) *Conservatives and Conservatism* (London: Maurice Temple Smith).

Olson M. (1965) *The Logic of Collective Action: Public Goods and the Theory of Groups* (Cambridge, MA, & London, England: Harvard University Press).

Olson M. (1982) *The Rise and Decline of Nations* (New Haven & London: Yale University Press).

Otake H. (1996) 'Forces for Political Reform: The Liberal Democratic Party's Yound Reformers and Ozawa Ichiro', *The Journal of Japanese Studies* 22(2): 269–94.

Ottone P. (1966) *Fanfani* (Milano: Longanesi).

Ozbudun E. (1970) 'Party Cohesion in Western Democracies: A Causal Analysis' in Eckstein H. and Gurr E., eds., *Comparative Politics* Series No 01-006 Vol. 1 (Beverly Hills: Sage Publications) pp. 303–388.

Pammet J. and Dornan C. eds. (2001) *The Canadian General Election of 2000* (Toronto: Dundurn Press).

Panebianco A. (1988) *Political Parties: Organisation and Power* (Cambridge, MA: Cambridge University Press).

Pansa G. (1975) *Bisaglia: una carriera democristiana* (SugarCo: Milan).

Pappalardo A. (1980), *La Politica Consociativa nella Democrazia Italiana', Rivista Italiana di Politica* pp. 73–123.

Park C.H. (2001) 'Factional Dynamics in Japan's LDP Since Political Reform', *Asian Survey* 41(3) 428-461

Parker S. (1996) 'Electoral Reform and Political Change in Italy, 1991–1994', in Gundle S. and Parker S., eds., *The New Italian Republic: From the Fall of the Berlin Wall to Berlusconi* (London and New York: Routledge).

Pasquino G. (1972) 'Le radici del frazionismo e il voto di preferenza' in *Rivista Italiana di Scienza Politica* 2: 353–68.

Pasquino G. (1975) 'Crisi della DC e evoluzione del sistema politico', *Rivista Italiana de Scienza Politica* 5: 443–72.

Pasquino G. (1980a) 'The Christian Democrats: A Party for all Seasons?' in Lange P. and Tarrow S., eds., *Italy in Transition* (London: Frank Cass & Co).

Pasquino G. (1980b) *Crisi dei Partiti e Governabilita* (Bologna: Il Mulino).

Pasquino G. (1982) *Degenerazioni dei partiti e riforme istituzionali* (Bari: Laterza).

Pasquino G. (1983) 'Sources of Stability and Instability in the Italian Party System', *West European Politics* 6(1): 93–110.

Pasquino G. (1986) 'Modernity and Reforms: the PSI between Political Entrepreneurs and Gamblers' *West European Politics* 9: 1.

Pasquino G. (1991) 'The De Mita Government Crisis and the Powers of the President of the Republic: Which form of Government?' in Sabetti F. and Catanzaro R., eds. *Italian Politics: A Review* Vol. 5, pp. 40–54 (New York and London: Pinter).

Pasquino G. ed. (1993) *Votare Un Solo Candidato: Le Consequenze politiche della preferenza unica* (Bologna: Il Mulino).

Pasquino G. (1995) *La politica italiana: dizionario critico 1945–95* (Roma: Laterza).

Pasquino G. (1996) 'Italy: A Democratic Regime under Reform' in Colomer J., ed., *Political Institutions in Europe* (London and New York: Routledge).

Pasquino G. and McCarthy P. eds. (1993) *The End of Post-War Politics in Italy: The Landmark 1992 Elections* (Boulder: Westview Press).

Pasquino G. and Mershon C. eds. (1995) *Italian Politics: Ending the First Republic* (Boulder, San Francisco, Oxford: Westview Press).

Passigli S. (1971) 'Proporzionalismo, frazionismo e crisi dei partiti: quid prior? in *Rivista Italiana di Scienza Politica* August 1971: 125–38.

Patten C. (1980) 'Policy-Making in Opposition', in Layton-Henry Z., ed., *Conservative Party Politics* (London & Basingstoke: Macmillan).

Patterson D. and Maeda K. (2007) 'Prime Ministerial Popularity and the Changing Electoral Fortunes of Japan's Liberal Democratic Party', *Asian Survey* 47(3) 415–433.

Pedersen M.N. (1980) 'On Measuring Party System Change: A Methodological Critique and a Suggestion', *Comparative Political Studies* 12: 387–403.

Pempel T.J. (1986) 'Japan: The Dilemmas of Success' in *Foreign Policy Association Headline* Series No 277 January–February (Ephrata, PA: Science Press).

Pempel T.J. ed. (1990) *Uncommon Democracies: The One-Party Dominant Regimes* (Ithaca and London: Cornell University Press).

Penniman H.R. ed. (1980) *Italy at the Polls: The Parliamentary Elections of 1979* (Washington, DC: American Enterprise Institute for Public Policy Research).

Penniman H.R. ed. (1981) *Canada at the Polls, 1979 and 1980: A Study of the General Elections* (Washington and London: American Enterprise Institute for Public Policy Research).

Penniman H.R. ed. (1988) *Canada at the Polls, 1984: A Study of the Federal General Elections* (Washington and London: American Enterprise Institute for Public Policy Research).

Pennings P. and Lane J.E. (1998) *Comparing Party System Change* (London and New York: Routledge).

Perlin G. ed. (1987) *Party Democracy in Canada: The Politics of National Party Conventions* (Scarborough, ON: Prentice Hall).

Perlin G. (1990) *The Tory Syndrome: Leadership Politics in the Progressive Conservative Party* (Montreal: McGill-Queen's University Press).

Perlin G. (1991) 'The Progressive Conservative Party: An Assessment of the Significance of Its Victories in the Elections of 1984 and 1988', in Thorburn H.G., ed., *Party Politics in Canada*, 6th ed., pp. 298–316.

Pinto-Duschinsky M. (1972) "Central Office and 'Power' in the Conservative Party", *Political Studies* 20(1): 1–16.

Piper R.J. (1991) 'British Backbench Rebellion and Government Appointments, 1945–87', *Legislative Studies Quarterly* 16(2): 219–38.

Pomper G.M. (1992), 'Concepts of Political Parties', *Journal of Theoretical Politics* 4(2): 43–159.

Powell B. (1982) *Contemporary Democracies: Participation, Stability and Violence* (Cambridge MA: Harvard University Press).

Pridham G. (1988) *Political Parties and Coalition Behaviour in Italy* (London & NY: Routledge).

Prior J. (1986) *A Balance of Power* (London: Hamish Hamilton).

Przeworski A. and Sprague J. (1971) 'Concepts in Search of Explicit Formulation' *Midwest Journal of Political Science* 15: 183–218.

Przeworski A. and Sprague J. (1986) *Paper Stones: A History of Electoral Socialism* (Chicago: University of Chicago Press).

Pugh D.S. ed. (1990) *Organization Theory: Selected Readings* (London: Penguin Books).

Putnam Robert D. (1993) *Making Democracy Work: Civic Traditions in Modern Italy* (Princeton, NJ: Princeton University Press).

Quango Debate (1995) *Parliamentary Politics* 48(2).

Quinn T. (2005), 'Leasehold or Freehold? Leader-Eviction Rules in the British Conservative and Labour Parties', *Political Studies* 53(4): 793–815.

Rae D. (1968), 'A Note on the Fractionalization of Some European Party Systems', *Comparative Political Studies* 1(3): 413–418.

Rae D. (1971) *The Political Consequences of Electoral Laws* (New Haven: Yale University Press).

Rae D. and Taylor M. (1970) *The Analysis of Political Cleavage* (New Haven and London: Yale University Press).

Ramseyer J.M. and McCall Rosenbluth F. (1997) *Japan's Political Marketplace* (Cambridge, MA and London UK: Harvard University Press).

Ranney A. (1975) *Curing the Mischiefs of Faction: Party Reform in America* (Berkeley: University of California Press).

Rapoport A. (1960) *Fights, Games and Debates* (Ann Arbor: University of Michigan Press).

Rapoport A. ed. (1974) *Game Theory as a Theory of Conflict Resolution* (Dordrecht, Holland: D. Reidel).

Rapoport A. and Chammah A.M. (1965) *Prisoner's Dilemma, a Study in Conflict and Cooperation* (Ann Arbor: University of Michigan Press).

Rawnsley A. (2007a) 'Peace and War: The Reckoning 1997–2007', 'The Blair Years 1997–2007' *The Observer*, April 2007.

Rawnsley A. (2007b) *The End of the Party* (London: Viking).

Reed S.R. (1990) 'Structure and Behavior: Extending Duverger's Law to the Japanese Case', *British Journal of Political Science* 20(3): 335–56.

Reed S.R. (2009) 'Party Strategy or Candidate Strategy: How Does the LDP Run the Right Number of Candidates in Japan's Multi-Member Districts?', *Party Politics* 15(3): 295–314.

Reed S.R. and Thies M.F. (2001) 'The Causes of Electoral Reform in Japan', in Soberg Shugart M. and Wattenberg M.P., eds., *Mixed-Member Electoral Systems: The Best of Both Worlds?*, pp. 152–172 (Oxford University Press).

Reuter O.J. (2009) 'Dominant Party Regimes and the Commitment Problem', *Comparative Political Studies* 42(4): 501–26.

Rhodes R.A.W. and Dunleavy P. eds. (1995) *Prime Minister, Cabinet and Core Executive* (New York: St. Martin's Press).

Richard J. (2008) 'Polarized Pluralism in the Canadian Party System: Presidential Address to the Canadian Political Science Association, June 5, 2008', *Canadian Journal of Political Science* 41(4): 815–34.

Richardson B.M. and Flanagan S.C. (1984) *Politics in Japan* (Boston: Little, Brown).

Richardson J.J. and Jordan A.G. (1979) *Governing Under Pressure* (Oxford: Martin Robertson).

Riddel P. (1985) *The Thatcher Era and Its Legacy* (Oxford: Blackwell).

Ridley R.F. ed. (1995) Parliamentary Affairs: A Journal of Comparative Politics; Special Issue: 'The Quango Debate'.

Riker W.H. (1962) *The Theory of Political Coalitions* (New Haven: Yale University Press).

Riker W.H. (1976) 'The Number of Political Parties: A Reexamination of Duverger's Law, *Comparative Politics* 9: 93–106.

Riker W.H. ed. (1993) *Agenda Formation* (Ann Arbor, MI: The University of Michigan Press).

Robertson D. (1976) *A Theory of Party Competition* (London: Wiley).

Robertson D. (1986) 'A Comparative Analysis of Post-War Election Programmes in 20 Democracies' (Pamphlet).

Robins L., Blackmore H. and Pyper R. (1994a) *Britain's Changing Party System* (London: Leicester University Press).

Robinson J. (1942) *Economics of Imperfect Competition* (London: Macmillan).

Rose R. (1964) 'Parties, Factions, and Tendencies in Britain' *Political Studies* 12(1): 33–46.

Rose R. (1974) *The Problem of Party Government* (London and Basingstoke: Macmillan).

Rose R. (1980) *Do Parties Make a Difference?* (Chatham, NJ: Chatham House), 2nd ed. (London: Macmillan, 1984).

Rose R. (1997) 'The New Labour Government: On the Crest of a Wave', in Norris P. and Gavin N.T., eds., *Britain Votes 1997*, pp. 242–8 (New York: Oxford University Press).

Rossi M. (1979) 'Un partito di 'anime morte'? Il tesseramento democristiano tra mito e realta', *Democrastiani*, Istituto Carlo Cattaneo: Centro per Ricerche e Studi dell'Associazione il Mulino.

Rossignol M. (1987) *Crossing the Floor and the Party System*, Political and Social Affairs Division, Library of Parliament Research Branch (Ottawa).

Ruin O. (1974) 'Participatory Democracy and Corporativism: The Case of Sweden', *Scandinavian Political Studies* No 9, p.174.

Rustow D.A. (1955) *The Politics of Compromise: A Study of Parties and Cabinet Government in Sweden* (New York: Greenwood Press Publishers).

Sakamoto T. (1999) 'Explaining Electoral Reform: Japan versus Italy and New Zealand', *Party Politics* 5(4): 419–38.

Sanders D. (1992) 'Why the Conservative Party Won – Again', in King A. et al.,eds., *Britain At The Polls 1992* (Chatham, NJ: Chatham House Publishers).

Sani G. (1995) 'Toward the Second Republic? The Italian Parliamentary Election of March 1994' in Sechi S., ed., *Deconstructing Italy: Italy in the Nineties* (International and Area Studies: University of California at Berkeley).

Sani G. and Radelli C. (1993) 'Preference Voting: before and after the 1991 Referendum', *Italian Politics and Society* No 38.

Sartori G. (1971), 'Proporzionalismo, frazionismo e crisi dei partiti', in *Rivista Italiana di Scienza Politica* August 1971: 629–55.

Sartori G. ([1976] 2005) *Parties and Party Systems: A Framework for Analysis*, Vol. 1, (Cambridge: Cambridge University Press). Published by ECPR Press (Colchester, UK) in 2005 with a new preface by the author and an introduction by Peter Mair.

Sartori G. (1994) *Comparative Constitutional Engineering: an Inquiry into Structures, Incentives, and Outcomes* (Basingstoke: Macmillan).

Sato S. and Matsuzaki T. (1986) *Jiminto Seiken* (the LDP's rule) (Tokyo: Chuo Koron-sha).

Sauger N. (2010) 'District-Level Dominance and the Vulnerability under the French Fifth Republic', in Bogaards M. and Boucek F., eds., *Dominant Political Parties and Democracy: Concepts, Measures, Cases and Comparisons*, chapter 4, pp. 60–72 (Abingdon, New York: Routledge).

Savoie D. (1999) *Governing from the Centre: The Concentration of Power in Canadian Politics* (Toronto: University of Toronto Press).

Sayers A.M. (1999) *Parties, Candidates, and Constituency Campaigns in Canadian Elections* (Vancouver: University of British Columbia Press).

Scalapino R.A. and Masumi J. (1962) *Parties and Politics in Contemporary Japan* (Berkeley: University of California Press).

Scarrow S.E., Webb P. and Farrell D. (2000) 'From Social Integration to Electoral Contestation: The Changing Distribution of Power within Political Parties', in Dalton R.J. and Wattenberg M.P., eds., *Parties without Partisans: Political Change in Advanced Industrial Democracies* (Oxford and New York: Oxford University Press).

Schattschneider E.E. (1942) *Party Government* (New York: Rinehart).

Scheiner E. (2006) *Democracy without Competition: Opposition Failure in a One-Party Dominant State* (New York: Cambridge University Press).

Schelling Thomas C. (1960) *The Strategy of Conflict* (Cambridge, MA: Harvard University Press).

Schelling Thomas C. (1978) *Micromotives and Macrobehavior* (New York and London: W.W. Norton and Co. Inc.).

Schepis R. (1963) 'Analisi statistica dei risultati', in Spreafico A. and LaPalombara J. (1963) *Elizioni e comportmento politico in Italia* (Milano: Edizioni di Comunità).

Schlesinger J.A. (1965) 'Political Party Organisation', in March J.G., ed., *Handbook of Organisations* (Chicago: Rand McNally).

Schlesinger J.A. (1984), 'On the Theory of Party Organisation', *The Journal of Politics* 46: 367–400.

Schlesinger J.A. (1985) 'The New American Political Party', *American Journal of Political Research* 79: 1152–69.

Schlesinger J.A. (1991), *Political Parties and the Winning of Office* (Ann Arbor: The University of Michigan Press).

Schmitt S., Guasti L., Laude C. and Scott J. (1977) *Friends, Followers and Factions: A Reader in Political Clientelism* (Berkeley, London: University of California Press).

Schofield N. (1987) 'Stability of Coalition Governments in Western Europe: 1945–86', *European Journal of Political Economy* 3: 555–91.

Schofield N. and Laver M. (1985) 'Bargaining Theory and Portfolio Payoffs in European Coalition Governments 1945–83', *British Journal of Political Science* 15: 143–164.

Schofield N. and Laver M. (1990) *Multiparty Government: The Politics of Coalition in Europe* (New York: Oxford University Press).

Schumpeter J.A. (1943), *Capitalism, Socialism and Democracy* (London and New York: Routledge).

Schwartz M. (1990) *The Party Network: The Robust Organization of Illinois Republicans* (Madisoon, WI: The University of Wisconsin Press).

Searing, D. (194) *Westminster's World: Understanding Political Roles* (Cambridge, MA, and London, England: Harvard University Press).

Sechi S. ed. (1995) *Deconstructing Italy: Italy in the Nineties* (Berkeley, CA: International and Area Studies, University of California at Berkeley).

Seldon A. (1994) *The Conservative Century Since 1900* (Oxford: Oxford University Press).

Seyd P. (1972) 'Factionalism within the Conservative Party: The Monday Club', *Government and Opposition* 7: 464–87.

Seyd P. (1975) 'Democracy within the Conservative Party', *Government and Opposition* 10(2): 219–37.

Seyd P. (1993), 'Labour: The Great Transformation', *Britain at the Polls 1992*, Anthony King (New Jersey: Chatham House Publishers).

Shapley L. and Shubik M. (1954), 'A Method for Evaluating the Distribution of Power in a Committee System, *American Political Science Review* 48: 787–92.

Shefter M. (1977) 'Party and Patronage: Germany, England, and Italy', *Politics and Society* 7(1): 404–51.

Shepherd R. (1991), *The Power Brokers: The Tory Party and Its Leaders* (London: Hutchinson Press).

Shepsle K.A. (1989) 'Studying Institutions: Some Lessons from the Rational Choice Approach', *Journal of Theoretical Politics* 1(2): 131–47.

Shepsle K.A. and Bonchek M.S. (1997) *Analysing Politics: Rationality, Behavior, and Institutions* (New York and London: W.W. Norton).

Shugart M.S. and Carey J.M. (1992), *Presidents and Assemblies: Constitutional Design and Electoral Dynamics* (Cambridge: Cambridge University Press).

Sidoti F. (1993) 'Italy: A Clean-up after the Cold War', *Government and Opposition* 28(1): 104–14.

Simon H. (1965) *Administrative Behaviour*, 2nd ed. (New York, Free Press: Collier-Macmillan).

Simon H. (1982) *Models of Bounded Rationality*, Vol. 2 (Cambridge, MA: MIT Press).

Simon J. (1995) 'Relations between Prime Ministers and Cabinet: From Wilson to Thatcher', in Rhodes R.A.W. and Dunleavy P., eds., *Prime Minister, Cabinet and Core Executive* (Basingstoke and London: Macmillan Press Ltd; New York: St Martin's Press).

Smith D. (1985) 'Party Government, Representation and National Integration in Canada', P. Aucoin, ed., *Party Government and Regional Representation in Canada* (Toronto: University of Toronto Press).

Smith D. (1992) 'Party Government in Canada', in Carty R.K., ed., *Canadian Political Party Systems: A Reader* (Peterborough, Ont.: Broadview Press).

Smith G. (1989) *Politics in Western Europe: A Comparative Analysis*, 5th ed. (Aldershot: Gower).

Smith G. (2010) 'Hard and Soft Dominance: Assessing the Case of the Bavarian CSU', in Bogaards M. and Boucek F., eds., *Dominant Political Parties and Democracy: Concepts, Measures, Cases and Comparisons*, pp. 98–108 (Abingdon and New York: Routledge).

Spicer M. (1992) *A Treaty Too Far: A New Policy for Europe* (London: Guardian Books).

Spotts F. and Wieser T. (1986) *Italy: A Difficult Democracy – A Survey of Italian Politics* (Cambridge, London, New York, Melbourne, Port Chester, Sydney: Cambridge University Press).

Spreafico A. and LaPalombara J. (1963) *Elizioni e comportmento politico in Italia* (Milano: Edizioni di Comunità).

Stevens A., Miller A. and Mann T. (1974), 'Mobilisation of Liberal Strength in the House, 1955–1970', *American Political Science Review* 68: 667–81.

Stone, D. (1996) 'The Influence of Think Tanks in Britain', *West European Politics* 1(4): 675–92.

Strom K. (1984) 'Minority Governments in Parliamentary Democracies: The Rationality of Non-Winning Cabinet Situations", *Comparative Political Studies* 17(2): 199–227.

Strom K. (1990) 'A Behavioral Theory of Competitive Political Parties', *American Journal of Political Science* 34(2): 565–98.

Strøm K. (2000) 'Delegation and Accountability in Parliamentary Democracies', *European Journal of Political Research* 37(3): 261–89.

Strom K., Budge I. and Laver M. (1994), 'Constraints on Cabinet Formation in Parliamentary Democracies', *American Journal of Political Science* 38(2): 303–35.

Studlar T.D. (1998) 'The Last Westminster Electoral System? Canada, not Britain?' *Representation* 35(3): 70–8.

Swaze M.A. (1996) 'Continuity and Change in the 1993 Canadian General Election', *Canadian Journal of Political Science* XXIX: 3 (September 1996) 555–66.

Swingle P. (1970) *The Structure of Conflict* (New York and London: Academic Press).

Taagepera R. and Shugart S. (1989) *Seats and Votes: The Effects and Determinants of Electoral Systems* (New Haven & London: Yale University Press).

Tarrow S. (1967) *Peasant Communism in Southern Italy* (New Haven: Yale University Press).

Tarrow S. (1977) 'The Italian System between Crisis and Transition', *American Journal of Political Science* 21: 193–222.

Taylor M. (1987) *The Possibility of Cooperation: Studies in Rationality and Social Change* (Cambridge, New York, Melbourne: Cambridge University Press).

Taylor M. and Herman V.H. (1971) 'Party System and Government Stability', *American Political Science Review* 65: 28–37.

Thatcher M. (1995) *The Downing Street Years* (London: Harper Collins).

Thayer N.B. (1969) *How the Conservatives Rule Japan* (Princeton: Princeton University Press).

Theakston K. (1987) *Junior Ministers in British Government* (Oxford: Blackwell).

Theakston K. (1999) 'Junior Ministers in the 1990s', *Parliamentary Affairs* 52(2): 230–45.

Thomas P.G. (1989), 'Parties in Parliament: The Role of Party Caucuses', Tanguay A. and Gagnon G., eds., *Canadian Parties in Transition*, 2nd ed. (Toronto: Nelson Canada).

Thorburn H. ed. *Party Politics in Canada*, 6th ed. (Scarborough, ON: Prentice-Hall Canada).

Tsebelis G. (1990) *Nested Games: Rational Choice in Comparative Politics* (Berkeley, Los Angeles, Oxford: University of California Press).

Tullock G. (1969) 'A Model of Social Interaction', in Herndon J.F. and Berndl J.L., eds., *Mathematics Applications in Political Science I*, pp. 4–28 (Charlottesville, VA: University of Virginia).

Underhill F. (1958) 'The Revival of Conservatism in North America', *Transactions in the Royal Society of Canada II Series* 3, June 1958: 1–19.

Underhill F. (1960) *In Search of Canadian Liberalism* (Toronto: University of Toronto Pres).

Van Deemen A.A. (1989) 'Dominant Players and Minimum Size Coalitions', *European Journal of Political Research* 17: 313–32.

van Wolferen K. (1989) *The Enigma of Japanese Power: People and Politics in a Stateless Nation* (New York: Alfred A. Knopf).

Von Beyme, K. (1984) *Political Parties in Western Democracies* (Aldershot: Gower).

Ward H. (1987) 'The Risks of a Reputation for Toughness: Strategy in Public Goods Provision Modelled by Chicken Supergames', *British Journal of Political Science* 17: 23–52.

Ward H., Samways D. and Benton T. (1990) 'Environmental Politics and Policy', in Dunleavy P., Gamble A., and Peele G., eds., *Developments in British Politics 3* (London: Macmillan).

Ware A. (1996) *Political Parties and Party Systems* (New York: Oxford University Press).

Warner S. and Gambetta D. (1994) *La retorica della riforma. Fine del sistema proporzionale in Italia* (Einaudi: Turin).

Watanabe T. (1964) *Habatsu, Nihon Hoshuto No Bunseki* (Tokyo: Kobundo).

Wearing J. (1979) 'President or Prime Minister?' in Hocking T., ed., *Apex of Power: The Prime Minister and Political Leadership in Canada*, pp. 242–60 (Scarborough, ON: Prentice Hall).

Wearing J. (1980) *The L-Shaped Party: The Liberal Party of Canada 1958–1980* (Toronto: McGraw-Hill Ryerson).

Wearing J. (1988) *Stained Relations: Canadian Parties and Voters* (Toronto: McLennan & Stewart).

Wearing J. (1989) 'Can an Old Dog Teach Itself New Tricks? The Liberal Party Attempts Reform', in Gagnon A. and Tanguay B., eds., *Canadian Parties in Transition: Discourse, Organization and Representation* (Scarborough, ON: Nelson Canada).

Webb P. (1995) 'Reforming the Labour Party-Trade Union Link: An Assessment', in Broughton D., Farrell D., Denver D. and Rallings C., eds., *British Elections and Parties Yearbook 1994* (London: Frank Cass).

Webb P. (2000a) 'Political Parties: Adapting to the Electoral Market', chapter 9 in Dunleavy G. and and Peele H., eds., *Developments in British Politics 6*, pp. 151–68. (Basingstoke and London: St. Martin's Press Inc.).

Webb P. (2000b) *The Modern British Party System* (London, Thousand Oaks, New Delhi: Sage).

Webb P. (2002) 'Political Parties in Britain' in Webb P., Farrell D. and Holliday I., eds., *Political Parties in Advanced Industrial Democracies* (Oxford, New York: Oxford University Press).

Weingast B.R. and Marshall W. (1988) 'The Industrial Organisation of Congress; or Why Legislatures, Like Firms, Are Not Organised as Markets', *Journal of Political Economy* 96: 132–64.

Weir S. (1995) 'Quangos: Questions of Democratic Accountability'. The Quango Debate, *Parliamentary Affairs 48* (2).

Weir S. and Beetham D. (1999), *Political Power and Democratic Control in Britain* (London and New York: Routledge).

Wertman D.A. (1981), 'The Christian Democrats: Masters of Survival', in Penniman H.R. ed., *Italy at the Polls: The Parliamentary Elections of 1979*, pp. 61–84 (Washington, DC: American Enterprise Institute for Public Policy Research).

Wertman D.A. (1983) 'The Christian Democrats: Masters of Survival', H.R. Penniman ed. Wertman ed. *Italy at the Polls, 1983: A Study of the National Elections* (Durham, NC: Duke University Press).

Wertman D.A. (1987) 'The Christian Democrats: The Big Losers', in Penniman, H.R., ed., *Italy at the Polls 1983: A Study of the National Elections* (Durham, NC: Duke University Press).

Wertman D.A. (1988) 'Local Involvement, Central Control' in Callagher M. and Marsh M., eds., *Candidate Selection in Comparative Perspective* (London, Newbury Park, Beverly Hills, New Delhi: Sage Publications).

Wertman D.A. (1995) 'The Last Year of the Christian Democratic Party', in Mershon C. and Pasquino G., eds., *Italian Politics: Ending the First Republic,* pp. 135–50 (Boulder, San Francisco, Oxford: Westview Press).

Whitaker R. (1977) *The Government Party: Organizing and Financing the Liberal Party of Canada, 1930*–58 (Toronto: University of Toronto Press).

Whitaker R. (1992) 'The Government Party' in Carty R.K., ed., *Canadian Political Party Systems: A Reader* (Peterborough, Ont.: Broadview Press).

Whiteley P. and Seyd P. (1994), *True Blues: The Politics of the Conservative Party Membership* (Oxford, UK: Clarendon Press).

Whiteley P. and Seyd P. (1999) 'Discipline in the British Conservative Party: The Attitudes of Party Activists toward the Role of Their Members of Parliament', Bowler S. Farrell D. and Katz R., *Party Discipline and Parliamentary Government* (Columbus: Ohio State University).

Wildgen J.K. (1985) 'Preference Voting and Intraparty Competition in Italy: Some New Evidence on the Communist-Christian Democrat Stalemate', The Journal of Politics 47(3): 947–57.

Williamson O. (1985) *The Economic Institutions of Capitalism* (New York: Free Press).

Wood D.M. and Jacoby W.G. (1983), 'Intraparty Cleavage in the British House of Commons: Evidence from the 1974–1979 Parliament', *Legislative Studies Quarterly* 8: 203–23.

Wright V. (1984) *The Government and Politics of France,* 2nd ed. (London, Melbourne, Sydney, Auckland, and Johannesburg: Hutchinson).

Young H. (1989) *One of Us* (London: Macmillan).

Zariski R. (1960) 'Party Factions and Comparative Politics: Some Preliminary Observations', *Midwest Journal of Political Science* Feb. 1960: 372–90.

Zariski R. (1962) 'The Italian Socialist Party: A Case Study in Factional Conflict', *American Journal of Political Science* (June 1962).

Zariski R. (1965) ' Intra-Party Conflict in a Dominant Party: The Experience of Italian Christian Democracy', *Journal of Politics* 27: 3–34.

Zucherman A.S. (1975) *Political Clienteles in Power: Party factions and cabinet coalitions in Italy* (Beverly Hills, CA: Sage).

Zucherman A.S. (1979) *The Politics of Faction: Christian Democratic Rule in Italy* (New Haven, CT: Yale University Press).

Index

ACLI. *see* Italian Christian Workers' Association (ACLI)
Adscam scandal, 116, 119
African National Congress (ANC), 6, 12, 13
Alitalia, 30
Allum, P.A., 30, 125, 129, 145
Åmark, K., 18
ANC. *see* African National Congress (ANC)
Andreotti, 130, 131, 132, 148,153, 154–7, 159, 160, 161–2, 164, 165, 166–76, 178–9
Andrews, J.T., 48
Argentina, 20
Arian, A., 11, 25
asymmetric competition
and party dominance, 7, 10–12
Australia, 6
federalism in, 62
legislature, 61

Baerwald, H.H., 183, 189
Bagehot, W., 52
Baker, D., 58, 80, 86–7, 91, 97, 221
Baker, K., 97
Banzhaf index of power, 23, 24, 25, 46–7
Christian Democrats (DC) of Italy, 137, 138, 146, 148–9, 154, 159, 165, 172
Banzhaf, J., 46
Bardi, L., 125, 128
Barnes, S., 11, 25
Base faction, 148–59, 165–6
Bavaria, regional based cleavages, 13
Beer, S.H., 58
Beetham, D., 32, 78, 80
Berlusconi, S., 179, 180–1, 216, 225
Berrington, H., 51, 60
Besson, J., 170
Bianco, W.T., 218

Bibes, G., 170
Biffen, J., 74, 78, 85
bipolar competition, 18, 22, 50–2, 63, 128, 170, 180, 204, 208–9
see also Britain, majoritarian institutions in; Canada, majoritarian government in; Italy; Japan
'Black Wednesday,' 85
Blair, T., 1, 15–16, 19–20, 42, 53, 54, 56, 58–9, 67, 69, 71, 96, 117, 206
defeat of Conservative government in 1997, 206
dissent and disunity attitude to, 42, 54, 117; perception of, 53; under, 58
Iraq war, 53, 58–9, 67
Labour Party leadership selection and eviction, 67
media and 'spinning,' 20
non–ideological politics, 19
potential new government during Maastricht bill passage, 96
threats from second–in–command, 56, 69, 71
Blais, A., 215, 218
Blake, R., 73, 75
Blick, A., 56
Bloc Québécois, 16–17, 52, 63, 116, 117
Blondel, J., 7, 11
Body, R., 85, 93, 97
Bogaards, M., 7, 9–10
Borisyuk, G., 215
Boucek, F., 6–7, 9–12, 15, 17, 35–6, 44, 53, 60, 70, 73, 124, 127, 133, 142, 156, 167, 186
Bourassa, R., 113
Brams, S., 47, 220
Breton, A., 55
Britain, majoritarian institutions in
bipolar competition, 50–2, 208
cabinet conflict, 57

candidate selection, 64–5
career advancement, 61, 65
civil service autonomy, 29
coalition government, 56, 70
Conservative-Liberal Democrat
    coalition, 16
correlation between party
    unity/disunity with party
    popularity, 52–4, 58
disincentives to factionalism, 37,
    39, 50–2
executive concentration, 37, 58
leadership selection, 66–7
legislative dissent, 54, 57–9, 61
party splits, 71, 206–7
party unity and responsible
    government, 5, 54–5
policy selection, 69
political spinning, 20
prime minister's role; power of,
    55–7; vulnerability of, 56
public perceptions and party unity,
    52–3
restraints on freedom of
    information, 21
single-member plurality (SMP),
    15–6, 51, 52, 70
state nationalisations, 29
two-party democracy, 16
unitary state, 3
British Election Studies, 53
British House of Commons, 21, 48,
    56, 58, 61, 78, 83–5, 96, 134,
    218
British Leyland, 72
British National Party (BNP),
    19–20
Brittan, L., 80
broadcasting monopolies, 20–1
'brokerage politics,' 13, 105–6
Brown, G., 54, 67, 71
    as Chancellor of the Exchequer, 56,
    69
Bruges Group, 81
Budge, I., 20, 85, 96–7, 216
Budgen, N., 85, 97
Bufacchi, V., 178
Bull, M., 177
bureaucracy, 11, 29

Burnett, S.H., 20, 162
Bush, G.W. (President)
    issue cleavages, 13–14

Caciagli, M., 168, 171, 173
Callaghan, J., 73
Cameron, D., 67, 71, 100
    candidate selection, 65
Cameron-Clegg coalition, 60
Campaign Group, 71
Campbell, A., 20
Campbell, J., 72
Canada Pension Plan, 104
Canada, majoritarian government in,
    1, 2, 3, 6, 10
    automatic leadership review, 68,
        109, 112, 117, 211
    bilingualism, 106–7, 219
    bipolar competition, 50–2, 63
    candidate selection, 65
    career advancement, 61, 116, 118
    'catch-all' strategies, 13, 19
    Charter of Rights, 110
    Conservative Party of Canada, 102,
        205
    consociational norms, 63
    Constitution, 63; repatriation of,
        110
    correlation between party
        unity/ disunity with party
        popularity, 52–4
    corruption scandals, 31; *see also*
        Adscam scandal
    disincentives to factionalism, 3, 37,
        39, 50, 52; and legislative
        dissent, 57
    dissidence in, 56
    federalism, 3, 19, 39, 62–3, 70, 208;
        see also partisanship
    leadership selection, 67–8, 102
    Liberals; 'business Liberals,' 103,
        107, 108, 113, 116, 121; 'social
        Liberals,' 103, 108, 113, 114,
        116, 121
    'national unity' and 'national
        question,' 63, 107, 121, 205,
        215, 221–2
    one-member-one-vote (O.M.O.V),
        68

Canada, majoritarian government in – *continued*
  party unity and responsible government, 5, 54–5
  partisanship, 3, 16, 19, 117; and partisan conflict, 39; *see also* federalism
  'polarised pluralism,' 215, 222
  policy selection, 69
  'prime ministerial government,' 57, 208
  Progressive Conservatives; 'losing party syndrome,' 101; implosion, 102, re–election, 113–14; 'tough love' budget, 109
  public perceptions and party unity, 53, 218
  regional based cleavages, 13
  single-member plurality (SMP), 16–17, 51, 52, 70
  single-party government in, 16–17
  volatile elections, 16
  see also Liberal Party (Canada)
Canada National Energy Program, 110
Canada Royal Commissions, 63, 106, 219
Canada-US Free Trade Agreement (FTA), 103, 113–14, 121
Canadian House of Commons, 16, 54, 61, 101, 112–3
'capitalist developmental state,' 30
capolista, 125
careerist politicians, 2, 38, 50–1, 141, 153, 181, 183, 185, 196, 203
Carlisle, J., 85, 91, 93
Carlisle, M., 73
Carttiss, M., 91, 94
Carty, R.K., 52, 62–3, 65, 68–9, 105–6, 116, 121
Cash, W.Bill, 85
'catch all' parties and strategies, 13, 18, 32, 36
Centre for Policy Studies, 73
'centrifugal' competition, forces, pluralism, polity, 36, 37, 39, 121, 123, 152, 155, 181, 193, 206, 208, 214

'centripetal' competition, forces, factionalism, 36, 37, 39, 50, 62, 70, 208, 210
Centrismo Popolare faction, 148–51, 153–5
Charest, J., 117
  candidate selection, 135–9
  centre-left coalitions, 152–7
  centre-right coalitions, 145–52
Chrétien, J., 5, 54, 56, 61, 65, 68, 102–3, 108, 111–12, 114–22, 138, 149, 205, 209, 211, 221, 222
  authoritarian leadership, 61, 65, 102, 114–17
  'lame duck,' 119
  offensive to oust, 119
  return to power due to implosion of Progressive Conservatives, 102, 114
  rivalry with Paul Martin, 103, 114–20, 122
  selection of candidates, 65
  snap elections, 56, 117–18, 211
Christian Democratic Party s (DC) of Italy (*Democrazia Cristiana* (DC)), 1, 2, 17–18, 22–8, 32
  agenda control, 28
  Banzhaf index of power, 137, 138, 146, 148–9, 154, 159, 165, 172
  candidate selection, 135–9
  centre-left coalitions, 136, 152–7
  centre-right coalitions, 145–52
  collapse of, 27–8, 163–80
  communist delegitimation, 20, 145–52
  communist exclusion, 25–8, 145–52
  communist inclusion, 27–8, 152–63
  corruption scandals, 28, 29, 31, 156, 164, 173, 176, 179
  decline in dominance, 10
  effective number of factions, 145–6, 149, 151
  electoral reforms, 163, 173, 175–6
  exit costs, 42–3
  factionalism, 34–5; and electoral market, 42; measurement of, 44–7
  'historic compromise,' 26, 144, 157–63, 181; end of, 164

monopoly over state resources, 29–30, 125

national executive committee (NEC), 125, 135

party fractionalisation and bargaining power, 137–9

'polarised pluralism,' 22–8, 181, 206

strategies, 129–30, 131, 132

successful repositioning, 20

Chasseriaud, J.P., 138, 149

Christensen, R., 18, 31, 126, 185, 188, 190–1, 193, 201, 203

Chubb, J., 125, 167

Churchill, W., 81

Clarity Act (1998), 116

Clark A., 82

Clarke, K., 66, 85, 87, 93, 97

Clark, J., 108, 109–10, 221

Clark M., 129

Clarkson, S., 106, 107, 108, 109, 110, 118–19, 215, 222

Clean Government Party, 185

'Clean Hands' (*mani pulite*) investigation, 28, 31, 178–9

cleavage theory of party dominance, 12, 13

issue-based, 13–14

regional bases of, 13

cleavages

cross-cutting, 121, 158

intra-party and factional, 80, 101–2, 114, 145, 185, 205, 215

societal, 123

Clegg Commission, 73, 74

coalition dominance, 21–2

agenda control, 28

Christian Democrats (DC), of Italy, 22–8

and partisan resources, 29–32

coalitions, 11–12

advantages of factions in, 42, 46, 128–9

Christian Democrats (DC), of Italy, 22–8, 32

Liberal Democrats (LDP) of Japan, 34, 130

majority, 22–3

pivotality of, 23, 24, 25

political parties as coalitions of individuals and factions, 35; Conservative Party (UK) 92; Liberal Party of Canada, 106, 108

theory, 7, 46–7, 54

Coldiretti (Italy's Catholic Association of Peasant Proprietors), 151

Colombo, 131–2, 150–2, 154–6, 159–60, 164–5, 170–1, 223–4

Common Agricultural Policy (CAP), 94

Communist Party (PCI) of Italy, 20, 25–7, 125, 147, 161–9, 175

competitive factionalism, 36

Confederation of British Industry, 74

Confederation of Small Farmers (*Coltivatori Diretti*), 14

Confindustria, 30, 151–2, 168

confidence vote or motion of, 34, 40, 208, 223; British Conservatives, 57–9, 61–2, 67, 73, 86–90, 93–6, 98, 109; and Canadian liberals, 112, 116, 120; Italy 133, 161; Japan, 183, 190, 197

Congress Party, 1

factionalism, 34–5

consensus model of democracy. *see* non-majoritarian democracies

Conservative Party Conference, 58

Conservative Party of UK, 14

Cameron, D., 67, 71, 100; candidate selection, 65

campaign of disobedience, 97–8

'catch-all' policy, 19

coalition with Liberal Democrats, 65, 70–1

deflationary budget (1981), 75–9, 100

denationalisation of public services, 19

dissidence, 78

European Communities (Finance) Bill, 64, 92–8; game pay–off matrix, 94–6; 'hardliners,' 93; John Major's strategy, 94–8; rebels' strategies, 94–8; 'softliners,' 93; Ulster Unionists, 96, 98

'Fresh Start' group, 84, 98

Conservative Party of UK – *continued*
   levels of rewards and deprivation in
      caucus in, 1979–97, 59–60
   Maastricht treaty and John Major,
      43, 53; blocking of ratification
      by rebels, 48–9, 58, 84–5, 86,
      87–90; divergent preferences of
      rebels, 85; game pay-off matrix,
      87–90; leadership selection,
      66–7; 'nightmare scenario,' 86,
      89; opt-out policy, 86–7; Social
      Chapter, 85–6, 87, 89; under
      Margaret Thatcher, 80–1, 83,
      85; Ulster Unionists, 89, 91;
      unstable consequences, 91–2
   policy selection, 69
   scandals, 98
   and single-member plurality (SMP),
      15–16
   'wets' and 'dries,' 69, 72, 73–9
   see also Thatcher, M.
consociationalism, 63, 181,
   206
consociativismo, 20
convention ad excludendum, 25
Cook, R., 59
cooperative factionalism, 36
'cooperative federalism' Pearson's
   model of, 106
Copps, S., 114, 119
Cossiga, F., 159, 164, 169, 170, 175–6,
   224
Council on Economic and Fiscal
   Policy (CEFP), 201
Cowley, P., 58–9, 83, 98
Cox, G., 11, 13, 15, 18, 51, 127–8,
   140, 142, 184–5, 191–3, 197
Craan, J., 85, 93
Craxi, B., 27, 144, 161–8, 170–1,
   206
Cronache Sociali, 146–7
Cross, J., 104
Cross, W., 116
Curtis, G., 31, 35, 183, 189,
   191

Day, S., 120
dealignment, 180

De Gasperi, A. (Prime Minister), 20,
   25, 135, 137, 145–50, 152, 158,
   170, 178, 181
degenerative factionalism, 36–7, 163
Della Sala, V., 133
Delors, J., 81
Delors Report, 82
demand theory, 43
Democrazia Cristiana. see Christian
   Democratic Party s (DC) of Italy
   (*Democrazia Cristiana* (DC))
De Mita, 131–2, 135, 154, 156–7, 159,
   166–73, 175, 181, 211, 216, 225
Denver, D., 65
Di Palma, G., 133–4, 153, 157–8, 160
dissidence, 2, 11, 34, 78
   burden on party leaders, 70
   caveats in collective action by
      dissidents, 42–3
   exit for voice, 42–3
   incentives for, 43
   internal, 11
   likelihood under party dominance,
      40
   voice, 36, 43
   voice for exit, 41, 43
Docherty, D.C., 121
Doern, B.G., 118
Dogan, M., 129
dominance of parties
   identification of, 8; by longevity, 8;
      by multi-level concept, 8–9; by
      size of legislative majority, 8
   as relative, 10
   intra-party dimension of, 34–5
   resource theory as reason for, 11
Dornan, C., 118
Dorotei (Moro faction), 132, 148–9,
   151–6, 159–60, 165–6, 170–1
Dossetti, G., 146–7
Douglas-Hamilton, J., 92–3
Downs, A., 19
Downsian competition, 19
'dries' and 'wets,' 69, 72, 73–9
   pay-off matrix, 75–7
'dual monarchy,' 56
Dunleavy, P., 9, 10, 14–15, 20, 44, 80,
   170, 174

Duverger, dominance as question of influence, 8
Duverger, M., 7–8, 15, 16, 37–8, 51, 64, 124

'early day motion' (EDM), 84
E-Committee (economic committee), 79
The Economist, 92
'effectiveness advantage,' notion of, 9, 10
effective number of electoral parties, 17
effective number of intraparty factions, 44–6
effective number of legislative parties, 17
'effective number of parties' index, 44–6, 137–9, 145–6, 149, 151
Eisaku, S., 191
'elective dictatorship,' 55–7
electoral dominance, 12–21
    institutional explanations, 14–18
    sociological explanations, 13–14
    strategic and spatial explanations, 18–21
electoral market, and factional behaviour, 40–3
    elastic demand, 41, 169
    market for consent, 40–1
electoral strategies
    of incumbents, 13
    social engineering, 14
electoral systems
    mechanical effects of, 15
    permissive, 15, 17–18, 21, 39
    reductive, 14–15, 21, 39, 51
Epstein, L., 59, 64
Esping-Andersen, G., 14
Euro-communism, 157
European Central Bank, 82
European Communities (Finance) Bill, 64, 92–8
    game pay-off matrix, 94–6
    'hardliners,' 93
    John Major's strategy, 94–8
    rebels' strategies, 94–8
    'softliners,' 93
    Ulster Unionists, 96, 98

European Council (EC), 81, 82
European Court of Auditors' report, 93
European Economic Community (EEC), 57, 72–3
European Monetary Union (EMU), 80, 83
European Union (EU), 61, 71
    fraud in, 93, 94
Euroscepticism, 43, 61, 66, 71
Exchange Rate Mechanism (ERM), 82, 83, 85, 88
exit costs, 2, 10, 34–5, 38–9, 41–3, 51, 70, 207–8, 212
    DC, 144, 153, 163, 169, 173–6, 180
    effect of coalition government on, 22–3
    interaction with electoral market, 172, 212
    LDP, 135, 141, 183, 185, 193, 197, 203, 206, 227
exit for voice (trade-offs between), 42–4, 169–70, 172–6, 180, 182, 185, 193, 206, 213
'Expo 67,' 104

factionalism, 35–7
    competitive, 36, 144; in the DC, 152–63; in the LDP, 186–8
    cooperative, 36, 144; in the DC,145–52; in the LDP, 184–8
    defined, 35–6
    degenerative, 36–7; in the DC, 163–81
    and electoral market, 40–3
    and institutional incentives, 38–40, 50, 123; of coalition government in Italy, 128–30; and Japan, 130, 134–5; and Japan's LDP, 139–42; of legislative incentives in Italy, 133–4; and of party organisation in Italy's DC, 135–9; role of non-majoritarian rules; preference vote in Italy, 124–6; and SNTV in Japan, 126–8

factionalism – *continued*
  and institutional disincentives; *see*
      Britain, majoritarian
      institutions in; Canada,
      majoritarian government in
      measurement of, 43–9; Banzhaf
      index of power, 23, 24, 25, 47;
      effective number of factions,
      44–6; game theory, 46, 48–9;
      power indices, 46–7
  and party dominance, 37, 44
Fianna Fáil, 21
Fine Gael, 21
Falklands war, 20, 79
Fanfani, 29, 125, 131–2, 136, 147–53,
      154–62, 164–71, 216, 224
Farlie, D.J., 20
Farrell, D., 68
federalism, 62–3
  in Canada, 39
'First Republic,' 133
Fixed-term Parliaments Act, 57
Flanagan, T., 66
Fleet Street, 20
Follini, M., 173, 176, 178
Food Prices Review Board, 107
Foot, M, 71
Ford, H.J., 52
Foreign Investment Review Act, 107
Forlani, A., 154–6, 158–60, 164–7,
      170–2, 176, 178
Fox, M., 93, 98
Forze Nuove faction, 131–2, 153–4,
      156–7, 159, 164–6, 171
  see also Fanfani
France
  bureaucracy, 29, 216
  Radicals, 8
  study of district–level dominance, 9
  two-ballot plurality rule, 179, 215
French Canada, 103–6
  see also Québec
French Socialist Party, 9
  dominance of, 214
  under Mitterrand, 168
Friedman, E., 33, 35
Front de Libération du Québec (FLQ),
      104

Fukuda, 187, 188, 189, 190–2, 199,
      202, 203, 226
Fukui, H., 135
Furlong, P., 129, 133

Galeotti, G., 55
Gallagher, M., 64
Galli, G., 150, 153, 157, 159, 165, 168,
      172, 173
Gamble, A., 19, 58, 80, 86–7, 91, 220,
      221
game theory, 46, 48–9, 72, 100, 208
'Gang of Four,' 51–2, 71
Gardiner, G., 91
Geddes, A., 99
German Christian Social Union, 13
Germany
  as 'unitary federal state,' 62
Gerring, J., 210, 217
Giannetti, D., 37, 48, 124
Gidengil, E., 218
Gill, C., 85, 93
Gilmour, I., 73, 78
Giovagnoli, A., 172, 178, 224
Golombiewski, R., 37–8
Gomery Inquiry, 116, 119–20
Gow, I., 72, 75
Gray Report, 107
Greene Kenneth, F., 10–13, 29, 214
'The Grindstone Group,' 109
Gronchi, G., 146–50, 152, 155
Guadagnini, M., 223

habatsu politics, 126, 139–40, 185
Hague, R., 60
Hague, W., 66
Hall, P., 39
'hard dominance,' 12
Harper, S., 17, 57, 119, 120, 222
  'open federalism,' 120
Harris, M., 117
Hashimoto R., 195, 198, 226
Hata-Ozawa faction, 34, 197
Hatoyama I., 186, 226
Heath, A., 72–3, 81
Heathcoat-Amory, D., 99
Heath, E., 66, 72, 81
hegemony, 1, 101–2, 183, 185, 205
'heroes' and 'reptiles,' 75–9

Heseltine, M., 67, 73, 83, 98
    cabinet defection, 72, 79–80
Hine, D., 26, 133
Hirschman, A., 170, 173–4
Hix, S., 48
Holmes, M., 73, 75
Hosokawa M., 197–8, 227
Howard, M., 67, 87
Howe, G., 74, 75, 81–2
    resignation speech, 83
Huber, J.D., 223
Hunt, B., 20
Hurd, D., 83, 87
Husbands, C., 20

IDS. *see* Smith, Ian Duncan
    (IDS)
Ikeda, H., 185, 188, 194, 223, 225
Ike, N., 183
Impegno Democratico faction, 131, 137,
    153–6, 160
Imperiali quota, 124
implosion, 28, 33–4, 37, 102, 103,
    114, 117, 144, 205, 207, 212
incumbents, advantages of, 3, 18,
    28–31, 153, 188, 207, 211
    in definition of dominance, 9–11,
        13, 21, 32, 214
    rates of incumbency among MPs
        and elite turnover, 59, 121, 158,
        160, 167–8, 194–6, 207, 211,
        223
    threats, risks and challenges to
        incumbent leaders, 35, 38, 56,
        62, 66, 67–8, 72, 135, 189, 191,
        194, 209
India, 1
    factionalism, 34–5
    federalism in, 62
Ingham, B., 20
Iniziativa Democratica (Fanfani's
    faction)
Institute for Industrial Reconstruction
    (IRI), 30, 172
Institutionalism and 'new
    institutionalism,' 3, 37, 184
Institutional Revolutionary Party, 1,
    11

institutions
    defined, 39
    incentives, 38–9
    see also, Britain, majoritarian
        institutions in; Canada,
        majoritarian government in;
        coalitions, Christian Democrats
        (DC), of Italy; dissidence;
        factionalism; Italy; Japan;
        Liberal Democratic Party (LDP)
        of Japan; legislative dissent;
        majoritarian parliamentary
        democracies; non-majoritarian
        democracies
Inter Governmental Conference
    (1996), 97
intraparty disequilibrium, 2, 206
intraparty harmony, 2, 4
Iraq war, 53, 58–9
Ireland, coalition politics, 21
'Iron Lady,' 79
Irving, R., 151, 155
Ishida, T., 183
Ishiyama, J., 33
issue cleavages, 13–14
    see also cleavages
Italian Christian Workers' Association
    (ACLI), 14
Italian Confederation of Labour
    Movement (CISL), 14
Italy, 1, 2, 6, 10
    bipolar competition, 51, 18, 22, 128
    Catholic Church, 20, 30, 145, 147,
        163–4
    Chamber of Deputies, 23, 26–7, 124,
        133, 161, 163, 169, 176, 215
    coalition politics of Christian
        Democrats (DC). *see* Christian
        Democrats (DC) of Italy
    Communist Party (PCI). *see*
        Communist Party (PCI) of Italy
    electoral reform, 18, 35, 128, 163,
        175–6, 224
    factionalism, 34–5; and electoral
        market, 42
    legislative incentives, 133–4
    Mafia, 28, 164, 169, 170, 175, 178
    MSI (Social Movement) 24, 25, 27,
        149–51, 177, 224

Italy – *continued*
non-majoritarian democracy, 37, 39, 123
party system, 8
permissive electoral system, 17–18, 124–6; impact on intraparty competition, 128
Socialist Party (PSI). *see* Socialist Party of Italy (PSI)
theory of 'polarised pluralism,' 8, 22

Jacoby, W.G., 58
Janda, K., 44, 58
Japan Communist Party, 185
Japanese Diet, 18, 45–6, 126–7, 134–5, 140–3, 183, 186–7, 189–92, 195–7, 199–201, 210, 227
Japan New Party (JNP), 196, 197
Japan, 1, 2, 6, 42
bipolar and party competition, 18,198
coalitions in, 130, 143
electoral reform, 18, 31, 127, 128, 130, 134, 139, 183–4, 193–99. 203–4, 223
economic performance, 192, 226
factionalism, 34–5; and electoral market, 42
House of Councillors, 188, 192, 194, 198, 201, 226
House of Representatives, 185, 187, 192, 194, 198, 201, 202, 226
institutional incentives, 39, 126–8
and institutionalisation of factions, 39, 126–8, 191
legislative incentives, 134–5; *see also* Japanese Diet
Ministry of Construction, 216
monopoly over state resources, 30–1
partisan and non-partisan politics, 19, 48, 143, 210
party splits, 130, 183, 212
permissive electoral systems, 39, 124; *see also* single non-transferable vote (SNTV)
prime minister, 134, 186, 210, relations with USA, 185, 225
single-member plurality (SMP) 196–7

single non-transferable vote (SNTV), 17, 126–8
'the 55 system,' 130, 139, 184, 203, 209, 223
see also Liberal Democratic Party (LDP) of Japan
Jeffrey, Brooke, 68, 112, 115, 118–19
Jesse, N.G., 66
Johnson, C., 30, 31
Johnston, R., 16–17, 215, 222
Jones, G.W., 83
Joseph, K., 73

Kabashima, I., 141, 200
Kaifu T., 193–4, 196
'Kaku-Fuku War,' 190
Kam, C., 53–4, 61, 218–19
Kanemaru, S., 195–6
Kang, W.T., 9
Kato, J., 225, 227
Katz, R., 50, 125, 128, 133, 169, 223
Keidanren (Japan Federation of Economic Organizations), 226
Key, V.O., 9
King, A., 61
King, M., 105–6
Kinnock, N., 53, 80
Kirchheimer, O., 18
see also 'catch all' parties and strategies
Kishima, T., 226
köenkai, 31, 126–8, 130, 142, 185, 194, 196, 203–4, 209
Koizumi, J., 130, 141–2, 199, 203–4
opposition to LDP factions, 130, 141–2, 183, 199–201, 204–5, 211
privatisation of postal service, 183, 200, 201–2
re-election as LDP leader, 198–202
Kogan, N., 155, 157
Kohno, M., 35, 127, 134, 141–2, 184–6, 196–7, 223, 225
Kolodny, R., 59, 218
Kōno, I., 187, 188
Kōno, Y., 189, 190
Krauss, E., 19, 31, 124, 126–7, 134, 139, 141–2, 184, 186, 192, 199, 201, 225

Kuomintang (KMT), 1, 34–5
Kyubin scandal, 195–6, 226

Lalonde, M., 104
Lamont, N., 85
Landsorganisationen federation, 14
LaPalombara, J., 29
Laporte, P., 104
La Rete, 28
Labour Party of UK, 1, 14, 53
  'Blairites' and 'Brownites,' 69
  dissent, 53, 59, 64, 71
  disunity, perceptions of, 53, 58
  elections, 16, 52
  electoral reforms, 15
  factions, 71, 51
  'Gang of Four,' 51
  leadership selection, 67
  'New Labour,' 53
  non-ideological politics, 19
  policy selection, 69
  rival governments, 56, 69
  split (1981), 51
  support, 20
  and single-member plurality (SMP),
    15–16
Laver, M., 11, 20–3, 37, 48, 124, 129,
  216, 225
Lawson, N., 74–5, 77–82, 219
LeDuc, L., 218
legislative dissent
  disincentives to, 57–9
  and size of legislative assembly, 60–1
legislative dominance, 21–2
legislative incentives
  Italy, 133–4
  Japan, 134–5
Leigh, E., 97
Leiserson, M., 187
Leonardi, R., 35, 125, 132, 136, 138–9,
  147, 151, 154–5, 157, 159, 165,
  168, 172, 223
Lévesque, R., 107, 109
Liberal Democratic Party (LDP) of
  Japan, 1, 2, 13, 17–18, 42
  Banzhaf index of power, 47–8
  breakdown of, 183, 193–8, 202–4
  'clean government' campaign,
    188–9

coalitions, 130; competitive, 186–8;
  co-operative, 184–6; reasons for
  instability, 187–8
corruption scandals, 31, 183, 184;
  Kyubin scandal, 195–6;
  Lockheed scandal, 140, 188–9;
  Recruit scandal, 193, 195;
  Tanaka scandal, 140, 193
defeat, 204
dissidence, 203
effective number of factions, 45, 186
electoral reforms, 127–8, 130,
  183–4, 193–8, 199, 203–4
exit costs, 135, 183
factionalism in, 34–5; and electoral
  market, 42; measurement of,
  44–7
faction institutionalisation, 126–8,
  139–42, 191–3; in '55 system,'
  139–40; new institutional
  regime, 140–2
flexible politics, 19
formation, 185
leadership selection, 39
legislative incentives, 134–5
monopoly over state resources, 30–1
oil shocks, 185, 188
origins of, 184–5
party realignment, 184–8
patronage distribution, 30–1
single non-transferable vote (SNTV),
  17–18, 39, 45, 124, 126–8; '55
  system,' 130, 139, 184
support, 14
voice for exit, 41
warning signs about internal
  discord, 1
see also Japan
Liberal Democrats of UK, 15
Liberal Party (Canada), 1, 2, 13, 17
  'catch-all' policy, 19
  constitutional amendments, 68
  corruption scandals, 31, 106, 115,
    119–20; *see also* Adscam scandal
  decline in dominance, 10, 33, 101,
    205
  dissidence, 118, 122
  factionalism, 102, 112

Liberal Party (Canada) – *continued*
leadership selection and leaders, 67–8, 102, 221; *see also* Chrétien, J; Martin, Paul; Trudeau, P.; Turner, J.
policy selection, 69
warning signs about internal discord, 1
see also Canada, majoritarian government in
Lijphart, A., 5, 15, 22, 45, 50, 55, 57, 123, 124, 217, 219, 222
Lilley, P., 85
'Lionheart,' 200
Lockheed scandal, 140, 188–9, 190, 224
'Logrolling,' 134
lottizazione, 30
Lowell, L., 52
Ludlam, S., 58, 80, 86–7, 91, 219–21
Luebbert, G., 80

Maastricht treaty, 43, 53
blocking of ratification by rebels, 48–9, 58, 84–5, 86, 87–90
divergent preferences of rebels, 85
game pay-off matrix, 87–90
leadership selection, 66–7
'nightmare scenario,' 86, 89
opt-out policy, 86–7
Social Chapter, 85–6, 87, 89
Ulster Unionists, 89, 91
under Margaret Thatcher, 80–1, 83, 85
unstable consequences, 91–2
'machine politics,' 125, 128, 209
Macnamara, K., 91
Madisonian democracy, 55
'Madonna strategy,' 194
Maeda, K., 200
majoritarian parliamentary democracies, 3, 5, 50
careers, 55, 57, 58; incentives, 59–62, 64
constraints on factionalism, 208–10
disincentives to legislative dissent, 57–9

institutionalism in, 37, 39
party organisation, 63–9; candidate selection, 64–5; leadership selection, 66–8; policy selection, 68–9
Major, John, 10, 54, 57, 58, 82, 84
confidence vote, 61–2, 86–7, 88
dissent under, 58, 71
European Communities (Finance) Bill, 64, 92–8; game pay-off matrix, 94–6; 'hardliners,' 93; John Major's strategy, 94–8; rebels' strategies, 94–8; 'softliners,' 93; Ulster Unionists, 96, 98
divide-and-rule strategy, 91, 93
levels of deprivation under, 60
and Maastricht treaty, 43, 53; blocking of ratification by rebels, 48–9, 58, 84–5, 86, 87–90; divergent preferences of rebels, 85; game pay-off matrix, 87–90; 'nightmare scenario,' 86, 89; opt-out policy, 86–7; Social Chapter, 85–6, 87, 89; under Margaret Thatcher, 80–1, 83, 85; Ulster Unionists, 89, 91; unstable consequences, 91–2
'Magna Carta of the Prairies,' 110–11
Mair, P., 50
majority coalitions, 22–3
Mantovani, L., 20, 162
Manuale Cencelli, 129
Maor, M., 129, 161–2
Marchand, J., 106
Marlow, T., 85, 92, 97
Marshall Aid, 25, 146
Marsh, D., 64, 146
Martinazzoli, 171, 178–80
Martin, Paul, 102, 103
'asymmetric federalism,' 120
battle with Jean Chrétien, 68, 114–19
'business Liberals' association with, 121–2
government marred by controversies, 120
selection of candidates, 65

Masayoshi, T., 195
Masonic Lodge P-2 (Propaganda 2) scandal, 164
McAlpine, A., 85
McCall-Newman, C., 101, 105
McCall Rosenbluth, F., 139
McCarthy, P., 145, 157–8, 162–3, 171, 176
McGann, A.J., 22
Medium-Term Financial Strategy, 75
Meech Lake Accord, 103, 112–15, 121, 222
Mexico, 1, 11
  factionalism, 34–5
Meisel, J., 104, 108, 110–11, 221
Meyer, A., 82
Michael, P., 85
Middlemas, K., 74–5, 78, 220
Miki, T., 140, 187–90, 192, 203, 225–6
Milazzo S., 150
Miliband, D., 14, 67
Miller, G.J., 83
Misgeld, K., 18
Mitsuzuka faction, 34
Moate, R., 85
Molin, K., 18
Montreal Olympic Games, 106
Mori, Y., 198
Moro, A. (Prime Minister), 26, 27, 147, 151–2, 155–8, 159, 161
  murder of, 162
Mount, F., 78
Movimento Laureati (the Movement of Catholic University Graduates), 14
Mulé, R., 108, 221
Mulroney, B., 111, 113
Mussolini, 30, 147

Nakane, C., 183
Nakasone, 188–9, 203
Nakagawa, I., 190–1
Nenni, P., 150, 152
  and faction institutionalisation, 188–9, 191–3
Nash equilibrium, 77, 220
National Energy Program (NEP), 110
National Health Service (NHS), 19

New Democratic Party (NDP) of Canada, 17, 52, 104, 107, 114
Newell, J., 177
New Labour, 1, 53, 69
New Liberal Club (NLC), 135, 189–90, 192
No. 10 Policy Unit, 79, 82
non-ideological politics, 18
non-majoritarian democracies, 3, 55, 123
  incentives for factionalism, 208–10
non-temporal approach, to dominance, 8–9
  advantage of, 9
Norris, P., 52
Northern Ireland, 91
Northern League, 28
Norton, P., 58, 64, 73, 79, 218

Obuchi, K., 196–8
Occhetto, A., 175
October Crisis (1970), 104
Official Languages Act (1969), 106
Ogata, 186
Ohira, 189–91
oil shocks, 75, 157, 162, 185, 188
one-member-one-vote (OMOV), 53
  Canada, 68
opposition parties, 11
  coalition dominance, 21–2
  focus of incumbents on failures of, 13
  resource disadvantages of, 11
organisation of party, 63–9
  candidate selection, 64–5
  leadership selection, 66–8
  policy selection, 68–9
Otake, H., 195–8, 226
Ottone, P., 151
Ozawa, I., 34, 183, 195–9, 202
Ozbudun, E., 58, 64

Pammet, J., 118
parastato, 30
PARC. *see* Policy Affairs Research Council (PARC)
Park, C.H., 200
parliamentary mass-membership hybrid system, 67

Partido Revolucionario Institucional (PRI), 34–5
Parti Québécois, 107, 110, 217
partisan resources, monopoly over, 29–32
    in Canada, 31
    in Italy, 29–30
    in Japan, 30–1
    in UK, 29
party longevity, 6, 8, 10
partisanship, 3, 19, 39, 51–2, 55, 62, 117, 128, 133, 143, 185, 208, 210
party organisation. *see* organisation of party
party splits, 2, 33–4, 38, 48, 51, 57, 71, 130, 147, 183, 206
party system categories
    criticism of, 8
    multiparty, 7
    'one hegemonial party in polarised pluralism,' 7
    predominant, 7
permissive electoral systems, 15, 17–18, 21, 39, 124–8
    in Italy, 17–18, 124–6
    single non-transferable vote (SNTV) in Japan, 17–18, 39, 45, 124, 126–8
Pasquino, G., 20, 157
Patten, C., 72
Patterson, D., 200
Pearson L., 106, 119, 221
Pekkanen, R., 19, 31, 124, 126–7, 134, 139, 141–2, 184, 186, 192, 199, 201, 225
Pempel, T.J., 11, 31, 183
Perlin, G., 101, 221–2
Petro-Canada, 107
Pinto-Duschinsky, M., 71
Piper, R.J., 61
Pitfield, M., 101, 105
Policy Affairs Research Council (PARC), 131, 134, 141, 192, 201, 210
Politica Sociale, 146
'poll tax,' 19, 53, 80, 83
Popular Party of Italy, 145
Portfolio allocation, 63, 129
Portillo, M., 66

power indices, 46–8. *see also* Banzhaf index of power
    criticism of, 47
Preston Manning, 117
Pridham, G., 133, 158
Primavera faction, 148–51, 153
Prior, J., 72–4, 78, 168, 219
Progressive Conservatives of Canada, 17, 52, 54, 108–9, 120, 122
    implosion of, 16–17, 102, 103, 116–7, 205
    'losing party syndrome,' 101
'protected core,' notion of, 9
public information, control of, 20–1
public sector, 11, 29
Pym, F., 40

Québec, 10, 13, 17, 63, 101–2, 106–7, 109–22, 209, 215, 217, 221–2
'Quiet Revolution,' 103–4
    see also French Canada
Quinn, T., 67

Rallings, C., 215
Ramseyer, J.M., 139, 184, 187
Rate Support Grant, 74
'Rat Pack,' 114
Rawnsley, A., 56
realignment of politics, party and party systems, 13, 34, 70, 130, 184, 185, 196–7, 199
    see also dealignment
Recruit scandal, 193, 195
'Red Book,' 117
Red Brigades, 27, 158
reductive electoral systems, 14–15, 21, 39, 51
Redwood, J., 85, 98
Reed, S.R., 126–7, 142
Reform Act (1832), 51
Reform Act (1867), 51
Reform Party of Canada, 52, 63,116–7, 118–19, 219
Rengō (Japanese Trade Union Confederation), 226
Repeal of the Corn Laws, 80–1
representative government, theory of, 50, 55, 123

resource theory of party dominance, 11–12
responsible party government, theory of, 50, 55
Reuter, O.J., 214
Rhodes, M., 177
Richardson, J., 107
Riddel, P., 79
Riker, W.H., 11, 22
Robertson, D., 20
Rock, A., 119
Roland, G., 48
Rosenbluth, F., 128, 139–40, 142, 184–5, 187, 189, 191–3, 197
Rose, R., 53, 71–2
Rossi, M., 157, 163
Royal Canadian Mounted Police, 108
Royal Commission on Bilingualism and Biculturalism (1963), 106
Royal Mail, 92
Rumor, 130–1, 147, 150–2, 154–7, 159–61, 165, 166, 216, 224
Russo, 150, 178
Ryan, C., 110

St. Laurent, L., 105–6
Sakamoto, T., 194–5, 197
Sakigake (Harbinger Party), 34, 197–8
Sanders, D., 14
Sani, G., 126
SAP, 14
Sartori, G., 7–9, 22, 37–8, 44, 46, 131, 181, 214
    party 'fractionism' and concept of factions, 44, 46
    theory of 'polarised pluralism,' 8, 181, 214
Sauger, N., 9, 214
Savoie, D., 57
Sayers, A.M., 65
Scandinavia, coalition politics, 22
Scarrow, S.E., 64, 68
Schattschneider, E.E., 37, 64
Scheiner, E., 31
Schelling, T.C., 48
Schlesinger, J.A., 226
Schofield, N., 11, 21–3
Seawright, D., 58, 219

Segni, 155, 163, 175, 176, 179–80, 222, 224
Second World War, 1
Seldon, A., 19
Sened, I., 219
Seyd, P., 64
Shapley, L., 23, 46–7
Shapley-Shubik index of power, 23
Shefter, M., 29
Shepherd, R., 85, 93, 96, 220
Shepsle, K., 48, 129, 225
Shinseito ('New Born' or 'Renewal' Party), 34, 197
Shubik, M., 23, 46–7
Shugart, M., 44, 218
Sidoti, F., 178
Simon, H., 226
Single European Act (SEA), 81
single-member plurality (SMP), 14–15, 37, 39, 51, 70
    in Canada, 16–17
single non-transferable vote (SNTV), 17, 39, 124
    in Japan, 17–18, 39, 45, 124, 126–8
Smith, D., 66, 93
Smith, G., 11, 12
Smith, Ian Duncan (IDS), 66–7
Smith, J., 53
Smyth, R., 219
Social Democratic Party (SDP) of UK, 71
Socialist Party of Italy (PSI), 24–7, 147, 151–2, 158, 167, 177–8, 216, 224–5
Socialist Party of Japan (JSP), 18, 194, 198
Social Movement of Italy (MSI), 24, 25, 27, 149–51, 177, 224
Solidarity, 71
sottogoverno, 29
South Africa, 6, 12
    cleavage theory of party dominance, 13
    regional based cleavages, 13
    see also ANC
South Korea, 30
'sovereignty association' referendum on (1980), 110

spatial conceptualisation of
    dominance, 6
  problems of, 9–10
Spicer, M., 85, 91, 93
Spotts, F., 134, 216
'stalking horse' candidates, 66
state resources
  monopoly of, 11, 29–32
Steel, G., 141, 200
Strom, K., 216
Suzuki, 190
Sweden, 6, 12, 14
  coalition politics, 22
Swedish Confederation of Professional
    Employees, 14
Swedish Social Democrats (SAP), 12
  'catch-all' policy, 18
Swingle, P., 94

Taagepera, R., 44
Taiwan, 1, 30
  factionalism, 34–5
Takeshida N., 193, 195–7, 226
Tanaka, K., 140, 188–9, 190–3, 195,
    197, 226
Tanaka scandal, 140
Tariff Reform, 80–1
Tarrow, S., 11, 20, 26
Taviani, 150–2, 154–6, 224
Taylor, T., 85
Tebbit, N., 74, 85, 99
temporal approach, to dominance, 6,
    8, 10, 11
  and strains on unity, 3, 5, 10
tessitore, 162
Thacker, S.C., 210, 217
"Thatcher Cabinet," 79
Thatcher, M., 5, 14, 16, 20, 42, 51, 53,
    56, 59–60, 66–7, 71–100, 107,
    111, 114, 202, 206, 209, 211, 219
  anti-Europe views, 53
  deflationary budget (1981), 75–9,
    100
  and deteriorating intraparty
    relations, 79–84
  dismissal of, 60, 83–4
  early years, 72–3
  'Iron Lady,' 79
  political spinning, 20

'poll tax,' 19, 53, 80, 83, 100
  refusal to join European Monetary
    Union (EMU), 80–1, 83, 100;
    support to free marketeers, 85
  rival governments, 69
  social engineering, 14
  'stalking horse,' 72
  Westland affair, 53
  'wets' and 'dries,' 69, 72, 73–5
  see also Conservative Party
    Conference
Thayer, N.B., 134, 183
Theakston, K., 218
theory of 'polarised pluralism,' 22, 181
  see also Sartori, G.
Thies, M.F., 126, 142, 184
Thomas, P.G., 101
Thrasher, M., 215
Thursday Breakfast Group, 79
The Times, 60, 99
time-series analysis, 45
'tipping point,' 28, 83, 91, 118, 198,
    206, 212
Tokyo land boom, 190
Treaty of European Union (TEU), 84
Tribune Group, 71
Trudeau, P.
  bilingualism, 106–7
  controversial constitutional
    reforms, 110
  divorce, 108
  economic interventionism, 103,
    106, 107, 110–11
  federalism, 3, 39, 62–3, 57, 70, 102,
    103, 106–7, 108
  government policies of, 106–9
  government reforms fostering
    dissatisfaction, 105–6
  inclusive politics of, 103–4
  identity of, 103–4
  retirement from politics, 111, 121
  rivalry with John Turner, 101, 103,
    107–8, 111–13, 205
'Trudeaumania,' 104
Turner, J., 103, 107–8, 111–14
  exit from Trudeau's cabinet, 108,
    112, 222
  as Leader of the Opposition, 112

opposition to the Canada-US Free Trade Agreement (FTA), 103, 113–14
rivalry with Pierre Trudeau, 101, 103, 107–8, 111–13, 205
support for Meech Lake Accord, 103, 112–15, 121
weak and divisive leadership, 54, 68, 103, 111–14
Tsebelis, G., 64, 97

UK Independence Party (UKIP), 19–20
Ulster Unionists, 79, 89, 91, 92, 96, 98
United Nations Educational, Scientific and Cultural Organization (UNESCO), 120
United Russia, 9
United States, 9
identification of multilevel dominance, 9
issue cleavages, 13–14
Madisonian democracy, 55
'median' appeals to voters, 13
'United States of Europe' speech, 81
unity, of party, 33
difficulties of maintaining, 37–8
as necessary but insufficient condition for political dominance, 2, 33, 205, 206
and party organisation, 63–9; candidate selection, 64–5; leadership selection, 66–8; policy selection, 68–9
and public perceptions, 52–4
and responsible government, 54–5
US Congress
careers, 55
legislative factionalism, 59, 218
majoritarian logic, 52
'Utopia Political Study Group,' 195

van Wolferen, K., 31, 35, 140, 216, 223
Vespa, 146, 148, 149
voice for exit, 41, 43, 169–70, 173, 206
Von Beyme, K., 7

vote of no confidence. *see* confidence vote
voters
'catch-all' appeals to, 13, 32
'median' appeals to, 13, 18–9

Walters, A., 79, 82
Ware, A., 7, 11
War Measures Act, 104
Watanabe, T., 195
Wearing, J., 109, 221
Webb, P., 65, 68, 81
Weir, S., 32, 78, 80
Wells, C., 115
Wertman, D., 35, 125, 132–3, 135–6, 138–9, 145, 147, 151, 154–5, 157, 159, 161–2, 165, 167–8, 172, 179, 223
Westland affair, 53
Westland Helicopters, 79–80
Westminster systems. *see* majoritarian parliamentary democracies
'wets' and 'dries,' 69, 72, 73–9
pay–off matrix, 75–7
'whipping' system, 58, 134
Whitaker, R., 31
Whitelaw, W., 72
Whiteley, P., 64
Wieser, T., 216
Wildgen, J.K., 124–5
Wilson, H. (British Prime Minister), 16, 57, 61
Wilson, W., 52
'winter of discontent,' 73
Winterton, A., 85
Winterton, N., 85
Wong, J., 33, 35
Wood, D.M., 58

Young, H., 77, 79
Young, L., 116

Zaccagnini, B., 132, 147, 156, 158–63, 164–7, 171, 173, 181, 211, 216, 224
Zariski, R., 152
Zucherman, A.S., 216

Printed and bound in the United States of America